LEVERAGING THE NEW HUMAN CAPITAL

LEVERAGING
THE NEW
HUMAN CAPITAL

Adaptive Strategies, Results Achieved,
and Stories of Transformation

SANDRA BURUD AND MARIE TUMOLO

Davies-Black Publishing
Mountain View, California

Published by Davies-Black Publishing, a division of CPP, Inc., 1055 Joaquin Road, Suite 200, Mountain View, CA 94043; 800-624-1765.

Special discounts on bulk quantities of Davies-Black books are available to corporations, professional associations, and other organizations. For details, contact the Director of Marketing and Sales at Davies-Black Publishing; 650-691-9123; fax 650-623-9271.

Visit the Davies-Black Publishing Web site at www.daviesblack.com.

09 08 07 06 05 10 9 8 7 6 5 4 3 2
Printed in the United States of America

Library of Congress Cataloging-in-Publication Data
Burud, Sandra L.   Marie Tumolo
    Leveraging the new human capital : adaptive strategies, results achieved, and stories of transformation / Sandra Burud and Marie Tumolo.
        p. cm.
Includes biographical references and index.
    ISBN 0-89106-205-X (hardcover)
    1. Human capital. 2. Quality of work life. 3. Work and family. 4. Emotional intelligence. 5. Adaptability (Psychology). 6. Organizational change—Case studies. I. Tumolo, Marie. II. Title.
HD4904.7.B87 2004
658.3'14—dc22

                                                                        2004015276

FIRST EDITION
First printing 2004

To my husband, Larry Remlinger, whose incredible love and wisdom enrich my life beyond measure
—*Sandra Burud*

To my mother, Dee Tumolo, whose love, encouragement, and interest in my journey enable me to travel to places beyond my imagination
—*Marie Tumolo*

CONTENTS

PREFACE

The employee today is a whole different animal. In the fable of the giraffe and the elephant,[*] the giraffe, who is a successful carpenter, wants to expand his woodworking enterprise, so he invites the elephant (a capable craftsman) to join him. Left alone to begin his work, the elephant inadvertently smashes into walls and damages equipment in the narrow workshop, which was designed and equipped for the giraffe. The giraffe returns and surveys the damage and arrives at a solution: The elephant should join a gym to lose weight and take up ballet to become more graceful. In his giraffe-centric view, the giraffe overlooks the inherent differences between giraffes and elephants and misses the opportunity to capitalize on them.

American businesses, like the giraffe's workshop, have also been designed with giraffes in mind. These giraffes may differ in appearance—they are both male and female and come from different ethnic backgrounds—but they are still all giraffes. The "gene" they share is not visible. Their giraffe-ness—the trait they have in common—is that they are "work-primary": they put work first. Work is their primary role, and they are singularly focused on it. They do whatever it takes to get the job done and they have had the invisible system of support in their private lives that makes that singular focus possible.

Throughout the Industrial Age, certainly for the past half-century, giraffes made up the bulk of the workforce, and giraffes remain at the helm.

---

[*] Roosevelt Thomas, *Building a House for Diversity*. We have "embroidered" Thomas's fable and used it to make a different point than he makes.

Elephants, however, now outnumber giraffes three to one. Most workers no longer focus exclusively on work even when they are at work, nor is work their sole priority. They lack the system of invisible support that would enable them to do so. Without a mate devoted to managing life's nonwork tasks—essential to operating as a giraffe—these elephants operate in "dual-focus" mode, with work alternating with other priorities. Elephants require new equipment, but they can do things that giraffes cannot.

The influx of elephants is occurring just as work itself (woodworking, in our story) is evolving in a way that makes elephants' strength essential. The heavy lifting these adaptive, multidimensional, and collaborative animals are particularly adept at will make the critical difference in the woodworking enterprise's adaptation and success.

Business thinkers have suggested ways to improve the output of the workshop: reengineering its work processes, crafting new business strategies, and changing its culture, to name a few. But it has consistently escaped their notice (perhaps because most of them are giraffes themselves) that the worker is an entirely different animal. As the base around which all organizational performance revolves, this concept is a deceptively simple but profound element in the dynamics of the workshop. Understanding it is essential to accomplishing any other organizational change.

This book is designed to help business managers understand these structural changes and turn them to an advantage. It presents a new framework for managing, testing it against research data and the real experiences of four very different companies. It is organized in four parts, each beginning with a statement by a thought leader—Peter Senge, Mihaly Csikszentmihalyi, Robert Reich, and Rosabeth Moss Kanter—that connects that leader's insightful work in management, psychology, or economics to the book's central ideas.

Part 1 describes the three converging forces that are shaping a new American business environment. As organizations grasp this new reality, described in Chapters 1 through 3, it alters who can help them succeed best. Chapter 4 describes the qualities of these contributors and the talents they bring.

Part 2 (Chapters 5 through 9) describes five strategies organizations can use to adapt to the new reality. These adaptive strategies build on one another and begin with fundamental decisions about people and organizational values.

Part 3 offers research evidence showing how the adaptive strategies described in Part 2 affect business results. Chapter 10 shows how employee performance is measurably affected. When employees are more effective, customers have a superior experience, as the research in Chapter 11 shows. And when employees are more productive and customers have a better experience, shareholder value is improved, as shown in Chapter 12.

And finally, Part 4 (Chapters 13 through 16) presents the stories of four very different companies, exploring what made them decide to manage in an adaptive way, what approach they used (each is unique), and what happened as a result. These real-life examples show how it all comes together.

ACKNOWLEDGMENTS

This book is enhanced by many people's contributions. It builds on the work of thought leaders in disciplines ranging from anthropology to finance. The ideas were shaped and challenged by senior executives, nurtured by thoughtful questions from formal and informal advisors, and buoyed by the support of a visionary funder. The book and research were sponsored by an academic institution of superb scholarship and executed with the help of a great team. We thank them all.

The thought leaders are too numerous to mention; their names appear in the bibliography, but the book's ideas build on theirs. Twenty-one senior executives let us interview them; their candor helped ground the book in reality and hopefully ensure its relevance to real-world challenges. Our Advisory Committee guided us and opened doors. Its members include Jim Renier, chair emeritus of Honeywell Corporation and founder of Success by Six; Ron James, executive director of the Center for Ethical Business Cultures; Sarah Meyerrose, executive vice president for employee services of First Tennessee National Corporation; an economist, who must remain anonymous since he acted unofficially; and Mike Csikszentmihalyi, director of the Quality of Life Research Center at the Peter F. Drucker and

Masatoshi Ito Graduate School of Management and author of brilliant books including *Flow*.

Four guest authors—Robert Reich, Rosabeth Moss Kanter, Peter Senge, and Mihaly Csikszentmihalyi—contributed their unique perspectives to this book, a phenomenal gift, particularly given their other time commitments.

The David and Lucile Packard Foundation, which consistently focuses on systemic approaches to creating a better world for the next generation, funded our work. Their support gave us time to pursue this project thoroughly and thoughtfully, which is a rare opportunity. We particular appreciate the support of our project officer, Marie Young.

Four companies, whose stories appear in the book, allowed us to spend time with them and graciously shared their secrets to success. We particularly appreciate the assistance of Alice Campbell and Harry Kraemer of Baxter International; Pat Brown, Sarah Meyerrose, and Jennifer Nieman of First Tennessee National Corporation; Rich Vintini and Irene Shadoan of DuPont; and Trent Smith and Diane Fuqua of SAS.

The Claremont Graduate University provided the perfect institutional home base for this project, as a community committed to learning that crosses disciplines. We especially appreciated strategic support from David Drew, dean of the School of Educational Studies, and Kees DeKlyver, dean of the Peter F. Drucker and Masatoshi Ito Graduate School ofManagement, who understood the transdisciplinary nature of the work. Jay Prag, finance professor, also shared his time and ideas.

Sandy Cunningham coauthored Chapters 13, 14, and 16 with us, and Marci Koblenz, of MK Consultants, helped us shape the ideas in Chapters 6, 7, and 8. Other friends and colleagues shared their thoughts, in particular Faith Wohl, former executive at DuPont and later director of the Office of Workplace Initiatives at the General Services Administration during the Clinton Administration; Stephanie Trapp, former executive director of the Alliance for Work-Life Progress; and Mary Ellen Dallman of Valdosta State University. Karen Woodford, of Summa Associates, and Kathy Lingle, current executive director of the Alliance for Work-Life Progress, reviewed and commented on drafts. Susan Seitel and Joan Fingerman of Work & Family Connection were incredibly helpful in tracking down sources of studies. WFD, a consulting firm, gave us permission to use their work for the DuPont story in Chapter 13.

We were assisted by a staff that helped us gather and catalog an immense amount of research data. We thank Mary Stetcheson, Donna Kaner, and Virginia Lee in particular. Shelley Gupta and Teresa Wilborn also supported us technically and skillfully.

We especially appreciate the team at Davies-Black, in particular Senior Acquisitions Editor Connie Kallback and Publisher Lee Langhammer Law, who understood and believed in the book and knew where it fit in the book publishing world. Their open-mindedness and willingness to listen to our ideas made the publishing process a pleasure.

I appreciate the complementary knowledge and skills my coauthor, Marie Tumolo, brought to this work. The book would not have been what it is without Marie's breadth of knowledge on management thought and trends, her academic and experiential perspectives, her carefulness, and her enormous intellectual capacity.

I also thank Linda Wall for her consistently wise counsel, and my husband, Larry Remlinger, whose breadth of intellectual knowledge, wisdom about human dynamics, and willingness to endlessly explore ideas were invaluable. I thank him even more for the joy he brings me.

—Sandra Burud

I thank Sandy Burud for the opportunity to work on this book and appreciate the many ways in which she has expanded my thinking and my horizons, leading me safely beyond my comfort zones. I also thank my family and friends for their willingness to listen, to share their ideas and support my endeavors.

—Marie Tumolo

ABOUT THE AUTHORS

Sandra Burud is a researcher, analyst, writer, and consultant who specializes in issues relating to the new workforce. For fifteen years her Pasadena-based consulting practice, Burud & Associates, has helped organizations as diverse as Microsoft Corporation, Warner Bros., Los Alamos National Laboratory, the California State University System, and Caterpillar create effective organizational responses to the new workforce dynamics. With a keen interest in measuring the impact of positive change on key stakeholders, she has conducted research studies measuring the return on investment of innovative employee practices and developed other metrics to assess results.

Previously, Burud conducted a national study of child care benefits and coauthored an earlier book, *Employer-Supported Child Care: Investing in Human Resources* (1984), which was highlighted by the White House. The how-to guide for employers also reported the results achieved by organizations that adopted these new benefits. She is a past president of the Alliance for Work-Life Progress and led the development of a professional certification for work-life balance practitioners. Burud directed the research and writing for this book in her position as visiting research faculty at the

Peter F. Drucker and Masatoshi Ito School of Management and the School of Educational Studies at the Claremont Graduate University in Claremont, California, where she also serves on the Board of Visitors. She holds a Ph.D. degree in education. She can be reached at sandy@burud.org.

Marie Tumolo is a researcher, writer, teacher, and management consultant specializing in strategy implementation. She is interested in research that contributes to management theory and practice and finds fertile ground for research topics in the experiences and challenges facing her consulting clients. For more than twenty years she has worked with companies to improve strategic, operating, and financial performance, focusing on the effective management of people, processes, and technology. Recent research addressed human capital effectiveness and client relationship management. Her client list includes Fortune 50 as well as middle-market companies in a variety of industries. As a teacher, Tumolo brings her real-world knowledge and research findings into the classroom to enrich the learning experiences of her business school students.

Tumolo holds a Ph.D. degree in executive management from the Peter F. Drucker and Masatoshi Ito Graduate School of Management at Claremont Graduate University and an MBA degree from the Wharton School at the University of Pennsylvania. She received a B.S. degree in accounting from St. Joseph's University and is a certified public accountant.

PART 1

THE NEW WORKFORCE REALITY

Three forces are converging upon U.S. businesses, creating a new reality that directly affects an organization's ability to succeed. The first two forces—the rise of human capital and the shift from an industrial to a knowledge society—have been written about extensively, although their implications for the way people work has not. The third force—the rise of the dual-focus worker—is an entirely new phenomenon in the history of paid market work, and it has not been considered in the management literature. The core workforce relates to work in a very different way from workers of earlier generations—no longer as the top priority, not with a singular focus, but as one priority that competes with others for attention. This third force changes how we define "good work" and has a powerful complicating effect on the other two forces.

The convergence of these three forces requires fundamental changes in the way organizations manage people. American businesses operate in an economy that is now more knowledge- and idea-based than it was throughout most of the twentieth century. It is also more global. The number of service jobs has increased relative to manufacturing jobs, making knowledge and service work a greater component of U.S. jobs. The aging of the U.S. population and the lagging birth rate point toward a more competitive labor market in the future. These factors, which have already happened, as Peter Drucker likes to point out, present a significant challenge for organizations, one most are completely unprepared to face.

The rise in unemployment and decrease in turnover among remaining employees may convince managers and executives that the talent wars of the 1990s were an aberration—a product of an exceptional period of economic growth—not to be seen again for another twenty to thirty years. It may be more comfortable to assume that the current state of the labor market will continue, and that history—a history based on the twentieth-century industrial economy—provides an accurate indicator of the future labor market, but we challenge that assumption. We believe current conditions reflect short-term adjustments and are providing false signals about the future state of the labor market. Despite current appearances, human capital is one of the most important ingredients of organizational success today and in the future, and we believe that few organizations are adequately prepared to address the realities of the labor market and competitive landscape.

Part 1 is organized into four chapters, which describe the new reality facing organizations. Chapter 1 addresses the *why*: why human capital has become so important to organizational success. Chapter 2 provides the *what*: what workers today actually do, given the shift in the nature of work from traditional manufacturing or industrial occupations to knowledge and service occupations. Chapter 3 discusses the *who*: who today's workers are and why they are more likely to have a dual focus rather than a singular focus on work. Chapter 4 contrasts the industrial idea of the ideal worker with a new definition of the ideal worker and describes the abilities that make the new ideal worker fit the new reality.

These chapters provide the groundwork for Part 2, the adaptive strategies that organizations need to deploy to be successful given these converging forces, and Part 3, the evidence developed thus far that demonstrates the benefits to organizations of adopting these strategies.

We begin this part of the book with some thoughts from guest author Peter Senge, who reflects on the idea of *seamlessness*—that people cannot separate who they are from what they do. As whole people, they can bring many skills to their work, the skills organizations need to be effective in the new reality.

WHOLE PEOPLE
by Peter Senge

Rhonda Staudt was a thirty-four-year-old systems engineer at Xerox, with three kids and a project engineers dream of. She was part of the "Lakes Project," a team directed by John Elter and chartered with creating Xerox's next major product platform. "This was a bet-your-company project," says Elter, who was nominated for the National Medal of Technology for the many patents the product eventually included. The product, released as the Document Center 265, was Xerox's first fully digitized offering. Early on in the design work, Elter and his team also created a vision of a product where nothing would ever go into a landfill, that all components of the product would be either remanufacturable or recyclable. The result was a host of technical breakthroughs, including a final design with fewer than two hundred parts (about one tenth of its predecessor's), of which 92 percent are remanufacturable and 98 percent recyclable. Its sales met or exceeded all expectations.

When Xerox hosted a group from the SoL (Society for Organizational Learning) Sustainability Consortium in late 1999, we entered the manufacturing facility under a giant banner that read, "Zero to Landfill, for our children." You could feel the energy just walking through the facility. Every piece of equipment you saw had a tag on it—indicating where it was to be used and, when done, where it would go. The plant had no waste storage areas because it generated no waste—for the people had also decided that this would be a zero-to-landfill manufacturing facility as well. Even the shipping cartons from suppliers—most of whom had also embraced the zero-to-landfill vision—were returnable.

That afternoon the visiting SoL group was packed into a hot, stuffy meeting room adjacent to the assembly area, the site of the design team's regular 7:00 A.M. "sunrise meetings." Rhonda was reviewing the system design process employed for the product. She had just started talking about how meaningful it had been for her to be part of such an innovative team when she was interrupted with an unusual question. David Berdish, a veteran of many organizational learning projects at Ford, asked, "Rhonda, I understand what a great opportunity this was for you, and how exciting it was. I work with engineers and I know the intellectual excitement of pushing the technological envelope. But what I really want to know is why you did this. What I mean is, what was the stand you took and who were you taking that stand for?" Rhonda looked at David for a long time in silence and then, in front of many peers and a few superiors, began to cry. "I am a mom," she said.

Seamlessness

I imagine many of us will never forget that moment. There was a silence that filled the room. Roger Saillant, formerly of Ford and Visteon, and now CEO of Plug Power, a pioneering fuel cell manufacturer, turned to me and whispered, *"Seamlessness."* I knew immediately what he meant—when what we do becomes inseparable from who we are.

We have all spent much of our lives in institutions that force us to be someone we are not. We manage appearances. We commit ourselves to the company's agenda. We act professionally. After a while, we have lived so long in the house of mirrors that we can easily mistake the image we are projecting for who we really are. The poet David Whyte (1994) quotes an AT&T manager who wrote, "Ten years ago, I turned my face for a moment . . . and it became my life."

Purpose

The first question all members of an organization ask, either publicly or privately, is *why*. "Why should I invest my whole self in this endeavor?" "Do I believe in the organization's purpose, or do I believe that my purpose is truly in line with what I am working on?" The answer, unfortunately, for most is no. As former IKEA CEO Goran Carstedt puts it, most organizations do not have "a purpose worthy of people's commitment."

Dr. W. Edwards Deming, famous pioneer of the worldwide quality movement, was in a meeting with executives of a Detroit automaker in the early 1980s. Interest was growing, in Detroit and elsewhere in American manufacturing, in total quality, just-in-time inventory, and what eventually became known as the lean manufacturing revolution. The auto executives had set aside several days of their busy schedule to learn from the master, but things were not going well. Every time the executives asked Deming to explain some part of the total quality philosophy and practice, he retorted by asking them a question, the same question. Since they never seemed to answer the question to his satisfaction, he told them little of what they wanted to know. The meeting ended after less than a day. The question with which Deming kept confronting the executives was "What is the purpose of this company?" "Unless you can answer this question beyond the normal business of maximizing shareholder return," said Deming, who had little reservation about confronting powerful senior executives, "you are not ready for the knowledge of quality management."

Profits are not a purpose. They are a requirement. "Profits for a company are like oxygen for a purpose," says Peter Drucker. "If you don't have enough, after a while you are out of the game." But people who think life is about breathing have missed something. The same can be said for companies who think that profit is their purpose. They too are missing something, starting with the commitment of their people.

The basic problem with profit as a purpose is that no one actually cares that much about it. A hundred years from now, few will know or care what profits your company made last year, or this year, or next. But they might care about what your company created and what effects this had on the world.

Focusing exclusively on profits also diverts attention from creating more meaningful aspirations. Instead of seeing their purpose as generating profits, employees could see themselves as creating something that matches their deeper concerns as people, as parents, and as citizens, the way the Lakes team did. Engineers will not go home and talk to their children about their contribution to ROI, but they will talk about a product that expresses their personal values. Only through aligning what employees do at work with what they would want to share with their children do organizations tap the power to fully engage people and, in turn, to command their loyalty, commitment, imagination, patience, and perseverance.

The mistaken notion that maximizing return on invested capital is a company's purpose goes hand in hand with the idea that people are hired hands, or, if you prefer the more contemporary jargon, hired brains. If the relationship between enterprise and employee is purely transactional—an honest day's labor for an honest day's wage—then it makes little difference what the company's larger purpose is. Indeed, contracted employees are suspicious of lofty-sounding corporate mission statements. They will see the business as being, *at its essence,* about making money because their relationship is defined by money. Alternatively, if the relationship is based on shared principles and aspirations, people will insist on higher aspirations than just financial return. Few people will actually invest their spirit in return for boosting an investor's dividend check.

Parent Leaders

"Isn't it a shame," said William O'Brien, retired CEO of Hanover Insurance, "that companies spend untold sums of money on 'leadership development' at the same time that they work relentlessly to destroy the greatest training ground that exists for developing leadership, parenting." O'Brien regarded the greatest strengths of leaders as "advanced maturity," conceptual skills to understand and explain complex issues without trivializing them, and the capability to lead through "moral suasion." He believed that, as necessary as it might be in a crisis, giving orders was an indicator of leadership failure in everyday circumstances. "Ordinances, orders, and enforcement . . . are an attempt to compel the kind of behavior that organizations fail to induce," says VISA International's founding CEO, Dee Hock (1999, pp. 89–90).

Leaders like O'Brien and Hock appreciate that good leading, like good parenting, involves using influence instead of positional power, fostering reflection and deeper thinking, and nurturing genuine aspiration. It is one part encouragement and one part setting high expectations in areas where the person truly seeks to achieve. (All too often parents' expectations are in areas where *they* want their children to achieve.) It is ultimately all about the growth of the other.

Today, more and more innovative firms are reaching out to legitimate and support people's lives as mothers, fathers, and family members. For example, when Lotte Bailyn and her colleagues (Rapoport, Bailyn, Fletcher, & Pruitt, 2002; Rapoport & Bailyn, 1996) conducted some of the original research on the balance between work life and personal life, they interviewed engineers in product development teams about the dilemmas they faced that pitted work demands against family and personal demands. Almost without exception, the engineers valued the opportunities the researchers created to talk about these issues, so much so that they requested team meetings on the subject. But what was most surprising to the researchers was that many of the teams in which they worked also showed improved performance in getting new products out on time. This development surprised the researchers because there was nothing in their questions or analyses that dealt overtly with shortening product development times. Eventually, they came to realize that a work environment that allows people to talk openly regarding concerns about their home-related problems encourages people to express their concerns about work-related problems as well. Difficult professional subjects that were traditionally "un-discussable" (Chris Argyris's term) became discussable. People started to trust one another and, from there, to naturally help each other in solving their engineering, as well as work-life balance, problems.

So What Are We Afraid Of?

Moving from transactional to developmental relationships between firms and their members has great benefits but also some costs. Companies must be prepared to give up some things, starting with the mental model that, for successful professionals, work comes first.

It can be done. Anne Terry (pseudonym) was promoted to group vice president of a Fortune 50 global firm shortly after she had her first baby. She went to group CEO John Rolph and told him that she was thrilled by the opportunity but that he needed to understand something: "My child comes first in my life." She felt he should know that up front, in case he felt that her priorities might be out of line with what was expected. Rolph, who is single and known for his drive and long hours, responded, "That is one reason you have been selected. We need more of what you stand for in the organization—just don't expect the same from me."

The work-comes-first mental model has shaped much of current management practice. It has justified the view that it is not the role of employers to be concerned or invested in the other parts of employees' lives. It has shaped expectations of time commitments, assuming employees' time is a boundaryless resource available to the organization for breakfast and dinner meetings, weekends, and endless travel. It has influenced how work is organized, establishing schedules that cannot be customized to meet people's other commitments. And it subtly reinforces persisting biases underlying recognition and reward. For example, sociologist Joyce Fletcher (1999) has shown that teamwork, interpersonal skills, and relational approaches to work in general, though espoused widely by businesses today, often disappear in male-dominated management hierarchies in the sense of going unnoticed and unacknowledged. When it comes time for promotions, those whose dedication is "compromised" by commitments outside work can find themselves at a significant disadvantage.

Companies must also be prepared to give up other facets of traditional mind-sets around control. For example, most companies seek to build what they call *shared vision*. But, in reality, what passes for shared vision is the vision of one person or a small number of people imposed on larger groups. Real shared visions grow from deep understanding of the business reality and deep personal commitment. The soil from which shared visions emerge is an environment rich in opportunities to reflect, clarify, and commit to personal visions. No personal vision, no shared vision. But personal visioning is inherently integrative. Our visions for our lives integrate across all dimensions of our lives: as professionals, citizens, church members, parents, and human beings. Creating environments that acknowledge and even nurture personal vision is a large step beyond the traditional dichotomy between the professional and the personal.

While this dichotomy has represented a lost opportunity for synergy between work and one's larger life, moving toward integration is inherently risky for businesses. After all, a talented manager or engineer at the age of forty, just reaching the peak of value to the organization, may discover that what truly matters is to be a writer or to spend a great deal of time with the kids. In other words, moving from transactional to developmental relationships between firms and their members—just as between people—rests on shared values and vulnerability.

This is why businesses are understandably fearful. But the courage to face these changes is the gateway through which, I believe, truly innovative organizations must pass.

1

PEOPLE, THE ENGINE OF SUCCESS

When we think about what makes a successful company, we usually think about profits—successful companies generate profits. And when we think about the sources of those profits, we think of things like quality products, excellent service, the right location, good customers, access to capital, controlled costs, low-rate financing, and being in the right industry at the right time.

Yet we all know that quality products come from the minds of people who generate ideas, the labor of people who turn the ideas into products, the imagination of people who package and promote the products, and the enthusiasm of the people who sell them. Excellent service is, by its very nature, an exchange between people, reliant on the responsiveness and know-how of service personnel. Someone, some person, has to pick the right locations, analyze who the good customers are, investigate the alternative sources of capital, monitor costs and negotiate discounts, work with people at financial institutions to obtain the best financing, and keep an eye out for opportunities in the industry. We tend to forget that business is commercial activity between and among people. We have developed a business lexicon that describes the things we do without mentioning the people that do them. It's as though people are of secondary importance. And that's a problem.

Likewise, when we think about managers, we think about what they manage. In most cases, if you read their titles, they manage functions, processes, geographic regions, products, or services. There are managers of IT, of research and development, of the western sales region, of operations, of software development, of benefits, of coatings and polymers. Rarely does a manager's title indicate anything about people, which is really what a manager manages. At the same time, ask any manager to name the most difficult part of the job, and most will say, "managing people." It's as though we think being a manager is about some*thing*, not some*one*. And that's a problem.

One of the most successful business books of recent years is *Good to Great* (Collins, 2001), an analysis of companies that had fifteen years of returns at or below market followed by fifteen years with cumulative returns at least three times the market average. These companies weren't in great industries, didn't have celebrity CEOs, didn't deploy strategies far superior to comparison companies. What these companies did have was disciplined thought, disciplined action, and disciplined employees. In these companies *who* was more important than *what*. One of the main reasons these companies went from good to great is that their managers understood how important people are to success, making sure they "got the right people on the bus, the wrong people off the bus, and the right people in the right seats." Many companies employ rhetoric about the importance of people, but few actually match the rhetoric with action—companies like Nordstrom, Southwest Airlines, Rosenbluth Travel, where reliance on people is so well understood that all aspects of the management system (culture, compensation practices, autonomy levels) reinforce the message. Most companies are still at the stage of talking about how important people are to success, without building the infrastructure that makes success through people possible. And that's a problem.

It's a problem because today employees are increasingly the best way for companies to achieve and sustain a competitive advantage—more so than traditional sources of sustainable advantage, such as new products, technological superiority, and regulated markets (Pfeffer, 1994). More often, the skills, relationships, and motivation of employees determine long-term competitive success. The ability of employees to make on-the-spot decisions that enhance customers' experience is a key part of the value proposition delivered by Nordstrom. At Southwest, the culture of employees' pulling together to deliver customer service and turn planes around quickly contributes to the success of the company's low-cost strategy (C. O'Reilly & Pfeffer, 1995). Even outside the service industries, employees are often the drivers of innovation and process improvement.

It's a problem because talent—human capital—is in limited supply, and that supply is dwindling; by 2010, with Baby Boomers retiring, there will potentially be 10 million jobs for which there will be no available workers (Herman, Olivo, & Gioia, 2003). With this kind of shortfall, the companies that understand and appreciate the value of human capital—of people and what they can do—will outperform those that do not.

It's a problem because we need to move away from our comfortable places—away from managing things instead of people, away from thinking people are secondary to the function of our work—and start building organizations that enable people to do their best work and make the contributions to organizational success that only they can make. We need to understand and manage human capital.

What Is Human Capital?

Some say *human capital* is the ability of people to innovate—to create new products and new services, and to improve business processes (Stewart, 1997). Others say it is skills, experience, and knowledge (T. O. Davenport, 1999). For purposes of this book, we will define it as the application of intellectual capital (knowledge, skills, and talent) plus relational capital (connections and relationships with customers, peers, vendors, and external associates) in the pursuit of an organization's goals.

Traditional Sources of Competitive Advantage

As the economy has changed significantly over the past twenty years, traditional sources of competitive advantage have become obsolete. During the Industrial Age, which lasted from approximately 1938 through 1974 (Atkinson, Court, & Ward, 1999), a company's competitive advantage could be based on having a product that dominated the market, developing a proprietary technology to produce products or deliver service, or relying on the protection of regulated markets. In today's Information Age, competitive advantage most often derives from knowledge, ideas, and technology.

Product life cycles are short and getting shorter. Companies can't assume, as Xerox did in 1959, that a product can dominate the market for thirteen years (Pfeffer, 1994). A better product often comes to market before a company has fully recouped its investment in the old one.

Technological superiority is also a tenuous base for building competitive advantage. Consider the handheld computer market. Palm created the handheld market—but by 2002 it found its market share shrunk to 36 percent. In 2003, facing tough competition from makers of smart devices that combine cell phones and handheld computers, the company announced plans to acquire a company with that capability. It chose Handspring, the company founded by the original founders of Palm itself (Tam, 2003).

Regulated markets, formerly a good source of competitive advantage to those within them, have just about disappeared in the United States—and other parts of the developed and underdeveloped world are not far behind. Deregulation in trucking, airlines, telecommunications, and financial services has made these industries more competitive, driving down prices and making it difficult for any one company to stand out.

Globalization has forced companies to seek new sources of competitive advantage. Firms that used to compete for customers locally now deal with competitors in every marketplace. Communication technology continues to fuel this growth in globalization by increasing consumers' access to information about products and services around the world (Ohmae, 1990) and by creating Internet-based marketplaces that facilitate *e-commerce*, the buying and selling of products and services without regard to physical location.

New Sources of Competitive Advantage

In a global, highly competitive world, companies need to continually innovate their products, services, and processes; react quickly to changes in existing and potential markets; and mobilize to serve customers in diverse geographic locales, all while providing individualized, customized service to customers. Like it or not, people are the only way to do that—through their creativity and knowledge, their relationships with customers and co-workers, and their professional networks. Companies like eBay, Apple, Amazon.com, and others illustrate the truth that "people and their ideas are the most significant drivers of wealth creation in today's global economy" (Low, 2002). Traditional industries also find people key to competitive advantage. Ken Iverson, president of Nucor Corporation from 1962 to 1996, attributes over half of its 17 percent annual compound growth rate to the company's culture, citing people as the engine of success (Iverson & Varian, 1998).

Businesses need three things in particular that only people can bring: creativity, knowledge, and relationship capital.

Creativity

People are critical to a company's ability to innovate, to create new ideas and new products and services, to develop better ways to do things, and to reduce costs. Competition limits the ability of companies to raise prices, requiring them to continually improve efficiency and reduce costs. Improving process efficiencies through technology is necessary to stay competitive but not sufficient to outperform other companies, who can easily duplicate or replicate any software-based improvements. People, then, become critical to improving efficiency as they devise ways to increase the capacity of existing machinery, reengineer processes for optimal performance, and identify ways to eliminate waste. Their increased productivity from these efficiencies is critical to reducing costs.

Intense competition requires companies to continually innovate—to create new products and services for new markets. DVDs replace VCRs, digital cameras replace film, handheld computers replace day planners, and pocket calculators replace slide rules. The marketplace rewards companies that are successful at developing new products and markets. In fact, the pace at which a company develops new products compared to that of its rivals matters more in global competition than the absolute pace of learning and innovation (Barkema, Baum, & Mannix, 2002). Competition intensifies as firms innovate in response to each other, requiring an endless stream of new ideas (Cairncross, 2002). It is easy to fall behind, even when a firm looks like it is undergoing rapid change and innovation (Barkema et al., 2002). High-tech companies once felt this pressure more intensely than other industries; today even traditional manufacturing companies are feeling the pressure to innovate rapidly. And it's worth repeating: Innovation can only come from the minds and hearts of people—their ability to produce novel ideas, their knowledge of the domain that enables them to adapt the idea to a problem or opportunity, and their determination and perseverance when it comes to implementing novel but appropriate ideas (Amabile, 1997).

Knowledge

People are both the holders and transmitters of knowledge. As the economy migrated away from the Industrial Age, when capital and the tools of production were the primary factors of wealth creation, and entered the Information Age, wealth became concentrated in knowledge (Tapscott, 1996). In an information economy, knowledge assets are more important than physical assets in determining sustainable business success. Knowledge assets reside in individuals who have specialized knowledge or rare skills that cannot be easily replicated or replaced. Certainly knowledge work—accounting, architecture, law, systems programming, medical technology, and so on—is dependent on specific expertise, but even manufacturing work has become more reliant on specialized knowledge and skills, particularly for complex machinery and processes.

Although computers accumulate data and generate information, only people can make the information usable, can turn it into knowledge that results in calibrating a machine for a particular application, that interprets the results of an MRI, that analyzes the daily take from thousands of cash registers to determine what products are selling and why. Since expertise is relatively more expensive and more mobile than physical assets and can easily walk out the back door (Cairncross, 2002), organizations need to maximize its use.

Knowledge is enhanced through human collaboration. Collaboration and coordination among people can leverage individual performance, leading to new types of differentiation and higher levels of firm success. DuPont's fluoroproducts plant in Louisville, Kentucky, created a more collaborative working environment that reduced plant emissions by 50 percent and saved more than $1 million annually (Chin, 1997). Collaboration is a function of relationships, the other thing that people uniquely bring.

Relationship Capital

People's connections with others, both within and outside their organization, contribute to the creation of wealth in organizations. The research scientist's work is enhanced by collaboration with a colleague at another university. The systems programmer knows the person developing a new product and configures the program to process its sales. The purchasing agent gets a long-term vendor to telescope normal delivery time in an emergency. The salesperson's solid relationship with a customer provides instant awareness when a new sales opportunity arises.

These sustained connections have been termed *social capital* or *relationship capital*. They are the sum of the "trust, mutual understanding, and shared values and behaviors that bind the members of human networks and communities and make cooperative action possible" (D. Cohen & Prusak, 2002, p. 4).

Relationships serve many purposes, supporting collaboration, creativity, and interaction and enhancing commitment and initiative. Knowledge work in particular is done in the context of relationships and these relationships facilitate knowledge exchange. In fact, knowledge work cannot be done without "persuasiveness, shared decisions, the pooling of knowledge and the creative sparks people strike off one another," which depend on relationships with others (D. Cohen & Prusak, 2002, p. 17).

Service work is also relationship-driven—employees' relationships with the organization and each other affect their relationships with customers, and those relationships have become key to profitability. Customers have more power to make demands on suppliers as the number of competitors and access to suppliers have increased through the Internet. At the same time customers' expectations have risen as they themselves must deliver better, faster, and cheaper products to their own customers. They must have swift, customized responses, which only come through people who maintain customer relationships, respond to customer demands, and anticipate future customer needs.

Relational capital also acts as a lubricant; organizations rich in relational capital can be more efficient. As Robert Reich (2003) says, a strong bank account of relational capital enables people doing business together to know who knows whom, who knows what, and who can be relied on. In durable relationships where people know and trust one another, things move more smoothly and swiftly; extra steps are avoided, and communications are expedited. Participants avoid false starts and corrections, lowering transaction costs. These efficiencies happen only with a presumption of trust, built up over many experiences, which is why relationships are hard to replicate quickly.

These mutual and meaningful connections also create value to the people in them. They help people gain a sense of purpose, which feeds their commitment, engagement, and initiative, creating a virtuous circle. They can be energizing and rewarding; they even improve self-understanding (Walsh, Bartunek, & Lacey, 1998).

Relational connections are distinctly individual—they are exchanges and relationships between individuals; some people are better at developing them than others. Even so, organizations have a part in facilitating relationships. Relational capital grows when the organization is stable and is destroyed through the volatility of mergers and rapid organizational changes that do not recognize the human element in these activities. It requires an ecology of trust, mutuality, shared understandings and goals, and common frames of reference shared by people (D. Cohen & Prusak, 2002).

When Human Capital Takes Center Stage

If people are the engines of business success, several things become more important than they were before, such as understanding how human beings operate, including the dynamics of human attention and aptitudes related to human interaction. Employee frame of mind and alignment with organizational goals and objectives also become critical considerations.

Humans: A Unique Form of Capital

Humans are unlike other capital (machine or financial capital). With Jean-Jacques Rousseau (1911), we believe they are more organisms than mechanisms. They are unpredictable. They are idiosyncratic. (No one is like anyone else—ever, in the history of the world, which is amazing.) Most important, as organisms, people have the innate capacity "to self-assemble . . . change constantly, reproduce, learn and self-organize" (Ehin, 2000, p. 7). They have their own requirements as complex, whole, "biological systems seeking to fulfill their needs and aspirations" (p. 8). Bio-logic and not machine logic prevails, which is why efforts to control people inevitably fail. Machine logic is mechanistic; you can dissect a machine into parts, and its inputs generate the same outputs every time. Bio-logic is organic: people don't all react the same way, nor do they just react; they act upon and co-create.

When managers understand this difference, they manage more effectively. The very evolutionary urge to change that Charles Darwin observed in all living creatures—the urge to burst out of existing constraints that is responsible for our evolution itself—is the same urge that is thwarted when organizations attempt to manage humans as if they were machines. People naturally resist. What works better is to shift from organizational behavior that seeks to control to behavior that seeks to support positive self-organization. "The new model for organizations is the biological world, where uncontrolled actions produce stunningly efficient and robust results, all through adaptation and self-organization" (Petzinger, 1997, cited in Ehin, 2000).

We need to meet with individuals and treat them as learners to be engaged and potential decision-makers, rather than as pets to be trained and recognized. (Kohn, 1998, cited in Ehin, 2000)

Peter Drucker suggests that seeking to manage human beings is itself the wrong idea (Drucker, Dyson, Handy, Saffo, & Senge, 1997). Instead, organizations should give up any illusion of control over human capital and not confuse control with order (Ehin, 2000). Order will arise, but only when self-organizing humans are allowed to act naturally—to participate in the creation. Leaders must understand and create the conditions that will generate spontaneous effort, conditions that create what Mihaly Csikszentmihalyi (1990) calls flow. Management approaches must leverage the individual differences of employees and support rather than resist employee initiative.

Human Attention: A Critical Currency

Regardless of the job, in a human capital environment human attention is a critical currency. It is in one sense the commodity being exchanged (T. H. Davenport & Beck, 2001). Certainly this concept is true in the "attention-giving service sector"—health care, education, and the like; but in a knowledge society, the delivery of information also relies on an exchange of attention, whether to the information itself, to the processes that manage it, or to the people exchanging it.

Attention is a highly perishable commodity and in increasingly short supply. We are bombarded by demands on our attention. Sixty thousand new books are published every year in the United States, and four hundred thousand scholarly journals worldwide and billions of Web pages pour out information. The average supermarket carries forty thousand different items—two hundred brands of salsa alone (T. H. Davenport & Beck, 2001).

Humans have only so much mental space. If attention goes one place, it cannot go another. We "cannot process more than a few bits of information at any single moment, roughly 110 bits of information. Understanding what another person is saying to us requires about forty bits—which is why we cannot understand what two people are saying at once." This space limitation is the reason that multitasking is "more a myth than a reality. Humans cannot really successfully multitask, we are in fact moving attention rapidly, but consecutively attending, not simultaneously" (Csikszentmihalyi, 2003, pp. 77–78).

Attention is about quality as much as quantity. When our attention is constantly broken into micro-units, there are certain kinds of thinking we simply cannot do. And shifting attention from one thing to another creates a more superficial result than when attention is focused for a sustained period (Csikszentmihalyi, 2003). If we spend our allotment of available attention sifting through a hundred e-mail messages, we have no attention left to consider what any of them means (T. H. Davenport & Beck, 2001).

> *What information consumes is the attention of its recipients. A wealth of information creates a poverty of attention.*
>
> —Herbert Simon, Nobel prize–winning economist
> (cited in T. H. Davenport & Beck, 2001)

What humans attend to falls along a spectrum of what's important to them. Attention is a physiological phenomenon and it follows a hierarchy, with survival always getting first priority. Because humans are biological and not mechanical creatures, no one (not even a manager) can legislate what will command their attention. The first four priorities (described in Abraham Maslow's hierarchy of needs) show clearly what commands our attention first if threatened (T. H. Davenport & Beck, 2001).

1. *Survival and reproduction:* Food, water, sex and protection of offspring
2. *Safety:* Shelter, trusted friends, and family

3. *Belonging:* Connection and intimacy

4. *Esteem:* The drive to achieve, be competent, gain approval and recognition

Only after these basic needs are met can a person attend to growth needs such as understanding, aesthetics, achieving individual potential, and going beyond oneself (Huitt, 2003).

When basic needs are met, people can focus attention elsewhere. But when their jobs are insecure (which threatens their basic sense of safety), or when their children are in worrisome care, when a spouse or close friend is in crisis, it consumes their attention. It cannot do otherwise. (Children draw instinctive attention because both men and women have a primal drive to protect their progeny.) When managers understand this dynamic as a biological and psychological reality, they can make better decisions about how to maximize attention to work goals. They may realize the pointlessness of punitive approaches and see the value of providing resources that help remove chronic worries about children's care or of giving employees time to deal with family emergencies. They can also better appreciate the importance of reducing the complexity that compromises focused attention — information overload, work interruptions, crisis mode, lack of downtime, and the like.

What Becomes Important

When human capital moves center stage, three things increase in importance: the ability to foster positive human interactions, employees' state of mind, and employees' belief that the organization shares their values.

Aptitudes Related to Human Interactions

The ability to foster positive human interactions — between employees, with customers, or across organizations — becomes a critical part of organizational success. Human interaction skills, for both managers and workers, become as valuable as technical skills and content knowledge. The following paragraphs describe key skills.

Communication skills. The ability to communicate effectively with others requires more than the one-directional communication skills used to express ideas. It requires two-way communication skills: the ability to listen effectively, read cues, recognize what's happening emotionally with people, and pick up on the contextual nuances of different environments. It requires understanding and managing the differences between the various forms of communication—written, verbal, and electronic—and the subtleties of gender, age, culture, and other influences on communication styles. Higher-order communication skills like the ability to facilitate, model, observe, teach, and so on become essential to leaders and valued in team members.

Interpersonal skills. Employees must be able to understand and relate to a wide range of people. They must be able to build relationships, to establish trust, to work interdependently, to collaborate and cooperate. They must value others and have an appreciation for other points of view. These abilities are essential if knowledge is to be exchanged, good service is to be delivered, and team-based production environments are to work effectively. Competitiveness and self-promotion, contrarily, destroy value in today's environment; they are counterproductive when cooperation and knowledge sharing are essential (Ehin, 2000). In place of individualism, which was valued in an industrial production environment when tasks were separated, people need the capacity to work together for the good of the whole. The ability to persuade, guide, and empower people is important for employees and leaders alike. Leaders must also be able to do more than command; they must accurately assess others' frame of mind and build a genuine sense of collective spirit.

Intrapersonal skills. Employees must develop intrapersonal skills (emotional skills) if they are to have the potential for loyalty, engagement, and commitment in an environment where security is no longer explicit. They also must be able to deal with change, complexity, and ambiguity, to be responsible and act with integrity. They must be able to trust and to earn trust in others and be persistent. They must be self-motivated, confident, and comfortable making decisions, and be wise risk-takers. To do these things they must have self-understanding and be able to manage their emotions. Self-understanding is the basis for emotional intelligence; it is also required if employees are to find meaning in their work. These personal skills are important to the individual employee's success and to the organization's functioning as a whole. It is almost impossible to succeed without employees who have the sound emotional footing that enables them to commit to goals and persist in the face of disappointment.

Employee State of Mind

Whether employees are bored or enthusiastic, engaged or tuned out, inspired or demoralized—all matter very much in a human capital environment. These issues particularly matter in knowledge and service environments where frame of mind triggers creativity, motivation engages and inspires customers, and initiative fuels innovation.

Match of Individual with Organizational Values

People will only be engaged fully when they understand and are allied with what the organization is about. The essence of the organization—what it stands for, what it values, and how it behaves—will attract employees with those same values. "Values matching" becomes integral to the ability of workers, particularly knowledge workers, to find meaning and to be fully present in their work. It is in the making of meaning that the spiritual aspect of human capital comes into play.

In Conclusion

People—with all their complexity and complications—are the only way for organizations to generate the ideas, relationships, and attentive service that success now requires. But managing human capital is an entirely different challenge from managing to maximize physical and financial capital. While people are the differentiator in organizational success, they are also people—they are organisms, not mechanisms. No two are alike. Their individuality and humanness is what enables them to create, to care, and to connect.

Organizations could perhaps once manage people like replaceable parts—as if they were extensions of the machinery—and still succeed, but they cannot do so anymore. They must understand what influences human attention and supports human interaction, and what facilitates engagement and belief in the organization's values.

2

KNOWLEDGE AND SERVICE WORK

As the new engine of business success, people drive results through their relationships, creativity, and knowledge. This fact reflects a fundamental change in the nature of work itself, a change that requires a completely different contribution from workers. Work once involved primarily hands; now it requires minds (intellect) and hearts (emotion). Where most workers once ran a lathe, poured steel, or sewed clothing, now they design buildings, write computer code, edit legal briefs, design marketing brochures, or create financial statements. They teach, sell real estate, care for the sick, or do social work. They are knowledge and service workers, and their minds and hearts are central to their performance.

Knowledge and service work represent the majority of today's jobs— 85 percent, according to Peter Drucker (2001). By his definition and estimate, knowledge workers now comprise 60 percent of all workers, and service workers are another 25 percent, numbers that will only increase. Manufacturing, manual, and farm work make up the remaining 15 percent, and even this work has become more knowledge-intensive and interactive. These workers also analyze and convey information and use technology on the job. Warehouse workers use computers to track inventory. Production workers are in self-managed teams. Family farmers measure crop moisture and yield with computers in their combines.

Knowledge and service work is as different from yesterday's industrial work as industrial work was from farm labor. Understanding the implications of these differences and how they are affected by the increasing dual focus of the workforce, discussed in Chapter 3, is essential for managers and organizations.

Knowledge Work

We traditionally think of knowledge workers as doctors, lawyers, scientists, and professors. Peter Drucker ("Survey: The New Workforce," 2001) describes people in these jobs as high-knowledge workers, and they are not a new phenomenon, though their numbers have increased. The greater increase has come in what Drucker calls "knowledge technologists—people who do much of their work with their hands (and so are the successors to skilled workers), but whose pay is determined by the knowledge between their ears, acquired in formal education rather than through apprenticeship. They include X-ray technicians, physiotherapists, ultrasound specialists, psychiatric case workers, dental technicians and scores of others." These workers, he believes, within twenty or thirty years will become the dominant group in the workforce, as unionized factory workers once were.

Knowledge workers generate value in a fundamentally different way from manual workers, creating intangible products as a result of their thinking and relating. They can turn products into services and make physical products smaller or more valuable (Magretta, 1993). They develop new products such as pharmaceuticals or software and file applications for FDA approval (T. H. Davenport & Prusak, 1998). They manage customer relationships—coordinating processes and information from various touch points within the customer organization and managing customer knowledge to provide one face to the customer (Grisaffe, 2001). They leverage their knowledge about customers with technical knowledge to improve the overall quality of the service they provide (Hitt, Bierman, Shimizu, & Kochhar, 2001).

Knowledge workers apply knowledge to improve existing products and processes and they develop new knowledge, producing software, books, and scientific developments (Amar, 2002). They have firm-specific knowledge; general and specific knowledge in a field, industry, or function; and experience and skills (Dess & Shaw, 2001). Their tacit knowledge, which is based on experience, reasoning, expertise, judgment, and insight, has become as important as their explicit knowledge, if not more so (Ehin, 2000).

A Different Management Approach

The distinctive characteristics of knowledge workers require that they be managed differently from industrial workers. In various books and lectures, Peter Drucker has discussed these characteristics, which we summarize in the box below.

To create high performance with knowledge workers, the management approach requires flexibility, results orientation, and empowerment. The more intense the knowledge application, the more important it is for organizations to organize organically and flexibly. To be effective, knowledge workers require nonhierarchical organizational structures. Hierarchies are counterproductive because knowledge workers cannot be managed as subordinates. They see themselves as equals and expect to be managed as partners, not underlings ("Survey: The New Workforce," 2001). Instead,

---

CHARACTERISTICS OF KNOWLEDGE WORKERS

- Knowledge workers carry the means of production with them.
- Knowledge workers know their jobs better than their supervisors do.
- Knowledge workers are highly mobile and do not work in linear patterns the way manual workers do.
- Knowledge workers see themselves as equals and behave like volunteers.
- Knowledge workers contribute ideas and imagination, so they must be engaged in their work.
- Work is a source of meaning to knowledge workers, so they seek a match between their values and those of the organization.
- Knowledge workers choose work that enhances their own capital.

adhocracy (an ad hoc, or fluid, approach) is often the best structure (Newel, Robertson, Scarbrough, & Swan, 2002). An adhocracy deemphasizes bureaucracy and replaces it with a dynamic environment of self-formed and self-managed work teams with few formal roles and procedures, where decision making is decentralized to the workers themselves (Mintzberg, 1993).

With knowledge work, the quality of output is usually more important than its quantity. Outputs and not inputs must be the basis of performance measures—not hours invested but results. Knowledge work is not easily monitored or checked (Amar, 2002), and things that undercut quality, such as overwork, overload, and distractions, deserve special attention.

Knowledge workers are motivated primarily by job content and quality and are best managed as though they were volunteers who work primarily for the satisfaction of the work itself, rather than the paycheck ("Survey: The New Demographics," 2001). They seek personal achievement and responsibility and prefer to make their own decisions ("Survey: Will the Corporation Survive?," 2001). Successful empowerment—the delegation of responsibility that gives employees increased decision-making authority—significantly increases their job knowledge, which is key to their performance (Leach, Wall, & Jackson, 2003). Because the ability to think, process, and internalize information as knowledge and the ability to create new concepts, solve problems, and make judgments are critical to the performance of knowledge workers, work processes and cultures that foster these outcomes are crucial.

The role of managers is different with knowledge work. Both knowledge technologists (such as paralegals and lab techs) and high-knowledge workers (such as nurses and scientists) often know more than their managers about how to achieve results, particularly in jobs and careers that have become highly specialized ("Survey: The New Demographics," 2001). No longer have supervisors come up through the ranks and done the job they now supervise. Also, knowledge content changes rapidly, so knowledge workers know how to execute their work better than anyone (Drucker, 1993). Only they can know how to structure it for best results. The supervisor facilitates the best outcomes not by organizing the work and giving instructions or assignments but by helping make connections and ensuring each knowledge worker has the resources required to do the job. Knowledge managers must be able to assess and support the invisible achievements that are part of knowledge work (T. H. Davenport, 2002).

With knowledge work the power dynamics of management change. Most important, because knowledge workers carry the means of production with them in themselves, the power that management once had to make demands no longer exists at the same level. "The knowledge worker . . . may realize that he depends on the organization for access to income and opportunity, and that without the investment the organization has made—and a high investment at that—there would be no opportunity for him. But he also realizes, and rightly so, that the organization equally depends on him" (Peter Drucker, in *Business: The Ultimate Resource*, 2002, p. 984). Knowledge workers recognize that their internalized knowledge is not easily replaceable and they can be highly mobile ("Survey: The New Workforce," 2001), taking their knowledge capital with them from organization to organization.

Portable Capital

"Portable capital" gives knowledge workers more employment options; they can work in a diverse pattern of employment relationships as contractors or consultants, as well as in the traditional employee role ("Survey: Will the Corporation Survive?," 2001). They can also work to later ages because knowledge work is not physically demanding ("Survey: The New Demographics," 2001). As knowledge workers of the Baby Boom generation approach retirement, many will choose to work part-time as independent contractors or consultants because work is satisfying to them, or to replenish their diminished retirement accounts, or both. To get these *wisdom workers*, organizations will have to accept part-time status in knowledge-intensive jobs; the status and higher pay these workers will expect will redefine part-time work.

Continual learning is vital for knowledge workers because knowledge rapidly becomes obsolete; knowledge workers must continually improve the quality of their capital ("Survey: The New Workforce," 2001). Recognizing this fact as key to their marketability, they choose employment opportunities that advance their knowledge.

Because knowledge work is a source of meaning as well as income, knowledge workers seek organizations whose values mirror theirs. Peter Drucker writes, "Increasingly, the knowledge workers of tomorrow will have to know and accept the values, the goals, and the policies of the organization—to use current buzzwords, they must be willing—nay, eager—to buy into the company's mission" (*Business: The Ultimate Resource*, 2002, p. 984).

Certain skills are essential to knowledge work. Knowledge workers must be able to think abstractly, solve problems, and know how to learn—to sense, to judge, and to create (Stewart, 1999). They must be able to connect, extend, and disseminate ideas (Amar, 2002). These are highly complex skills, and the work environment can either support or inhibit them. Bureaucracies and inflexible work environments stifle these skills; flexible environments that reinforce employees' self-organization and autonomy support them.

Service Work

The distinction between knowledge work and service work is not neat; by some definitions the two overlap. Services are generally understood to be work whose output is not a tangible product: "anything sold in trade that could not be dropped on your foot," as the *Economist* defines it, pointing out that it is consumed at the time it is produced and provides value to its consumer in an intangible form—in improved health, comfort, convenience, or entertainment (cited in Quinn, 1992). Clearly this definition includes much knowledge work.

There are *service industries*: transportation, communication, financial services, wholesale and retail trade, most utilities, professional services (law, consulting, and accounting), entertainment, and health care, as well as government social services in the public sector. There are *service activities* within other industries that allow products to be stored, transported, distributed, financed, and repaired: personnel, accounting, finance, maintenance, legal, research, design, warehousing, marketing, sales, market research, distribution, repair, and engineering activities, and the list goes on. According to one estimate, in most manufacturing companies 65–75 percent of employees are performing *service tasks*, defined as information systems, legal, marketing, advertising, clerical, product design, customer information, or research and development (Quinn, 1992).

Service functions have grown to be a higher percentage of all jobs because improvements in manufacturing and agricultural technology have enabled products to be produced with less labor. A pound of food or piece of furniture can be produced with fewer hours worked. At the same time our society has became more affluent; people seek a better quality of life through services that offer comfort, health, entertainment, travel, communication, and convenience.

The service aspects of products have also become a more important part of an organization's wealth-generating capacity. Customer service and service reputation often differentiate one company's product from another's (Quinn, 1992). The service aspects of a physical product do the same—adding value to a car, for example, by enhancing the design or the engineering so it improves the experience of the customer. Customers pay extra for this service-generated value. According to the Bureau of Economic Analysis, the service sector (finance, insurance, real estate, retail and wholesale trade, transportation, and communication) accounted for three fourths of gross domestic product in 2001, while the total goods sector (all manufacturing, construction, mining, agriculture, forestry, and fishery outputs) accounted for only the remaining fourth (U.S. Department of Commerce & Bureau of Economic Analysis, 2002).

Improved service functions—better distribution, inventory, warehousing, and so on—can lower costs and improve productivity as effectively as cutting direct labor or investing in machinery or product features (Quinn, 1992). So service work is increasingly important to an organization's financial performance, whether it is in the service business per se or has service functions related to its products, which nearly every business does.

Many service workers perform what Robert Reich (2003) calls an "attention-giving service." They treat patients, rescue people, handle customer complaints, clean hotel rooms, or care for elderly. They work in what are often traditionally thought of as "service occupations" as defined in the *Dictionary of Occupational Titles* (U.S. Department of Labor, 2003). However, if one considers everyone working in service functions (everyone who doesn't produce something that can be dropped on your foot), the list of people doing service work would be much broader. It would, for example, include a wide range of managers, salespeople, communications workers, and many higher-level professionals. (The overlap with knowledge work is apparent in many of these jobs.) However one defines service work, two key things are true:

- *Service workers and employees performing service functions have a powerful influence on customer experience.* They are usually in direct contact with customers, and may be the only person who is. They are the link in the service-profit chain—the retail clerk at Sears or the insurance company's customer service rep. In the airline industry, the interaction with the gate agent has such a powerful effect that it determines whether a passenger thinks the plane left on time—regardless of the actual departure time.

- *Much service work has an emotional component.* State Farm wants agents and claims adjusters to care. Nordstrom wants sales associates who are enthusiastically interested in the customer. Southwest Airlines wants employees to have fun. Evoking certain emotions as part of the job is why some describe service workers as performing *emotional labor*—because managing their own emotions and evoking certain emotions in other people is part of their job. The masseuse's job is partly to induce a feeling of relaxation; the worker's job at Disneyland ("the happiest place on earth") is to make visitors feel happy; the police officer's job often involves helping people calm down. Having studied the intensive training invested in generating and managing emotions among airline personnel, sociologist Arlie Hochschild (1983) suggested that the emotional work—the genuine smile and warmth of the flight attendant that makes the flyer feel safe and as welcome as a family guest with the airline, for example—is in fact the very commodity being sold.

The box below highlights the distinctive characteristics of service work.

CHARACTERISTICS OF SERVICE WORK

- The employee is the instrument of action—the product is delivered directly through a person.

- The worker has a direct effect on value delivered to customers and is often the principal contact with customers—in direct contact, face-to-face, or voice-to-voice.

- The work may have an emotional component—so workers' ability to work with emotions (their own and others) may be part of the product. Workers' emotional state and abilities have an increased influence on output.

The emotional quality of the workplace directly affects the success of service workers and ultimately the success of their organization. Whereas it is certainly desirable for mill workers not to be cranky or feel disrespected, when customer service representatives feel that way, the customers they deal with can perceive it and start feeling that way too. When physical therapists genuinely want their patients to heal, the patients are all well aware of it.

Certain qualities are important in service workers, in particular self-esteem, social skills, and a tolerance for conflict. These intrapersonal (emotional) skills and interpersonal skills are more important when the "self is the instrument of action" and when workers are often called upon to involve their feelings in the situation (Albrecht & Zemke, 1985, p. 114). Managing a service business, with its intangible outcomes, requires "a tolerance for ambiguity, ease in dealing with lack of direct control over every key process, and a finely tuned appreciation of the notion that the organization is equally dependent on soft (or people-related) skills and hard (or production-related) skills" (p. 18).

Because workers' authentic emotions have more power than emotions they assume artificially when it comes to evoking desired emotions in customers, emotions also become part of managers' responsibilities. They must understand that workers who are expected to care for customers do that better when they feel they are cared about by their organizations. They are genuinely enthusiastic about the service they sell when they believe in it. They make customers feel respected when they are respected. Managers must understand the danger of manipulating emotions—with superficial rhetoric or cosmetic team building—and know how to apply mutuality and work toward genuinely aligning emotions.

Recognizing the emotional component of work also suggests attention to job design. As with other work, the de-skilling of service work—breaking it down into standardized segments (like factory work)—subtracts from workers' autonomous control. It can destroy value for service workers, making them feel disconnected (Hochschild, 1983). For example, when health care workers' jobs are structured so they can treat patients holistically, rather than performing disconnected individual tasks, it enables them to care and be more fully present in their work.

Manufacturing

The manufacturing sector has undergone significant changes in the past forty years. Increased use of technology and high-performance work practices, which place more control in the hands of employees, have changed the roles workers play and the skills their jobs require. No longer interchangeable parts who follow directions while managers think (Appelbaum, Bailey, Berg, & Kalleberg, 2000), workers now participate with highly specialized skills and knowledge, in ways that can be critical to many U.S. manufacturers' ability to compete globally. Computer-aided manufacturing has cut costs, reduced waste, and saved energy (Atkinson et al., 1999). Repetitious tasks have been automated for the most part, leaving the more complex tasks to be done by skilled workers.

> *"We don't need people who work like robots anymore,"* one VP of HR says. *"We need people who watch robots."* (Levering & Moskowitz, 2001)

The specific knowledge and skills of manufacturing workers often make the difference between average and high levels of production, quality, and efficiency. Small manufacturers, in particular, must make something different and difficult for customers to do without if they want to compete with larger manufacturing firms. Sustaining this capability requires new designs and processes (Ansberry, 2001b)—and the people who make such innovation possible.

As manufacturing work becomes more knowledge-intensive and manufacturing processes more complex, requiring the use of computers and other technology, specialized skills and knowledge become essential for manufacturing workers. At the same time, interpersonal skills have become more important. As with many types of knowledge and service work, manufacturing now also requires workers who can establish and maintain connections with co-workers in work teams as well as with people in other parts of the organization or in other companies. Workers who are trained to work autonomously in teams can help a company save money. For example, a Miller brewery operating in Ohio has a 50 percent higher productivity rate than the company's next most productive factory, as a result of a lean overnight crew that has been trained to work without oversight in autonomous teams (Atkinson et al., 1999).

Manufacturing companies in most industries today must be concerned with the effectiveness not only of their own company but also of other organizations in the industry's supply chain. Close collaboration with such entities as distributors, raw material suppliers, and assemblers can improve the effectiveness and profitability of a manufacturer, so employees must interface with employees from other companies in the chain. Establishing good working relationships and networks becomes more important with this increased interdependency of all links in the supply chain.

The following box highlights changes that have taken place in manufacturing work.

CHARACTERISTICS OF MANUFACTURING WORK

- The work is becoming knowledge-intensive and complex.
- Workers need interpersonal skills.
- High-performance systems require increased employee involvement and autonomy.

Managing in a Knowledge and Service Economy

Traditional ways of managing—ways that worked just a few decades ago—have become an anachronism because they are based on an industrial model that no longer applies. Table 1 highlights the key differences and begins to reveal how the new human capital can be a lever to help with the heavy lifting that organizations must now perform.

In Conclusion

As the nature of work changes for nearly all kinds of workers—knowledge, service, and manufacturing workers—what is required for workers to be fully effective and generate the greatest results changes too. Whereas organizations operating in the Industrial Age required a contribution of employees' hands alone, in the Information Age intellect and passion—mind and heart—are also essential. This fact—and the fact that workers' knowledge or caring attention essentially defines the goods being sold—alters the

TABLE 1
FROM INDUSTRIAL AGE TO INFORMATION AGE

Industrial Age MACHINE-DRIVEN	Information Age HUMAN CAPITAL-DRIVEN
Work must be • Synchronized • Standardized • Centralized	**Work must be** • Customized • Flexible • Mobile
Valued in Workers • Homogeneity • Compliance	**Valued in Workers** • Diversity • Initiative
Output maximized by . . . • Synchronized work schedules • Central work locations • Identical work practices • Hierarchical structures • Managerial-driven work design	**Output maximized by . . .** • Flexible work schedules • Virtual and flexible work locations • Customized work policies and practices • Adhocracy (a fluid approach) • Employee-driven work design

conditions under which the best performance is produced. Factors that affect workers' attention, attitude, and initiative become paramount. Maximizing the output of this human capital requires a new management approach.

The effect of the shift toward knowledge and service work is significant, particularly when combined with the force explored in Chapter 1—people as the engine of business success. In Chapter 3 we add the third force—the increase in the number of workers who focus on work and other responsibilities simultaneously—and begin to see the new, very different reality in which organizations now operate.

3

THE RISE OF THE DUAL-FOCUS WORKER

At this point in time, when unique human contributions drive results and employees must bring all of themselves—minds and hearts as well as hands—to work, an entirely new phenomenon has taken shape. The majority of workers no longer relate to work with a singular focus; instead, work is just one critical priority that competes with others for their attention. In this chapter we describe this third force and how it alchemically unites with the other two, producing a radically different workforce that can be either gold or lead, depending on how it is managed.

The Former Reality and Typical Worker

Until fairly recently, the core workforce was somewhat homogenous in terms of the type of work people performed, who the workers were, and how they worked. The typical worker was characterized by three commonalities.

1. A person doing work in which standardization and individual achievement were valued and competition was less intense

2. A male head of household whose primary role in the family was as provider, who was singularly focused on work during work hours and had a partner who managed family and home

3. A regular employee working full-time year-round from entry through retirement without interruption

In the industrial environments of the past, a worker's idiosyncratic qualities were not assets. What a machine required for quality output was the same input every time. The best industrial workers were the most consistent and compliant; they did not rock the boat. Managerial control was vital.

In a service and knowledge economy, the reverse is true. Knowledge work requires diverse ideas, perspectives, and inputs. The best workers are those who give personalized (individualized) service and who innovate on the job—create new ideas, solve problems in new ways. Personalized service is given not by compliant employees but by employees who take initiative and decide for themselves what the situation requires. The traditional values of an industrial environment—homogeneity, consistency, and an emphasis on control—are a liability in the new environment. Creativity, initiative, and an emphasis on self-direction replace them in importance.

Whereas isolated individual achievement was a worthy and practical goal in an industrial environment, in a knowledge economy, the creation and sharing of knowledge and the building of relationship capital (durable personal networks) require cooperation and an emphasis on *collective* accomplishment.

NEW REALITY #1

Whereas the former reality was represented by a person doing work in which standardization and individual achievement were valued and competition was less intense:

Today the typical worker is doing knowledge or service work in a highly competitive environment that requires innovation and relies on collective achievement of work results.

In the rest of this chapter we focus on the second and third characteristics of the typical worker, sole breadwinner and full-time employee, and the social changes that are reshaping how most people work. Some of these changes may sound familiar; some facts are so often repeated that their meaning to the workplace has been lost. We hope to describe what is happening in a fresh way, so that organizations can determine how they will need to respond.

The Dual-Focus Worker

Until recently, the core workforce was made up of primarily men working full-time year-round—throughout their lives—as regular employees. This image was fairly universal, with a few exceptions: entry-level workers, part-time workers, and women who worked before they married and some after their children left home.

The "Breadwinner" Profile

The core worker was typically a male head of household (56 percent of employees in 1950; Bailyn, Drago, & Kochan, 2001), and his primary role in the family was as *breadwinner*. His family usually relied on him alone for its income; if he was out of work, the family had no other earner with employment options that paid very well.[1] His wages were supposed to be enough for the family to live on that single income. In fact, there was a presumption of a *family wage*—the idea that the breadwinner's pay should be enough to support a family.

Work was this man's primary source of identity and self-worth, and it was essential to his family's economic survival that he be successful at work. By putting work as a top priority he met both his work and personal responsibilities, so he was highly motivated to be accommodating to his employer.

When an employer hired this worker, instead of one employee the employer got two—the employee himself and a second invisible partner who managed the personal side of his life and made it possible for him to focus on work. This partner packed his lunch, made sure he had clean clothes, managed his children, arranged for the plumber, helped ailing parents, and handled emergencies. This singular-focus, two-for-the-price-of-one worker is now a small minority (21 percent in 2000)—that is the first thing that has changed.[2]

Women in the Workforce

That change is driven by a second: For many families a single wage has become insufficient.[3] Families with two adults can no longer live well on a single income. Men's real wages have dropped in the past thirty years.[4] At the same time, women have access to a wider range of better-paying occupations and have become more significant direct financial contributors to their households.[5] The shift is so dramatic that, for a variety of reasons, in 55 percent of families, women earn more than half the household income (Cubed, 2002). In one in five families, since no male is present, women are the sole support.

Women's financial contribution is the reason it is not just socially acceptable these days for women to work outside the home, it is necessary. The economics—the rewards, costs, and risks of being full-time homemakers—have shifted. For the first time, women can reap greater economic rewards working outside the home than in; women can contribute more to a household's standard of living in terms of goods—though not perhaps in intangible terms—by being employed.[6] The goods a woman used to produce with her labor (laundry, cooking, sewing) can be purchased now at a price close to what it would be if she did it herself. An electric blanket now costs $35 at Wal-Mart. In contrast, one of the authors' great-grandmothers made each of the woolen blankets that covered the family beds. First she raised the sheep, then sheared them, spun the wool, dyed it from plants growing on her farm in Norway, and then wove it on a loom that her husband had built. She spent much of the rest of her time cooking meals from ingredients she and her family raised; she didn't have the option of picking up "Happy Meals" for $1.99 at McDonald's. While Happy Meals and electric blankets are not exactly the definition of the good life, we suspect she might at times have happily taken both.

Which women are employed and *when* in their life cycle they work are dramatically different today. Although historically more women have been employed than is often realized,[7] most women left their jobs when they married; they raised children and some reentered the labor force twenty or more years later. Now they are marrying later, having fewer children spread over a shorter time period, divorcing, and continuing to work while raising children. Most married women are now employed (an increase from 37 percent to 61 percent between just 1967 and 2000). (As recently as the 1940s custom and the law in some places actually barred married women from paid employment.)[8] Women will work more years of their life, which (along with the likelihood of divorce and rise in single parenthood) compels them to remain in the labor force to ensure their employability and economic viability.[9] It is no longer accurate to view women as unattached and impermanent workers whose skills growth is likely to be halted or organizational attachment severed by long periods out of the workforce (Appelbaum, Bailey, Berg, & Kalleberg, 2002).

Women are employed for longer hours (averaging thirty-six hours a week in 1998; P. N. Cohen & Bianchi, 1999), including mothers of young children, 75 percent of whom work full-time. More women work year-round (Spain & Bianchi, 1996),[10] often in more demanding (and better paying) jobs than before, which their families can less easily risk jeopardizing (National Women's Law Center, 2001). As of 2002, the workforce was approaching an even split — 53 percent men to 47 percent women (Bureau of Labor Statistics, 2002). Some professions tend to remain gender segregated (in 1998 women were still 98 percent of secretaries and 92 percent of nurses), but women are much less thoroughly confined to so-called pink-collar professions (Heintz, Folbre, & Center for Popular Economics, 2000). In 2000, women were 31 percent of math and computer scientists, 53 percent of economists, 30 percent of lawyers and judges, 56 percent of editors and reporters, 50 percent of financial managers, and 56 percent of accountants and auditors (U.S. Census Bureau, 2002d).

More mothers of very young children are employed—in fact, the majority are working outside the home. Now, 51 percent of mothers of infants under a year old and 56 percent of mothers of children under six are employed (Bureau of Labor Statistics, 2003). More women with children under eighteen are employed (73 percent) than women without children (55 percent; Bureau of Labor Statistics, 2001c).[11] In fact, the proportion of mothers of children under eighteen who are employed (73 percent) is roughly the same as the proportion of all men employed (75 percent; Bureau of Labor Statistics, 2001c).

IN A NUTSHELL

- Dual-focus workers outnumber two-for-the-price-of-one workers (people with a partner at home) by three to one.
- Most employees have dependent children, dependent elders, or both.
- Mothers of children under eighteen are now employed at about the same rate as men.
- Half of U.S. families live on less than $42,000/year (a quarter earn less than $25,000), with limited means to replace what the stay-at-home adult once did.

What It Means to Employers

Workers' lives have changed in the new reality. The effect of these dynamic changes in the labor force is twofold.

More Options

First, since most families have two incomes and the second income pays better and has more growth potential than it used to, each earner in a middle-income household has more options. One can take time out to retool, return to school, be more selective about a job change, or simply not abide a boring job or poor manager. The already tenuous hold an employer has on employees, particularly knowledge workers who carry the inventory in their heads, is further weakened.[12]

Less Support

Second, extra flexibility—for most employees, regardless of income—is more than offset by the lack of the invisible support system at home that once allowed them to focus primarily on work. Men no longer have it, nor do women. Most employees don't have a spouse or partner at home seeing that children and elders have what they need, that groceries and toothpaste are in the house, and that home tasks get done. Neither can most employees (male or female) count on being able to work without interruption during the day, to put in extended hours or show up on any schedule their organization needs, or to travel on demand.

While many tasks the nonworking partner used to handle can be contracted out—for those who can afford it—others cannot. Take-out meals, housecleaning services, child care, and even help to take an ailing parent to the doctor can be purchased. These services are costly; child care alone is the equivalent of a second mortgage. But it is nearly impossible to find someone who can be with your kindergartener from 5 A.M. to 7 A.M. if you are a bus driver and leave for work at the crack of dawn. Nor would you want to hire out the task of calming your scared teenager whose school isn't safe, or being with your grandmother when she awakes from surgery. In short, tasks the silent partner in the family enterprise used to perform have not been systematically rethought either within families or more broadly within society.

Juggling Responsibilities

Now typical employees—outnumbering those with a spouse at home by more than two to one—are dual-focus workers with no one at home to tend to family and manage life's other tasks. With most employed adults working nearly full-time,[13] both men and women juggle major responsibilities outside work. The majority (53 percent) of employees have either children or elders for whom they care—a remarkable number.[14] The care responsibilities are often very demanding; for example, one in five of elder adults being cared for has Alzheimer's disease or dementia (Fredriksen-Goldsen & Scharlach, 2001).

With a median household income of $42,000 (in 2000), most families do not earn enough to contract out the things the stay-at-home partner used to do. Their income does not cover the cost of child and elder care, even if care were available (U.S. Census Bureau, 2002a).[15]

It is easy for organizations to think this change doesn't concern them and to miss the fact that it causes an enormous disruption of work performance. In a Harvard study, 30 percent of working parents had cut back on work at least one day in the past week to meet the needs of family members, 12 percent had cut back on two or more days, and 5 percent had cut back on three or more days (Heymann, 2000).[16]

These trends will also directly affect the quality of the future labor pool, a serious problem for employers of whom 43 percent already have to provide remedial training on basic proficiency skills (Committee for Economic Development, 1998). The complex skills essential in a knowledge economy—the ability to reason, solve problems, and create new ideas—are at even greater risk. These skills are not inborn; 80 percent of brain development is the result of experiences before age two (Shore & Families and Work Institute, 1998). Regrettably, 43 percent of infants under a year old are in child care (Lombardi, 2003), and only one in twelve child care situations have enough attentive and knowledgeable adults to help children develop thinking skills, emotional stability, and traits like responsibility and initiative that workers and employers will need (Helburn & Bergmann, 2002). Unless something changes, employers are facing a whole generation of ill-equipped future workers.

Because much of what the silent partner did was hidden and unnamed, it was easy to underestimate both the energy and the expertise the role required and the important contribution it made to the smooth functioning and quality of people's lives (Burggraf, 1999). Harriet is now employed just like Ozzie, but we have not yet figured out how to get done what Harriet always did—shaping Ricky and David into good citizens, helping Ozzie decompress, supervising the house painters, serving on the PTA, and creating a place of refuge from the rest of the world. Harriet made *home* more than another place of assignments and tight schedules; it was a place where people were cared about, where they could be rejuvenated and feel joy (Jackson, 2002).

Underestimating what it took for Harriet to accomplish these tasks often means underestimating their value and what it would take to replace her—if indeed Harriet can be replaced. Often she cannot—and if her absence eats away at employees' overall quality of life, the job is often where the price is paid. As one man said, "If the trade-offs become too great, I can always get another job; I can't get another family."

The ultimate price an employer can pay is the loss of valuable talent. Robert Reich, secretary of labor in the Clinton administration, resigned at the end of his first term of office. He had in essence missed four years of his adolescent sons' lives, working the long hours with frequent late-night meetings that typified the Clinton White House. He decided that another four years would mean missing too many never-to-be-recovered teenage years in his two sons' lives, and so he quit. Reich said, "It was the best job I ever had, but it was the best family I ever had."

Organizations may think these are family or social changes that individuals must deal with themselves. But at the same time organizations require the additional labor the old employment patterns brought.

NEW REALITY #2

Unlike the former typical worker, who was a male head of household whose primary role in the family was as provider and who was singularly focused on work with a partner who managed family and home:

Today the typical worker is as likely to be female as male, is not a primary breadwinner, and does not have a full-time system of support at home. Such a worker does not have and may not want a singular focus on work.

Selecting Leaders

It is difficult for senior leaders to recognize the meaning of these changes because most have not experienced them directly. Most have a spouse at home who makes it possible for the leader to devote enormous undivided attention to building the organization. As noted in Chapter 13, DuPont actually found that in 1995 its male exempts (most managers) were *more* likely to have a stay-at-home spouse than they had been ten years earlier. The increasing rigors of the job made it more difficult to do without a singular focus, so single managers and those with employed spouses apparently were not advancing. This situation creates a dual challenge—managing workers who lead vastly different lives from their own, and developing new leaders who reflect the realities of the employee population.

Developing leaders who can truly understand how to work with employees whose personal responsibilities take as much precedence as their work is hard because leaders are identified early in their careers specifically by their willingness to focus heavily on work. Since this willingness is required at the same time most people are beginning to start families, the people identified as young leaders are often those willing to compromise or sacrifice this option (Bailyn, 1993), perhaps not even recognizing the consequences of the choices they make. Old leadership patterns are thus reinforced when this cycle is perpetuated. It is hard to manage well what you do not fully understand.

Change in Employment Patterns

One final key difference separates today's typical workers from their predecessors. Uniformity and continuousness in employment patterns is a thing of the past. The typical worker used to work in a fairly straightforward, linear employment pattern, as a full-time regular employee without interruption from the first job through retirement. Today people increasingly vary their employment, mixing periods of part-time work, full-time work, and no work and spreading them over multiple cycles of learning, work, and rest. As people live longer they have more time to pursue a second cycle of education, work, and time off. They need added income to support longer lives and have nearly two additional decades in which to earn it.[17]

The uniform employment pattern has evaporated because knowledge workers can work under a host of arrangements. Unlike brawn workers, they can work at older ages, because they are not limited by the physical demands of work. As noted earlier, they may not necessarily want to work full-time. By 2008, 18 percent of men and 9 percent of women over sixty-five are expected to be employed, slightly higher than in 2000 (U.S. Census Bureau, 2002b). Eight in ten Baby Boomers plan to work after retirement. Most of them expect to work part-time; a third say they will work part-time out of sheer interest in the work and a quarter to earn extra income (Keilly, 2002).

Knowledge workers don't have to be regular employees to earn a living. They can readily contract out their talents—as freelance writers, *e-lancers* (electronically connected freelancers; Malone & Laubacher, 1993), consultants, and independent contractors—or do project work as short-term employees. They may interrupt employment trajectories to acquire more education or reinvent themselves. A second earner in a family gives all kinds of workers a cushion that makes interruptions possible.

The shift away from uniformity is also driven by dual-income families who must take time out to raise children or care for other family members. More men are increasingly determined not to miss out on the things their fathers did, like connecting with their children or keeping a marriage intact. By 2000, 45 percent of men with young children had taken some amount of family leave under the Family and Medical Leave Act (FMLA; Waldfogel, 2001). As women's income has increased, men are sometimes the ones holding down the home front when children are young or relocating for a wife's employment. With two earners in a family, a man whose job is eliminated is under less pressure to find another at once and has more leeway to increase his marketability by taking time out to get or finish a degree.

Taking time out is nothing new for women, but with women now in mainline jobs as managers, investment bankers, and engineers, the fluidity in career patterns has shifted from jobs once considered peripheral to those now considered central to organizations.

For both men and women, there is a fundamental evolution toward greater diversity in careers in general. Careers are more individually driven and less organizationally driven. That is, people measure their success more by their own standards and less by external signposts like position (Hall, 2002). Knowledge workers in particular affiliate with their profession or specialized branch of knowledge, not their organization, and so they are more mobile ("Survey: The New Demographics," 2001).

Finally, more workers have directly experienced the breakup of the old employee-employer contract and its presumed job security. One in two American workers has either been downsized, worked for a company that has been merged or acquired, or been transferred to another city because of job requirements (Ellsworth, 2002; Maharaj, 1998). In 1996, 11 percent of employees thought there was a significant chance they could lose their job

---

NEW REALITY #3

Unlike the former reality, where a regular employee stayed on the job full-time year-round throughout a working life without interruption:

Today the typical worker will eventually be employed under a variety of employment arrangements: working on a contingent basis, interrupting or changing careers, or working well beyond retirement age. Most workers have experienced the breakup of the old employer-employee contract.

within the next year, an increase from 3 percent in 1989 (Mishel, Bernstein, & Boushey, 2002). In 1980 and 1981, 79 percent of management and 75 percent of nonmanagement employees rated their job security as "good" or "very good." By 1992–94, those confidences had fallen to 55 percent and 51 percent (Ellsworth, 2002; B. O'Reilly, 1994).

Consequences of the New Realities

These new realities create a very different employment environment. What is considered *typical* has changed at a basic level. Dual-focus workers— those with simultaneous work and personal responsibilities—used to be the exception. Now they are the rule. Once considered peripheral to organizational success, they are now—by the jobs they hold and by their sheer numbers—carrying the essential weight in organizations. In a knowledge and service environment, managing these individuals for their success will determine if the organization's structure is on a solid foundation.

Shift in the Balance of Power

Most noticeably, employers have less power to command certain behaviors of employees. The workforce is "more mobile, better informed, more individualistic than ever before and confident in its ability to move" (Towers Perrin, 2001).

Knowledge workers must be managed like volunteers. They consider themselves equals in the enterprise, not subordinates, and they expect to make decisions about their work ("Survey: Will the Corporation Survive?," 2001). They know that if they leave, their tacit knowledge (the internalized information forged by experience that only resides in people) and their relationship capital (the network of relationships that expedites action) go with them. They are *portable* ("Survey: Will the Corporation Survive?," 2001). When someone works for the satisfaction of it, not just the paycheck (as knowledge workers do), retention becomes even more important and not as simple to resolve as when compensation is a prime motivator.

A different dynamic happens with service jobs, but the result is the same—management's power to command essential outcomes shrinks. Service workers often have little overt power, and many are relatively low paid. But the very thing that their employer is selling is their genuine enthusiasm, warmth, or caring about customers or clients and their ability to generate emotions in customers. This emotional labor cannot be produced in the same way a can of soup can be. An artificial version can be commanded—a phony smile or phrase repeated mechanically—but the real *passion* that sells products better and real *caring* that clients recognize as personalized service are emotions that belong to the employee (Hochschild, 1983). They cannot be commanded, coerced, or successfully manipulated, but they can be cultivated (Cheever, 2001). Organizations must pay attention to what is going on with customer service people, health care workers, and sales clerks because they are often the only people in the organization who make direct contact with customers. Their power to affect the customers' perceptions and the organization's outcomes is great.

Short-term economic downturns may mask the shift in power for knowledge and service workers, but only temporarily. In all kinds of industries, competitive pressures will continue to require decisions to be pushed down and success will rely more heavily on employees' making on-the-spot decisions.

Employers also have less power to command certain behaviors such as an exclusive focus on work or perfect attendance, because when people don't have a support system at home, these behaviors are simply not possible.

Altered Expectations

Employees are less trusting and more tuned in to and protective of their own requirements. Because they have been downsized (reorganized, rightsized) themselves or have otherwise personally felt the change in the old implied employer-employee contract, they no longer expect an employer to protect their interests. They know that it will be up to them to get what they need.

The old employer-employee contract promised that giving an employer your all would be rewarded. Loyalty on both sides was met with reward on both sides. Employees gave 110 percent to work and the organization responded with long-term security. There was an expectation of later reward, whether in eventual promotions or other future benefits. It was in a sense a parental relationship. Now, the employee-employer relationship has shifted to an adult-adult relationship in which each party takes care of its own interests. Employees become more self-protective. This is not news, but what follows from this change is not well understood.

Employees who have gone through a traumatic separation from work have often cocooned themselves in an almost involuntary reaction to the trauma. They have pulled away to recover, whether literally or figuratively—and in the process have examined what is important to them. Those who have gone through this self-examination have often discovered important nonwork sides of themselves that they have been neglecting: they may have postponed giving attention to their health, family relationships, or spirituality, or participating in community life.

Once they become reacquainted with these aspects of their lives and recognize their loss in the emotional or temporal space that cocooning provides, their willingness to continue to postpone these important aspects of themselves evaporates. This resolve holds particularly true in the new transactional employer-employee relationship, where little binds either party beyond the immediate payoff. Employees become more insistent about meeting their needs for health, balance, and meaning, rather than waiting for a sense of value and belonging to come from a long-term employment relationship. The urgency is particularly acute for those with the most knowledge and social capital—the midcareer and wisdom workers—who realize they don't have unlimited time remaining in their lives to recover, rebuild, or make up for what they have missed.

The motivation to not sacrifice oneself for one's employer acts together with the fact that most workers now have more personal tasks to attend to while they are working. The combination makes employees even less willing to always put work first.

New Requirements for Success

A different way of organizing work, measuring performance and commitment, and identifying high-performers is required. Managing employees becomes more complicated and requires the exercise of judgment instead of the uniform application of rules. Instead of one-size-fits-all policies, or under-the-table exceptions that supervisors make at risk of censure, an overtly individualized approach to managing today's workers is required. In fact, pushing the decisions down and off the manager can be, as we will discuss in Part 2, simpler and more effective.

The work environment must promote creativity, individual expression, and social contacts. The old ways of increasing productivity must be re-examined—for example, longer hours in a knowledge environment don't necessarily yield more great ideas; the effect may be just the reverse. What is valued changes; passion may have limited value in a steel mill (although some would argue), but in the design of a building or discovery of a new drug, it can give an enormous advantage. Social networks are not a distraction, they are a core asset.

There are limits to when, how, and how much employees can work. Organizations must organize activities and people differently. The 9-to-5 workday was much simpler, and given that work and personal life have become simultaneous 24/7 undertakings, coordinating both lives has become quite dificult. Whereas early morning meetings, after-hours planning sessions, professional development that involved travel, and work over weekends were once reasonable to expect (Rapoport & Bailyn, 1996), these practices are no longer realistic for most men or women. The flexibility required to coordinate workers' lives today puts a very different spin on such expectations.

New resources (benefits) become essential for high performance. Benefits become a vehicle for offering key resources required for productivity. Benefits designed for a family headed by a single earner no longer fit the typical worker. And large numbers of workers have no benefits at all. In 2000, only 52 percent of employees in private industry participated in medical care plans, and only 48 percent were covered by retirement benefits (Bureau of Labor Statistics, 2000). Medical, retirement, and other benefits are certainly still highly desirable, but 53 percent of the workforce have dependent children or are caring for an elderly relative. Different benefits—certainly child care, elder care, and other family care—not needed before, thus become essential and affect employees' ability to be productive.

The belief that benefits should be equitable and the old definition of equity (the same for everyone) must change. Some employees will simply need to receive benefits that are worth more than others if they are to be effective at work. The conception of employee benefits as having value only for employees, instead of also having value for management as a tool to improve organizational effectiveness, must also change. Benefits become a way of providing resources.

Employee commitment must be redefined. Employee commitment must be measured by the person's willingness to take full responsibility to get the work done at the essential level, and by the quality and appropriateness of output—not by willingness to put work first or to follow orders without objection (Bailyn, 1993). A new definition of commitment might also recognize how discretionary efforts contribute to the goals of the organization, such as the willingness to contribute to the effectiveness of others, to build teams, to smooth the way.

Rise of Intrinsic Motivation

Employees are increasingly motivated by intrinsic factors. These include control, the ability to work flexibly around competing time demands, job content, and overall quality of their life. In the past, if workers could not control their work schedules, it did not affect them and their family's overall quality of life as it does today. Today, with all adults in the household employed, the ability to protect time can be as important as compensation to the family's quality of life.[18]

Employees are more selective and self-protective about working for an organization whose values they believe in (the organization also requires this match to get full engagement and passionate contribution); making sure the job matches their talents, interests, and long-term growth and is a source of meaning, not just a paycheck; and having a job that does not threaten the quality of their personal and family life.

Increasing Legal Risks

Employers who continue to hold expectations that are best met by workers with stay-at-home spouses are potentially exposed to a claim of gender discrimination. Organizations that hold workers to old ideal-worker standards risk a gender-discrimination claim, because workers who cannot meet the standard are predominantly female. If the firm consistently promotes employees who are not also caregivers (whether they are male or female), or pays a lower rate to less-than-full-time workers who do the same job as full-time workers and then does not promote them *because* they are part-time, the workers involved have potential grounds for a gender discrimination claim. Such practices have a disparate, greater, effect on women, who are the majority of family caregivers (Williams, 2000). Although these practices may not be discriminatory on their face, they are in fact, which is the definition of de facto discrimination.

A survey of cases in which family caregivers have been successful in the courts reveals many different legal theories that can be used to resolve such cases.

> *Though no federal statute specifically protects workers from adverse employment actions based on family care-giving, roughly ten legal theories have emerged: Title VII disparate treatment; Title VII disparate impact; Title VII hostile work environment and constructive discharge; Title VII retaliation; the Equal Pay Act (EPA); the Family and Medical Leave Act; the Americans with Disabilities Act (ADA); Section 1983; state statutes protecting workers with family responsibilities, state common law actions based on violations of public policy; and actions based on employment contracts, handbooks, and collective bargaining agreements.* (Williams & Segal, 2003, p. 124)

The wage gap between women who are mothers and other women has also been documented, which further supports possible claims (Anderson, Binder, & Krause, 2003). After controlling for differences in employment experience, the gap in wages between mothers and other women is 5 percent per child (Budig & England, 2001).

Renewed Emphasis on Education

Employers will have to pay closer attention to early education issues and ensure that children's early environments are developing the skills needed in the future. There are basically three possibilities for ensuring that the future labor force, now in child care, will develop the skills employers will require: reduce the time children spend in nonparental child care, or improve the quality of child care, or both. This objective can be accomplished through voluntary action by employers, including some of the adaptive practices mentioned in Part 2, or through collective action, where costs are spread and solutions are spurred by public policies with government support.

Early childhood education has been called the watershed education issue of this century, as significant as creating the public school system was in the past century. Employers will want a voice in ensuring good education because it is essential to their success as well as to the growth and competitiveness of American business on the world stage.

Organizational Implications

Table 2 sums up what the changes discussed in this chapter mean for organizations.

The revolution in employees' lives, when added to the fundamental changes in the business and work environment described in Chapters 1 and 2, is what we refer to as the "new human capital." It calls for a metamorphosis in workplace practices. Without metamorphosis, organizations will not achieve the maximum employee performance they need to succeed in a human capital–driven world.

TABLE 2

IMPLICATIONS FOR ORGANIZATIONS

The Old Reality	The New Reality
The typical worker A person working in industry, where processes were standard, competition less intense than it is today, and individual achievement primary.	**The typical worker** A person doing knowledge or service work in a highly competitive environment that relies on innovation and collective performance.
A regular employee working full-time year-round throughout a working life without interruption.	A worker with access to a variety of employment arrangements—apt to work as a contingent worker, interrupt a career, or work well beyond retirement age (probably part-time), and to receive some income from nonsalary earnings.
A head of household whose primary role in the family was as provider, who was singularly focused on work during work hours and had a partner who managed family and home.	A male or female in a household where all adults work virtually full-time with no full-time system of support at home. This makes a singular focus on work undesirable and often impossible.
The working environment Managers determine how the work is to be carried out by workers.	**The working environment** Workers participate in the design and organization of their work.
Extrinsic rewards are given for individual performance.	Intrinsic rewards encourage collective and individual performance.
Technical skills are more critical than interpersonal skills.	Both technical and interpersonal skills are recognized and rewarded as critical to organizational success.
Consistency and uniformity are critical.	Individuality and diverse contributions are valued and encouraged.

Full-time continuous employees are presumably better contributors and leaders.	Employees who work in a variety of employment patterns are equally valuable and judged, rewarded, and promoted based on their contribution, not their full-time or part-time status.
Definition of loyal employees includes only full-time continuous workers.	Definition of loyal employees includes those working in fluid arrangements.
Employee commitment can be gauged by whether work is top priority and workers are willing to sacrifice other interests.	Employee commitment is best gauged by work outcomes and discretionary effort that furthers the organization's goals.
The employee's time is a virtually unlimited—boundaryless—resource to the employer.	The employee's time is a limited resource to be shared between employee and employer and managed with both interests in mind.
The number of hours invested in work is a reasonable measure of results.	Direct measures of results and effectiveness are used rather than proxies such as time invested.
Work and personal life do not mix.	Work and personal life can be integrated for the mutual benefit of both.

Clearly, we are in a time of transition. In 2001 the president of Cerner Corporation shot a tirade via e-mail to managers berating employees' work ethic. He stormed that he saw few cars in the parking lot at 8 A.M. or after 5 P.M. anymore and therefore would withhold approval of all new employee benefits, among other things. He was operating from an old ideal-worker norm. Cerner had outperformed the Dow Jones technology software index for the past year—whereas in the previous five years it had underperformed it. Still, the president equated long standard hours at the office and employees at their desks (and their cars in the lot) with high performance. In an age when work can be done remotely (sometimes more effectively) and hours invested don't equal results (never mind that hours at work don't mean hours worked), he was using a proxy for performance that was no longer valid. The president's e-mail was posted to a Yahoo Web site with employees' comments, and Cerner's stock dropped 28 percent within weeks. As the *Wall Street Journal* put it, "It takes years to earn a reputation as a great place to work. But damaging that can take only seconds, as medical-software maker Cerner Corp. discovered this month" (Burton & Silverman, 2001, p. B3).

In Conclusion

Most workers today are different from those of the past. No longer singularly focused on work, they are juggling other major responsibilities as well. They have dependent children, dependent elders, or both. Their career patterns are more varied than their predecessors'; they change or interrupt their careers, work on a contingent basis, or work well past retirement age. Because most of these employees are knowledge and service workers, managers have less overt power to command their performance and must manage them in new ways.

Many organizations manage these dual-focus workers as if they still fit into the former reality. But where these management practices made sense and were effective before, now they no longer work. New management practices are needed to fit a new reality, practices that promote creativity and connections, recognize limits on work schedules, and increase employee engagement. In Part 2 we describe a new management approach that fits this new reality.

The convergence of the three forces described thus far—people as the engine of business success, the shift toward knowledge and service work, and the rise of the dual-focus worker—raises questions about successfully managing human capital in this new reality. What does the organization need to achieve success now? Given that, who are the best workers and what behaviors should be promoted? And how does the organization manage workers for maximum performance? In Chapter 4, we discuss how to redefine the image of the ideal worker to fit the new reality.

4

THE NEW
IDEAL WORKER

In this chapter we address a subtle concept—the notion of an *ideal worker*—and why it matters. People don't talk about this concept, but they do have a mental image of an ideal worker, and that image matters because it is at the heart of any organization's expectations. The sense of what is ideal influences what behavior is rewarded—who is considered an A player, who is thought to be a serious contributor, who is competent, who is promoted and developed, and even how work is distributed and organized (Rapoport et al., 2002).

Many organizational choices are made to support the success of those considered to be the *best workers*. Assumptions about best workers are based on impressions about the core workforce—the typical employees—and what kind of performance is most important (Bailyn, 1993). In each organization, the characteristics regarded as ideal define success and ultimately affect the results the organization can achieve (Williams, 2000). Further, it is an important survival strategy for any organization to set its standards of ideal on current reality. You might say, what you reward determines what you get, so you'd better be sure what you are rewarding is what you want.

In the past, as described in Chapter 3, the typical employee in the core workforce was someone who could be singularly focused on work while at work, an approach made possible by virtue of being a male head of household with a partner who managed family and home. He was a regular employee who worked full-time year-round until retirement without interruption, in an environment where standardization and individual achievement were valued. From that *norm*, the image of the typical worker, the image of the ideal worker emerged. Regardless of the type of work being done, the ideal worker was an individual achiever who put work first, a full-time and accommodating employee. In simple terms, if managers could describe the kind of worker they would prefer, it was the person for whom other priorities did not interfere, who did his job well on his own, who did what was asked of him, and who was always available as needed. He kept his personal life out of work. This was the person who would be chosen over others; this was the behavior that was valued, rewarded, and promoted.

THE FORMER IDEAL WORKER

The person for whom other priorities do not interfere with work, an individual achiever who always does what is asked and is always available as needed, keeping personal life out of work.

Not only did this employee work independently, he was predictably consistent, as his work required. He did not challenge the rules or his superiors, or stray too far from "the way things are done around here." He didn't question whether assignments were necessary, but instead did whatever it took to get the job done. His sense of identity and self-worth came largely from work; he either regarded other responsibilities as secondary or saw work as the route to achieving them, as with supporting his family (Bailyn, 1993; Rapoport et al., 2002). He worked full-time year-round, which made him readily available and his schedule and career trajectory relatively easy to manage (Williams, 2000). His attention and concentration belonged fully to his work. He was rarely absent or late. When something was asked of him at work, he almost always said yes. His time at work was expandable.

He was the first one in and the last one to leave. When the definition of a star is "someone who doesn't know enough to go home at night," it's a sign that this old ideal worker image is operating (Bailyn, 1993; Rapoport et al., 2002).*

This mental image of the ideal worker, though unarticulated and often unconscious, has been the basis for many of today's management practices. It is now obsolete—and that makes the traditional management systems (rewards, promotions, work organization, and workplace rules and policies) based on it equally obsolete. Many traditional practices must be radically revised if organizations are to achieve their goals in the new environment.

Who Is the New Ideal Worker?

This new reality—in which people are the engine of success, where work requires more of them and yet most people simultaneously navigate work and personal responsibilities—calls for a new ideal.

To cope with today's complex demands, organizations must deliver service that is increasingly customized, create new knowledge, and rapidly innovate, collaborate, and continually change in an interconnected world. They must push decisions down to respond nimbly to customers. As a result, they require workers who function in more complex ways. Whereas the former reality required consistency, predictability, and individual achievement, the current reality requires flexibility, adaptability, and collaboration. Instead of being accommodating, workers must challenge, be self-regulating, and take initiative. Straying from "the way things are done around here" is precisely what is required for survival and success. In a knowledge environment, the best workers are those who think for themselves, not those who follow instructions without question. In a service environment, the best workers are those who care—not those who leave their emotions at home. In a networked society, the relationships and interests employees have outside work add to their effectiveness on the job; they don't detract from it.

In a world where most people no longer have a partner at home full-time, employees must be able to successfully integrate rather than separate the parts of their lives. It is impossible for employees to keep their personal

---

* Lottie Bailyn and her colleagues at MIT have done much thoughtful work on the norm of a "career-primary" person.

lives out of work when both work and home have become intertwined in a 24/7 technological, temporal, and spatial overlap. Instead of keeping their two lives separate, employees must be able to perform at a higher level while managing the other responsibilities that compete for their attention.

The work-only focused individual achiever once considered ideal is replaced by a dual-focus individual who can bring heart, mind, and hands to work, be effective in navigating work and personal life simultaneously, deliver results collaboratively, create new knowledge, challenge existing ways of doing things, and work well under diverse arrangements as employee or non-employee.

THE NEW IDEAL WORKER

The multidimensional individual who is effective in dual-focus mode (managing work and personal life simultaneously) can deliver results collaboratively, can innovate and challenge, works well in diverse employment arrangements, and possesses meta-competencies that leverage technical skills: a whole person who can bring heart, mind, and hands to work.

These new ideal workers are efficient with their energy and attention, know when enough is enough, and can say no. They can integrate the various aspects of their life and bring all of who they are to reach the organization's goals without compromising their personal needs. They can establish boundaries and distinguish between work and private life, but also calibrate them in a redefined way that fits today's more fluid circumstances. They are managers of their own nonlinear careers and variable work schedules, which in turn can give their organizations greater options.

As organizations consider what are the truly essential worker traits for both leaders and employees in this new environment—how *success* and *good employees* are defined—they might ask these questions:

- Can someone who is absent twenty times a year with an asthmatic child but beats all sales records be "best-in-class"?

- Can someone who works three days a week man~~~~
- Can someone who works two years on and every t~~~~ a foreign country be a potential leader?
- Can a person who must leave by 5 P.M. produce gr~~~~

60

Distinctive Capabilities of the New Ideal Worker

Today's workers lead complex lives, juggling work, family, friendships, interests, and obligations. This very complexity could be seen as irrelevant, a nuisance, and a potential drain on their work performance. We assert, instead, that these experiences create an enormous advantage to organizations precisely because they enable workers to develop high-level social skills—relational, communication, and emotional skills—that today's complex environment demands. However, these skills are a plus only if organizations recognize their worth and use them.

Workers with technical skills and content expertise have always been valued in organizations. Unfortunately, technical skills and content expertise are insufficient in a knowledge environment. People must also possess well-developed intrapersonal and interpersonal skills—at every level in the organization. The customer service representatives, team-based production staff, and tech support staff must have them as well as the researchers and managers. These skills are highly developed in today's new ideal workers, precisely because of the more complex lives they lead.

The value of nontechnical aptitudes cannot be overestimated; sometimes they are more important than technical competency. The National Association of Manufacturers (National Association of Manufacturers & Center for Workforce Success, 2001) found, for example, that the lack of a basic work ethic in the workforce, more than a lack of reading or math ability, was what prevented production levels from meeting customer demand.

Unfortunately, workplaces where content knowledge is valued often deemphasize abilities such as receptive communication skills that enable knowledge to be used effectively. One insightful researcher who studied engineering firms found that these abilities are often not considered abilities at all, and their exercise is not seen as "real work." The person who encourages a co-worker to stick with a stubborn problem through resolution, who takes time from an assignment to show a new colleague the nizational ropes, who defuses tension with humor and helps team members mend a fragile working relationship can have an enormous influence on a work team's performance (Fletcher, 2001). But what do you call that and how do you manage for it? Many organizations do not recognize or reward these behaviors because they do not recognize them as skills. They either do not even notice them, or they consider them personality traits (being *nice*), which devalues them. This lack of recognition causes them to shrink because what is not encouraged is discouraged in these lean times (Fletcher, 2001). Successful organizations, however, identify the value of this distinctive set of aptitudes, and then discover who has them and how they are encouraged.

Our analysis leads us to believe that the intrapersonal and interpersonal skills new ideal workers typically possess are *meta-skills*, competencies that trigger other skills, and so are critical to performance. Meta-skills make it possible for people to work together, to build cohesive teams, and to make collective achievement happen. For a financial analyst, for example, they are the difference between simply exercising analytical and quantitative skills and getting essential information from other departments in a timely way. To do the job well such an analyst must relate successfully to the people who have the data—time the request, grasp their situational constraints, and motivate them to cooperate (Rapoport et al., 2002). Meta-skills make the difference between delivering technically competent service to customers and making sure customers feel heard, understood, and attended to—and ultimately satisfied.

The rest of this chapter describes the distinctive talents and skills that the new ideal workers possess. The list represents a set of possibilities; no one has all of them, and mastery occurs on a continuum. The more they are present, though, the better a worker will function in the new environment.

Ability to Deal with Ambiguity and Complexity

The ability to deal with ambiguity allows someone to persevere when the outcome is unclear. Unlike the industrial economy, where production yielded an easily measurable result, the information economy makes quality of output more difficult to ascertain. Workers need to be comfortable with ambiguity to persevere and derive satisfaction from their work.

Trust-based environments, which are critical to learning organizations, require accepting responsibility for issues over which an individual has limited control and taking actions in an environment in which measurable outcomes are unclear. The ability to thrive under conditions of ambiguity is essential. Organizational management experts Sumantra Ghoshal of the London Business School and Christopher Bartlett of the Harvard Business School (Ghoshal & Bartlett, 1997) said that creating such an environment "requires a more organic *family-like* emotional bonding in which people rely on each other's judgment and depend on each other's commitments" (p. 93).

Dual-focus workers develop the ability to deal with complexity by juggling multiple relationships and responsibilities. This makes them highly effective in organizations with competing priorities, conflicting demands, and complex challenges—characteristics of most business environments. The ability to deal with ambiguity and uncertainty is cultivated by a variety of experiences, but successful personal relationships—such as managing a home and raising children—develop this capability powerfully. Parenting is a role with high stakes and little control over outcomes. One cannot successfully issue performance objectives to children or partners or command their compliance; subtler skills and strengths are required. Active mothers and fathers, who are closely involved with their children or aging parents, have many opportunities to practice these subtler skills. They know from experience that people are unique and unpredictable, and that control over others, whatever their size, is illusory.

Resilience and Adaptability

In a fast-moving economy, where the pace of innovation results in ever-shorter product life cycles and the only constant is changing conditions, the ability of an organization—primarily its people—to embrace change, to experiment with new processes and ideas, and to apply problem-solving skills to entirely new challenges can make the difference between mediocre and exceptional company performance. Resilient employees can adapt in the face of adversity and significant sources of stress. They can bounce back from workplace and personal stressors. Resilience is a *learned skill* that is associated with the ability to communicate effectively, solve problems, and manage strong feelings and impulses (Halpern, 2003). Resilient and adaptable workers are more versatile.

Today's new ideal workers have been forged on the anvil of social, economic, technological, and personal change—abrupt shifts in job security and family situations—which can bring incredible personal growth and learning. Among other priorities, these workers are committed to maintaining healthy personal relationships, which in turn help build and maintain resilience.

Emotional and Relationship Management Skills

Emotional and interpersonal skills are critical in holding together effective work units and sustaining relationships with customers, suppliers, and associates. Organizations once led by powerful individuals who made decisions now require leaders who can lead without overt power. Leaders must be able to understand, relate to, and effectively move disparate groups to achieve real (not coerced) agreement and bring differing groups and individuals into a common direction. In colleges, for example, whereas the president once decided whether to build a new building or create a new degree program, that decision and many others now require buy-in from often competing constituencies—boards of trustees, academic senates, and student organizations, for example. College presidents once had clear positions of power and hierarchies to support them; they now must constantly navigate multiple constituencies and bring them to consensus (Lewis, 2003).

People who have typically not had the power to command but still had responsibility (such as women and ethnic minorities) have had to develop the ability to manage complex relationships. They understand how to bring order, which is quite different from control, to complex environments (Wheatley & Chodron, 1999).

Similarly, the ability to recognize, understand, manage, and express emotions is a high-level set of skills, not an inborn trait. The capacity to maintain emotional equilibrium in interactions with co-workers, supervisors, customers, professional colleagues, and vendors is critical to good performance. The skills that enable someone to take criticism and learn from it without getting defensive, to handle stress without getting paralyzed or hostile, to maintain hope and be tenacious in the face of disappointment are as critical to an individual's effectiveness as technical aptitude. Their strength or lack of it determines where managers will need to invest energy, whether talented people stay or go, whether attention is focused on the work product, and the degree of satisfaction from work. Managing one's emotions is critical in a human capital environment, as is the ability of both managers and workers to facilitate the emotional dance between others.

Some less recognized relational skills include the ability to help people establish connections, to create the conditions in which relationships will thrive, to use emotional data to understand situations and develop strategic responses, to listen, and to defuse tensions. These skills are often associated with women and shaped by caretaking roles. Inaccurately considered natural personality traits, they are associated with being *nice* or *afraid of conflict*—and trivialized, rather than recognized, labeled, and rewarded as the highly developed skills they are (Fletcher, 2001).

These misread skills also include the ability to understand others' experience (empathic competence), the ability to admit not knowing and seek help (vulnerability), the ability to respond to others but not lose one's own reality (response-ability), and the ability to think holistically (Fletcher, 2001). In organizations, these skills promote mutual empowerment, the creation of real teams (in contrast to more superficial team-building exercises), and more effective task completion because the focus is on getting something done rather than assigning credit for it. They also facilitate organizational learning, preventing future problems and project delays.

The risks of not recognizing these skills as valid are twofold. When they are not valued or considered real work, the time they require is not considered in planning or rewards and so they are discouraged. On a deeper level, the opportunity they offer to transform an organization to one rooted in mutuality and empowerment, instead of autonomy and individual achievement, is missed (Fletcher, 2001).

Although emotions at work erupt in an environment very different from private life, emotional management skills developed at home are highly transferable to work. People who were managers both before and after they became parents say they manage employees more holistically now. Parents (and adults who care for elders) develop conflict resolution skills, and they learn how to defuse emotional tension and to put minor emotional eruptions in perspective. A study conducted by a recruiting organization found that a majority of working adults thought their mothers could perform as well as or better than their bosses at resolving employee disputes (67 percent) and communicating (75 percent), and thought their mothers would also do a better job at handling company finances (62 percent; "Mom As CEO," 2003).

Multidimensional Integration

Multidimensional, integrated workers can tap into other rich aspects of their lives as sources of inspiration and creativity. They integrate who they are in their personal life with who they are at work (Rapoport et al., 2002). Besides being a welder or mail carrier, they may be an avid cyclist, cellist, or collector of jazz. They may love volunteering at a homeless shelter or being a Girl Scout leader or race-car driver; they may have a special needs child or a brother with AIDS. They bring this richness to their work. In fact, one could say they bring their souls to work (Whyte, 2001). This integration enables them to better understand the complicated lives that customers live and identify with them. Some of the features that differentiated a highly successful Ford van were developed by engineers who were also active mothers. They knew what design features other mothers would want to buy.

Integration makes it possible for workers to develop a shared sense of purpose with their organization. The sense of shared mission and purpose and the importance of cohesiveness are never more pronounced than in people's home lives. The family unit, however defined, has mutual well-being as its primary goal, so it is a superb training ground for the development of shared purpose. The subtle skills that develop and sustain this one-ness are honed in family life; those who use them can translate them to work environments. And because they seek organizations in which their values can be aligned, integrated workers are less likely to make decisions that are inconsistent with the goals of the organization. They require less supervision and communicate a consistent message to customers and suppliers (Bailyn et al., 2001).

The ability to be integrated enables people to bring both the feminine and masculine sides of life and self to work. (These terms here refer to aspects of human life that often have gendered meanings, not to men or women per se.) In one sense bringing home and work closer together is an integration of the female side of life (the private or home side) with the male (the public or work side). The old ideal worker was quintessentially masculine—focused on being separate from others—individuated. He was independent and competitive. (From infancy boys establish their identity by being *different*—differentiating from the mothers who raise them; girls establish their identity by being the *same* as their mothers. For men the driving force becomes individuation; for women it becomes connection.) Boys are generally socialized to compete; girls are socialized to cooperate (Chodorow, 1978).

New ideal workers—both male and female—can access both the masculine and public (independent, separate, self-reliant) and the feminine and private (connective, relational, receptive) aspects of themselves. They can be independent and self-reliant and at the same time connect with, care about, and nurture the development of others. Whereas old ideal workers felt the need to constantly demonstrate their worth, the new ideal workers are also aware that much important work is unseen—preventing problems, empowering others, influencing, mentoring, connecting people with resources, encouraging. Such supportive behaviors reflect a feminine style (Fletcher, 2001).

The masculine style sees things in black and white—choose A or B; the feminine style sees varying grays and asks, "Is there another way?" These days the best workers are able to blend both styles as circumstances require.

People who can employ both styles have greater range and avoid the extremes of either style. They can be strong and sensitive, creative and rational, receptive and decisive as the situation requires. They know their own mind but can also listen and learn from others. The importance of legitimizing the so-called feminine ways of relating in the work environment—being receptive, empathic, and comfortable with a certain level of vulnerability in the business environment—is new. In the old work environment the feminine style was dismissed as weak; the male style was tough and uncompromising—and was considered necessary. Today, organizations that recognize the value of a variety of styles and those who can use them with facility will be better equipped to deal with the challenges of the times.

Capacity for Passion and Intellect at Work

The capacity and desire to be fully engaged by their work makes people seek work they can put their minds and spirits into and enables them to believe in their work. Beyond what often passes for employee engagement, they see their employer as making it possible for them to have personal input (Ghoshal & Bartlett, 1997). Service Master employees who clean hotel rooms and Warner Bros. cartoonists who work on feature films both can take enormous pride in their company and their work.

These workers are not naive; they know all too well about the breakdown of trust between employers and employees and recognize that not all organizations match rhetoric with action. They read the newspapers. But instead of closing themselves off, they have learned to be more discerning, to question platitudes, to compare espoused values with lived ones, to assess the integrity of leaders carefully. They have the capacity to affiliate with an organization whose purpose and practice match their own—a capacity grown out of self-reflection and self-knowledge, and exercised with great discrimination.

These are the kind of people that Jim Collins could be speaking of in *Good to Great* (2001) when he says that "getting the right people on the bus" is more important for organizations than deciding where to drive it. You first have to start with people who can give their passion and their intellect in full measure and genuinely align with an organization's purpose. For such employees work is not drudgery but rather a source of personal growth and sense of purpose (Csikszentmihalyi, 1990, 1993, 2003). It is a powerful way to express their unique identity (Whyte, 2001). This passion is essential if they are to challenge, critique, create, and innovate.

Other-Orientation

An other-orientation facilitates the sharing and leveraging of knowledge and the collaboration and cooperation that are critical to innovation and profitability. This orientation is more important than individualism and competitiveness to organizational success in a networked environment. It is at the heart of the ability to work behind the scenes toward a shared goal, regardless of the direct personal reward (Fletcher, 2001).

An other-orientation does not mean forgoing one's own interests; it is the ability to access the part of oneself that considers the good of the whole. The vision beyond the self transforms workers from self-centered, static individuals into entities yearning to grow and connect with other beings (Csikszentmihalyi, 2003). The desire to contribute to something beyond oneself is also essential to achieving any organizational vision. But people can only subordinate themselves to larger effort when it doesn't violate their own well-being and when it contributes to a purpose they consider worthwhile.

We all come into this world with both innate self-centered drives (e.g., concern for control, rank, status, territory, possessions) and other-centered innate drives (e.g., concern for attachment, affiliation, altruism, care-giving, care-receiving). Unfortunately, most current organizations with their prevailing top-down, command-and-control administrative systems are unknowingly targeting their people's self-centered drives. At the same time, their leaders are asking these people to be good team players and committed to institutional goals. Obviously, this style is not an effective way to run knowledge-intensive businesses where the exchange of tacit knowledge is the key to success and, therefore, the other-centered drives need to have an opportunity to be expressed. . . . If organizations are serious about increasing their knowledge assets to achieve increased competitiveness, they must first place primary emphasis on developing . . . a social foundation that will facilitate the balanced expression of both sides of human nature necessary before voluntary sharing of tacit knowledge can take place. (Ehin, 2000, pp. 2–3)

An other-orientation is part of keeping the *whole* in mind—the overall result, the long-term goal, the bigger picture. This orientation enables one to focus on preventing problems, eliminating the need to engage in heroic individual action after they develop. Preventing problems from happening can have a substantial effect on efficiency, outcomes, and costs (Rapoport & Bailyn, 1996). An other-orientation is valuable in leaders as well as workers. Visionary business leaders see their organizations as much more than simply a way of generating profit; they pursue wider goals beyond the interests of owners and shareholders (Csikszentmihalyi, 2003). Such leadership is critical to organizational excellence.

Corporate leadership that focuses primarily on the returns generated for shareholders, rather than on broader purposes or shared values, offers only a limited sense of purpose to the organization's members. Outstanding performance comes from the "hearts and minds" of employees who are attracted to and motivated by higher values and purposes. (Ellsworth, 2002, p. 89)

The orientation toward others and the sense of interdependence are natural and highly developed in one's private life (Bailyn, 1993). At home

one cares genuinely about the well-being of others; in healthy personal relationships what is good for one is literally good for the other. This turns out
to be a transferable skill that is highly relevant at work.

Communication Skills, Including the Ability to Negotiate and Persuade

Communication skills are commonly recognized as important, but the ones
that have traditionally been valued in the workplace are primarily about
expression—developing ideas, writing, and speaking. *Receptive* communication skills are also essential in a human capital environment. The abilities
to read the other party, to listen, to appreciate another's perspective and
express one's own in a way suited to the receiver—are increasingly important in a networked (interdependent) environment. They are essential to
effectively communicate ideas.

The ability to know, and care, whether the other person understands, to
communicate effectively in different contexts—that is, to consider the
dynamics of the receiver—are also skills that are polished in private life.
The ability to hear between the lines, to ask good questions, to listen without judging to the unspoken as well as the spoken, are skills that parents and
family members develop. They develop them out of a genuine interest in
one another, from a desire to see things the way the other person sees them
and to accommodate other points of view. Learning to adjust conversation
topics to a spouse's mood, seeing a child's reaction to a harsh tone of voice
(the same reaction an adult who reports to you might mask), knowing that
a friend will only open up under certain conditions, these are communication experiences that can form an aptitude over time. At the highest level
this skill enables one to read *meta-messages*—what someone is really saying,
which may differ from the literal words.

Only with receptive communication skills can knowledge workers
comprehend the explicit and implicit messages being sent, interpret their
meaning in context, grasp the implications, and effectively share learning.
Only with them can service workers read customers' needs and confer effectively with supervisors and co-workers about how to respond. They enable
people to persuade and negotiate more effectively and to arrive at genuine
agreement and mutually beneficial results.

The value of relationship capital increases the importance of communication skills of all kinds, even as technology changes the form of com-

munication. As e-mail and voice mail shift face-to-face interactions to virtual ones, effective communication gets trickier (Hallowell, 2000) and the underlying skills of good two-way communication become more important. Even though feelings and tone are not readily transmitted via e-mail, people still read feeling into it. There is a tendency to be curt, less polite, to forgo the social niceties like warm-up and exit lines, all of which affect the emotional and social content and tone. Sensitivity to nuances, taking them seriously and recognizing the need to be especially careful in the absence of other cues, is even more important for good two-way communication.

Ability to Guide, Empower, and Mentor

Clearly, the ability to develop people is critical to organizational success—and development must happen all the time, not just during planned sessions or by assigned trainers. The ability to develop others is constantly being polished and practiced at home and in one's personal life. Active parents constantly guide, empower, and mentor their children. Ideally, they learn how to coach without destroying self-confidence, how to give freedom without overwhelming, how to teach without talking down, and how to recognize when to "give them wings and let them fly."*

While empowerment at the workplace can take on a superficial character, a parent understands the stakes involved in a child's becoming genuinely independent and is intent on making it happen. Parents adopt a long-term orientation by making a long-term commitment to raising their children. They have learned to pick their battles and order their priorities (having a chronically ill child or a dying parent makes arguments over office space pale in importance). Along with these traits, active parents can bring enormous patience and tenacity to the workplace, acquired by this concentrated experience in their personal lives.

Margaret Wheatley (2001) has said that "leaders are those who have more faith in people than they do in themselves . . . hold them in the song of their promise and possibility until they can sing that song for themselves." Nothing could be a more accurate description of the spirit of good family and personal relationships.

---

* Parents learn the value of establishing clear expectations, giving consistent reinforcement, and allowing children to experience the consequences of their decisions. Clearly not all parents learn good parenting (or management) skills, but those who know what works and what doesn't have the principles indelibly embedded in them.

People Process–Orientation

The person with a people process–orientation is aware of the process for getting results and attentive to how it is experienced by the people involved. This ability is in contrast to a task-orientation that places primary importance on the outcome without regard to the effects on people. It comes from an appreciation for the *experience* of work as well as its result and contributes to work being intrinsically rewarding for workers. This skill is particularly important in a knowledge and service environment, where workers find satisfaction in their work and their experience influences that of others, especially customers. It is the ability to pay attention to what people need and want while the work is getting accomplished (Kossek, Colquitt, & Noe, 2001). This skill is nurtured in personal relationships, which are enhanced when one is attuned to the experience of the other person.

Self-Awareness and Self-Reliance

Although the new ideal workers can collaborate and connect and be other-oriented, they also recognize that they cannot rely on any organization for long-term security. They have become self-reliant by necessity. The other-orientation and pursuit of mutual goals only happen, then, in a particular context—when the individual's needs are also recognized and met. These employees and managers know themselves well; they recognize what is good for them and pursue it. Their self-knowledge enables them to be conscious and direct about finding where their interests, values, and goals line up with an organization's. As a result they do not always say yes to management requests. They may find a better way to organize a task or question whether a status report is essential. They may not be willing to work long hours consistently.

Self-awareness helps workers understand their strengths and weaknesses; it enables them to find the best match between their skills and specific work challenges. This match is critical for them to experience flow in their work—the condition that leads to personal satisfaction, growth, and intense concentration and focus (Csikszentmihalyi, 2003). "Money, security and comfort may be necessary to make us happy, but they are definitely not sufficient. A person must also feel that his talents are fully employed, that he is able to develop his potentialities, and that his everyday life is not stress-ful or boring, but holds deeply enjoyable experiences" (Csikszentmihalyi, 1990, pp. 18–19).

Self-aware workers calibrate decisions about where to work and what level of energy and self to invest from a more informed, clear-headed point of view. This clarity makes them easier to manage when they are ap-proached with mutual respect and open communication. With these conditions, self-aware workers do not require close supervision and tight structures—an important consideration in today's flatter organizations where employees on the front lines with customers and suppliers need to be able to make critical decisions. They are self-managing and responsible and accountable for work outcomes. While they may not always say yes to man-agement requests, ultimately they achieve the important work results.

Self-awareness, self-worth, and self-reliance balance traits like an other-orientation, which might otherwise make new ideal workers vulnerable to exploitation and burnout. The new ideal worker is not the twenty-first-century equivalent of Super-worker—doing it all. Instead these workers know what they need and want because they have reflected on their priori-ties and pursue them. But part of what they want is an organization aligned with their values so that they can invest themselves enthusiastically in its goals.

The meta-competencies described in this section are interrelated and often derive from the same life experience. They are especially valuable in a human capital environment where knowledge and service work predom-inate, leveraging the technical skills and content knowledge that have always been required.

These meta-competencies can be found in the new *ideal* worker. As with the old ideal, no worker can ever achieve this level of perfection. The defining qualities must be continually developed and enhanced. Develop-ing these capabilities requires action by both the individual worker and the organization. Workers need to become more aware of the skills they are developing in other aspects of life and how these skills can be brought into the work experience to improve performance. They also need to contin-ually improve existing skills and seek to develop new ones. The orga-nization must motivate employees to develop and deploy skills in the work-place, create opportunities for employees to cultivate them, and reward their use and improvement. Fundamentally, the greatest challenge for organizations is recognizing the value of the person (whether worker or leader) who can use both personal life skills and technical skills and shift gears as the situation requires—to attend to the experience of the people doing the work and the work product, to process and content—and ultimately, contribute most to their organization's success (Kossek et al., 2001).

In Conclusion

Most organizations see the increasing complexity in workers as a negative, regretting their higher expectations and the outside responsibilities that compete for their attention. This chapter describes why this complexity can be leveraged as strength for organizations, but only if it is managed as such. We suggest there is a new ideal worker, the dual-focus worker—a whole person who can bring mind and heart as well as hands to work—to replace the work-focused individual achiever once considered ideal. These individuals also possess valuable meta-competencies—self-awareness and relational skills—that leverage their technical skills.

These are the people whom organizations must recognize as essential to performance, whose success must be made real. Organizations have increasingly complex demands placed on them by the marketplace; multi-dimensional individuals who can bring more of themselves to the work, be effective at work and personal life simultaneously, deliver results collaboratively, and navigate diverse employment arrangements (as employee or non-employee) are essential for responding to these demands. Leveraging this new human capital with all its complexity is key to organizational success. In Part 2, we describe the adaptive strategies that will enable organizations to leverage this new human capital.

PART 2

THE POWER OF ADAPTIVE STRATEGIES

When forces as powerful as those we described are converging, the adaptation required by organizations is pervasive. This part of the book offers a contemporary theory for managing in the context of the new reality, along with some practical methods for adapting. It examines why some organizations excel in managing a dual-focus workforce in a knowledge and service economy in ways that contribute to business performance.

We have studied the strategies that business enterprises have begun to design and implement and their specific contexts and purposes, and have found important points of consensus. From our synthesis, we present on the following page five interrelated strategies for managing today's human capital that will enable organizations to successfully adapt to current and future realities.

Adaptation takes place at a number of levels:

- The culture itself, along with all its implicit and explicit values, beliefs, and assumptions
- The practices, policies, and programs that govern day-to-day activities
- The role of managers

Marci Koblenz of MK Consultants contributed to this discussion.

THE FIVE ADAPTIVE STRATEGIES

1. Choosing to *invest* in people
2. Adopting a new set of beliefs
3. Redefining the organizational culture
4. Transforming management practices
5. Ensuring fit: beliefs, culture, and practice

For many organizations, these adaptive strategies are entirely new ways of thinking and behaving—a truly radical departure from how business has traditionally been done. But it is precisely a *radical* departure that is in order, given the dimensions of the changes happening in the business environment, in society, and in individuals. Future survival will depend on foundational change. Businesses that thrive in the future will be those that can let go of ways that have successfully brought them to where they are and recognize the wisdom of changing even the fundamentals.

Adaptive strategies are much more than a collection of tactical actions or programs. They start much further back in the fabric of the organization. They are *strategic* in the basic sense of the word, in that they use all possible forces in planning and development to support policies that will ensure success. Although the strategies suggest specific tactics, they are first and foremost systemic—new ways of thinking about how to achieve business results, a reexamination of how work is organized, and a transformation in how people are managed—that is, a deep rearrangement of form, appearance, and structure, and of the relationship among the organization's parts.

The strategies are *adaptive* because they alter the form or structure to fit a changed environment. Adaptation, even more than strength, was the quality Charles Darwin found to be the key to survival. By adapting, the organization becomes better fitted to survive and grow.

The end goal is not static, nor is it a particular collection of new practices; rather, it is a process toward a particular state for the organization and the individuals and groups within it. It has been referred to as a "state of satisfaction" where optimal performance is reached. It is both dynamic (ever-changing) and synergistic (the important elements work together for a greater result). The state of satisfaction is highly individualized and varies between groups and individuals, and it evolves over time for individuals, groups, and organizations as situational elements change.

The five strategies begin with a choice to invest in people, rather than manage them as costs. This first strategy is followed by adopting a new set of beliefs that fit what the organization requires now, redefining the culture, transforming management practices, and ensuring that all of these elements are congruent across the organization. Each is described in turn in Chapters 5–9.

THE PARADOX OF WORK
by Mihaly Csikszentmihalyi

By the age of twelve, most American children associate the word *work* with something one must do that is boring and unpleasant. Many adults, when prompted at work to fill out a survey, say they would rather be anywhere else but on the job (this despite the fact that when they fill out the same questionnaire anywhere else they are likely to rate themselves less creative, active, and focused, and more bored and passive than at work).

This paradox is deeply rooted in our attitudes. On the one hand, the majority of people in the United States say they would want to continue working even if they did not have to do so for financial reasons. On the other hand, the "TGIF" mantra, "Dilbert" cartoons, and a tsunami of data on job dissatisfaction suggest a much darker picture. And this paradox is reflected in the diametrically opposed positions on work that thinkers have taken over the centuries. For Aristotle and his fellow philosophers in Greece, human nature was expressed only in leisure. Work was a necessity one tried to avoid at all costs. Conversely, most modern philosophers would agree with Karl Marx that it is through productive work that the possibilities inherent in human nature can best be expressed and developed.

Part of the reason for this confusion is that the word *work* applies to such entirely different experiences. It applies to jobs that are dreadfully demeaning and to jobs that are wonderfully liberating. In our studies of creative individuals, we heard over and over variations on this theme: "I could say I have worked every moment of my life. And I could say I have never worked in my life. Both statements would be true because I never think of what I do as work." Or, in the words of historian John Hope Franklin: "I always say TGIF, because on the weekend I can go home and work for two solid days without the interruptions I have at the office."

Some jobs are so exciting and rewarding that they don't feel like what we usually mean by "work." Surgeons, software developers, artists, geneticists, entrepreneurs, and workers in many other occupations seldom experience the boredom and alienation most people associate with the word. But that's only part of the story. The other part is that any job, no matter how routine and apparently demeaning, can be experienced as exciting and fulfilling provided that the work is seen as contributing to some larger good. Your job as a hospital orderly is demeaning if you think of it as emptying bedpans and washing soiled linen. It is much less so if you think of it as a vocation that helps patients live in a clean, inviting environment.

What makes the difference between a job and a vocation? Two things matter most: how much value a person is able to find in the product or outcome of the activity, and how much value he or she can find in the activity itself. The value of the outcome is something the worker may not be able to influence. If, for instance, the only job in the region is at a factory that makes cigarettes, it would be delusional to think of it as adding value to the consumer. But many jobs that seem worthless have the potential to be genuine vocations, if approached with the right attitude.

Finding value in the activity itself is something much more accessible to any worker in any job. When a person is able to focus attention on clear goals in work that are neither too difficult nor too easy, and get timely feedback on his or her actions, eventually that individual is likely to enter a state I have called *flow*—deep involvement that leads to a sense of serenity and joy. When an assembly-line worker breaks down his simple job into separate challenges and tries to improve on the efficiency, speed, or precision of his actions, the job begins to be interesting, exciting, and intrinsically rewarding. We have found this to be true in a great variety of occupations, from farming to surgery, and from teaching to sheepherding.

These reflections lead in two different but complementary policy directions. The first concerns management, and it suggests ways of structuring work
ing environments that make it possible for workers to find value and flow in
what they are doing. This should have positive consequences for the organization: increased productivity, employee loyalty, creativity. But even if it
doesn't, it would be irresponsible management not to do one's best to encourage the growth and satisfaction of one's employees. The second direction concerns everyone who works, and it suggests that we can all do something to
make our job more valuable and enjoyable by paying greater attention to the
possibilities inherent in it. Even surgeons and professional basketball players
can become jaded and dissatisfied with their work if they approach it as just
a money-making job rather than as a vocation.

It is never too early to take these suggestions seriously. When American
teens are asked what job they expect to have after college, one out of five
answers "physician" or "lawyer." Most of the rest expect to do something professional or at least white-collar. Almost none expects to do the kind of job
that keeps the infrastructure of society from falling apart; future farmers,
builders, and tool makers are very difficult to find. When these teens are asked
how much money they expect to make five years after they complete their last
degree, $250,000 a year is the average figure.

Unless the upcoming generation learns that money and status are not
the only rewards of work, the next cohort of our society will be sorely disap-
pointed. Of course, young people are unlikely to learn the true rewards of work
unless they see ahead of them credible role models who find rewards in the
work itself and in its outcomes. As long as what we show them are boredom
and greed, who can blame them if they turn into dissatisfied workers whose
only goal is to milk the system for all it's worth?

5

CHOOSING TO *INVEST* IN PEOPLE

Despite everything written about the importance of human, intellectual, and social capital, many managers and executives have at best a vague notion of how these factors affect results in their business. The concepts are clear—people are more important in the Information Age than they were in the Industrial Age because of the unique knowledge and relationships that only people can have. But their specific importance varies by type of industry, function, and organization. For example, an organization that differentiates itself by service relies heavily on employees who affect the service experience, while an organization that competes on product innovation relies heavily on people in R&D.

Financial services firm Edward Jones differentiates itself through service—using the tagline "focus on people"—and by providing individual investors and business owners with high-quality, low-risk investment advice through face-to-face contact. The corporation doesn't invest its human capital efforts in creating new financial products. Instead, it invests in improving the ability of its financial consultants, who operate out of small neighborhood offices and are active in their local community, to develop trusting relationships with their clients and the community. Information technology people develop tools that enhance those relationships; these tools are available in local offices so financial consultants can, face-to-face, help clients easily manage their investments. In this company employees on the front lines and in the back office are critical to the success of the face-to-face service strategy.

Few organizations have attempted to identify where human capital has the greatest influence on organizational success—how people's knowledge and relationships contribute to the overall business strategy. Yet this information is critical to the successful implementation of any business strategy, as illustrated in the Edward Jones example. Without it, how can an organization's leaders determine how much and in what ways they should invest in people?

The first strategy, choosing to invest in people, involves the essential factors that enable people in organizations to see where human capital plays a role. In some organizations, much of this information is understood but may not be explicit. Making it explicit allows managers to make more appropriate decisions about resources and improves the capacity of the organization to create value.

Adaptive organizations choose to invest in people, to consider people as *human capital* and worth investments of various kinds, rather than as costs to be minimized. This choice, based on an understanding of how human capital affects results in the organization, represents a response to the converging forces described in Part 1. It also recognizes the reality that the demand for qualified knowledge and service workers exceeds the supply in many labor markets and will continue to do so for some time to come.

The first strategy is the foundation for the next four; they all depend on the decision to invest in human capital. Without that decision, organizations lack a coherent approach to managing people. Practices tend to be implemented on an ad hoc basis or to conflict from one part of the organization to another. As long as beliefs and assumptions in the organization that reflect traditional ideas about work and people remain ingrained in the culture, practices that characterize the new ideal will be largely unusable.

Choosing to invest in people requires an examination of the importance of human capital to a particular organization in pursuit of a specific business strategy. For leaders to choose to invest in people and to know which investments will yield the greatest payback, they must understand the human element in the work itself, how human capital affects results, what

---

CHOOSING TO INVEST IN PEOPLE

Steps in the Investment Choice

1. Identify the human capital element in each type of work
2. Understand how the human capital aspects of work affect results
3. Identify the factors that drive human performance
4. Evaluate the workforce profile, needs, and trends
5. Recognize people as assets, not expenses

---

drives human performance, and the nature of the workforce itself. We suggest the above steps. Each step is critical to making an appropriate decision — a decision that has enormous consequences for an organization's profitability and long-term viability.

Step 1: Identify the Human Capital Element in Each Type of Work

The application of *intellectual capital* and the execution of *relational* (or *social*) *capital* make up the human capital element of work. They are uniquely human (as compared to things that machines can also do).

Intellectual capital refers to the knowledge element in each job—the application of the employee's knowledge and skills to create, invent, improve, advise, use, deploy, or develop some thing or process. It is the combination of experience and education (both formal and informal) that enables the analyst to pick up a financial statement and immediately see where a company is making or losing money or helps the sales rep translate a customer's need into the sale of the company's product.

Relational (or social) capital is the employee's ability to connect with others as well as the ability to access a network of contacts and relationships and thereby find answers more quickly, locate resources, and elicit cooperation both inside and outside the organization. The waiter who automatically pours you a cup of decaf at your regular lunch spot is exercising (and building) relational capital, as is the pharmacist who asks if you're still getting those headaches. Intellectual and relational capital overlap and reinforce each other, enhancing the value of the service or product delivered to the customer or the efficiency of the company's operations.

A Process to Find Human Capital Elements

To assess how critical people are to the success of any business, the first step is to determine to what extent each job is dependent on the knowledge and relationships of people—and what the full cost of replacing those people would be. Most managers have a sense of how important the people element is to a job based on their experience hiring and training people within their department, although the information may not be formally captured. The human capital element is often more critical in those positions that are difficult to fill. If people have trouble being successful without extensive training, it suggests the position is human capital–intensive.

The process of determining the importance of the human capital element in work doesn't have to be onerous. It can be done for broad categories of jobs—customer service, sales, accounting management, logistics coordination. Or it can be derived from the organization's performance management process by analyzing to what degree the work objectives rely on knowledge or relationships. This analysis works best when the objectives are linked to the organization's business strategy. In that analysis it will become clear what specific skills are required in the job and how success is defined.

An example may help illustrate this step. An objective of a customer service department in a computer services company is to reduce the time it takes for customers' computers to be repaired from three days to one, supporting the business strategy of delivering fast, reliable computer repairs. It is clear in this example that the customer service rep affects the customers' experience of service—whether they believe their problem was understood, its urgency was recognized, and the technician was dispatched—and by identifying obstacles in the company's process or systems that prevent the objective from being achieved. If a rep lacks relational and intellectual capital—is, for example, new and poorly trained—you can imagine the effect on results, especially in the usual service call situation where margins are so tight that a few mistakes can more than offset the profits earned on other, successful service calls.

The analysis of the human capital element in work needs to be deliberate to ensure that conclusions reflect reality and don't simply reinforce previously held assumptions. The presumption that support areas, for example, are less connected to results than professional positions misses the fact that a customer service person can be the deciding factor in keeping a customer. Likewise, a purchaser can negotiate contracts or identify suppliers that enable the company to produce a superior product at a lower cost. Intellectual capital–intensive professional functions are often assumed to be more closely tied to performance, but, if they're not part of a company's core competency, are better outsourced (Drucker, 2003). So the analysis must consider positions and people not only in terms of their knowledge and relationships but also on their contribution to value creation—the direct line of sight to customers and results.

Continual Analysis

Analysis must be ongoing because the element of human capital within each type of work isn't static—it changes continually in response to technological advances, customer demands and expectations, and legislative and regulatory changes. Technology replaces some workers while increasing the level of knowledge required by others. A good accounts receivable function twenty years ago was staffed by people who made sure customer payments were posted to the proper account. Today, computers post payments automatically and a good accounts receivable person uses Internet databases to assess customer credit and helps manage the company's positive cash flow. The human capital element also varies across markets. In some markets customers increasingly demand customization, raising the human capital element involved in understanding, translating, and responding to their needs.

Human capital elements—the knowledge and relationships essential to knowledge and service jobs—are increasingly found in production jobs as well, so determining the role of human capital applies to all types of work. Automobile assembly workers no longer lift and bolt parts—they operate the robots that do the lifting (Stewart, 1999). Health care work involves much greater knowledge of and compliance with regulation than it did fifteen years ago. Some jobs—research and development, consulting, engineering, and so on—are almost entirely knowledge based; and many manufacturing, and other, employees now work in self-directed teams.

To assess how critical people are to the success of any business, the first step is to understand how much of each job depends on the knowledge and relationships of people—and what the full cost of replacing those people would be. Most managers have a sense of this based on their experience hiring and training people within their departments, although the information may not be formally captured. Employee performance objectives and position descriptions that outline the requirements of the job and also define criteria for success in the job contain important clues regarding the human capital element of any position.

Step 2: Understand How the Human Capital Aspects of Work Affect Results

Once the human capital element in each type of work has been identified, the organization must determine how human capital–intensive positions affect organizational results. Some will be clearer than others. In retail, service personnel seem to have a much more direct effect on revenues than do accounting personnel, but accounting personnel play an important role interpreting and analyzing data used to improve store performance.

The degree to which particular knowledge affects organizational results may vary depending on the specific strategies the organization is using to compete in the marketplace, as these examples demonstrate.

- A low-cost differentiation strategy will depend heavily on employees' abilities to continually improve the efficiency and effectiveness of processes. Wal-Mart's success is largely attributable to superior logistics. It completely changed the dynamics of retail by focusing on distribution and purchasing—two support functions rarely considered strategic until Sam Walton came along. By continually improving its processes, Wal-Mart makes it difficult for competitors like Kmart to ever catch up.

- A high-quality differentiation strategy will rely on employees' ability to continually innovate, market, and relate to target customers. Mountain Travel Sobek offers unusual trips to exotic locations (ski Antarctica to the South Pole, hike the old Silk Road from China through Nepal). They continually develop new, more exotic, trips; ideas for trips are fueled by the exploration dreams of their employees, the passion their trip leaders have for certain locales or activities, and the responses or inspirations of customers in their target market. Customers eagerly open the catalog the day it arrives to see what new travel adventures have been put together by the company.

The connection between human capital skills and organizational performance is important for leaders to understand. It helps them know the value of recruiting people with the required skills or the capacity to develop them, of managing people in ways that enhance, develop, and apply these skills, and of retaining employees with difficult-to-replace knowledge and relationships. Imagine how hard it would be for Sobek to create a memorable travel experience for its customers without a trip leader who intimately knows the region and its people and can arrange lunch with a Turkish family or a safe trip rafting through Class V rapids. Similarly, what would 3M be without its inventors, Southwest without friendly attendants, or Nordstrom without its shoe sales force?

Step 3: Identify the Factors That Drive Human Performance

Each organization must come to a clear sense of what promotes the best performance of its people. Performance is generally affected by people's degree of commitment, motivation, and productivity. The adaptive strategies identified in this chapter increase employee commitment, engagement, and productivity and improve organizational performance across industries and types of workers. Substantial scientific evidence supports this relationship (see Part 3).

Because performance starts with having the right employees in the right jobs, leaders and managers must also know what attracts the right employees. Generally, attracting the right employees, motivating employees, and gaining their commitment and productivity depends heavily on the following conditions.

- Rewards and recognition are fair, competitive, and commensurate with performance.

- Opportunities exist for growth, advancement, and skill development.

- Managers are effective, behave consistently, and act on employee suggestions.

- Work is meaningful and engaging and allows employees to use their skills.
- Employees have a reasonable degree of autonomy over their work and schedules.
- The employer recognizes and supports employees as whole people with lives and responsibilities outside work.
- Employees have the necessary tools and resources to do their jobs well.
- The organizational culture is supportive, inclusive, and respectful.
- Employees feel secure about their jobs.

All of these factors are important. It would be difficult, for example, for an employee to stay motivated while working for someone who provides a wonderful opportunity to develop new and marketable skills but who rewards high-performing and low-performing employees alike. It doesn't require much math ability to calculate how long after mastering the new skills the employee will be out searching for a new employer. Nor would an employee feel respected if a supervisor dictated every aspect of the job.

The factors affecting human capital performance will be specific to the organization and the people within it, particularly those in the most critical functions. The Kenya trip leader at Mountain Travel Sobek requires different tools on the job than those required by Wal-Mart's East Coast distribution manager. The organizational culture at a software development company would vary considerably from the culture of an investment bank, but both cultures should still be characterized by respect for people, employees as well as customers.

Step 4: Evaluate the Workforce Profile, Needs, and Trends

To leverage human capital, leaders and managers must understand their people. Barry Libert, author of *Cracking the Value Code*, asked five hundred CFOs, CEOs, and other leaders to identify their most important assets. Although all listed customers, employees, or suppliers, none of them could answer these follow-up questions: "What are their names?" "Do you keep track of them?" "Do you spend money measuring them?" "Do your technologies enable them?" If these are your most valuable assets, you should know them ("Know Your Assets," 2001).

Knowing your employees requires genuine effort and investment in a continuous process involving the reexamination of assumptions. Typical profiles of employees—by ethnicity, age, gender—can miss significant trends, which can adversely affect performance. The rise of the dual-focus worker (see Chapter 3) has gone virtually undetected by standard demographic analysis, yet it has enormous implications for organizations.

Needs vary—not all employees require the same thing from their organization to be effective in their work. Employees' expectations and requirements differ by gender, age, experience, lifestyle, ambitions, values, and goals, and they change over time as life circumstances change. Some people, including most hourly workers, need a greater sense of participation or respect, because their jobs don't naturally give that. Some people need time to retool their skills, pursuing more education or more challenge. Some with young families or elders need resources that support them in caregiving responsibilities. Some expect and require extra latitude in how they go about achieving results. Some need to sustain their health through athletic pursuits or to have time for activities that give their life meaning, such as volunteering in their community.

On the surface, some of these needs may seem not to be the concern of the organization for which employees work. But attitudes, job satisfaction, and a well-balanced life affect employees' overall health and well-being, their full engagement at work, and ultimately their effectiveness. Adaptive organizations, having decided to invest in people, create cultures and implement practices that enable employees to fulfill these needs while delivering results for the organization.

It is important to be aware of the expectations and requirements of prospective workers as well as those of the current workforce, especially given the projected decline in the U.S. labor force over the next twenty years. Studies have shown that people entering the workforce today have different expectations of work from those of their grandparents' or even their parents' generations (Bennis & Thomas, 2002; Tulgan, 2000; Zemke, Raines, & Filipczak, 2000). There is no reason to expect future workers to fit existing molds. Being aware of the kinds of workers the organization will need to attract in the future is a critical part of a long-term strategy.

It may be unrealistic for employers to respond to every expectation or need of every employee, but it is still important to pay attention to those that influence employee effectiveness. Conscientious investigation is required to understand employees' needs and determine an appropriate role for the organization in meeting them. Periodic employee surveys and focus groups, exit interviews, and employee suggestion processes, when done well, gather relevant data about employees' expectations and their ability to be effective. Ideally, a way is found to satisfy the expectations and needs of employees while fulfilling those of the organization. Baxter Healthcare (2000) identified two alternative approaches for addressing both:

- *Competitive:* "One approach for dealing with the two sets of needs is an approach where each party (the company and the employee) holds the perspective that 'my' needs are more important and must be addressed first, even when that means the other's needs are ignored."

- *Collaborative:* "A second approach to addressing the convergence of employee and company needs is one where each party holds the perspective that the other's needs must be incorporated into the solutions in order for 'me' to be successful."

A collaborative approach doesn't just sound better—it works better (see Chapter 14 for the Baxter story). The employment relationship is like any other relationship—it prospers when both parties are moving in the same direction and find common solutions to each other's needs. BP America bases its policies on this concept.

> *The policies of the new BP are summed up in . . . our belief* that all relationships, if they are to endure, must be driven by mutual advantage. . . . *Lasting success demands something more from companies.*
>
> —BP America

Precise knowledge about the profile, trends, and needs of current and future employees, when integrated with the information regarding the importance of human capital, its effect on business results, and the factors that drive human capital performance, gives a composite picture of just how human capital functions in the organization and what it requires.

Step 5: Recognize People As Assets, Not Expenses

Once the connection between human capital and organizational performance is made, managers and executives face a decision: whether to treat people as assets or as costs. Do they choose to *invest in people* or not? Facing this decision is like facing a fork in the road leading to different destinations. Some organizations have already made the decision to invest. The four companies profiled in Part 4 have clearly decided to invest in people, as have organizations that are implementing the adaptive strategies described in this book. Others, including those shipping jobs off to low-wage countries, have made the decision to pay.

But many organizations have yet to decide. Unclear about the importance of human capital to their strategy, the way individuals contribute to success, or which positions have the greatest effect on results, many managers are unable to make the right decisions for their organizations and their employees. They lack the knowledge that will clarify the best road for them to take.

When Mary, the best estimator in the company, asks Tom if he'll allow her to work part-time after her maternity leave, he is faced with a difficult decision: either lose a valuable employee or establish a management practice he thinks will lower overall productivity. Pursuing the decision to invest in people, letting Mary work part-time, would enable him to weigh the part-time loss against a full-time loss based on the importance of skills and experience to the estimator job, the effect estimators like Mary have on the company's ability to be successful, the difficulty of replacing a good estimator given the current labor market, and the knowledge and experience good estimators need in order to perform effectively. Information on these factors is not difficult to obtain, nor is the decision hard to make once you have the necessary information. As we note in Part 3, research indicates that implementing part-time scheduling will improve overall productivity rather than lower it.

Choosing to Invest in People

The five steps in Strategy 1 provide a logical way of thinking about people and clarify for managers how important human capital is to each business.

Lower levels of importance require lower or no investment. Higher levels require higher investment but produce superior results.

Certain industries, those involving significant knowledge or service work, may explicitly recognize how important people are to the organization's success.

> We know that our continued success and growth relies upon building fulfilling and trustworthy relationships with our employees. Attracting, growing and retaining great talent is critical to sustaining Cisco's competitive advantage.
> —Cisco Systems

Recognition that people are real assets is only the starting point. It must lead to the decision to invest in people, a decision that is reinforced by the information gained in going through the steps identified in this chapter.

The decision to invest in people as assets involves more than the issue of how much to invest. In general, choosing to invest in people calls for the following measures, which we discuss in Chapters 6–9.

- Adopt a new set of beliefs and assumptions to replace existing ones more suited to the decision to treat people as costs.
- Create a culture that genuinely values employees as assets.
- Institute practices that reflect the importance of people to the success of the organization.
- Find a way to bring all the pieces of the puzzle together—the beliefs, culture, and practices—in a coherent whole.

In Conclusion

The process of leveraging the power of the structural changes in work and workers described in Chapters 1–4 begins with the conscious decision, at every level of the organization, to treat people as assets rather than expenses—to willingly *invest* in people rather than attempt to minimize their costs. This choice involves developing an understanding of the role human capital plays in work and how it affects results, as well as identifying the drivers of human performance and evaluating the needs of the workforce.

It is important to have honest assessment, throughout the organization, about taking this position. The other four adaptive strategies require this foundation; they are impossible to execute well without it. Examining the role of people in the various types of work and understanding what drives their performance will ground the decision to invest in people even when weighed against financial pressures or historical patterns.

Once made, the decision to invest in people leads to the second strategy, ensuring that the beliefs and assumptions held throughout the organization support this decision. We explore those beliefs and assumptions in Chapter 6.

6

ADOPTING A
NEW SET OF BELIEFS

Once the decision to invest in human capital has been made, grounded in a thorough analysis of the actual relationship between human assets and business results for the specific organization, the next step is to make sure this decision is implemented well. Investments in human capital will be ineffective without a solid set of beliefs underlying management practices, behaviors, or policies. Organizations that have attempted to make such investments have found these practices are neither used nor accepted, and never become sustainable.

Baxter Healthcare, which did create a strong foundation, based its "new model for working" on this statement: "We begin with the foundation upon which the rest is built—the core beliefs that organizations hold about how to achieve results and the operating principles that arise from them. These beliefs and principles comprise some of the key elements that create an organizational culture. From them flow the strategies themselves, the systems, processes and practices."

Because beliefs, consciously and unconsciously held, are at the core of every organization's culture, systems, processes, and practices, a critical step in developing adaptive strategies is to uncover and evaluate the beliefs and assumptions currently shared by individuals within the organization. One way to do this is to ask what the organization's practices and norms indicate about the beliefs its people hold and the assumptions they share (Schein, 1992b).

Underlying beliefs and assumptions can often be traced back to those of the original founders and subsequent leaders of the organization. They are shaped by experiences—successes and failures—and reinforced over time as individuals with similar beliefs are drawn to the organization. Subgroups within the organization may have had different experiences or hold different beliefs, and those need to be examined also.

Beliefs and assumptions—about what is right and what is wrong, what behavior is appropriate, what works and what doesn't—forge the culture of the organization and the effectiveness of its management practices and strategies. Anyone undertaking organizational change must first recognize which beliefs form the foundation and determine whether they will facilitate or hinder the new direction. This is an enormous challenge, since beliefs and assumptions are not always consciously recognized or easily changed.

Beliefs and assumptions are often an unconscious "of course" to those who hold them. They became ingrained because they were effective and became associated with survival and success. They may not always remain so, however, and that is why it is important to become aware of what beliefs and assumptions are held and examine them in the light of current realities. Because they function as a framework for construing situations, or as a filter when analyzing new events and experiences, beliefs and assumptions can get in the way of accurately perceiving reality. Edgar Schein (1992b) notes that most groups and individuals develop defense mechanisms to protect their beliefs and assumptions—making it even harder to change them.

Traditional Beliefs and Assumptions

In this section, we describe a set of beliefs and related assumptions that underlie many current management practices, but that have become obstacles to the success of human capital management practices. They primarily revolve around three core concepts—the nature of business, human nature, and the nature of work—that evolved out of the Industrial Age and its social and business environment.

The Nature of Business

Business is a competitive, masculine-oriented activity.

- Business is about dominating the marketplace, about winning or losing. One party must win and the other lose.
- Individuation—separateness—is the goal for people in business.
- The best business leaders are alpha males—single-minded in the pursuit of success and warrior-like in their approach, tough and not swayed by emotion.
- Business is purely rational; it is the polar opposite of home, where emotion rules.

Human Nature

Workers are not naturally motivated to work hard.

- People are not naturally as ambitious as the times require.
- Workers are subordinates and for the most part replaceable and interchangeable.
- The interests of labor are at odds with those of management.
- Workers are qualitatively different from management and are less motivated to achieve the organization's goals, so managers must direct, control, and modify workers' actions to fit the organization's needs (McGregor, 1960).

The Nature of Work

Work is not engaging or rewarding by itself.

- Work is something workers have to do, not something they want to do. Given a choice, most people would not be working.
- The rewards from work generally come from what it brings (income, security, and so on), rather than from the work itself.
- Much work is boring or repetitive because routine processes, in manufacturing jobs and elsewhere, are the most efficient.

- The most valuable work is observable, and results can be measured by effort or time invested.

If These Beliefs and Assumptions Are True

These traditional beliefs and assumptions have implications for management practices. Both the way work is assigned and the way rewards are allocated will reflect this view of the world.

The Nature of Business

If business is purely competitive, then cooperation and collaboration are not important. Cooperation may be useful in the service of competition, but to win—to beat others—is the ultimate goal. You (the individual and the organization) must be on top to succeed. If you don't win, you lose. You cannot trust. You cannot cooperate with or consider the needs of others (as competitors cannot) if you want to win. As the author Gore Vidal said, "It is not enough to succeed. Others must fail" (Brandenburger & Nalebuff, 1996, p. 3).

If this is true, then competitive behavior is recognized and collaborative behavior is ignored. Individual achievement is rewarded—in performance expectations and advancement decisions—while contributions to the collective goal are not considered either directly or indirectly. Rewards reinforce the importance of individual efforts, leading to increases in this type of work as employees are, logically, drawn to what gains recognition and stop doing what is ignored.

If business is competitive, then the best leaders are warriors. Warriors are action-oriented and must have greater strength and be tougher than everyone else. Emotions and relationships must be subsumed to the larger goal of winning the war. Warriors are not empathic; such "soft" behavior endangers the group. Survival is key.

If business is about dominance, then displays of power are important—dominating markets and displaying dominance through hierarchies and aggressive behavior. Behavior that is respectful is weak. Having an edge is desirable, being aggressive an asset. Giving away too much information makes you vulnerable.

Dominant leaders are celebrated because the group survives best when the strongest members get to the top. The pack supports the existence of the alpha male—the leader who exerts authority by aggressive behavior—shouting, glowering, and demonstrating power through sheer physical presence. Richard Conniff has comically observed the similarities between the behavior of human alpha males such as Larry Ellison at Oracle and that of other alpha male mammals. It is about power—you are either powerful or powerless; power is not shared. To have power you must exercise and display dominance (through the corner office), with an entourage that insulates you from assault (a large department), and by not sharing or giving away power (not empowering others).

If hierarchies are essential, separateness (individuation rather than connection) is valued. The emphasis is on difference. How do I differentiate myself from others? The emphasis on individualism and individuals' differentiating themselves in order to move up the hierarchy affects the way work is done and the types of work that are considered critical or noncritical. Business processes, decision making, employee development are affected by an emphasis on individual effort—often negatively, because this focus tends to ignore connections and unintended consequences. Individual tasks take precedence over the effectiveness of the entire process, decisions have unexamined consequences in related areas, and employees become focused on their individual goals to the detriment of group or organizational goals. The focus is not on the good of the whole.

> *Have you ever noticed that the managers rise to the top by not taking risks? They get to the top by not making too many waves. But what organizations need is leaders who will take risks and lead with courage. If you ask "why don't leaders consider the big picture—the overall success of the organization in making decisions?" Why do they watch costs almost exclusively instead of the returned value of something to the company? Is it because organizations are siloed or is it the market pressure for short-term results? I don't think so. It's because managers are busy managing their careers, instead of the organization.*
>
> —Paul Orfalea, founder and chairperson emeritus of Kinko's, Inc.

If business is a purely rational and competitive activity, then it is the opposite of home, which is the place of emotions, where people care.

Business is the public domain—where private matters don't belong. It is guided by different standards and different values than those in effect at home. Business values and promotes independence; home values and develops interdependence. Business and home are not only separate; they conflict (Bailyn, 1993). Concerns, interests, emotion, and the skills of home or private life have no relevance at work.

A problem with this belief is that it doesn't encourage the passion and energy needed to believe in an organization's vision and make it come true or convey the care for customers that builds long-term relationships. To have workers care passionately about customers or the organization's goals requires legitimizing their emotions in general.

Beliefs about the nature of business form the foundation for beliefs about who the best workers are: Are they competitive individual achievers, not swayed by emotion, who work with a singular focus? Do they keep skills important in the private sphere (relational, empowering, self-understanding, the ability to read emotional data) away from the public sphere of work?

To help examine the beliefs and assumptions about the nature of business that may operate in a given organization, the following questions are worth asking.

- What do the organization's objectives convey about the nature of business? Is it competitive or collaborative?

- Are the organization's strategies designed to support a collaborative or competitive strategy?

- Are compensation systems and policies designed to reward individual or group achievement?

- What sort of people are developed as leaders in the organization? What skills, abilities, behaviors determine who is a good leader?

- How is success for employees defined, and what skills, abilities, and behaviors determine success?

Human Nature

If workers are not naturally motivated to work hard, if they are not naturally as ambitious as the times require, then managers must direct and control employee actions. If workers are unmotivated and irresponsible, they can't be trusted—so they must be watched constantly.

Beliefs and assumptions about worker motivation reflect beliefs about human nature. These unspoken beliefs follow the same debate that has raged for centuries about whether people are naturally inclined toward bad behavior, are a blank slate and entirely influenced by environment (as John Locke, 1632–1704, proposed), or are born with naturally constructive tendencies (although corruptible) as Jean-Jacques Rousseau (1712–1778) wrote.

Stated another way, are people more like mechanisms or organisms? In modern business terms, McGregor's Theory X reflects this same question: Is the average person like a computer, for example, a mechanism that must be switched on to become active, putting out only what is programmed in (garbage in, garbage out)? This view sees workers as unambitious (indolent) by nature, static and resistant to change, and gullible—easily influenced by outside forces (McGregor, 1960). They must be *extrinsically motivated*—pushed or pulled by others (persuaded, punished, directed, or controlled) to perform the desired tasks. In contrast, if people operate like *organisms*, as McGregor's Theory Y describes, workers have an internal drive toward action and change, and they are highly differentiated—as organisms are. Organisms (from slime mold to ants) are naturally self-organizing, active, ambitious, and driven toward growth and evolution (S. Johnson, 2001). They are capable of creativity—of generating entirely new outputs. They are *intrinsically motivated*. If that is so, the best results come when managers facilitate rather than direct their efforts, ensuring they have what they require.

Beliefs about motivation determine how people are treated and managed at work. If they are presumed to require extrinsic motivation (Theory X), they will be closely monitored and controlled, given the minimum information necessary, and subjected to strict rules. Trust and connection will be minimal and the emphasis will be on control.

Beliefs about motivation also determine how work is organized, who sets work objectives, and how rewards are determined. If people are presumed to be extrinsically motivated (Theory X), they must be told what to do and when, where, and how to do it. They are rewarded extrinsically for following the rules and achieving the objectives determined for them.

Under Theory X, employees are considered to be subordinates. They are for the most part replaceable and interchangeable—differences among employees are more liabilities than assets because they make management more complex and open to claims of unfairness. People are a *cost* to the organization, not an *asset*, and their associated expenses should be kept as low as possible. Investments in employees—training, development, and stress management—are considered a waste of resources.

Under Theory X, employee selection and fit with the right job or career path is not important. Retention is not important, because employees are easily replaced. The employees' experience of work—whether they find it satisfying, challenging, or meaningful—is not a management concern. The organization's responsibility to workers is limited to providing compensation for work performed and complying with relevant employment laws and regulations.

When employees are believed to be extrinsically motivated, it follows that some employees will require more motivating than others—those in lower-level jobs or with less pay or less responsibility, for example. Meanwhile, it is often assumed that professional employees get greater satisfaction from work than nonprofessional employees whose jobs are by definition less rewarding, which translates to a belief that professionals can be given greater latitude than nonprofessionals are allowed.

If workers' interests are at odds with those of management, negotiations between management and labor are a battle, where one party wins at the other's expense. It is difficult to find points of common interest. Although this situation occurs in many organizations, it is not true everywhere. Compare United and American Airlines with Southwest or General Motors with Toyota. United, American, and General Motors have been hampered by battles with unions, while Southwest and Toyota have not, a strong factor in the differences in performance among the companies. Although one might say the existence of labor unions at United, American, and General Motors raises costs and increases contentiousness between labor and management, there is an old saying that unions exist because the labor-management relationship has already broken down. Organizational alignment is difficult to achieve when management interests are at odds with those of workers.

If workers are qualitatively different from managers, they cannot be relied upon to deliver results and act in the best interests of the organization. Managers have a greater sense of responsibility for work results and the welfare of the organization than employees do. The manager's role is to determine how work should be organized and assigned and to control when, where, and how work gets done. Workers cannot be relied upon for input or decisions in these matters because they lack the motivation and commitment to do so. Managers need to make all decisions to ensure that organizational goals are met. In general, managers are considered to be more responsible, trustworthy, and motivated, as well as better able to see the big picture.

These assumptions about the role of management were formed by Frederick Taylor (1856–1915) nearly a century ago: ". . . what the manager really ought to do is discover the best way to do the job, provide the right tools, select the right man, train him in the right way of doing the job, give him incentives if he does perform the job correctly, and by doing all of these things, he should motivate the worker to work" (Herzberg, 1966, p. 56).

The idea that managers are qualitatively different comes in part from a notion embedded in our social consciousness that the fittest (as in the "survival of the fittest") rise to the top. Called social Darwinism, this view assumes that those at the top (from midlevel managers on up) are somehow different (better) and earned their power by being more highly evolved or more worthy. As Herzberg also points out, this view affects beliefs about who should make decisions and whether employees should be empowered.

To examine the beliefs and assumptions about human nature that may be operating in a particular organization, the following questions are worth asking.

- What do we believe about why people come to work and whether employees seek or naturally shun responsibility, growth, and change? What do we think motivates employees to commit to organizational goals?

- How much authority do employees at various levels have to make decisions?

- To what extent are employee decisions reviewed, monitored, or allowed to stand?

- Are performance appraisals and compensation used to motivate employees or to reward them for achievement of results?

- What resources and rewards are available to management but not available to employees?

The Nature of Work

If work is not engaging or rewarding by itself—employees are not excited by, inspired, or involved in the work for its own sake—management must motivate employees extrinsically—pushing or pulling them to perform.

In this view, work has a natural element of pain and sacrifice: one must force oneself to work; it is not intended to be enjoyable. ("That's why they call it 'work,'" people say.) This belief is a remnant of the Protestant work ethic, which considered work a tool for redeeming mankind from a sinful nature (Herzberg, 1966), not something done for the joy of it. Being concerned about how happy employees are is not only irrelevant to managers, it is potentially counterproductive. If employees are enjoying themselves, they aren't working hard enough and standards need to be set higher. When work is toil and employees are not motivated by the work itself, managers must actively oversee them to ensure that they are doing the job. Extrinsic rewards—pay, recognition—are believed to have the greatest power to get results, because the rewards of work come from what it brings, rather than from the work itself (see p. 75).

If work must become routine to be efficient—as the Industrial Age required—the fact that it is boring or repetitive to the worker is inescapable. Industrial processes further eroded any intrinsic rewards by separating work into steps. Workers did not see the results of their labor in a finished product, one intrinsic reward of work. Machines require the same inputs every time, so standardization is necessary and workers' idiosyncratic contributions and characteristics are not. The reverse is true in a knowledge society: standardization kills innovation and creativity, the lifeblood of success.

If the most valuable work is observable, and results can be measured by effort or time invested, then the more time it inherently takes, the more valuable the work must be. Under this belief, work that is not observable or measurable—thinking, creating, listening, managing, and so on—is not valuable. This view is also a holdover from the Industrial Age, when outputs came directly from inputs and time invested was a fairly good measure of results. Rewarding employees for the amount of time they put in rather than the results they generate works well only when the input is relatively standard. When more time invested equals greater output, the employee working the most hours is by definition the top performer. Rewards based on time invested do not work well for knowledge work, where the amount of input cannot be directly tied to output and there may even be a reverse effect from long hours. How much thinking time is required to generate a new product idea or advertising concept? In service work, the quality of the customer experience is what matters.

To examine the beliefs and assumptions about the nature of work that may be operating in a particular organization, the following questions are worth asking.

- Is work deliberately designed to be engaging and intrinsically rewarding for employees?
- Does the organization actively develop employees by providing them with opportunities to stretch and grow, or does it only seek employees with proven ability to do a particular job?
- What criteria are used to identify high-performers?
- How does the organization gauge employee commitment?
- Does the organization, either explicitly or implicitly, reward face time, long hours, and other measures of observable work or results achieved?

Situational Examples

The following situations illustrate how beliefs and assumptions affect decisions about management practices and human capital in an organization.

Example 1: A Professional Employee

A high-potential graphic artist requests permission to work remotely from a loft in the Colorado mountains. How that request is processed illustrates the beliefs and assumptions at work in the organization.

- Will he perform as well if he is not supervised in person? (human nature)
- How will we know he is working? How can we evaluate his performance and potential for advancement? (human nature and the nature of business)
- Will he be working a normal schedule? Will he be accessible to others who need to reach him? Do we care how long the job takes him; what

if he doesn't work as many hours as he would in an office? (nature of work)

- Do we believe high-quality work can be done in such an environment? Will it contribute to or distract from his best work performance? (nature of business and nature of work)

- How can we be sure he contributes to both team and organizational performance? (nature of work)

Example 2: A Tech Support Person

A tech support person requests permission to work two hours from home each morning (5–7 A.M.) so he can be at home and transport his children to school when it opens at 8 A.M., and then work the rest of the day at his normal location. How would his request be processed?

- Would it be different or the same as a request from a management-level employee in terms of the perceived sense of responsibility and trustworthiness? (human nature)

- Work hours: Does it matter when he puts in the extra two hours? (five in the morning, midnight, Saturday?) (nature of work)

- How can this work be done from home? (nature of work)

- How will his supervisor know he is working? (human nature)

Do These Beliefs and Assumptions Still Fit?

It is time to examine the beliefs and assumptions we may unknowingly hold. Do we still find them valid? Are they consistent with our current reality? Do they make sense?

Although the implications we attribute to these traditional beliefs and assumptions may seem extreme, it is clear that they are still operating in many organizations. They provide the foundation for a whole range of structures, systems, and processes, but if the beliefs don't fit reality, the structures don't fit reality either.

Adopting a new set of beliefs and assumptions requires first honestly identifying existing beliefs and contradictions. A manager who purportedly believes that properly selected and trained employees are naturally motivated to act in the best interests of the organization and perform at a high level should not feel the need to closely monitor or review every customer service decision employees make to determine if it was appropriate.

This story illustrates old beliefs that are challenged by the new reality.

THE BUS MECHANIC

The mechanic at an urban transit company came to work dressed in full Harley-Davidson regalia—black leathers, long hair wrapped in a bandana, and a full gray beard: the image of a tough male employee in a masculine work environment, someone whose personal life would not interfere with work. But he was afraid his teenage son and stepdaughter would engage in sexual activity when they were home alone in the summer (he had reason for concern from past experience). So he had asked to flex his lunch hour—taking it at odd times—so he could drop in at home unannounced some days.

His supervisor denied the request, saying, "Can't your wife do that?" (She worked full-time across town, so, no, she could not.) The request wouldn't compromise the work output, but the supervisor did not consider the effect on the work itself. It just didn't fit with "the way things are done here" and might open a Pandora's box of other requests. The supervisor referred to the labor agreement for justification, even though it was developed for a different era and unclear about this circumstance. The work rules were designed to control, from a presumption that either the supervisor or the employees, given the opportunity, would take advantage. The mechanic got a "no" that made no sense to him, and the decision reinforced his status as a subordinate.

In Conclusion

We have recommended that organizations reexamine the hidden beliefs and assumptions behind their current practices to see if they support the decision to invest in people as assets. Traditional assumptions that business is a competitive, win-or-lose proposition, that people are not motivated, and that work cannot be engaging or rewarding create barriers to organizational success when they are not in sync with current reality. It is critical that managers be right about their assumptions because of the enormous waste of organizational resources when they are wrong. Managing *against* laziness instead of *to* unleash natural inspiration involves a very different set of actions.

Replacing traditional assumptions and beliefs is both possible and wise, but it is not a superficial undertaking. It begins with candidly assessing the beliefs that lie beneath the organization's current behavior. Changing long-held beliefs takes time. Deeply held unconscious ideas rooted in decades of experience do not change easily or quickly. They are, however, the place where the adaptation process begins.

In Chapter 7 we present a new set of adaptive beliefs that replace these traditional assumptions and help redefine the organizational culture, the third adaptive strategy.

7

REDEFINING THE ORGANIZATIONAL CULTURE

Every organization has a culture, whether weak or strong, consistent or varied throughout the organization. The third strategy is to redefine the organizational culture based on examined and deliberately chosen beliefs, values, and assumptions.

What Is Organizational Culture?

Culture is subtle, complex, and hard to recognize if you are inside it; it is like the water fish swim in or the air we breathe—we are not conscious of it. Culture is resistant to change because it has worked well for the organization. It arises, as we have said, from the beliefs, values, and assumptions of the organization's founders, modified over time by experience and reinforced by the infusion of new members who are selected in part because they fit the culture (Schein, 1992a). It forms the principles, systems, structures, behavioral norms, traditions, common language, practices, and policies, and it determines how employees, vendors, customers, or other stakeholders are treated. Culture acts as a unifying force, uniting people in ways that take precedence over individual differences.

Practices that are inconsistent with the underlying culture will not be used. If the culture doesn't support a decision to invest in and treat people as human assets, all the programs and policies in the world won't change behavior or results. Why? Because culture—not to be confused with written policy—is what determines how a company operates.

What Is an Adaptive Culture?

Adaptive organizational cultures respond proactively to the new reality. They manage people as assets rather than costs and share a number of common values. In general, they take a long-term perspective, particularly on issues pertaining to business, people, and work, and so they make investments in individuals, relationships, and processes. Assuming that managers and employees will be around and that the fruits of labor will be realized over time affects many things, including internal and external relationships, what data are included along with financial information in making decisions, and what outcomes are considered important. It affects hiring, firing, and promotion decisions and how employees are treated from day to day. It affects decisions about customers. Adaptive cultures are about building clocks rather than telling time (Collins & Porras, 1994); they seek to develop one-hundred-year managers, not one-minute managers (Csikszentmihalyi, 2003).

> We really try to act like this company is going to be here a hundred years from now.
> —Yvon Chouinard, founder of Patagonia (quoted in Csikszentmihalyi, 2003)

Adaptive Beliefs, Values, and Assumptions

An adaptive culture must have a set of adaptive beliefs, values, and assumptions at the core of its operating principles and specific practices. In this section, we describe these beliefs, the values that relate to them, and examples of operating principles consistent with them. In the next chapter, we discuss the practices that emerge from them.

The Nature of Business

Adaptive Belief: Business today is both a competitive and collaborative enterprise. The trick is to know when and with whom to compete or collaborate. This belief leads to the following observations.

- Joint effort and collaboration have become increasingly important, both within the organization and with strategic partners. At the same time, competition is also essential in the external marketplace.

- Leaders must be strong, but warrior-like toughness that disregards what is happening with others becomes a liability. Strength is redefined to include the abilities to connect, persuade, develop, and empower others, rather than pure individuation and isolation.

- Connection becomes more important, relationship and communication skills become critical.

- Business and private life become more integrated. Some qualities of private life, such as interrelatedness and the sense of belonging, can be desirable at work, as are skills developed in private life, such as the ability to listen, guide, and understand others.

This adaptive belief gives rise to the following organizational values.

- Integrity and respect
- Aligned interests
- Empowering leadership
- Integration of public and private spheres

Integrity and Respect

No one will collaborate with someone else without believing the other party will act with integrity and respect their opinions, skills, and ideas. In adaptive cultures, integrity is expected of all stakeholders—shareholders, partners, employees, and everyone else involved. Management is responsible for upholding a high standard of ethics. Employees and managers treat one another with respect and accord that same respect to customers, vendors, and shareholders. Open communication fosters trust and respect. Communication flows in all directions. Both management and workers are responsible for honest communication.

Three key components of respect are dignity, recognition of the employee as a whole person, and equity (Campbell & Koblenz, 1997). All aspects of the organization recognize and support the dignity of every person, regardless of position, rank, race, gender, or personal choices. These values must actually operate and govern behavior in organizations, not merely show up in printed reports or in lists that hang on walls. Equity is about fairness and recognizing diverse needs. It is not the same as uniformity—which may be perceived as equity but can have disparate effects—or equality. Equal treatment can have unequal consequences. True equity focuses on creating a level playing field, for example, by enabling everyone to attain plum assignments (Catlette & Hadden, 1998).

> *Treat each other as you would like to be treated.* (Baxter Healthcare, 2000)

Aligned Interests

For collaboration to be effective, participants must realize that the interests of stakeholders can and should be aligned. The traditional view of managers and employees being at odds or employees being catered to at the expense of shareholders or customers fails to recognize how each group benefits from and relies on the right behavior of the other. The best results are achieved when everyone recognizes that employees play an important role in developing and delivering customer satisfaction, which generates revenue growth and ultimately profits to be distributed to shareholders. The right employees have a vested interest in the success of the organization as a whole as well as the success of their own careers. Organizations have a vested interest in the well-being of employees, without whom it is not possible to serve customers, generate growth, or compensate shareholders for their investment. Alignment of interests is the reverse of one party's achieving all of its goals all of the time at the expense of other stakeholders. Aligned interests are part of the human resource strategy for mutual gain, rather than a zero-sum game where one wins at the expense of the other.

> *The interests of the company and the individual are inseparable.*

> *We believe that doing what's right for the business with integrity will lead to mutual success for both the company and the individual. Our quest for mutual success ties us together.*

We encourage stock ownership and ownership behavior.
(Procter & Gamble, 2002)

An adaptive culture has a *we*, rather than an *us-versus-them*, orientation.

Empowering Leadership

The organization values—and therefore develops, promotes, and rewards—leaders who demonstrate the ability to connect to others and build organizations that incorporate adaptive beliefs and principles. In an increasingly interconnected world, effective leaders must be able to access a full complement of leadership styles: relational skills (the ability to collaborate, contribute, and mentor) that enable them to contribute to others' success; instrumental skills that enable them to empower, persuade, and sustain social networks; and direct skills (the ability to master their own tasks; to take charge, excel, and outperform; Lipman-Blumen, 1996). In a less connected, more competitive business environment, leaders who excelled at taking charge and outperforming others were highly valued and often very successful. An adaptive culture, necessary for success in a collaborative and interconnected world, requires very different skills.

Integration of Public and Private Spheres

Business and private life (home and work) are increasingly interconnected and integrated as technological innovations enable people to work anywhere and any time, and as a singular focus on work becomes impossible (see Chapter 3 for a description of the changes in the workforce). Work and home overlap—blurring boundaries of time and tasks. Work comes home (e-mail read at night) and personal life comes to work (children's school conferences and grandparents' medical appointments during work hours).

Although the integration of home and work may bring additional stress and make it more difficult for workers to focus completely on either sphere, it also has benefits, such as the ability to use skills necessary in one sphere to enhance performance in the other. The other-orientation, interdependence, and interconnectedness (Bailyn, 1993) that are valued at home are becoming recognized as increasingly important for organizational success. Skills and abilities honed in the private sphere—such as relational skills and intrapersonal intelligence—are increasingly valued in the work environment (see Chapter 4 for a description of such skills). As the public and private spheres become integrated, they no longer have to conflict but can act synergistically (Bailyn, 1993).

A climate of caring and sense of affiliation are other values usually associated with home that are gaining importance in the workplace. Caring—the sense that people are important and traditionally considered a hallmark of home—has become legitimate in the workplace. It is personal. "Caring is an attitude, not a program. First you feed the troops. Motivation doesn't necessarily follow money. Caring about people means really listening to them" (Catlette & Hadden, 1998, p. 85). Allstate Insurance defines care as one of its core values—permeating relationships with stakeholders.

> Our business is one that is built on caring—a value that has been at the core of our relationship with customers, employees and agents for more than 70 years.

—Allstate Insurance

Human Nature

Adaptive Belief: People are naturally self-motivated, open to change, and eager to learn. They are interested in performing their jobs well. This belief leads to the following expectations.

- Employees possess intrinsic motivation to perform their work well under the right conditions, that is, when they are matched with the right job and find the work rewarding. This principle applies to all types of jobs and all types of employees.

- The work environment can enhance or detract from the natural motivation of people to perform their jobs well.

- The individuality of each employee is a potential asset—everyone brings tacit (internalized) knowledge and relationships (social capital) to the job, and these are not easily reproduced.

- There is no qualitative difference between managers and employees in terms of inherent worth, capacity to contribute value, nature of motivation, or potential for acting responsibly.

- The role of managers is to facilitate rather than dictate. In a knowledge society, workers possess more specialized knowledge than their managers and know best how to organize their work. With technology, managers are no longer needed to convey information up and down the organization, so the role of management shifts to one of coordination among highly motivated skilled workers across the organization.

This adaptive belief gives rise to the following organizational values.

- Trust
- Flexibility
- People as assets
- Diversity and individuality
- Wholeness
- Shared responsibility
- Results orientation

Trust

Because employees are naturally self-motivated, trust is possible between workers and management and among workers. Trust is based on shared interests, careful selection, alignment of rewards systems, and consistent values. Trust enables employees to have the freedom to meet their personal needs while achieving work goals. Trust is made real by organizational practices that focus on results rather than on time spent, and by eliminating artifacts of mistrust such as hierarchies and excessive rules. An environment of trust enhances efficiency as it reduces the need for and cost of supervision, rigid roles, and inflexible procedures, enabling workers to pinch-hit for one another as need arises (Hochschild, 1997).

Trust is an integral aspect of adaptive organizations. With it, organizations eliminate systematic signs of distrust (probation periods, time clocks, locked supply cabinets), dramatically increase discretionary authority levels, deal swiftly and harshly with those who break faith, and make people feel empowered, not powerful (Catlette & Hadden, 1998).

Flexibility

The organization is flexible rather than rigid, seeking to create a work environment that facilitates high performance based on the needs of individual workers, work groups, and required tasks. Work environments and locations are based on job requirements as well as the requirements of the individuals performing each job, and so they can change as requirements change. Mobile, virtual, and remote environments and traditional centralized locations are all considered legitimate.

Flexibility also applies to work schedules and career paths. Measures of performance and commitment do not rely on time metrics such as hours worked. Effort and outcomes, availability of employees to managers, and performance are not considered equivalents in a knowledge environment. The adaptive culture allows individuals with a wide variety of work styles and lifestyles to be successful contributors, to advance, and to lead. Reduced schedules, including part-time work and job sharing, are considered as valid and valuable as full-time work and feed into advancement tracks in the same way. Employees who take time off in midcareer are not viewed as lacking commitment. Assignments, pay, benefits, bonuses, advancement, and rewards are apportioned appropriately, replacing a full-time or no-time approach (Williams & Calvert, 2001).

People As Assets

As with other assets, the organization safeguards its people, protecting their attention and providing opportunities for them to replenish their energies. It is concerned about their short- and long-term health, well-being, and development. It pays attention to their physical, emotional, and social work environment and is careful not to overload them.

Leaders are concerned with future human capital as well. The education and development of children, who form the pool of future human capital from which the organization will later draw, is considered a legitimate business concern. The organization actively promotes and works toward improvements in early and later education, child care, and parental accessibility to children to ensure this resource is developed and well prepared.

Diversity and Individuality

The diverse aptitudes of individuals are leveraged to increase the quality and quantity of ideas, to improve service to diverse customers, to generate new products and services, and to increase suggestions for improvement. Recruiting, rewards, and advancement policies promote genuine diversity of workers, and thus of contribution. Genuine diversity is different from representation by members of different groups, which may give only the appearance but not the substance of diversity (Thomas, 1999). The natural tension that comes with diverse viewpoints is considered essential to continuous improvement.

Individuality means recognizing and valuing people as living systems with idiosyncrasies that are assets: their skills, knowledge, abilities, value systems, and life situations. Equity (justice and fairness) takes precedence over uniformity (S. Friedman & Greenhaus, 2000). Adaptive organizations not only accept the differences that make each individual unique—they capitalize on these differences, finding ways to identify and develop the strengths of each employee so that these strengths enable the employee to do meaningful work while fulfilling the goals of the organization (Buckingham & Clifton, 2001).

We believe that a diverse group of associates is the best way to serve the diverse and individual needs of our customers.

—Edward Jones

Wholeness

People are seen as whole (integrated) beings with legitimate responsibilities and interests beyond work. They are encouraged to bring their whole selves to work (their work and nonwork selves and their minds, hearts, and hands) because then they can exercise their full creativity, initiative, and engagement. While the nonwork self is welcomed at work, it is up to the employee to determine how much of that private self to bring to work. People can share aspects of personal life without fear of repercussions.

All employees, including those who are not "work-primary," can be high-performers. Employees with multiple priorities—people who have significant caregiving responsibilities, both male and female, are able to feel they fit in and have no need to overcome unnecessary roadblocks to high performance. Employees who have dual responsibilities are integrated into business strategies and assigned important and relevant tasks. Employees can discuss personal issues and needs along with work requirements in planning sessions without retribution. People who are not singularly focused on work but have other interests outside work—participating in their communities, spending time with their families, and so on—have equal opportunities for plum assignments, advancement, and development.

People who want to be effective and highly involved at work and outside work can do so, instead of having to choose one or the other.

We are committed to providing equal opportunity for all employees to reach their full potential; it is a fundamental value.
—Fannie Mae

Shared Responsibility

Because there is no difference between managers and employees in terms of work ethic, ability to contribute, or value, both share responsibility for work outcomes. Shared responsibility is a collaborative answer-finding process. It is an adult-adult relationship. It is not paternalistic, with managers helping employees or providing all the answers. The manager is a facilitator of solutions, someone who supports employees so they can do their jobs. The manager is responsible for eliminating barriers and ensuring that employees have access to a work environment, work processes, and resources that enable good results. Managers and employees are responsible for results. The employee is responsible for asking for help when it is needed and for raising issues to be jointly solved with managers.

Employees are accountable for their own results, for collaborating with colleagues as needed, and for contributing to the overall success of the organization. Employees have control over their time and how their work is organized because both are critical to their sense of ownership of and responsibility for work outcomes.

Results Orientation

Time is a valuable and limited resource, shared between the organization and employees. Work is organized to achieve goals in the most time-efficient manner. Nonessential, low-value work is eliminated even when doing so requires a reorientation of managers' roles or conflicts with convenience factors such as constant accessibility of employees to managers or co-workers. Performance is judged by results, not availability of workers, number of hours worked, or physical presence at work.

Results include individual as well as group performance. It is considered insufficient to evaluate the individual achievement of employees without considering how their performance affects the organization as a whole.

The Nature of Work

Adaptive Belief: Work is engaging and rewarding. This belief presupposes that the work is properly designed, and assumes the following.

- Work can be highly engaging and rewarding, regardless of the job level, when employees are in a job that is appropriate for their skill level, yet challenges them, and when they have the resources required to do the job well.
- Work can contribute meaning and value to life and bring fulfillment from the sheer satisfaction of doing it well.
- Work is a way to both express and develop who we are (Whyte, 2001).
- When people are doing work that fits them, they do their best work.
- Valuable contributions are not always observable.

This adaptive belief gives rise to the following organizational values.

- Challenging and rewarding work
- Egalitarianism
- An inclusive definition of valued work

Challenging and Rewarding Work

For work to be engaging and rewarding, the organization must ensure that employees are matched with the right work, provided with opportunities to grow and develop, and have some control over the objectives and process for performing their work. Employees must be actively involved in job selection, work design, skill development, growth plans, and so on to ensure that their individual interests, skills, and aspirations have an appropriate outlet. It requires a commitment on the part of both the individual and the organization to ongoing assessments and revisions of the work to sustain employees' focus and the appropriate level of challenge.

The organization sets clear standards and expectations, communicates both to employees, trains and develops employees to achieve them, and creates an environment conducive to attaining them. All this is done in the context of the other values, which align the interests of employees and the organization and respect employees as whole people with legitimate needs.

Egalitarianism

All work is valued and has the potential to be meaningful and challenging when properly designed. Though employees may fulfill different roles, all are valuable to the organization. The contribution of employees in line jobs is as important as the contribution of professionals and managers. Clear goals, immediate feedback, balance between opportunity and capacity, deep concentration, the ability to be present while working, control, and the ability to focus are required for meaningful work (Csikszentmihalyi, 2003).

Decisions about when and where work is performed consider personal constraints as well as business constraints. Adaptive cultures are not "on-demand cultures" where employees are at the beck and call of management, a chaotic environment in which it is difficult to balance individual and organizational needs. Instead, work is planned ahead of time, specifications clearly articulated, desired outcomes clearly communicated, and contingency plans created. When emergencies arise two questions are asked before workers are drawn off their existing plans: Is it necessary to do this? If so, what's the best way to accomplish it? (Bailyn, 1993).

An Inclusive Definition of Valued Work

Both individual achievement and other-oriented work are valued. There is a heightened effort to recognize the less visible work that typically has not been recognized—to name it, reward it, and allow time for it. Real work includes work that builds connection, prevents or solves problems, builds teams, and enables information sharing.

Model of Adaptive Beliefs

Establishing an adaptive culture (based on beliefs that business is collaborative as well as competitive; that human beings are naturally self-motivated, open to change, and eager to learn; and that work is engaging and rewarding; see Figure 1) facilitates the implementation of adaptive human capital management practices. Moreover, an adaptive culture encourages managers and employees to use these practices—enabling the organization to truly benefit from the decision to invest in human assets.

Changes in the business environment and advancements in our understanding of people suggest it is time for many organizations to redefine their

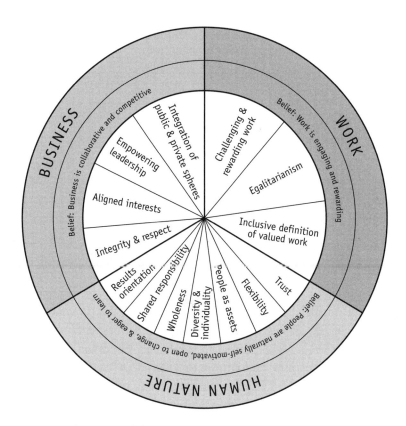

Figure 1 Model of Adaptive Beliefs

culture. And not just entrenched older organizations; young organizations also need to change if they embody the management model of the Industrial Age. In a knowledge economy, a successful business enterprise can no longer be an exclusively competitive, masculine-oriented activity; it must also be collaborative. Even leaders whose warrior-like toughness was once the ultimate strength are finding that command plays a much smaller role in the new reality and strength must be redefined to include the ability to connect, listen, and understand. Presuming that people are inter-changeable and not naturally motivated to contribute their best will not generate the kind of loyalty or performance the times require—better to assume that people generally want to perform their jobs well. It is also important to recognize that, rather than drudgery to be avoided, the work itself (whether planting trees, caring for the sick, or designing a Mars Rover) and satisfaction from doing a job well often provide the spark that inspires high performance.

In Conclusion

Organizational cultures need to be redefined to support the decision to invest in people as assets. This third strategy involves establishing a set of revised beliefs about the nature of business, human motivation, and the capacity of work itself to be rewarding and challenging—beliefs that then become an integral part of the organization's culture. Believing that business is collaborative as well as competitive gives rise to organizational values such as integrity and respect, aligned interests between management and employees, empowering leadership, and integration of work and private life. Believing that people are naturally self-motivated supports organizational values of trust, flexibility, treating people as assets, diversity and individuality, wholeness, shared responsibility, and results orientation. Believing that work can be engaging leads to values related to challenging and rewarding work, egalitarianism, and an inclusive definition of valued work. It is easier to espouse these values than to adopt them; many organizations will need to transform themselves to live them, because their cultures were formed before these values were essential to their survival.

With a redefined organizational culture, one that recognizes people as assets, organizations can then begin to adopt specific practices that enable employees to meet their personal goals while achieving the organization's objectives. We discuss these practices in the fourth strategy, presented in Chapter 8.

8

TRANSFORMING MANAGEMENT PRACTICES

Of all the adaptive changes, transforming practices is often what managers are most comfortable addressing. The transformation of practices alone, however, is insufficient and ultimately ineffective if not applied in the context of an adaptive culture.

In this chapter we describe the practices that would be found in adaptive cultures—practices that support the beliefs, assumptions, and values described in Chapter 7. The values of *respect, aligned interests, flexibility, shared responsibility,* and *diversity* are reflected in practices that provide employees with reasonable workloads, boundaries on work time, customized work schedules and career paths, the ability to participate in work design and restructuring, and equitably distributed work and rewards. *Trust* and *egalitarianism* are also reflected in employee-driven work redesign and restructuring, and in equitable distribution of work and rewards. Talent management practices such as selective recruiting and retention, control of complexity, contribution-based performance and advancement criteria, and professional development support *empowering leadership, results orientation,* and managing *people as assets.* When *diversity, wholeness,* and *flexibility* are valued, management practices include customized and flexible work schedules, appropriate resources and benefits, and boundaries on work time. And an organizational culture that values *challenging and rewarding* work will provide a high-performance work environment, professional development, and rewarding job content.

As with values, practices are sometimes stated but not lived. To evaluate lived versus espoused practices, one must look beyond the existence of practices in general to who's covered (realistically, who can and does use them) and specifically what's covered (Bravo, 2003). In adaptive organizations, the stated practices are available to be used by all employees and everyone shares responsibility for ensuring across-the-board access to the practices.

The adaptive human capital practices described in this chapter don't form an exhaustive list, they simply illustrate the range of possibilities. The appropriateness of a given practice will depend upon the needs of individual workers in the organization, the nature of the work requirements, and the goals of the organization. The box on page 123 provides a framework of the categories of practices we discuss.

Time

Adaptive practices about time are among the most central for managing in the new reality. They give employees greater control over time and shift the way work has been scheduled from a synchronized, standardized approach toward an asynchronous, variable approach to time. This allows an organization to adapt to requirements of customers who want anytime, anywhere service; takes advantage of technology; and capitalizes on the strengths of today's workforce. Greater employee control signals an evolution from work scheduled around static managers and machines toward work centered around customers, whose needs vary and who may be in another time zone or even on another continent. Variability in scheduling can reduce overhead through the use of technology that maximizes or reduces facilities loads. Adaptive practices involve new ways to organize, allocate, and manage time.

ADAPTIVE PRACTICES

Time

- Customization of work schedules, work hours, and career paths
- Reasonable workload and boundaries on work time
- Time off
- Minimal use of time as a metric

Organization of Work

- Employee involvement in work design and restructuring
- Work reorganization to eliminate nonessential work
- Flexible organization of work
- Elastic and rewarding job content and design
- Control of complexity

Talent Management

- Selective recruitment and intensive retention
- Equitable distribution of work and rewards
- Contribution-based performance and advancement criteria
- Human capital–oriented professional development

Resources and Tools

- Updated and redesigned benefits
- Efficient systems and processes

Customization of Work Schedules, Work Hours, and Career Paths

Self-determination is a critical aspect of adaptive time management. It involves giving employees and work teams more control over their schedules, including when to work and whether to work overtime. Technology, employee initiative, and responsibility enable a variety of scheduling possibilities.

Providing employees with control over their schedules reflects the fact that employees know best how to maximize their time to achieve the best results. Self-managing teams determine their work schedules based on the results required, while supervisors are redeployed as coordinators of self-motivated workers. Customization enables employees' personal responsibilities to be among the considerations in scheduling work, regardless of the employee's level in the organization, from top management to the front lines (Williams & Calvert, 2001). With aligned interests and shared responsibility, these practices reflect the values of respect, trust, and flexibility, as well as a results orientation, and will yield the best performance.

Applying the principle of self-determination in day-to-day and longer-term scheduling decisions lessens the burden on supervisors to coordinate complex schedules. Employees and teams have the authority and responsibility to restructure the work and coordinate schedules among themselves (Williams, 2000), considering the effect of schedules on work outcomes. Although federal and state regulations provide guidance on the use of overtime and compensatory time, these laws are changing in recognition of the changing demands of today's workers and employers.

> *Employees need to effectively manage demanding work schedules and their personal lives.* . . . *People are most satisfied, committed and productive, both at work and at home, when they have a support system in place and a sense of control over their time.*
> —Prudential

Work schedule customization comes in three forms: flexibility, predictability, and career paths.

Flexibility

Flexible scheduling practices are formal or informal arrangements that permit employees and managers to alter schedules occasionally or regularly. Alternatives to a standard eight-hour-day, five-day-week work schedule include modifying hours over the day, week, or even year, occasionally or regularly; compressing forty hours into less than five days; or working less-than-full-time schedules for jobs that are traditionally full-time. These flexible work schedules are accompanied by policies, training, cultural elements, and role models that make them possible for all types of employees, including promotion-track employees and managers.

A culture of every-day flexibility *puts our people in control of their time.*

—Deloitte & Touche Web site, 2002

Communication, cross-training of staff, and a culture that encourages flexibility make flexible schedules viable. Certain tools are also required, such as digitized mail and paper files so employees can read them from anywhere, team environments, nonterritorial offices, telework centers and virtual office space, and electronic and other software tools that facilitate schedule changes (Sims, Joroff, & Becker, 1996; Shellenbarger, 2001b).

EXAMPLES OF CONCRETE PRACTICES

- Compressed workweeks (4/10, 9/80, and so on)
- Flexible schedules that vary around core hours or are open-ended
- Situational flexibility that allows employees to make last-minute variations as situations demand
- The ability to shift hours across the month or year—reduced summer hours, or working more hours at peak times in the month, with time off when things are relatively slow
- The ability to make up missed work time
- The ability to swap shifts when necessary and rotate overtime and shift assignments
- Giving employee groups the option during a downturn to collectively reduce work hours to avoid layoffs, for example, by creating a thirty-two-hour workweek with prorated salary and benefits for employees and managers

---

Making flexible work schedules fully adaptive requires paying attention to the subtle gender implications that can affect their use. Fully adaptive organizations look deeply at flexibility across weeks and years and over careers to see who can truly use it without penalty. Many traditionally male jobs (whether held by men or women) require full-time continuous employment and involve extensive overtime, while some traditionally female jobs require regular hours with little mandated overtime. Taking time out of work altogether for child rearing may not remove employees from the promotion and growth ladder in traditionally female jobs, but it often does in traditionally male jobs (Williams, 2000).

Predictability

Predictability in shift rotations, required overtime, and required work schedule changes complement flexibility and also recognize that employees are not singularly focused on work but simultaneously managing other responsibilities. Reducing the unpredictability of schedule changes helps employees manage their lives better both at work and at home. Unpredictable changes in work shifts or hours (for example, mandatory overtime on short notice) force employees to make changes in existing child or elder care, break prior commitments, and inconvenience others. (Even predictable work shifts have a similar effect if they require night, evening, and weekend work, when substitute family care is difficult to find. Making such work hours voluntary or having more work done during traditional hours lessens the dilemma.)

Striving for predictability respects the reality of the dual-focus worker and acts to align employee and organizational interests. In production or service environments it may be more challenging for workers or teams to set their own schedules, although the flexibility principle can still work (see the First Tennessee National story in Chapter 16). What is important is to provide employees with as much control as possible.

Career Paths

Career paths have an element of timing to them. If timing of career trajectories can be customized, advancement becomes possible for more people, such as those who take time out of a career, or who work reduced hours, or who do not proceed at the same pace. Advancement-related practices are discussed later in this chapter, in the "Talent Management" section.

The adaptive practice ensures multiple career paths exist and criteria other than continuous full-time employment are used to identify highpotentials.

EXAMPLES OF CONCRETE PRACTICES

- Managers and employees strategize together how to make work demands more predictable

- Shifts set where possible to coincide with family care resources

- Advance notice for overtime and some flexibility for those with caregiving responsibilities

- Work organized to avoid crisis-response mode and, in a crisis, emergency requests evaluated for ways to avoid excessive demands on employees (Bailyn, 1993)

- Events—retreats and conferences, training, and so on—scheduled with awareness of employees' dual responsibilities

- Meetings scheduled when all employees can participate, considering personal constraints on a par with business constraints

- Business travel limited in amount and duration, with alternatives such as videoconferencing used when feasible; employee choice regarding travel on weekends; personal responsibilities considered when planning travel assignments

---

Reasonable Workload and Boundaries on Work Time

With continual downsizing, staff availability keeps shrinking without comparable effort to streamline the work performed by the people laid off. Given how little slack is left in most organizations and ever-rising performance expectations, making workloads reasonable is critical—by maximizing technology; improving the efficiency of processes, staffing, and coordination; continually reevaluating the effects of decisions on workload and deadlines; and improving communication, training, and equipment. Both the length of the workday and the workweek are at issue—including the structure, pace, predictability, and complexity of jobs and the potential for burnout.

Expanding options for work hours allows people with a variety of time constraints to be more productive contributors. Part-time work, for example, is seen by adaptive organizations as just as acceptable and valuable as full-time work. In the past, part-time work was often associated with lower rates of pay, less job security and employment protection, fewer benefits, and less career development potential. Part-time employees are typically considered secondary, less committed, or inferior. Part-time work is usually considered atypical or nonstandard work—qualitatively different from full-time work (Williams, 2000). In adaptive organizations, part-time work is valued, and salaries, benefits, bonuses, assignments, and advancement opportunities are set proportionally—to rates of full-time positions but prorated for the reduced time. Work assignments for part-time workers are just as challenging and desirable and have the same levels of responsibility as those for full-time workers. Reduced-hour positions may be used by any employee, regardless of level or managerial status. Part-time employees are not marginalized; they are considered equally committed and promotable.

MY OWN IDEA FOR WHAT MAKES FOR A GOOD PLACE *to work is laughably simple: Pay a living wage or better; require about 30 hours of work a week; then leave me alone to fritter away my non-working hours as I please.*

—Stamps, 1997

In adaptive organizations reasonable boundaries are set on work time. Extended workweeks—where employees normally work from forty-five to ninety-nine hours a week—are not the norm in adaptive organizations. When a deadline is set for a new system to be up and running, a new software version to be released, a new product to be in the stores in time for holiday shopping, a new office building to be ready for occupancy—these occasions where employees need to work especially long hours do not become everyday practices. Adaptive organizations ensure that extraordinary expectations about the number of hours worked are not reinforced by rewards, recognition, and promotion decisions. Promotion is not restricted to employees who put in excessive hours. A reasonable standard workweek is set, deadlines and models that influence behavior are considered, and common practices are monitored so that work-hour creep doesn't take hold

---

EXAMPLES OF CONCRETE PRACTICES

- Job-sharing opportunities
- Reasonable deadlines
- Reducing auxiliary time investments such as after-hours work-related social obligations and commute time due to work and plant locations
- Employee-driven process to make the work environment more efficient
- Reduced work hours (shorter standard workweek expectations and norms)
- Part-time positions at all levels, including managers and leaders
- Designing jobs for shared work—spreading work across more people through shorter workweeks, reduced work hours, flexible schedules, and job sharing
- Use of full-time equivalents instead of head count in reporting number of staff to avoid penalizing part-time work

---

(see the SAS story in Chapter 15 for a description of how to maintain a reasonable workweek).

Time Off

Adaptive policies about vacation, sick leave, personal time, and other time off support employees' quality of life, personal responsibilities, and peak performance. Employees have time for rest, renewal, and pursuit of other interests and priorities. Their use of time off is unrestricted by requiring advance notice or insisting that time be taken in one-week or even one-day increments, which restricts time off for personal emergencies, a primary reason employees need it.

Time-off policies are designed to protect people and the organization against burnout, reflecting the people-as-assets value. The organizational culture encourages time off, recognizing the benefit of having rested and focused employees. Employees who take time off are not considered less committed; instead, time off is understood as contributing to overall performance in a constructive way.

EXAMPLES OF CONCRETE PRACTICES

- Vacations treated as uninterrupted, protected time
- Vacation schedules not based on seniority, so that even new employees with school-age children can use vacation time during spring break and in the summer
- Personal time—to jog, pay bills, and so on—available in small increments during the workday to balance long hours
- Personal time banks for vacation, personal, and sick time, so that employees don't have to justify the need for time away from work
- Extensions of family care and disability leaves to cover emergency care, child rearing, caring for an ailing family member, or public service, beyond those currently available under FMLA
- Paid family leave
- Modified duty policies that allow employees to maintain active status while reducing work assignments so they can care for a newborn or newly adopted child

---

Minimal Use of Time As a Metric

Historically, time has been considered a proxy for employee commitment and performance: commitment and performance could be measured by the length of time specific work took. However, in adaptive organizations, employees are evaluated for contribution and results, not hours worked. Similarly, attendance policies, performance evaluations, and criteria for promotions do not evaluate employee performance by the number of hours put in on the job.

EXAMPLES OF CONCRETE PRACTICES

- Attendance policies that allow for legitimate reasons for absence beyond employees' control
- Provision for employees to make up missed time in lieu of earning an absence occurrence
- Performance measures that focus on results and not hours worked
- *Face time*—time present in the workplace—neither used to evaluate performance nor required to make employees accessible
- Head count deemphasized or not used for budgeting and measuring productivity
- Punctuality not considered a measure of commitment or responsibility; flexible schedules enable workers to handle last-minute emergencies
- Standards for achieving partnership or tenure distinguished from the amount of time in which the standards are met, so that employees with caregiving and other personal responsibilities work toward advancement under the same standards as other employees (American Association of University Professors, 2002)

Organization of Work

As organizations strive to boost the productivity of workers and realize how critical human capital is to business success, they increasingly focus on the connection between how work is organized and job performance. When employees, who know their jobs better than anyone else, are involved in designing and structuring work and work schedules and understand how their work relates to company goals, they can maximize efficiency and productivity. They can also better meet their simultaneous work and personal responsibilities and achieve a better quality of life.

Employee Involvement in Work Design and Restructuring

Adaptive organizations encourage employee input into job structure, work objectives, performance measurement, and organizational systems and processes. Because employees are seen as just as self-motivated as managers, they share responsibility for work outcomes and determining how work is designed and structured—eliminating unnecessary work and reducing inefficiencies.

EXAMPLES OF CONCRETE PRACTICES

- Self-managed work teams
- Quality circles
- Employee participation
- Joint decision making between employees and managers
- Safety practices
- Ergonomically sound equipment and a healthy, attractive, and safe physical environment

---

Work Reorganization to Eliminate Nonessential Work

The ongoing evolution of work requires continual assessment to determine which tasks are essential and which are not. Everyone has a favorite tale of a pointless procedure or process still in place within an organization—usually something that was developed to fix a system or process the company no longer uses. Peter Drucker advocates always asking, "Is this work essential to the main task?" In a knowledge economy, where work is not standard, it is more difficult to step back and evaluate which work tasks are essential, particularly when it is nearly impossible to determine where new ideas arise. Adaptive organizations hire talented people, providing them with clearly defined goals and objectives, and allowing them to design their work to make best use of their individual talents (Buckingham & Coffman, 1999b).

Although reengineering has eliminated some work practice inefficiencies, the task is never complete. Technological innovations constantly change work, which creates a need for periodic reexamination of work processes. At the same time, the roles and responsibilities of workers are changed by technology innovations or other business developments. An important adaptive practice then is to evaluate where employees add the most value to a process and change their responsibilities so they perform those tasks while computers or other machines perform the lower–value-added tasks.

EXAMPLES OF CONCRETE PRACTICES

- Reengineering of work processes to eliminate inefficiencies
- Redeployment of workers to positions with higher–value-added tasks
- Reorganization to eliminate nonessential positions and processes

---

Flexible Organization of Work

Just as flexibility has an important role in organizing, allocating, and managing time, it has a role in organizing and performing work itself. Some work groups act like a soccer team or symphony orchestra, occupying fixed positions and getting instructions from a leader. Others act like a jazz combo. In a jazz combo the leader is less of a factor; the important thing is that the small team can be spontaneous and calibrated to each member all at once (Drucker, 1993). In a knowledge environment, where teams are not static, members and leaders shift from project to project and team position to position. Organizing work flexibly enables employees and teams to fill in for each other and customize work for customers and others. It creates healthy experimentation with how goals are achieved by facilitating the questioning of assumptions, stereotypes, processes, and the goals themselves (S. Friedman & Greenhaus, 2000).

EXAMPLES OF CONCRETE PRACTICES

- Flexibility of work locations and environments: telecommuting or other virtual or remote work, hoteling, satellite offices, and shared work sites
- Flexible organizational structures
- Planned redundancy—sharing customer accounts, team coverage to minimize downtime and enhance coverage
- Flexible benefits (choice of benefits)

Elastic and Rewarding Job Content and Design

To create meaningful work, in adaptive organizations jobs are designed so employees participate in the creative process, see the end result of their work, find a good match between job requirements and their capabilities, and are challenged by the work. They have input into goals and objectives, and their job requirements are clearly defined. There is interactive inquiry, joint learning, and co-creation (Rapoport et al., 2002).

Having a common purpose that employees can personally identify with is an important element of rewarding work. When colleagues are united in support of a cause they find worthwhile, each is able to transcend personal self-interest and draw greater meaning from both the work and the relationships (Ellsworth, 2002). When people care about what they are doing, energy is produced, and when they believe deeply enough in it, it is hard for them *not* to make it as great as it can be (Collins, 2001). This ability to transcend and draw greater meaning depends heavily on having the right people in the organization: those who are both motivated and able to achieve a higher purpose (Collins, 2001).

Control of Complexity

In this complex world, focused mental engagement on a particular issue or item of information becomes more difficult (T. H. Davenport & Beck,

---

EXAMPLES OF CONCRETE PRACTICES

- Matching talent with job, so employees have the opportunity to be and feel competent
- Defining valued work more inclusively—designing jobs to include mentoring, guiding, problem avoidance, building team spirit, helping others, staying connected with the team (Fletcher, 2001)
- Creating opportunities for entrepreneurial employment—encouraging employees to start related businesses and create alternative sources of employment (Kanter, 1997)

2001). Since workers and managers have a finite amount of attention and much that competes for it, adaptive organizations are mindful of how important focused attention is to most work tasks and protect workers' focused attention.

EXAMPLES OF CONCRETE PRACTICES

- Control of information overload
- Providing focus through clear organizational purpose
- Managing pace—considering the effects of artificial deadlines on employees' lives and working to create a healthy, nonfrenetic pace
- Minimizing strain-based conflict—the stress experienced when two of a person's roles compete and fulfilling one makes it difficult to comply with demands of the other
- Clarifying expectations
- Managing effectively to reduce constant mergers, downsizing, reorganizations, and new initiatives that unnecessarily increase complexity

---

Talent Management

Adaptive talent management practices enable organizations to select the right employees (people who match the culture and the job), develop the full potential of all employees, and ensure retention of critical knowledge, skills, and relationships.

> *Get the right people on the bus, the wrong people off the bus, and the people on the bus in the right seats.* (Collins, 2001)

Selective Recruitment and Intensive Retention

In a study of good companies that became great companies, Jim Collins (2001) identifies hiring the right people and putting them in the right positions as a common practice among the most effective companies. This step eliminates problems of managing and motivating people—the right ones are self-motivated, are committed to the success of the organization, and see that success linked to their personal success. Collins points out that this allows organizations to rapidly change direction in response to market conditions or take advantage of opportunities. A culture that emphasizes shared responsibility—an adaptive value—creates a discipline where people support the goals of the organization and each other. Recognizing employees as whole people and encouraging employees to be responsible in their personal lives contributes to a broader culture of responsibility. The following are some specific recruitment practices.

EXAMPLES OF CONCRETE PRACTICES

- Clearly articulating organizational goals and people's specific responsibilities during the hiring process
- Careful hiring to ensure a match of values
- Hiring people who take responsibility for their work
- Providing ongoing opportunities for challenging work, professional growth, and success

---

Abbott strives to attract people of the highest skill-level, commitment, and personal standards. *That is why the company is committed to providing a work environment that will enable all Abbott employees to succeed in their careers and maintain a healthy balance in their work and personal lives. Achieving this balance can help employees do both more effectively.*

—Abbott Laboratories

Intensive retention is partly a result of selective and effective recruiting but is also affected by other adaptive qualities. Employees are more likely to stay if they find challenging and rewarding work, empowering leadership, an egalitarian and respectful culture that values their individuality and recognizes them as whole people, necessary tools and resources, the ability to control their work, and overall good quality of life.

In addition to the practices described throughout this book, following are some specific retention practices.

EXAMPLES OF CONCRETE PRACTICES

- Aligning expectations during and after hiring and as situations change
- Identifying what makes a great employee (using personality profiling, 360-degree feedback, performance appraisals, and interviews with current employees), while considering the values of diversity, individuality, and other adaptive values
- Creating an employee value proposition—why great employees want to work for your company—and managing so as to maintain it
- Customizing retention strategies to meet the needs of individual employees
- Making retention part of everyone's objectives

Equitable Distribution of Work and Rewards

Maslow's hierarchy of needs explains why salary is an effective reward for those whose basic needs (for food, shelter, and clothing) are not being met (lower-paid employees, for example). Once basic needs are met, however, salary is less effective at rewarding the type of superior performance generated when work has become a way to satisfy the need for a sense of belonging, self-esteem, or self-actualization. For this reason, it is important that organizations view rewards as having multiple elements, of which salary is only one (Csikszentmihalyi, 1990).

Perceived fairness is one of the most critical elements of adaptive rewards practices and applies within organizations for comparable jobs, within organizations at different levels, and across organizations. Inequity has been spotlighted as corporate scandals have revealed excessive compensation to senior executives while their employees have been forced into pay concessions, have been laid off, or lost their retirement funds. Employees in adaptive organizations know that rewards at all levels are distributed equitably and based on performance. In adaptive organizations the link between human assets and organizational performance is so clearly understood that rewards follow the same path.

We believe world-class results deserve world-class rewards.

—Household International

Contribution-Based Performance and Advancement Criteria

In adaptive organizations, the criteria for performance evaluations and advancement decisions are based on contribution. These organizations consider both visible and less visible contributions, including mentoring, guiding, coaching, team building, establishing networks, and coordination. Measures of competency and performance are the same for employees who work shorter hours, different schedules, or in different locations. These people are challenged with valuable work assignments and opportunities, and their evaluations reflect the results of their work, not the hours they work. In nonadaptive organizations, performance and advancement criteria still often include factors irrelevant for today's knowledge work and inconsistent with dual-focused workers, such as hours worked, face time, and 24/7 availability.

EXAMPLES OF CONCRETE PRACTICES

- Making sure employees share fairly in the results of their efforts
- Basing performance evaluation criteria and rewards on tasks accomplished rather than hours worked
- Designing reward and recognition systems that align employee and employer interests (such as stock purchase plans or profit sharing at all levels to create real ownership)
- Establishing team-based incentives
- Providing other forms of rewards than money, such as time off or discretionary time on the job, as an option for employees to choose
- Establishing shared rewards for shared responsibility between employees and management and among teams
- Rewarding all skills and contributions, including traditionally invisible skills such as mentoring, coordinating, team building
- Making compensation fair throughout the organization; minimizing pay disparity so that executive compensation is in line with that of employees and employees earn a living wage
- Employee involvement in determining goals and performance standards
- Multiple, flexible, equally viable career paths
- Advancement criteria consistent with adaptive values, including results-based performance and the ability to coach, mentor, and connect

---

Advancement criteria in adaptive organizations reflect an *inclusive meritocracy*; all those who merit advancement are considered (Bank of America, 2002). Multiple career paths provide opportunities for those who are unable to work full-time continuously throughout their lives. Men who participate in family care are not marginalized by doing so; and individuals on different career paths are equally considered for advancement, although advancement may be slower for those off the traditional career path (Williams, 2000). Career planning in adaptive organizations considers personal responsibilities and aspirations as well as work aspirations (Baxter Healthcare, 2000).

Managers in adaptive organizations are selected, evaluated, and promoted based on their ability to manage the new workforce. They are not held to a different standard from employees. Their performance or commitment is not judged by hours worked or constant availability, but rather by results achieved. The organization deliberately develops dual-focus employees as managers. Managers are evaluated based on their ability not only to achieve results but to recruit and retain all types of workers (Williams, 2000) and apply adaptive values and institute adaptive practices.

Human Capital–Oriented Professional Development

Because adaptive organizations are managed to enhance the performance of people—with selective recruiting, intensive retention practices, and challenging and meaningful work—professional development is considered a valuable tool in organizational success. It is designed to augment the skills and capabilities of employees while optimizing firm performance. Investments in professional development are considered investments in the firm's human assets. Professional development is different from remedial skills training—such as basic math, reading, and writing skills—that many U.S. organizations are required to supply. Rather, it is used to identify and enhance capabilities and provide outlets for those capabilities in pursuit of organizational goals.

Professional development practices are often a valuable recruitment and retention tool in that employees can gain skills that advance their careers. When professional development is not combined with strong recruiting and retention capabilities, organizations risk improving employee skills for the benefit of competing organizations—as employees take their new skills elsewhere. Unfortunately, this fear has caused many organizations to scale back on professional development investments, a tendency exacerbated by the recent downturn in the economy. However, adaptive organizations know that employees may be hunkered down today, but their need for professional development and growth will gradually overcome their reluctance to seek out new opportunities. For this reason, adaptive organizations provide professional development both as a retention strategy and to increase organizational capability.

In adaptive organizations, professional development is undergoing the same shift toward self-management as the scheduling practices and work design mentioned earlier. Unlike the ideal of the past, to move up within the hierarchy of an organization, today's ideal more often seeks skills development and has professional aspirations that transcend any one organization. In a *protean career* (after Proteus, the sea god who could change his shape at will), employees direct themselves toward work that will give a sense of success as they, not their organization, define it (Hall, 2002).

Professional development today entails providing employees with the opportunity to grow professionally, but it also requires employees to have a strong sense of personal identity; the capacity to acquire new skills and build on existing ones; self-awareness regarding values, needs, interests, goals, and abilities; and flexibility (Hall, 2002). Both management and employees share responsibility for meeting developmental objectives and for ensuring that knowledge acquired remains available to the organization (Finegold & Mohrman, 2001).

EXAMPLES OF CONCRETE PRACTICES

- Rotating assignments that allow growth in skills with or without promotion to higher jobs
- Retraining employees as jobs become obsolete
- Encouraging educational sabbaticals, external internships, or personal time-outs at regular intervals
- Identifying growth opportunities throughout the network of suppliers, customers, and venture partners
- Long-term employee development through career coaching and planning
- Tuition assistance for employees at all levels

Resources and Tools

Effective employees have the tools and resources (human and other) to accomplish their jobs in the most efficient way. These include a set of resources that enable employees to care for their families while they are working.

Updated and Redesigned Benefits

Updating traditional benefits involves adding some that the majority of workers now require, such as dependent care (see Chapter 3). The new benefits are much more than perks; they are *resources* that most employees must have to be present and to do their jobs well, as essential as the other tools—computers, trucks, or communications systems—they need to function.

Redesigning benefits requires rethinking them conceptually. It involves rethinking equitability—changing the definition of equity from the same for all (which fit a homogeneous workforce) to meeting the needs of all by providing a diverse set of benefit options (to fit a heterogeneous workforce) and recognizing that needs change over the life cycle and vary from employee to employee. Not all employees need a computer, a truck, or a high-speed Internet connection to do their work. Some jobs—and some employees—require more, or more expensive, equipment than others. Some jobs and some employees require more resources for dependent care than others. Jobs with odd hours, for example, require different family care services than 9-to-5 jobs do. Bus drivers who work split shifts (e.g., 5–9 A.M. and 3–8 P.M.) are a good example. Away from home for long hours, they must arrange almost two full shifts of care for children or dependent elders. Their schedules may run late or they may be asked to work weekends or change shifts at the last minute, so they must have highly flexible care, which is harder to find and more expensive. Dispatchers at the same transit company, who have more predictable and shorter shifts, do not need the same resources.

Notions of fairness—a traditional consideration for any employee benefit—must be reexamined and redefined. When dependent care resources and tools are provided through the benefit package, offering the same to all is no longer equitable or fair. Creating a level playing field where employees have the basic resources each requires has become a fairer metric: it applies the values of diversity and individuality.

Issues of fairness also need to be balanced by the organization's need to support productivity. Subsidizing the cost of dependent care for low-paid employees but not for high-paid employees may be necessary to retain a stable workforce of service workers, for whom the cost of this care would otherwise make it not worth working. Since low-income workers tend to use less stable forms of child care (relatives, neighbors, and friends), because they are less expensive than child care facilities, they also tend to have more lost work time. But low-paid workers also typically have less flexibility with which to manage emergencies than do high-paid workers. So, *not* giving more financial assistance to lower-paid workers can mean higher absenteeism and overhead costs for the organization. The justification for using hiring bonuses to recruit people for some hard-to-fill positions is similar; the organizational need supersedes the need to give the same to everyone.

Equitability cannot be handled simply by offering certain benefit options in a *cafeteria plan*, whereby employees choose the benefits they require. Given current total benefit levels, the large number of households headed by single parents (one in four; Acs & Nelson, 2001) would have to choose between two essential, and expensive, benefits—medical insurance and dependent care.

Instead, a reorientation of benefits is required so they are considered more like insurance (Bailyn, 1993): something available to all (although not all will take advantage) but not paid out to all at any given point in time. Across the whole organization, benefits are equitable over each person's life span, but there are times when some people receive costlier benefits than others, much like medical benefit payouts—higher for some employees at some times.

Redesigning benefits also means recognizing that they are not intended for the benefit of the employee only; they also benefit organizational performance directly. This is again particularly true for family care. Simply making benefits available is not enough; the organization must ensure they're used to reduce the lost work time, work disruptions, turnover, and compromised performance. Organizations must ensure that these redesigned benefits are universally accessible and affordable, that employees know about them, and that managers understand and encourage, rather than discourage, their use.

The connection between employee benefits, personnel policies, and employee services must also become more elastic and integrated. Low-income employees often require the most financial help to stabilize family care arrangements. With an employer-paid child care subsidy they can afford more stable care. High-paid workers already can afford to use child care facilities that are relatively stable. These employees may instead need the flexibility to work from home on the days their child is ill—or make up lost time, without getting an *absence occurrence* (a black mark on their attendance record), or perhaps to take a paid sick day. These personnel policies are not an employee benefit per se. Both low- and high-paid employees and employees with special needs children would also be aided by an Employee Assistance Program (EAP) or referral line that helps them find care services. These are examples of a *benefit*, a *policy* or *practice*, and an employee *service* helping employees with different child care needs, through the customization, elasticity, and integration required in these new complex times.

Budgeting for benefits must also be reconceived. Benefits decisions must now consider the effect of each benefit on organizational performance. The power of particular benefits to reduce lost work time and other overhead costs, enhance on-the-job performance, and so on should influence the choice of benefits and how they are structured. The benefits budget must, therefore, not be *siloed*—made an isolated line item in the organization's total budget—but connected to the operations budget and flexible enough to change with different needs. A situation may arise, for example, when a period of intense overtime or travel is going to be required by a whole work unit, creating increased difficulties for employees who need to arrange additional family care. In such a case, increasing expenditures for family care would make sense, as both the employee and the organization benefit.

Child Care

One of the two most essential new benefits is child care (see Chapter 3). Nearly half (45 percent) of employed people are raising children while all adults in the household are working (Economic Policy Institute, 2002), and most use some form of child care. Sixty-one percent of children under four are in child care, the majority from infancy on, and they often spend more hours in child care than their parents do at work.

Child care benefits should ideally ensure that *all* employees have access to the level of child care they need for children from birth through the teen years, so they can work effectively. This means regular care (all day for young children, before and after school for older ones), extra care (for overtime, when traveling), care for occasional predictable needs (teacher in-service days, holidays when schools close), and care for emergencies (children are sick, babysitters quit, or bad weather forces schools to close).

Child care must be of high quality. Unfortunately, much nonparental child care is impersonal, unsafe, and unhealthy, and children do not have the experiences that reinforce the intellectual and emotional circuitry they will need as adults. National research finds only 8–24 percent of child care center classrooms good for children and the rest stifling to their development or even dangerous (Cost, Quality, and Child Outcomes Study Team 1995).[1] Most care by relatives and other caregivers is also below "minimally acceptable" (Helburn & Bergmann, 2002). Poor care quality not only harms children, permanently affecting their brain development, it also reduces their parents' ability to concentrate on work. Good care quality is expensive and rarely possible when child care programs are funded by more than parent fees alone.

Child care benefits should be designed to fill the gap in community services, not to duplicate services. Most communities have a critical shortage of high-quality care of all types—whether in homes, schools, or child care facilities—and for all ages of children. Programs are usually open for limited hours and are not flexible enough to permit schedule changes or part-time use without extra cost. Employees who work long, rotating, or irregular shifts or nights can have extreme difficulty arranging care, and also pay a premium. Services may not be affordable to even middle-income employees. Even when families do not use quality programs (because they cannot afford them), child care still consumes 15–18 percent of total family income (Schulman, 2000; Mitchell, Stoney, Dichter, & Ewing Marion Kaufmann Foundation, 2001).

Adaptive organizations help with child care in a variety of ways: by helping employees pay for it (which increases employees' options), by creating services (such as work-site child care centers, summer camps, backup care centers), by providing referral information to help employees find resources, or by donating to community-based child care services to improve quality and availability. Alternatively, or simultaneously, employers can minimize the need for child care services through personnel policies and management practices. The most effective child care benefits increase the supply of good services, make them affordable to employees, and reduce employees' need for services through scheduling flexibility, reduced work hours, paid leave, more predictable work schedules, and job sharing.

The most direct way to make child care *affordable* is an employer-paid subsidy that supplements employee payments. Organizations typically shy away from such subsidies, because they are expensive and seem inequitable. A more widely accepted approach is Dependent Care Assistance Plan spending accounts (DCAPs), which enable employees to pay for child care out of their salary on a pretax basis. DCAPs are helpful but far from sufficient, because good care is still basically unaffordable. DCAPs also do not help lower-paid employees who use informal care, which is often not eligible for DCAP. Employers also make child care more affordable by subsidizing the many different child care programs and individual providers that employees use (a complicated undertaking), or by subsidizing their own child care facilities.

In contrast, subsidies paid to employees are the easiest child care benefits to administer. Accordion-like, subsidies can stretch or contract as needs change and, unlike facilities, can be offered across a multisite organization, but are still simple. Ultimately, with greater spending power (which a subsidy gives) in employees' hands, the shortage of supply, convenience, and quality in the child care marketplace would eventually disappear.

An example of such a subsidy, which Bank of America used to achieve its business objectives, follows.

BANK OF AMERICA'S "CHILD CARE PLUS"

Bank of America's primary child care benefit is a child care subsidy, called "Child Care Plus." Bank of America pays eligible employees (those working twenty hours or more with individual incomes of $30,000 or less and family incomes below $60,000) $152 per month per child for formal child care or $87 per month for informal, unlicensed child care. (The higher payment for formal care is to encourage use of more stable arrangements, which results in less employee absenteeism.)

New employees are eligible for this subsidy from their first day of work. The program was used by 18,914 children in 1998, approximately 12 percent of the total bank population. The bank invested $23 million in 1999 in this benefit to retain employees with otherwise high turnover. The turnover of employees using the subsidy was 52 percent of that of other employees earning $30,000 or less who work in the same departments—customer service centers, call centers, bank card centers, and banking centers (branches).

The bank has many other benefits for employees with family and other personal responsibilities, but it considers this subsidy its most effective child care benefit for two reasons. The number of employees affected by it is far greater than with other benefits, such as the five on-site child care centers. More important, employees who use it are the ones who "touch" customers most directly; turnover is felt most keenly when they leave. The subsidy program is easy to administer and communicate company-wide, and it is more consistently available than other programs, which vary by community.

Employers increase the *supply* of child care in multiple ways—indirectly or directly via employer-provided child care centers, summer camps, or partnerships with local schools to expand after-school programs. Not all improve work performance, although when done right they can. Work-site centers can be a good solution, but only when they are large enough to accommodate everyone and subsidized enough to make up the difference between what employees can pay and what the service costs to operate. Otherwise, only highly paid employees can use them and lower-paid employees still have productivity issues. Many adaptive organizations use other mechanisms, creating joint funds with other employers, for example. A group of twenty-one companies that form the American Business Collaboration for Quality Dependent Care created a $125 million fund to upgrade child care, elder care, and other family services in communities where their employees live (Mendels, 2002).

Referral and counseling services that connect employees with existing community services are an important benefit that complements the others but cannot stand alone. Often appealing to employers as the least expensive option, such services do not change the fact that there is a critical shortage of care, and most of what exists is both of poor quality and too expensive for most families to use. As a result, referrals and counseling typically do not eliminate existing productivity problems.

Adaptive organizations reduce the need for child care by allowing employees to legitimately stay home with a sick child, to make up lost work time when child care breaks down (babysitters get sick, run late, or quit at the last minute), to schedule vacation time around children's school schedules (instead of by seniority), to allow a workday to begin after a child is dropped off at school. Job-sharing and reduced work hours can lower the amount a family pays for child care, and sometimes enable a child's care to be shared between the father and mother. Paid family leave is the most efficient way to reduce the need for care. These effective and generally less costly ways to give child care assistance can be better all around, but only if they do not marginalize the workers who use them. Participants must not be labeled as less committed or knocked off the advancement track, or employees will not choose these child care solutions.

The challenge of truly resolving the child care dilemma is great for most organizations, because employees may be spread across multiple work sites and because their needs both vary and change. Managing such benefits is cumbersome and requires a whole new area of expertise. What is really required—what would be more efficient than employers' providing services in piecemeal fashion—is a comprehensive system of care (at a societal level) that fits both the variable needs and preferences of families and the need of organizations for readily available workers. It would eliminate the problem that now exists, where some employers invest in family care and others do not. Until such time as there is greater public investment in these essential resources, or the will to support paid family leave, a greater burden will fall on individual employers to fill the gap. They will continue to have to choose between providing these benefits and experiencing the inevitable drain on productivity.

For two reasons, employers may want to help design improved public policies and a system of good care and early education. They will experience an immediate reduction in benefits costs and improvement in productivity, and a long-term gain when the children are in situations that equip them to be successful in the future.

Elder Care

Elder care presents a somewhat different challenge for workers than child care does. One sixth of U.S. households provide care to an elderly or disabled adult, and 64 percent of the caregivers are working. Elderly or disabled adults require a range of care, including personal care (bathing, feeding), help with household chores (housecleaning, errands, transportation), and help with finances. Many people who work and care for an elderly relative provide that care in cooperation with a home health care provider (about one sixth) or other family member (about half), but one third have no help. More than 60 percent of working caregivers pay the caregiving expenses, which amount on average to 5 percent of their monthly income. About 7 percent of these caregivers report that the cost of care creates a financial strain for them (Fredriksen-Goldsen & Scharlach, 2001).

Elder care is generally not a happy experience, although there are exceptions. The direction of change for elders is not usually positive as it is for children. Ill or frail elderly people typically become increasingly incapacitated and uncomfortable, whereas children become stronger and more independent. Providing care for a parent can be emotionally charged and involve a shift of roles as the parent becomes dependent and ceases to be a source of strength and guidance.

The emotional strain of elder caregiving creates physical problems—fatigue, stress, sleep disturbance, and eating disorders. Eighteen percent of caregivers are clinically depressed—three times the rate of people with other care responsibilities (Fredriksen-Goldsen & Scharlach, 2001). The emotional strain is partly the result of watching loved ones become ill or disabled; trying to care for a depressed, uncooperative, or irrational person; and coping with the family conflicts and work disruptions that often occur (Fredriksen-Goldsen & Scharlach, 2001).

With elder care, the challenge is knowing about existing resources. The emotional and physical drain on employees caring for adults is greater than that on employees with children. Fewer caregivers of adults report difficulties affording care, perhaps because they are older and earning more than younger families who need child care.

As with child care, the challenges of elder care vary across the workforce and the most helpful benefits also vary. Some employees need help paying for home-health-care services or long-term care insurance. Many need information on how to find services and counseling to deal with the emotional issues. Some may need to take a leave of absence to be with a relative in the final stages of dying, without losing seniority or risking their job. Benefits options may help retain workers with caregiving responsibilities, 20 percent of whom leave their jobs temporarily or permanently (Fredriksen-Goldsen & Scharlach, 2001). Many caregivers need flexibility in their work schedule to deal with emergencies or to take the elderly person to the doctor, perhaps on short notice. Seventy-five percent of employees caring for adults report that their responsibilities at work conflict with their responsibilities in caregiving at home.

For many employees, working while giving care has positive effects for both work and the care they provide. Work is often a respite from the demands of caregiving and balances time that can be isolating and depressing. Also, there is evidence that caregivers may be more sensitive and effective in interactions with customers and may have greater self-confidence and feelings of competence that translate to work (Fredriksen-Goldsen & Scharlach, 2001).

Besides having benefits and policies that enable workers to arrange and give care, adaptive work cultures recognize the time and emotional demands of periods in employees' lives when people who are significant to them need their attention. Adaptive organizations reduce the stress and other health problems that can compromise the caregivers' well-being and effectiveness.

Other Family Care

Employees can have a variety of loved ones with care needs—disabled or ill adults, grandchildren, special needs children, adult children with care needs, spouses and domestic partners, and even close friends. Nationally, one in five children has special health or developmental needs involving regular medical appointments and need for special attention (Heymann, 2000). Healthy children in school still need help with homework, and parents need to meet with teachers.

Employer subsidies for care services are quite helpful (and nontaxable under Section 129 of the tax code, if the person cared for is a legal dependent). Referral and counseling services are helpful in finding community-based services, which are often available but little known. Adaptive organizations also give employees the flexibility to deal with their needs themselves through adaptive strategies, mentioned earlier in this chapter, such as customized work schedules or locations. They encourage sensitivity from supervisors; have a work culture that considers caregiving needs legitimate; and provide an environment of trust, respect, and mutuality that encourages employees to discuss their situation so solutions can be considered. In these cultures, such needs become part of how work decisions are made—decisions to require overtime and how much notice is given, absenteeism disciplinary policies, work scheduling, team processes, and cross-training—and managers understand the challenges and are supportive.

EXAMPLES OF CONCRETE PRACTICES

- Employer-paid dependent care subsidies to pay for child care, elder care, home health care, school-age care, special needs care, and extra costs such as travel-related and overtime care

- Extended (beyond FMLA) and paid family leave

- Summer apprenticeship programs for teenage children of employees

- Company-provided child care facilities, summer camps, and emergency backup care that are accessible and affordable to all employees who require it

- Arrangements to upgrade community based resources— before-school and after-school child care, adult day care centers, summer camps, and so on (purchased care or through contributions)

- Paid sick leave that can be used for family members, increased personal days to take children to doctor's appointments, and leave-sharing that allows employees to share unused time

- Referrals and counseling to connect employees with family services

- Elder care services—transportation to medical care, long-term care insurance, end-of-life counseling programs, EAP services that include family care

- Stress reduction, wellness, fitness programs and services (vouchers, facilities, trained staff, and time to use the services)

- Prenatal programs and maternal and child health services

- Access to adequate health insurance coverage

Efficient Systems and Processes

Technology plays an important role in facilitating many adaptive practices such as work location flexibility, work schedule customization, and redesigning jobs to make them more meaningful. Data lines, computers, and systems that enable offices to be open safely during off-hours provide employees with more options about when and how to work as well as with information they need to be effective.

A challenge for adaptive organizations is ensuring that technology supports people and the organization, instead of people supporting technology. In the past, organizations too often adopted technologies before fully understanding how they would affect processes, product development, or customer service.

In general, to ensure that employees have the tools and resources to accomplish their jobs in the most efficient way, problems and issues relating to human capital must be examined to see if they are systemic rather than individual. It is easy to dismiss issues as individual and isolated without considering how representative they are of larger problems in the organization that require systemic attention.

EXAMPLES OF CONCRETE PRACTICES

- Technology that supports workers and efficient processes
- Technology available for telecommuting, remote work, and time management
- Efficient and effective processes—information retrieval, authority, reporting, and so on
- Manager hiring, training, and evaluations that support other adaptive practices

---

In Conclusion

Changing management practices to adapt to the new reality is the fourth adaptive strategy rather than the first because practices do not happen in a vacuum; they must arise from and be consistent with the other strategies. Adaptive practices evolve out of the position that people are assets rather than costs, and are based on carefully examined beliefs and consciously chosen values that constitute an organization's culture. This chapter provides a framework for adaptive practices that has four sections: ways to schedule time, organize work, manage talent, and provide resources and tools. We offer some examples of concrete practices within each section of the framework but recognize that organizations may discover other practices that achieve the same objectives of scheduling time, organizing work, managing talent, and providing resources and tools. This framework is used in Part 3 to organize the research evidence showing the effects of these adaptive practices.

Organizations have enormous latitude to construct practices that fit their unique situation, but it is critical that they not adopt practices lightly or piecemeal, or simply copy what others do. They must see both old and new practices in full context—as part of a larger and cohesive pattern of organizational behavior.

In Chapter 9 we explore the fifth and final adaptive strategy: ensuring that the beliefs, culture, and practices fit together and support the decision to invest in human capital.

9

ENSURING FIT: BELIEFS, CULTURE, PRACTICES

The fifth strategy ensures alignment among all the adaptive strategies—so the beliefs, culture, and practices support each other and the decision to invest in human assets. Congruence is the glue that holds the adaptive strategies together and enables them to be really effective. Without a fit among the various elements, the organization hasn't truly committed to investing in people.

Congruence is more difficult to achieve in today's flatter organizational structures, which don't have layers of management to direct action and ensure a company's policies and practices are implemented consistently. In place of management hierarchy, flatter organizations can achieve congruence by having a consistent purpose that guides all activities, a strong culture that supports the purpose, and management practices and policies that are aligned with the purpose. In adaptive organizations, these same elements create congruence, but they must be supplemented by other elements, as we discuss in this chapter.

The story of First Tennessee National's (FTN) transformation to an adaptive organization is a good example of fit (see Chapter 16). The systems in the company have been reconfigured to support the employee-centered culture that is critical to customers' perception of service and the organization's overall performance. All measures of employee, leadership, and overall company performance used by FTN reflect and reinforce the reality that employee value and retention drive customer satisfaction and retention, which drive profitability. Leaders of the organization also reinforce the linkage between employees, customers, and profitability in promotion criteria, through communications both inside the company and to the external environment, and in all decisions made throughout the company.

In adaptive organizations like FTN, workforce needs are seen as strategic concerns. They are not isolated in formal programs or labeled as special interests or private matters; instead, the way they are handled and the placement of responsibility for addressing various needs are on a par with elements of the company's main product or service. If responsibility for addressing workforce needs is located only in the HR function, these needs will too often be evaluated based on their costs to the organization rather than on the value they contribute. If responsibility is distributed among business units and those reporting to senior management, the value is likelier to take precedence over cost, and responses are likelier to support the importance of human assets.

Senior management commitment to adaptive values and culture and expressions of management support are required components of adaptive organizations. At FTN, senior management drove the transformation and insisted that managers' and senior managers' regular discussions include concerns about what employees needed to be effective. Their experience clearly demonstrates that the more visible this commitment is, the better the fit of beliefs, culture, and practices. This fit occurs throughout the adaptive organization—in measurement systems, leadership, decision-making processes, and communication systems.

Measurement Systems

People pay attention to what is measured in an organization—measurement is a fundamental part of any management system. All types of measures—from measures used to manage revenues and expenses to those used to manage people—send clear signals about what matters in an organization. If the measures used in an organization are not consistent with stated practices, the practices will be ignored. An organization with fixed-fee contracts, for example, needs to measure the profitability of each project under contract and ensure that employees are evaluated based on how profitable their projects are. However, if employees are evaluated solely on billable hours (a common measure in this type of work), managers will find that employees put a lot of time into their projects, whether or not the projects are profitable. If an organization implements adaptive practices that focus on results rather than time spent at work, but continues to measure the number of hours worked per employee, the results-oriented adaptive practices will have no effect: employees will continue to deliver hours over results.

A good management system uses measures that provide information about the success of the chosen strategy, are consistent with the organization's culture, and support the practices the organization has adopted. In adaptive organizations, measures reinforce adaptive human capital practices; support adaptive beliefs and values about business, work, and people; and provide managers with information regarding how well the practices are meeting the needs of the organization and the employees.

Adaptive organizations recognize and support employees' personal as well as professional goals and aspirations. Their measures of a particular practice look at the effect on employees as well as on the organization (Rapoport et al., 2002). For example, it would be appropriate to look at effects of customized work schedules on the organization in terms of the following.

- Reduced costs related to absenteeism, lateness, and turnover
- Improved productivity as employees are better able to focus on their work
- Changes in the role of managers, such as increased focus on facilitating work, which results in productivity enhancements, and decreased focus on policing
- Improved customer satisfaction resulting from better coverage at peak times

  Simultaneously, the effects on employees would be indicated by

- Increased satisfaction with job and quality of life
- Improved sense of empowerment, control, and engagement
- Reduced stress and improved health

Although measures used by adaptive organizations will vary to reflect the specific strategies of each organization and the specific needs of employees, certain commonalities will exist within all their measurement systems.

- Measures used to evaluate employee performance in adaptive organizations are based on results, not face time or other traditional measures. It is essential to measure how well customer value is delivered, which may not be apparent from the number of hours invested (Hochschild, 1997).

- High performance is defined by how well the employee accomplishes the goals and meets or exceeds expectations. To be regarded as valuable, an employee need not always be available for additional work requests, because other responsibilities are recognized as equally valuable and important.

- Performance measurement systems do not require the employee to be singularly focused on work to be successful. Employees are not penalized for taking time to coach Little League or working part-time while raising their children.

- Measurement systems are informative. For example, if dual-focus workers are not being promoted into leadership positions and are leaving, the organization has evidence that there is a barrier—the culture and practices are not effective at retaining these employees.

- Baselines are established to measure progress. Measurement is an ongoing process—identifying and monitoring changing needs and to what extent they have been met (Locke & Henne, 1986). The organization needs to establish baseline metrics for future comparison so it can assess progress. It also needs to provide a means of benchmarking with other leading organizations and annual trend reports that offer a report card.

- Quality assessments are part of the metrics. For example, the Baldrige Award for Total Quality includes a measure by employees of the success of a "family-friendly work culture" (Hochschild, 1997, p. 248) or quality of life maintained. Measures use a whole-life approach—work life, home life, and community life. Employees evaluate how well the organization enables them to spend time with families, go to PTA meetings, or volunteer in the schools, just as the organization measures how productive, present, and valuable employees are.

- Measurement data are integrated into strategy discussions. Companies establish human capital metrics and incorporate them into monthly assessments of organizational performance. First Tennessee National uses an employee value score to track the value proposition for employees. These metrics are more in-depth than employee satisfaction measures; they provide feedback on how employees create value and how effectively the organization increases and supports their contributions.

Most important, performance measures and reporting systems in adaptive organizations measure "the building of human capital and the capabilities of people as thoroughly and frequently as [they] measure the building and use of financial capital" (Kanter, 1997). The measures are robust enough to balance short-term and long-term results, since human capital investments will have greater positive effect on an organization's long-term performance than on its short-term performance.

Leadership

Leadership plays a critical role in ensuring that the beliefs, culture, and practices of the organization fit together and support the decision to invest in people as assets. Four aspects of leadership have significant influence.

- The words and actions of leaders in the organization
- The types of people who are promoted into leadership positions
- The role leaders and managers play in the day-to-day operations of the company
- The process used to develop and promote leaders

Using words and actions, organizational leaders send clear messages to employees and the greater community regarding their support of adaptive practices or disregard for them. At Baxter Healthcare, the CEO reinforces the practices by living them and highlights these behaviors to legitimize them for other managers and for employees. He sends the message to employees that having and attending to responsibilities other than work is normal and acceptable—both are important. CEO support for adaptive values—in public statements and signaled through behavior and words (Williams, 2000)—facilitates their use and acceptance throughout an organization and is an important element for establishing congruence. The selection of leaders is an important element of congruence. If the organization promotes individuals who demonstrate commitment to adaptive beliefs, values, and practices, people see these elements as part of advancement criteria. In adaptive organizations, leaders are selected, coached, and rewarded based on their ability to manage the new workforce effectively. Increasingly, they are part of the new workforce themselves. They are "empowering leaders" of the type described in Chapter 7, skilled at facilitating collaboration, handling ambiguity, listening, feeling empathy, and appreciating differences.

In adaptive organizations the manager's role is to organize the work specifications, clarify goals, coordinate knowledge workers who know their jobs better than their supervisors do ("Survey: The New Demographics," 2001), facilitate the responsible application of knowledge, and ensure that workers—whether knowledge, service, or manufacturing—have the resources they require. Managers also provide feedback and mentor employees. They let employees handle the execution of tasks and operational decisions because they know careful selection procedures and development have ensured that the right people are in the right jobs and motivated to perform.

> *Shifting some workers to work from home as independent contractors caused the managers at Rank Xerox to shift focus from input (time put in, way of working) to output (the results of the work). This changed definition of managerial control was made easier precisely because employees were no longer visible. Managers were forced to be more precise about specifying job requirements and standards, and to learn to be unconcerned about how jobs were done. These out-of-sight workers produced the same as in-sight employees did, but they did it in half the time.* (Bailyn, 1993)

Managers are rewarded for adaptive behaviors; and they are skilled and trained in people management, not just content expertise or technical knowledge. They know employees and their individual differences and collaborate with them to develop options that meet both employee and organizational needs. Managers are informed about resources available to employees and encourage employees to use them. They "appreciate the unique life needs of employees" (Farren, 1999).

The selection and development of managers and leaders is part of a well-thought-out process that results in the placement and ongoing development of managers who value human assets. This aspect of congruence can be one of the most challenging for organizations. It may be difficult for managers who are producing other results (exceeding sales quotas or meeting project deadlines) to comprehend the importance of valuing human assets. It may be equally difficult for the organization to let someone go who produces bottom-line results but cannot treat subordinates and peers with respect. How difficult and often abusive managers are handled conveys volumes about organizational commitment to adaptive values and practices. Employees pay particular attention to these managers' fortunes as they decide whether to believe rhetoric about adaptive values and practices.

Leadership is developed at all levels within the organization. People learn leadership when the organization rotates leadership roles within self-directed work teams, encourages individuals to take leadership roles in addressing specific organizational issues, and employs similar measures that recognize the capacity of all employees to be self-motivated and responsible.

Managers in adaptive organizations give employees maximum responsibility and self-control (Drucker, 1999), including the control and authority to manage their work and their other life responsibilities, in order to allow success in both. They elicit employee input in job design and tasks, and in work environment decisions.

Ask what people want—don't institute programs based on assumptions. (Catlette & Hadden, 1998)

Decision-Making Processes

Both work and life outside of work involve a constant stream of decisions, all of which affect other people. For this reason, decision making—how decisions get made and who makes them—is an important aspect of achieving congruence in adaptive organizations, ensuring that beliefs, culture,

---

BAXTER HEALTHCARE WORK/LIFE
IN THE WORKPLACE GUIDEBOOK:
THE MANAGER'S PERSPECTIVE

Managers

- Represent a role model for work/life balance
- Know the work/life conflicts employees face
- Recognize results more than hours or visibility
- Express appreciation for employees' effort, work product, and commitment
- Seek ideas and input from employees
- Recognize and validate the "whole person"
- Treat employees courteously and with dignity
- Manage with compassion
- Know the employees
- Work collaboratively with employees
- Permit and support work/life integration

Source: Baxter Healthcare, 2000

---

and practices support the decision to invest in people as assets. Decision making in adaptive organizations has three main aspects:

- Employees participate in decisions.
- Decisions are evaluated based on their effect on employees.
- Decisions are consistent with adaptive values and beliefs.

One of the harsh realities of doing business today is the need for rapid responses, particularly among customers and suppliers. Few customers are patient about waiting for a supervisor to approve the return of merchandise or the transfer to another airline after a flight is canceled. Suppliers need to know quickly whether you want to take advantage of a last-minute volume discount or still want a product if the color doesn't match the earlier runs.

In adaptive organizations, such as Nordstrom and Southwest, employees often need to be able to, and are empowered to, make decisions on behalf of their employers—and they are qualified to do so.

Lines of authority and reporting structures within adaptive organizations reflect beliefs and values about human assets. Employees and management share decision-making power (Bailyn, 1993); employees have been carefully selected and developed to share responsibility for achieving the organization's goals. They can be trusted to make the right decisions.

All employees, regardless of the number of hours worked, location, or level, are considered important stakeholders of the organization and involved in decisions that affect their work and lives. They give input into decisions regarding the selection and use of tools, including technology and employee benefits. Employees participate in decisions about their work schedules, the organization of their work, and their professional development. Business unit managers participate in decisions about employee benefits because they are directly affected by the strategic value of benefits and often face less cost pressure than HR departments do.

The criteria used for decisions are clear, objective, and consistent, with a minimum of politicking involved, and they consider both the needs of the organization and those of the employee. Strategic decisions—growth through mergers and acquisitions, reorganization and decentralization, or contraction through divestiture—consider the effect on people's lives as well as the effect on the organization. Human capital is recognized as a strategic issue. The long-term overall success of the organization, which is the primary goal of strategic decisions, is not separated from the success of the organization's human capital.

Adaptive beliefs and practices, which acknowledge the value of individuals, are also reflected in relationships with other stakeholders (vendors, contractors, and partners).

Communication Systems

In today's fast-moving, flat organizations, effective communication links people all over the organization and reinforces their support of a common purpose. All aspects of communication are part of achieving congruence in adaptive organizations: the message and the delivery, verbal and nonverbal expressions, written and oral, speaking and listening.

Both formal and informal communication systems of adaptive organizations support the values and beliefs of the adaptive culture, advocate use of adaptive practices, and are consistent with the organization's decision to invest in human capital. Formal communications pertain to the official word in the organization and may include company newsletters, announcements, press releases, correspondence, memos, e-mail announcements, speeches, and meeting discussions. It is often easiest to ensure formal communication conveys a consistent message because people usually have a chance to review it before it is delivered. Informal communication can be both more powerful and less easy to control. It includes casual conversations between individuals, the unofficial grapevine, or the conversation around the watercooler. Informal communication often reflects what people actually believe and can highlight areas where adaptive values may not be fully in place.

How the message is communicated is often as important as what is being communicated. The form of a communication should support its purpose: the announcement of a decision to adopt a new adaptive practice will have more effect if it is reinforced by multiple forms of communication — formal announcement, press release, memo, and, most important, discussions between managers and employees throughout the organization. Facial expressions and gestures also function as communication mechanisms and, as with all forms of communication, should reflect adaptive values.

In adaptive organizations, the adaptive strategies are clearly stated, accurately understood by all, and reinforced by the actions of senior and middle managers as well as employees. Active listening is used to uncover and address places where adaptive strategies have not taken hold.

In adaptive organizations, there is transparency of communication: management may communicate frequently about the organization's strategy and employees' role in accomplishing it so that everyone understands their part in it. There are no hidden agendas. Transparency and a commitment to aggressive (regular, specific) communication to employees is also part of giving employees a context to consider as they organize their work. With a value of "aligned interests," the whole approach to communication is geared toward sharing of more rather than less information, because everyone is working toward the same ends. Communication must be open and frequent across all levels; transparent communication of information is essential to sustain trust.

Everyone in the organization is able to openly discuss issues about integrating work and personal life, knowing that individuals will be heard with respect and that the whole person is important in the organization. Open debates foster honest assessments of how well individuals and the organization are meeting the challenges of integrating work and personal life. They recognize that both are responsible for seeking solutions.

Employees recognize and communicate how they need to work for their peak performance and quality of life, for example, working actively in partnership with their employer to customize work arrangements, as the following real story from an employee illustrates.

THE ELECTRICIAN

The lead electrician position had been open for weeks. The business, a vineyard and winery that relied on having everything timed for maximum yield at harvest time, would be compromised if a good electrician could not be found. The vineyard was in a valley where skilled technical labor was not plentiful. It was the work of the electrician to ensure that the cellar temperature was regulated perfectly and production machinery was working smoothly.

Allen was a senior electrician who had been out of the workforce for some time but recently had been thinking he should go back to work. The company had sought him out, having heard about him from another electrician who used to work with him.

He told them he didn't need the income; he was over fifty and comfortable financially. But his wife had died three years before, and he found himself depressed staying at home. He had recently decided it would be better if he worked. He said he would accept the position only on condition that he had every Wednesday off, because Wednesday was the day he spent with his three-year-old granddaughter. That was what was most important to him now. It wasn't a negotiating ploy; that was the only condition under which he would accept the job. He didn't mind working longer hours on other days, or being paid on a part-time basis; it didn't matter, as long as he had Wednesdays off.

Allen and the company agreed on this arrangement, which seemed to work well for both of them. His expertise was just what the company had needed, and work at his trade—under the right conditions—was what he needed.

When communication systems are working effectively, messages are clear, rhetoric is consistent with action, implementation occurs properly, and assessments are honest and objective.

Ensuring a fit among adaptive beliefs, culture, and practices is not static; rather it is a process. Ensuring a fit becomes part of the organization's management system and requires continual examination and adjustment of existing work rules, expectations, and practices with evolving changes in the workforce and the business environment. All change efforts are grounded in adaptive beliefs and principles so that the effect of changes in businesses, operations, and locations on employee motivation and performance influences the decisions made.

Ensuring this fit requires the involvement of the entire organization — it cannot be relegated to HR departments. When there is a good fit across an organization, its systems, structures, and processes have the flexibility to capitalize on the diversity of employees and leverage the aligned employee-employer relationship.

In Conclusion

Ensuring that adaptive beliefs, culture, and practices fit together and support the decision to invest in people as assets requires measurement systems that reinforce adaptive practices and beliefs and measure the effect of decisions that affect employees. Ensuring fit also requires developing leaders whose words and actions support that decision. Fit occurs when decision-making processes include employee participation and decisions are evaluated based on their effect on employees. Communication systems also ensure fit when formal and informal modes of communication support and reinforce adaptive beliefs, culture, and practices.

The five adaptive strategies described in Part 2 enable organizations to adapt to the realities and opportunities of today's different work environment. This work environment is characterized by the three converging forces described in Part 1, where people are the engine of success, work involves knowledge and service, and dual-focus workers make up the majority of the workforce.

The five strategies represent major changes from common practice for most organizations, but they create an environment in which all employees, particularly those in knowledge and service work and dual-focus workers, can be successful. They give people the control and authority to bring all their capabilities to work and to manage their work and other life responsibilities, and thus make it possible for both them and their organizations to thrive.

None of the five adaptive strategies will work if implemented in isolation. The strategies are components of a system; all must be present for the practices to be effective and lasting change to take place. We must use systems thinking to address the challenges and opportunities of the current work environment, as Peter Senge (1990) describes: "*Systems thinking* is a conceptual framework, a body of knowledge and tools that has been developed over the past 50 years, to make the full patterns clearer and help us to see how to change them effectively" (pp. 69–70).

In Part 3, we provide evidence of the effects of adaptive beliefs, culture, and practices on human capital, customers, and organizational performance. We begin with human capital results, in Chapter 10.

EVIDENCE OF
RESULTS
ACHIEVED

If the three converging forces—the rise of human capital, the shift to knowledge and service work, and the rise of the dual-focus worker—described in Part 1 are as pervasive as they seem to be, there ought to be a noticeable effect on the performance of organizations that adopt strategies to harness their power. One would certainly expect such strategies to affect employee performance and attitude, the delivery of service to customers, and perhaps even the organization's financial performance. Part 3 weighs the evidence in each of those areas.

We have reviewed more than 550 pieces of research, which we describe in Chapters 10–12 using a framework that considers the interrelationship among them. For example, we describe research on how employee commitment is developed, how it contributes to employee performance and stability, and whether that in turn measurably affects customer retention and, ultimately, earnings. We then examine the research on the effects of the various adaptive strategies (individually and in clusters) described in Part 2 in these same areas: employee performance, customers and suppliers, and organizational performance. The framework shows the cumulative effects of adaptive strategies on organizational results.

Figure 2 The Human Capital Path to Results*

The total existing body of research evidence is larger than the research review presented here. We have selected the research that illustrates the most prevalent effects.

Note that a variety of terms are commonly used for certain clusters of adaptive practices described in this book. None of these terms individually represents all of these practices, nor do they create the same effect as when the clusters combine to form a whole as described in adaptive strategy 5. Because some of the research is about particular clusters, it is useful to discuss some of the terminology here. *High-performance work practices* typically mean employee involvement in work design, selective recruiting, and incentive pay for performance. *Flexible work arrangements* include many of the customized schedules described in Chapter 8, but often exclude reducing work hours expectations. *Work-life programs* usually include child care and elder care benefits, flexible work arrangements, and other programmatic practices; they sometimes omit cultural elements. *Family-friendly work environments* also include HR policies such as sick time and family leave that accommodate dual-earner families. The adaptive strategies described in this book include these but also incorporate cultural norms— advancement and performance criteria that do not require a work-only focus, along with human capital–oriented work processes, recruiting, rewards, and professional development.

Some caveats are in order. Although the research indicates that adaptive strategies have an overwhelmingly positive and powerful influence on business outcomes in a wide range of interrelated areas, some of the research evaluates only one side of the picture: results achieved by new adaptive practices. Current research rarely measures the effectiveness of traditional practices, which makes it difficult to compare them fairly with adaptive practices and can hold traditional practices to a less rigorous proof

*A more detailed model is shown on page 234.

standard. As one considers the evidence, it is worthwhile considering whether traditional practices would hold up to the same scrutiny.

Also, some adaptive practices have been studied more than others. A particular cluster of talent management practices and certain resources for dual-focus workers (child care benefits, flexible scheduling practices) have been studied more than the subtler aspects of adaptive cultures. These better-studied practices have been in place longer and are more self-contained; thus, it is easier to assess their effects.

Even with these qualifiers, the sheer magnitude of the evidence is overwhelming. Not only are the results potent and pervasive, they suggest that organizations may not be able to thrive if they fail to adapt to the new reality.

More details about many of the individual research studies, such as how the research was done and the number of employees or organizations studied, are in the Notes section for each chapter. Most of the research was performed by third parties and generally involved one of the following.

- Analysis of the effect of a change in adaptive practice on a department, business, or firm—comparing before and after data (most of these analyses are not longitudinal)

- Survey or poll of people's attitudes, activities, and intentions reflecting their need for and access to certain benefits or practices

- Analysis of firm performance or stock market returns based on adaptive practices used in comparison to a similar group of firms not using the practices

- Analysis of existing data, such as census reports, medical claims, attendance records, or test results

Many of the surveys and polls employed statistical methods and can be generalized to broader populations. However, there are limitations to statistical evidence. People often modify their responses to surveys and polls to conform to expectations of appropriate attitudes, beliefs, and intentions. As a result, it is necessary to consider the potential effect of these expectations when evaluating results. A number of the studies were conducted internally by the organizations. The results are interesting because of the pattern they establish, but there is little documentation of methods used and assumptions made.

We begin with some thoughts from guest author Robert Reich, who reflects on the idea of *relational capital*—the cumulative experiences, insights, and understandings of people—and the effect it has on organizational performance.

THE IMPORTANCE OF RELATIONAL CAPITAL
by Robert Reich

Two long-term structural changes in the economy operate like shifting tectonic plates, and businesses need to be prepared for them and understand them. The first is *globalization,* a term that has gone from obscurity to meaninglessness without any intervening period of coherence. The impact of globalization is that there will be no American products or companies and that everybody is competing around the world with everybody else.

The second great vector of change is *technological,* which in combination with globalization is changing the very pattern of work and the structure of industry. We used to have telephone operators, bank tellers, elevator operators, and service station attendants. Remember that? They have been replaced by technology.

We now have just three categories of workers: *routine production workers* (who can be replaced by software or other people around the world), people who deliver *in-person attention-giving services* (retail, restaurant, hospital workers, and the like—who cannot be replaced, but whose wages and job security are diminishing), and *symbolic-analytic workers* (marketing professionals, lawyers, engineers, and so on—who become more valuable as the service content of products grows and the value of the physical content declines).

It is the symbolic-analytic work that creates the service content of every physical and nonphysical thing bought. In a cell phone, for example, the design, distribution, marketing, and legal service is the symbolic-analytic work that is the value-added. The demand for symbolic-analytic workers is increasing because the value in products that is attributable to those services is increasing.

In the context of the shift to a world that no longer is based on high-volume, stable mass production jobs but increasingly is based on high-value customization production jobs, two factors become more important: lower turnover and the buildup of relational capital. One of the most misunderstood elements of a cost structure is the full cost of replacing workers, because all businesses are becoming more complicated and it is more critical to tailor what they do to the end uses of particular customers and clients.

Both private and public organizations are depending more and more on relational capital for their success. *Relational capital* is the cumulative experience of people in the organization in dealing with customers and clients—understanding their needs and developing those relationships. It is the cumulative experience of people in the organization in dealing with one another—understanding whose strengths can be built on, who knows what, how to collaborate, with whom. And it is the cumulative understandings and insights of people in the organization dealing with suppliers and subcontractors—who is reliable, who is good, who is knowledgeable. In other words, if you look at the true sources of productivity and success, much of it has to do with people's understanding of the needs and the capacities of other people around them, whether they are customers or suppliers, colleagues or supervisors or people working for them.

Put another way, employees are not *fungible* the way they would have been in an old system of high-volume, standardized, stable mass production. It matters who is in what position; it matters how long they are in that position, and it matters how much they are learning in that position. It matters how they deal with other people, customers, suppliers, and colleagues. Relational capital matters.

Who you hire and how you train them, how you recruit people, and how you retain people is a big part of the success of any enterprise. The accumulation of relational capital is a big part of whether an organization not only survives but also prospers, or fails to do so.

As I go to companies, I administer the pronoun test. I listen for the pronouns people use in describing the organization. If they use the pronouns *we* or *our*—for example, "*We* are trying to do this"—I know that it is one kind of organization. If they use the pronouns *they* and *their*—"This is *their* room"—

it is another. The first-person possessive pronoun organization—the *we/our* organization—is the one where relationship capital has been built up. People have a strong sense of affinity with one another, and with the organization's goals. They feel a degree of ownership. They understand that their fate and the fate of the organization are linked. It's an organization where people are going to stay and where they will go the extra mile in order to make the organization successful. There is a higher degree of trust than in *they/their* organizations.

To test relational capital I also look for the extent to which learning is going on, whether people talk in terms of what they are learning. The accumulation of relational capital—insights about customers and colleagues and suppliers and what's needed and how—depends on a continuous process of learning.

One of the things that employees are looking at more and more when they are hired, that enables them to develop relational capital and to learn and develop a sense of affinity with the organization, has to do with whether they feel the organization is taking full account of who they are as people in their private relations, not just their relations at work.

It is increasingly important that organizations pay attention to this concern. Without it, the very source of the capital that is essential to an organization's ability to survive and prosper is compromised; the value-added is lost. The potential that people—with all their complexity—can bring must be managed as an asset. The organization that does that will lead; those that do not will follow.

10

HUMAN CAPITAL RESULTS

We know that people have become the driving force of business success. Examples are so widely accepted that they are part of business lore: how employee empowerment at Nordstrom drives customer satisfaction and company profits, how fully engaged employees have built Southwest's growth and profitability, how employees made Nucor successful in the highly competitive steel industry.

In this chapter we consider the effect adaptive practices (see Part 2) have on employee performance—on creativity, commitment, productivity, and health and on the decisions employees make about their employment. Many factors must come together to create employee performance: the right employees in the right jobs, in the right frame of mind, with the right tools (supervisory and literal tools), and without distractions and hindrances. It requires a blend of skill and motivation and an organizational system that fosters creativity, commitment, engagement, and alignment with organizational goals. Employees must be able to be fully present— focused, enthusiastic, and with a sense of purpose—to operate at peak performance.

Creativity

Creativity drives the most important contributions employees can make—new ideas, process and product improvements—but creativity is not as simple to generate as widgets on an assembly line. Employee creativity is influenced by work environment, organizational culture, degree of support from supervisors and co-workers, time pressures and workload, clarity of goals, quality of feedback, and how well each individual's skills match opportunities (Csikszentmihalyi, 2003), to name a few. Studies have found four factors that affect employee creativity.

1. *Frenzy.* Frenzy reduces creativity. In a study of an economic research and development organization, creative thinking time decreased with the level of institutional frenzy. Institutional frenzy involved heavy workloads, crises, frequent change, lack of process support, constant interruptions, and much time spent in coordination. The frenzy also made it more difficult for workers to integrate work and personal lives effectively (Kellogg, 2001).[1]

2. *Time pressure.* Time pressure reduces creative thinking. On project teams in the chemical, high-tech, and consumer products industries, employees were 45 percent less likely to think creatively on days of high time pressure than on lower-pressure days, despite their perceptions to the contrary. A high level of time pressure also decreased creative thinking on the following two days. The most creative days noted in this study were those when employees were able to concentrate on a single work activity for a significant part of the day (Amabile, Hadley, & Kramer, 2002).[2]

3. *Downsizing.* Downsizing reduces creativity. A longitudinal study of a Fortune 500 electronics company with thirty thousand employees tracked creativity and productivity over time, finding both decreased during the downsizing period. Productivity returned to normal five months after the last downsizing, but creativity levels did not. Employees said they felt stifled, didn't take risks, worried about getting laid off, saw work quality drop, experienced decreases in sense of pride and teamwork, and worried more about protecting themselves than about doing the work (Amabile & Conti, 1999).[3]

4. *Supervisor support.* Supervisor support enhances creativity. Two studies illustrate the effects of supervisor support.

- *Among high-tech and manufacturing employees.* A study of manufacturing employees (from line operators to business analysts) found that employees' belief in their ability to produce creative results is enhanced by support from their supervisors and that actual creative performance improved as a result. Effects held true in both consumer products manufacturing and high-tech operations, despite diversity of occupations, educational level, and length of service (Tierney & Farmer, 2002).[4]

- *Among manufacturing employees.* A study of predominantly female knitwear companies in Bulgaria found friends and families contributed to employees' creative performance at work, above the contribution from co-workers and supervisors, and that married employees were more creative than unmarried ones (Madjar, Oldham, & Pratt, 2002).[5]

Creativity research suggests employees are more creative when the workload is reasonable and when they have the required tools, including supportive processes and supportive managers—in short, when they work in adaptive organizations.

Commitment

Employee commitment to the organization has never been of greater consequence or more threatened. Employee know-how and productivity are critical to efficient processes and cost reductions; employee ingenuity drives innovation, and employee relationships lubricate transactions with customers, suppliers, and other stakeholders. Yet employee commitment to organizations has suffered dramatically from continual corporate downsizing, the use of contingent workers, and the large-scale bankruptcies and acquisitions that have eliminated long-standing companies. The old psychological contract between employers and employees—where employers provide job security and predictable advancement to employees in exchange for their loyalty and performance (Cappelli, 1999)—has been damaged beyond repair. Organizational commitment is also being challenged by the tendency of knowledge workers to be more attached to their profession than to their organization. Organizational commitment must be generated in other ways.

Commitment comes in three varieties, all of which affect employees' behavior: job commitment, career commitment, and organizational commitment. *Job commitment* is the extent to which an individual identifies with the specific work tasks and responsibilities that make up the job (Bashaw & Grant, 1994). *Career commitment* is how important work and career are in a person's life (Greenhaus, 1971, cited in Bashaw & Grant). *Organizational commitment* is how strongly an individual identifies with a particular organization (Porter & Smith, 1970, cited in Mowday, Steers, & Porter, 1979). These three affect one another; for example, job commitment has been found to positively affect organizational commitment (A. Cohen, 2000).

Commitment differs from job satisfaction; commitment is about attachment to the organization itself, including its goals and values. When commitment exists, the individual believes in and accepts the organization's goals and values, is willing to exert considerable effort on behalf of the organization, and wants to maintain membership in it (Mowday et al., 1979)—all things organizations want to foster. Commitment also produces valuable behavioral outcomes. It affects an individual's performance on the job, intent to leave, and actual decision to leave (see Figure 3). By measuring commitment, organizations can determine whether other factors clearly tied to organizational performance are present.

Not all commitment is necessarily desirable. For example, organizational commitment has three components: *affective commitment* (the employee's emotional attachment to the organization), *continuance commitment* (the employee's desire to avoid the cost of leaving), and *normative commitment* (the employee's sense of obligation to the company; Allen & Meyer, 1990). Most commitment has aspects of each. Of the three, continuance commitment—employees remain to avoid losing their pensions, vested stock options, status, or other job benefits—is the least likely to result in desirable employee behavior such as high performance, engagement, and cooperation. Retaining employees whose continuance commitment is limited can actually be harmful to a company, causing productivity problems and possibly even sabotage (Flowers & Hughes, 1973).

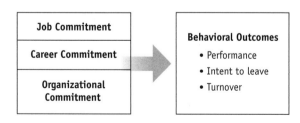

Figure 3 Commitment and Outcomes

To consider the value of commitment, ask, Commitment to what? Employees can be committed to their work team, their supervisor, their division, or to senior management. Though few studies have explored commitment in terms of these dimensions, they are important elements to understand. If an employee reports a high level of organizational commitment, but it is not clear whether the commitment is to the employee's supervisor, team, division, or organization, then changes made to increase employee commitment risk focusing on the wrong element. If an employee is highly committed to a supervisor, the organization risks losing that employee's commitment should the supervisor leave or change jobs.

What Affects Commitment?

To support commitment, one must understand what generates it in the first place. This topic has intrigued researchers, particularly in view of the recent decline in organizational commitment from the breakdown of the psychological contract between employers and employees. Three recent studies found personal development and growth, rewards, and alignment with organizational goals to be important drivers of employee commitment (Rodgers, 1998; Aon Consulting, 2000; Pfau & Kay, 2002). Respect was an important factor underlying commitment in all three studies.

Adaptive cultures as well as a number of adaptive practices (see Part 3) have been shown to have a positive effect on employee commitment (see Figure 4).

Overall, adaptive human capital work practices that give employees more control over their work and schedules, involve them in the organization of work, and provide essential resources such as dependent care benefits increase affective commitment for knowledge, service, and manufacturing workers, as evidenced by studies across the population and by individual companies.

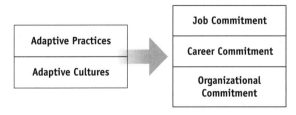

Figure 4 Adaptivity and Commitment

Adaptive Practices Increase Commitment

Studies show that adaptive practices tend to increase commitment almost without regard to the type of worker involved.

- *The general population.* The National Study of the Changing Workforce, a study of three thousand people, found that workers with more flexible time and leave options and more dependent care benefits reported greater loyalty to their employers and strong commitment to helping them succeed (Galinsky, Bond, & Friedman, 1993).

- *A cross section of U.S. workers.* A similar study of a cross section of U.S. workers found higher levels of affective commitment in organizations that offered family-friendly policies (parental leave, flexible schedules, child care assistance, and so on) *regardless of whether the employees anticipated directly benefiting from the policies* (Grover & Crooker, 1995).[6]

- *Business school graduates.* In a study of business school graduates, those working at companies with more programs to help employees with simultaneous work and personal responsibilities had higher levels of affective commitment to their organizations and lower levels of intention to leave (C. Thompson, Beauvais, & Lyness, 1999).[7]

- *Knowledge workers.* A study of part-time work schedules at a pharmaceutical company, a technology company, and two professional service firms found that 53 percent of employees who used part-time work arrangements, such as job sharing or reduced time schedules, increased their level of commitment to the organization, 48 percent increased their level of commitment to the job, and 42 percent reported no change (Catalyst, 1997a).[8]

- *Clerical employees.* A study of clerical employees in insurance companies found that flexible work schedules and organizational commitment were strongly related. Flexible schedules gave employees a sense of time autonomy, which in turn was connected to their organizational commitment (Pierce & Newstrom, 1983).[9]

- *Individual companies.*[10] At DuPont (see Chapter 13), employees who used programs designed for dual-focus employees (with work and personal responsibilities) were 45 percent more likely to say they would "go the extra mile" to assure the company's success than those who did not use the programs (Rodgers & Associates, 1995). Baxter Healthcare (Chapter 14) found that alternative work arrangements (job sharing, telecommuting, compressed workweek, part-time hours) had a significant positive effect on organizational commitment (Campbell & Koblenz, 1997). At Aetna Life & Casualty, where 59 percent of workers use flextime, employees say these arrangements have enabled them to retain their jobs; as a result, their commitment is deepened and they go "out of their way to make the job work" (Genasci, 1993). Case studies of twelve organizations in the United Kingdom found higher levels of commitment resulting from the use of flexible work arrangements (Coussey, 2000).

What Decreases Commitment

Studies identified four conditions under which employee commitment is reduced.

1. *Lack of awareness and underutilization of policies.* It is not enough for organizations to offer flexible work arrangements on paper; employees must actually be able to use them.

   - *Awareness affects commitment.* A study of 160 managers and executives found that women who perceived that their organization offered flexible work arrangements had higher organizational commitment than women who did not. Both men and women had higher job satisfaction (Scandura & Lankau, 1997).[11]

   - A study of four hundred professional and technical employees of seven biopharmaceutical firms found that when employees felt free to use flexible work arrangements, there was a significant effect on affective organizational commitment, while the existence of policies themselves, whether formal or informal, had no effect (Eaton, 2001).

2. *Overload.* Adaptive practices focus on the appropriate use of time for employees and the importance of reasonable and realistic workloads. It turns out that the most committed workers—those whom most employers want to keep engaged and involved—are not the most immune to, but are actually the most affected by, poor human capital practices.

   - *Work overload decreases commitment.* A study of the 75th Ranger Regiment, an elite light infantry unit specializing in attack missions—extraordinarily hardworking and dedicated personnel—found that those who cared most about their work were the most demoralized by work overload and other impediments to performance (Britt, 2003).

3. *Role ambiguity.* Ambiguity of work roles also has a particularly negative effect on highly committed employees.

  - A study by researchers from Bowling Green and the University of Wisconsin found the most committed nonfaculty employees at a western university reported the lowest levels of job satisfaction when their work roles were ambiguous. They were the most negatively affected by "impediments to good performance" (Britt, 2003).

4. *Inadequate resources.* Not having appropriate resources negatively affects commitment.

  - A study of three hundred hotel employees working in high-turnover functions, such as housekeeping and stewardship, and high–guest contact functions, such as front desk and department management, found that organizational commitment was significantly damaged when employees lacked appropriate resources to handle nonwork responsibilities. Child care and medical problems had the biggest effect on commitment, with transportation, home maintenance, and family problems also contributing to decreases in commitment (Cannon, 1998).

Adaptive Cultures and Commitment

In Chapter 7, we discuss the role organizational culture plays in sustaining and facilitating adaptive practices and enabling organizations to fully benefit from human capital investments. Adaptive cultures, which exhibit the values described, have been found in various studies to increase employee commitment.

  - *Commitment is found in empowering cultures.* An analysis of the relationship between organizational culture and employee attitudes and behavior, among 276 nurses working in obstetrics units of seven hospitals, determined how different types of organizational cultures affect employee commitment, job satisfaction and involvement, empowerment, and intent to leave. Organizational cultures that emphasized decentralized decision making, participation, teamwork, and horizontal communication had employees with significantly higher levels of commitment, empowerment, and job satisfaction, and lower intent to leave (E. Goodman, Zammuto, & Gifford, 2001).

Supportive cultures enhance commitment (and citizenship behavior). Studies of different worker populations illustrate the effects of culture.

- *Manufacturing employees.* A study at three manufacturing companies of the effects of organizational culture on employee commitment found employees who felt their organizations were supportive had stronger affective commitment, job satisfaction, performance, and citizenship behavior (Randall, Cropanzano, Bormann, & Birjulin, 1999).

- *University alumni.* In a study of alumni of an eastern university, employees who perceived more organizational support were more likely to have affective (emotional) commitment (Rhoades, Eisenberger, & Armeli, 2001).[12]

Commitment research suggests that organizations with more committed employees outperform others in sales and financial performance. Studies found that committed employees were more satisfied, empowered, productive, and active in serving customers, and they contributed greater discretionary effort. Adaptive practices and cultural elements contribute to commitment, affecting the most valuable workers most intensely.

Commitment and Organizational Performance

Companies whose employees are committed to their success generally outperform those without committed employees in three main areas.

1. *Net income.* A comparison study of matched pairs of six companies found, all things being equal, that companies that promote organizational commitment (HP, FedEx, GE, Southwest Airlines, Wal-Mart, 3M) would outgrow by four to one and outperform—increasing net income an average of 202 percent compared to 139 percent over a ten-year period—similar companies (Texas Instruments, Consolidated Freightways, GM, United Airlines, Sears, Xerox) with less committed employees (Catlette & Hadden, 1998).

2. *Sales.* A study of industrial salespeople in sixteen companies found organizational commitment, job commitment, and career commitment all positively associated with sales performance. Sales performance included technical competence, territory management, selling skills, relationships, and developmental strengths. Also, employees' intent to leave their current employer dropped when organizational and job commitment were present (Bashaw & Grant, 1994).

3. *Retention.* The link between employee commitment and retention has been studied extensively—both intent to leave and actual turnover.

- *Intent to leave signals future turnover.* In a study of nine thousand officers in the U.S. Navy, an intent to leave was strongly correlated with actual turnover. This longitudinal study of organizational commitment in officers (with service ranging from five to thirty-three years) is particularly instructive for large, hierarchical business organizations where employee length of service is important because of the associated skills, knowledge, and maturity it brings (Lee & Maurer, 1999).

- *Commitment increases intention to stay.* A study of medical library workers employed by hospitals, academic medical centers, social services agencies, and libraries in forty-one states found that workers with greater organizational and career commitment had less intent to leave. Workers with high levels of organizational and career commitment also reported higher levels of job satisfaction, felt more empowered, and were more willing to resolve customer service complaints (Carson, Carson, Roe, Birkenmeier, & Phillips, 1999).[13]

- *Commitment predicts retention.* A study at a West Coast financial institution surveyed employees, mostly knowledge workers, about their commitment to their organization, job involvement, job satisfaction, and intent to leave. The intent to leave was the strongest predictor of which people actually left, and organizational commitment, job involvement, and job satisfaction explained a significant proportion of why they had intended to leave (Lee & Mowday, 1987).[14]

- *Commitment-oriented HR practices contribute to retention.* A study of manufacturing workers in U.S. steel mini-mills found turnover reduced when human resource practices were used to increase organizational commitment. Mills with commitment systems had turnover levels half those of mills using control systems (J. B. Arthur, 1994). *Note:* Commitment-oriented human resource practices consist of employee involvement in management decisions, group problem solving, and a higher percentage of skilled workers. Control-oriented human resource practices are characterized by rules and procedures to which employees are required to adhere.

Productivity

Productivity continues to be a burning issue. With competitive pressures limiting a company's ability to raise prices, productivity is one of the few remaining profit growth sources. Physical capital was traditionally seen as the best source of productivity improvement, but companies like NEC, which began replacing robots with people (T. H. Davenport & Prusak, 1998), and 3M, whose productivity increased 100 percent from 1984 to 1994 (Stewart, 1997), have demonstrated the power of human capital in boosting productivity. Nucor's steel production success was due in part to workers' ability to use capital equipment beyond manufacturers' specifications (Maciariello, 2000). Measuring productivity is challenging, particularly with knowledge work, because of its qualitative nature and subjective results. Still, quantitative measures are possible—as the experience of Hoffman-LaRoche, which saved $1 million per day by streamlining the process of applying for new FDA drug approvals showed—and productivity matters in service work as well. HP leveraged the collective knowledge of its technical personnel to reduce average call times by two-thirds and cost per call by 50 percent in its service centers (T. H. Davenport & Prusak, 1998).

Many of the adaptive practices described in Part 2 influence productivity; most address two primary issues: ensuring that employees are able to work (whatever the location) and ensuring that they are effective while they are working.

Productivity that arises from employee effectiveness has different facets. The *quantity* of output, such as employees' ability to produce a high volume of work, to work quickly and accurately, and to meet deadlines, is important. The *quality* of output is also key and is affected by employees' attitude, stamina, and ongoing learning, and by their ability to focus and to share knowledge and ideas to improve processes and products. This productivity requires employees' maximum engagement, energy, and discretionary effort, and is compromised by burnout and physical exhaustion, which we discuss in the next section. It is enhanced when the workforce is stable and enriched by a range of talents from diverse workers and leaders. It requires effectiveness from both individuals and groups—smoothly functioning teams and managers who can focus energies on value-added tasks rather than on policing. It calls for synergy across efforts to improve performance, such as reengineering and restructuring. It increases when there is clarity of goals and a focus on key objectives and when the work is well organized. It requires efficient use of facilities and equipment. Each of these facets of productivity is enhanced by adaptive cultures and practices, as the research in this section details.

Attendance—ensuring that employees are able to work—is the other side of productivity. Absenteeism and other lost work time—work interruptions, cutting the workday short, and so on—are significant problems. On average, companies set aside a remarkable 5 percent of their budget to pay for unscheduled absenteeism. According to the 2002 CCH Unscheduled Absence Survey (CCH, 2002), losses due to unscheduled absenteeism have risen 29 percent since 2000. Absenteeism is a long-standing problem, but its root causes and therefore its remedies have changed. The new root causes are less attitude-driven and avoidable than those of the past, and must be managed differently if absenteeism is to be minimized. One of the predictors of higher absenteeism is *health status and parenthood.* A 1987 study found that health status was the best predictor of absenteeism—both frequency and length—and that having children under age six increased the likelihood of a woman's being absent, whereas having a child in child care increased the likelihood of a man's being absent (Vistnes, 1997).*

How Specific Adaptive Practices and Cultures Affect Productivity

A number of adaptive practices have been shown to significantly improve employee productivity, reduce absenteeism, and increase effectiveness at work. The evidence about specific practices—dependent care, flexible work arrangements, work redesign, and work-life balance initiatives—is discussed in the sections that follow.

---

* This finding is a reminder that men are sharing responsibility for children because their wives or partners are now employed. Children's doctor's appointments, parent-teacher conferences, and so on are schedulable, but require time off. Elder care crises, a breakdown in child care arrangements, or children's illnesses can neither be avoided nor scheduled in advance. Phone calls—from latchkey children to say they arrived home safe from school, from an ailing parent's doctor, or to coordinate activities (or referee quarrels) among older children at home alone—can cause employees to be distracted and/or interrupted while at work.

   These work disruptions are a normal part of life for employees with caregiving responsibilities. Even otherwise high-performing employees have these kinds of tardiness, absenteeism, and lost work time issues. When high-performers find themselves counseled or disciplined, punitive policies that presume absenteeism can be reduced by the exercise of self-discipline tend to backfire. Approaches that separate avoidable from unavoidable missed time and allow employees the flexibility to meet these obligations and still accomplish their work are more effective. Holding employees responsible for work outcomes rather than attendance per se is usually better from an organizational perspective and does not demoralize responsible workers with legitimate conflicting responsibilities.

Adaptive practices help reduce absenteeism related to pregnancy and childbirth.

- *Health insurance, job protection, supervisor support, and adaptive practices reduce absenteeism.* A study of women before and after childbirth found that workplace practices with these characteristics had lower absenteeism during pregnancy—a change from 3.4 to 2.1 days missed per person (Bond, 1992).

Resources and Tools—Dependent Care Benefits

The studies described here substantiate an immediate effect of dependent care benefits on productivity.

Lack of adequate child care reduces productivity. Employer-provided child care improves productivity because employees who cannot find high-quality, affordable care are often distracted on the job.

- A 1998 nationwide survey of a thousand working adults revealed 44 percent of those needing child care in the past five years had found it very or extremely difficult to find high-quality care and 51 percent had found it very or extremely difficult to find affordable care. As a result, 52 percent could not do their jobs well and 43 percent turned down a job (Taylor, 1998).

- Among employers who gave employees child care assistance, 54 percent reported decreases in absenteeism and 35 percent reported decreases in tardiness, according to a survey of the Conference Board's Work-Family Research and Advisory Panel (Parkinson, 1996).[15]

Child care benefits and leave policies improve attendance and productivity. In most cases savings from reduced absenteeism and improved productivity outweighed the cost of child care assistance.

- At Chase Manhattan, backup child care services for well children saved the company 6,900 workdays in one year, a return on investment of 115 percent on a service fully paid for by the bank and a net gain after expenses of $803,000 (D. Friedman, 1998). The usage rate also shows how often child care arrangements break down.

- AlliedSignal's on-site child care center reduced lost work time by 89 percent for employees using it (U.S. Department of Labor, 1998).

- Union Bank's on-site child care center cut absenteeism among its participants by 37 percent, compared to a similar group[16] of nonparticipants who had had the same absence rate the year before the center opened. It also improved morale of supervisors, who spent less time policing late or absent employees and were therefore able to focus on other tasks (Ransom, Aschbacher, & Burud, 1989).

- The 2002 CCH Unscheduled Absence Study found that paid-leave banks, which pool employees' time off and allow time off for a variety of purposes including family care, were among the most effective absence control programs, with an overall rating of 3.6 on a scale of 1 to 5 (5 being most effective). Also ranking highly for reducing unscheduled absences were flexible scheduling (3.78), on-site child care (3.62), and emergency child care (3.55; CCH, 2002).

Concentration and work performance increase when resources are sufficient. Employees report that their productivity increases when they are satisfied with the care their families receive. Productivity decreases when they are not.

- *Work performance.* In a study of thirty-nine employers with different types of child care assistance to employees, work performance was improved for 50 percent of employees using off-work-site services and 45 percent of those using on-work-site services (Dawson, Mikel, Lorenz, & King, 1984).[17]

- *Team performance and risk.* A teaching hospital's work-site child care center enhanced the efficiency of work teams and reduced risk. Surgeons scheduled surgeries around a particularly capable ICU nurse, who worked at the hospital because of the exceptional child care facility. Other operating rooms reported functioning short-staffed when personnel with less stable child care arrangements had unscheduled absenteeism (Burud & Associates, 2000).

- *Productivity.* Neuville Industries, a sock-finishing company, required 14–23 percent fewer production workers than industrial engineering standards recommended; and Neuville credited its lean staffing to its on-site child care facility, salaries 15 percent above market, and a work environment friendly to families (Burud, Aschbacher, & McCroskey, 1984).

The absence of elder care resources results in lost work time. Although currently an issue for fewer workers than child care, elder care responsibilities are expected to increase as life expectancies continue to lengthen.

- According to a 1997 study of U.S. households, approximately 12 million U.S. workers are taking care of elder relatives, with 25 percent missing at least one day a month of work as a result (Greene, 2001).

- At current levels, U.S. businesses lose an estimated $11.4 billion annually as a result of employees' elder care responsibilities—$398 million in absenteeism and $488 million from partial absenteeism—while workday interruptions cost $3.8 billion (Metropolitan Life Insurance Company, 1997).

Other family care requirements result in additional lost work time.

- A Harvard University study found that 30 percent of workers cut back time at work at least one day a week to care for family; 12 percent cut back on two days and 5 percent on three or more days. One in four men and one in three women interrupted their work for family care. Employees' children accounted for time away from work most often (42 percent); but 15 percent of the time it was taken to care for parents, 12 percent for spouses or partners, 7 percent for grandchildren, and 24 percent for other family members (Heymann, 2000).

Time—Customized Work Arrangements

Adaptive practices based on the values of respect, alignment of individual with organizational interests, results orientation, and diversity contribute to productivity, including those that recognize that employees have responsibilities outside work and that the organization does not own the employee's time. A poll of a thousand workers found 83 percent believe employers have an obligation to recognize employees' responsibilities outside work (Rayman, Krane, & Szostak, 2000).

- *Flexible work arrangements improve productivity and reduce absenteeism.* In a two-year study of more than fourteen hundred employees and managers, 70 percent of managers and 87 percent of employees reported that working a flexible arrangement improved productivity (Pruchno, Litchfield, & Fried, 2000).[18]

- *Compressed workweeks enhance productivity and reduce overtime.* In a study, financial center workers at HP almost doubled productivity and reduced overtime to less than half of former levels by changing to a compressed workweek (Martinez, 1997).[19]

- *Flexibility improves the ability to get work done.* In a study of flexible work arrangements at Chase Manhattan Bank, 66 percent of managers who supervised employees on flexible work schedules reported that the experience enhanced their management skills at work process coordination, team communication, and overall organization. Ninety-one percent saw no negative impact on (or a positive change in) teamwork and the ability to get work done with the new arrangements; 95 percent said it did not require more time to manage people; 90 percent said communications were easy to maintain (L. Friedman & D. E. Friedman, 1998).

- *Part-time schedules enhance productivity of professionals.* In a two-year study of part-time managers and professionals, 45 percent agreed that employees working flexible arrangements made productivity gains; 49 percent working part-time experienced no reduction in workload with the reduced hours and paycheck (Catalyst, 1997a).[20]

- *Customized work schedules enhance group productivity and attachment.* In a study of employees and managers at six large companies, job satisfaction scores among employees on flex schedules were slightly higher. The flex users were also more attached to their company, better educated, and more often in professional positions than employees overall. Seventy-five percent of managers reported no change in their workload with flex schedules, and nearly all found work group productivity greater (Pruchno et al., 2000).[21]

- *Flexible schedules support a results orientation.* A study of managers of women on flex schedules found them equally motivated, loyal, professional, productive, reliable, focused, and able to meet deadlines as other employees, if not more so: 56 percent found them more productive. Among the employees themselves, 90 percent reported being equally results-oriented as before, or more results-oriented (Flexible Resources, 1999).[22]

Organization of Work—Work Redesign and Telecommuting

Redesigning work enhances productivity. An in-depth study at the Fleet Financial Group explored the effects of workplace innovations that would help employees integrate rather than isolate the personal and work aspects of their lives. The work redesign effort increased productivity for both underwriters and sales managers studied. A concurrent redesign effort that among other things increased underwriter control over workload also resulted in significant time savings for both groups (Bailyn & Rayman, 1998).[23]

Three other studies reinforce the effects of work redesign on employee productivity, and two of them were intended specifically to coordinate work with employees' personal responsibilities.

- *Work redesign enhances work results.* An engineering product development team working long hours in a continual crisis mode experienced enormous pressure and an environment where high-visibility problem solving was more highly valued than low-visibility problem prevention. The team, with the help of researchers, examined how time was allocated and made it a priority to meet employees' personal life needs while accomplishing the work goals. The team also created uninterrupted quiet time when employees could focus on their objectives and managers could plan for and prevent problems. The result was the on-time launch of a new product and a number of excellence awards (Rapoport & Bailyn, 1996). The process that considered employees' personal life needs at the same level of priority as their work agenda made the difference, according to the researchers who conducted this study, rather than any particular way of organizing time or work (Rapoport et al., 2002).

- *Self-directed teams shorten production time.* Rower Furniture eliminated supervisory positions and reorganized five hundred manufacturing workers into self-directed work cells for each product line. Each cell designed its own process and procedures and obtained real-time access to all information needed—orders, output, quality, and so on. The study reported that productivity boomed: delivery time dropped from six months to ten days (Ehin, 2000).

Telecommuting improves productivity. Employees and managers report significant productivity enhancements as a result of offering employees the opportunity to work from locations other than the office.

- A survey of 159 senior executives from major North American companies found that every company with at least ten thousand employees offered telecommuting options, and 52 percent of them did so to increase productivity (William Olsten Center for Workforce Strategies, 1999).[24]

  According to managers. Managers find that results improve when they institute telecommuting. The number of teleworkers grew more than 20 percent from 1999 to 2000 (Nilles, 2000). Substantial evidence indicates that use of this adaptive practice improves productivity, as the following examples illustrate.

  - American Express gained $40 million in increased sales productivity by implementing telecommuting: the rate of sign-ups per sales call increased 43 percent, from 4.2 to 6+ calls per day; the number of account development calls increased 40 percent, from 2.5 to 3.5 per day; sales managers spent 60 percent more time in the field, increasing from 2.5 to 4 days per week; and sales administration productivity increased 60 percent (Sims et al., 1996).

- Among telecommuting travel agents at Holland America Line Westours Inc., telephone time spent with the customer and number of calls handled exceeded the levels of in-office agents. Revenue was 10 percent higher for at-home agents than for in-office agents (Washington State University Cooperative Extension Energy Program, 1998).

- Internal company evaluations of telecommuting programs at Illinois Bell found productivity increased 40 percent, and the use of satellite offices at GSA resulted in productivity improvements of 10–15 percent (Minnesota Center for Corporate Responsibility, 1997).

- AT&T, Mountain Bell, and Bell Atlantic reported average increases of approximately 30 percent in the amount of work done by telecommuters (Sims et al., 1996).

- Aetna recorded an annual 30 percent increase in claims processed after employees began working from home (Smith, 1996).

- Eliminating offices enabled IBM's Midwest operation to increase productivity 10–20 percent (Frank, 1995).

According to employees. Employees often report that their productivity improves as a result of their ability to telecommute.

- In a self-report study, 40 percent of one thousand U.S. workers reported that they were more productive when working from home, compared to 30 percent who indicated their productivity stayed the same (Heldrich Center for Workforce Development, 2000).

- In telephone interviews, eighteen hundred U.S. workers revealed that telecommuters in satellite work centers experienced a 30 percent increase in productivity, 15 percent for home-based telecommuters—a savings of $9,712 per worker per year (Nilles, 2000).

- Another self-report survey of teleworkers found 47 percent said they were more productive as a result of the practice; 42 percent found no change in productivity; 10 percent found their productivity dropped. On average, the effects created a net gain of $685 per worker (Pratt, 1999).[25]

Values—Integration of Public and Private Spheres

Personal life skills increase productivity. Interpersonal skills are among the meta-competencies described in Chapter 4. Integrating skills from one's personal life into work situations increases effectiveness.

- *Female executives.* Female executives found motherhood had increased their self-awareness, which enhanced their managerial effectiveness (Morrison, White, & Van Velsor, 1992, cited in Ruderman, Ohlott, Panzer, & King, 2002).

- *Male executives.* A parallel study of male executives found personal experiences such as coaching children's sports taught them lessons of leadership (McCall, Lombardo, & Morrison, 1988, cited in Ruderman et al., 2002).

- *Female leaders.* A study of female managers and executives that evaluated whether skills and outlooks developed outside work acted as resources on the job found women who were committed to multiple life roles (work and nonwork) had better peer and supervisor evaluations of interpersonal skills (sharing credit, personal presence, collaboration, managing complexity, and managing conflict), better peer and supervisor evaluation of task-related skills (personal motivation, vision, risk-taking, marketplace awareness, and standards of performance), and greater life satisfaction and self-acceptance. Their nonwork roles contributed resources to their managerial role performance in six major ways (Ruderman et al., 2002).[26]

  - *Enriched interpersonal skills* (mentioned by 42 percent): Skills developed included understanding, motivating, respecting, and developing others.

  - *Psychological benefits* (mentioned by 23 percent): Overcoming obstacles, taking risks, and succeeding in personal arenas bolstered self-esteem, confidence, and stamina.

  - *Emotional support and advice* (mentioned by 19 percent): Friends and family members acted as sounding boards and motivators.

  - *Handling multiple tasks* (mentioned by 9.7 percent): Juggling personal tasks and planning for family developed administrative skills and ability to prioritize and plan at work.

  - *Personal interests and background* (mentioned by 6.5 percent): Outside skills and perspectives proved useful at work.

  - *Leadership* (mentioned by 4.8 percent): Opportunities in volunteer groups, community organizations, or family settings provided leadership lessons (strategy, budgets, organizing, implementing systems, achieving goals through others) and increased comfort with authority role.

Values—Wholeness

Programs that enable employees to balance work and personal life enhance employee performance. Having a meaningful life outside work can enhance both employee productivity and performance.

- *Overwork leads to lack of sleep, which reduces productivity.* Lack of sleep affects workplace productivity and working long hours affects employees' ability to get sufficient sleep. A study found working more than ten hours a day made 46 percent of respondents too sleepy to do safe or quality work. The majority of respondents indicated lack of sleep makes work tasks more difficult: 51 percent said it reduces the amount of work done, 40 percent said quality suffers, and 68 percent said it interferes with both quantity and quality, reducing productivity an estimated 30 percent (National Sleep Foundation, 2000).[27]

- *Work-life balance benefits and programs contribute to quality improvements.* A study at Fel-Pro, an Illinois manufacturer of engine gaskets, found that employees who used and valued their benefits most, including a plethora of work-life benefits, were twice as likely to submit suggestions for product and process improvements as other employees. These employees showed higher levels of initiative, volunteered more for additional work, and helped supervisors and co-workers more (Lambert et al., 1993).[28]

- *Work-life balance programs cut absenteeism and increase morale.* In a survey of eight hundred U.S. organizations, the William Mercer organization found 47 percent of companies with work-life programs reported increased productivity, 64 percent of companies reported increased morale, and 50 percent of companies said work-life programs cut absenteeism (William M. Mercer, 1996).

- *Work-life balance programs reduce stress and increase job satisfaction and productivity.* According to a telephone survey of more than a thousand U.S. workers, those whose managers supported the use of work-life programs were more satisfied with their jobs; more productive; better able to balance work, family, and personal lives; and less stressed. Some 79 percent of nonmanagerial employees and 88 percent of managers rated work-life benefits as important or very important in improving employee productivity (Intracorp, 1997).

Values—Empowering Leadership

Empowering leadership enhances performance. A survey and study of archival data found that companies were more successful when managers shared knowledge and power with workers and when workers assumed increased responsibility and discretion. Equipment in steel mills operated with fewer interruptions, turnaround and labor costs were cut in apparel factories, and inventories of components and medical equipment were reduced. Jobs in participatory work systems often provided more challenging tasks and creative opportunities, had less involuntary overtime and conflict among co-workers, and had greater employee satisfaction (Appelbaum et al., 2000).[29]

Values—Respect and Integrity

Supportive cultures improve productivity and satisfaction and reduce burnout. A study found that supportiveness in the workplace and job quality are the most powerful predictors of productivity (including job satisfaction, employee commitment, and retention). Job and workplace characteristics are more important predictors of productivity than pay and benefits. Workplace support explained 37 percent of the variability in employees' job satisfaction (earnings and access to benefits explained only 2 percent, and job demands 3 percent), 24 percent of the variability in loyalty to employers, and 19 percent of the variability in burnout. The study suggests "a chain of effects in which excessive job demands lead to job burnout and job spillover from home to work which diminishes job performance." In contrast, the presence of support and better job quality reverses the trend (Bond, Galinsky, & Swanberg, 1998).[30]

Values—Diversity and Individuality

Organizations that actively value diversity have productivity enhancements as a result of accessing gender-specific skills. A study of female engineers identified four sets of relational skills that, according to the researchers, "are largely female," generally unrecognized and devalued, but important to individual and group performance (Fletcher, 2001):[31]

- Shouldering responsibility for the whole in order to preserve the life and well-being of the project by resolving conflict, anticipating and preventing problems, and placing project needs ahead of individual career concerns
- Expanding the definition of desirable outcomes to include increasing the knowledge or competence of others by teaching with awareness of the learner's needs and barriers, sharing information, facilitating connections, eliminating barriers, and giving help without making the receiver feel inadequate

- Using relational skills to enhance the ability to achieve goals by reflecting on personal behavior, and using feelings as a source of data to understand and anticipate reactions and consequences and strategize appropriate responses
- Creating background conditions in which group life can flourish by affirming individual uniqueness through listening, respecting, and responding; facilitating connections among individuals by reducing conflict; and creating structural practices that encourage interdependence

Values—Aligned Interests

Employee ownership enhances performance. Studies of employee stock ownership plans—a concrete way to align employee and organizational interests—suggest what aligning employee and organizational interests more broadly might achieve in enhancing productivity.

- *Employee stock ownership increases productivity.* An analysis of a large group of studies found productivity improvements averaging 4–5 percent in the year such a program is adopted—more than doubling the average annual increase in U.S. productivity for the preceding twenty years—and these levels are maintained in subsequent years (Kruse, 2002).[32]

- *Equitable rewards (employee ownership) lead to higher productivity.* A study of employee stock ownership plans found companies that adopted broad-based stock option plans tend to have higher productivity levels than other public companies. Holding constant total employment, capital intensity, and industry group, the study found, overall, companies with broad-based stock options had 27.7 percent more productivity than public companies as a group, 30.6 percent more productivity than their paired peers in 1997, and 29.4 percent higher productivity levels than all public companies during 1995 to 1997. Companies in which stock grants were shared broadly among nonmanagement employees reported 22 percent greater productivity than public companies as a group and 21.3 percent greater than their paired peers in 1997. Other corporations known to have broad-based stock option plans had 30.1 percent greater productivity than public companies as a group and 34.4 percent more than their paired peers in 1997. Companies that reported when their plans were adopted had 6.3 percent higher productivity levels than other public companies before adopting their stock ownership programs and 14 percent higher productivity levels after adoption (during 1995 to 1997; Blasi, Douglas, Sesil, Kroumova, & Carberry, 2000).[33]

Employee Health

Paying attention to employees' health is critical in protecting the inventory of human capital. The physical health of employees is also of keen interest because the cost of health-related benefits rises when employee health declines and because health has a negative effect on employee performance. Health insurance, wellness programs (smoking cessation, weight control), and the physical requirements and safety aspects of jobs all have an obvious effect on employee health and physical well-being; the adaptive strategies do as well. They give employees a greater sense of control and resolve major sources of chronic stress: conflicting responsibilities and an imbalance between demands and resources.

Stress is not a static thing; it is experienced differently by different individuals, depending on how each interprets external events. Further, while moderate amounts of stress can enhance performance in the short run, excessive or chronic stress can damage performance and even create physiological changes. There is a substantial body of knowledge about the multiple health and performance problems that result from chronic stress and the controllable job factors that contribute to it.

Stress creates physiological effects that affect health costs and performance. The effects can be severe and long-lasting if the stress is chronic or intense.

- *Chronic stress impairs the immune system and memory.* When the underlying physiological source of the stress response is activated too often or too intensely the immune system's ability to function is impaired, increasing the probability and severity of ill health. The results include impaired memory function and increased receptivity to disease. In a controlled experiment that exposed volunteers to a virus, interpersonal and work-related stressors were found to be more responsible for negative health results than smoking, diet, and lack of exercise (Cohen, Frank, Doyle, Skoner, Rabin, & Gwaltney, 1998; Herbert & Cohen, 1993; McEwen, 2002; and Sapolsky, 1994, all cited in Halpern, 2003).

- *Stress can inhibit learning.* Stress can inhibit learning because it encourages routine rather than creative responses. Job-induced passivity—from low-control jobs—can create learned helplessness. Various researchers have found that workers in repetitive jobs show a decline in intelligence over time, which does not occur with workers in intellectually demanding jobs. Older studies found, based on a longitudinal analysis, that intellectually simplistic jobs are associated with decreasing flexibility (Karasek & Theorell, 1990).

- *High demands coupled with low control and low support lead to poor health.* A Harvard study found that "a combination of high psychological demands with low control at work leads to mental and physical illnesses." Job strain not only predicted poor health, it also accelerated a decline in health over time as great as that from smoking. Solutions like relaxation therapy were considered ineffective because they dealt with symptoms, not causes (Cheng, Kawachi, Coakley, Schwartz, & Colditz, 2000).[34] Similarly, a study of male patrol officers found that diastolic and arterial pressure were significantly higher when the patrol officers had little control over their work (Bishop et al., 2003, cited in Halpern, 2003).

- *Low-control and nonengaging jobs increase mortality rates.* An analysis of twenty-five years of labor market information on twenty-five thousand workers found that people who spent the majority of their working life in low-control jobs (such as clerical and assembly workers) were at a 50 percent increased risk of dying early compared to those who worked in high-control jobs (such as lawyers and high-level managers). Those in passive, unengaging jobs had 35 percent higher risk. This difference persisted after controlling for other predictors of mortality such as income, health status, unemployment and other labor market experiences, and transitions such as retirement. Suggested solutions include giving workers increased control over their schedules and connecting them to what others are doing and to the end product of their work in order to reduce mortality rates (Ackerman, 2002). Likewise, a retrospective study of nonfatal myocardial infarction in men found high psychological job demands and low job control was a risk factor for manual workers—those with the least job control (Hallquist et al., 1998, cited in Amick & Mustard, 2003).

- *Job insecurity increases depression.* Job insecurity is related to increased levels of depression, anxiety, obsessive-compulsiveness, and anger-hostility, increased difficulties in interpersonal relationships; and complaints such as headaches, according to a study of manufacturing employees (Wichert, Nolan, & Burchell, 2000).

Stress is within the influence of organizations.

- *Stress, depression, and poor health result from a lack of control and job insecurity.* Demanding work is not the source of stress-related health risk; the real culprit is lack of control over how to meet job demands and how to use skills—the structure of the work (Karasek & Theorell, 1990). A body of research has found that the relationship between job demands and control is associated with "musculoskeletal disorders, diabetes, cancer, psychiatric illness, gastrointestinal illness, occupational and traffic accidents, suicides, total mortality, alcohol-related diseases, absence from work, use of medicine, sleeping problems, depression, reproductive problems, anxiety . . . and many more problems" (Halpern, 2003, citing Kristensen, 1996, p. 246).

- *Resource shortage and lack of control increase stress.* According to the stress literature, employed women are less depressed and report better physical health than women who are not employed. In the Framingham heart study (a large study of precipitating factors for cardiac-related illness), the only group of working women who had an increase in heart disease related to their employment were those who were in low-paid jobs that posed high demands and allowed little control, and who had several children at home and little support to help with the children (Barnett & Rivers, 1996, cited in Halpern, 2003). A change in the decision latitude (the power to make decisions) of a craftsman, nurse, foreman, or office supervisor is estimated to eliminate 23 percent of the risk for cardiovascular illness; greater social support could eliminate an additional 11 percent (Karasek & Theorell, 1990).

- *Adaptive cultures and practices reduce stress.* Adaptive cultures (with supervisor and company support for employees' work-life balance and benefits to assist employees in locating child care) increased employee commitment and reduced stress, according to a survey of fifteen hundred production workers at nineteen manufacturing plants (Appelbaum & Berg, 1997). And a survey of a thousand Canadian women working for a large food retail distributor or a health care company found that flexible schedules, part-time work, and job sharing reduced stress, improved morale, and increased employees' sense of competence at home, but only when employees also had a greater sense of control over their time or when the work overload was reduced (Kelloway & Gottlieb, 1998).

- *Streamlining work reduces stress.* A three-month pilot study at Marriott Corporation focused on identifying barriers to achieving both personal and business priorities. Managers were able to reduce low-value work by an average of 50 percent, substantially reducing the stress and burnout that increases turnover in these positions (Work/Family Directions, 2001).

- *Flexible scheduling reduces burnout.* Fifty-four percent of workers whose employers lack supportive work and family policies report burnout, compared to 27 percent of workers whose employers have them. This study of U.S. companies found that flexible scheduling of work hours reduced the number of workers reporting burnout from 39 percent to 28 percent (Northwestern National Life

Insurance Company, 1992). A study of emotional exhaustion among social welfare workers found that burnout affected job performance (as judged by managers) and was a strong predictor of turnover (Wright & Cropanzano, 1998).[35]

Work pressure has risen. Several studies illustrate how organizations affect employees' stress levels. In a telephone interview survey, 68 percent of workers reported they have to work very fast, 88 percent have to work very hard, and 60 percent do not have enough time to finish everything that needs to be done on the job—proportions that have risen substantially since 1977. About 25 percent frequently felt nervous or stressed, 26 percent felt emotionally drained by work, and 13 percent often had difficulty coping (Bond et al., 1998).[36]

Stress-related health costs are substantial. A study found that depressed employees' health care bills are 70 percent higher than those of other employees. Employees reporting high stress had 46 percent higher health care costs. Combined psychosocial problems—stress and depression—led to costs nearly 2.5 times higher than those incurred by workers who didn't report such problems (Goetzel et al., 1998).[37]

Attracting Employees

The increase in unemployment, from 4.4 percent in May 2001 (Ansberry, 2001a) to an estimated annual rate of 6 percent for 2003 (Schroeder, 2003), coupled with the post-2000 slowdown in the economy, has wiped the phrase "War for Talent" from the headlines of business journals and out of the minds of many managers. Yet a number of industries continued to struggle with the search for qualified workers throughout the recessionary period.

During 2001, 46 percent of employers experienced difficulty finding qualified workers, with 29 percent expecting the difficulty to continue despite the ongoing recession. Certain industries were feeling the pinch more than others: 71 percent of employers in finance, real estate, and insurance anticipated continuing problems, while those in retail had no trouble finding workers (Dixon, Storen, & Van Horn, 2002). The fields of nursing, elementary education, and information technology also had tight labor markets with the demand outpacing the supply of qualified workers in 2001 (Drizin, 2001). Even in the midst of a deep recession in manufacturing, 80 percent of companies in that area continued to experience a moderate to serious shortage of qualified job candidates. As of 2001, two thirds of manufacturers found a shortage of entry-level workers, operators, machinists and craft workers, and technicians and engineers, hindering their ability to meet production demands (National Association of Manufacturers & Center for Workforce Success, 2001). During 2002, with unemployment at 6 percent, there was little slack in the labor markets and highly skilled, highly productive workers were still in demand (Cooper & Madigan, 2003).

Given these facts, high-performing companies must continually improve recruiting practices to attract high-caliber people, particularly when the economy rebounds.

How Specific Adaptive Practices and Cultures Attract Employees

Selective Recruiting

Selective recruiting is integral to effective talent management. A number of companies are renowned for their recruiting practices and attribute much of their success to them. Southwest Airlines recruits people based on fit with organizational culture (Brannick, 2001) and attributes the company's success to employee performance. Leo Burnett, an advertising agency, has productivity 15–20 percent above its competition as a result of careful selection and extensive training of new hires (Reichheld, 1996). Highly selective recruiting practices, such as those used at Lincoln Electric (Pfeffer, 1994), include employee selection criteria, performance requirements, skill levels, values, and personal standards of integrity, responsibility, and commitment.

In *Good to Great* (2001), Jim Collins talks about the importance of getting the right people on the bus and in the right seats. But the right people for one company's bus may be the wrong people for another company's — as he and Jerry Porras describe in *Built to Last* (1994). Using examples from HP, Nordstrom, Wal-Mart, and others, Collins and Porras talk about the importance of fit to organizational performance. Numerous factors affect fit and combine to make the right choice for a "Nordie" very different from the right choice for Philip Morris. Yet both organizations have been extremely successful as a result of having the right people.

Fit enhances job satisfaction. Employees' perceptions of their fit with their job and their fit with the organization each contributed significantly and separately to employee job satisfaction, according to a survey of 104

office personnel and 127 truck drivers employed by a large national trucking company and examination of their employment records (Lawler,
Mohrman, & Benson, 2001). Determining how good the fit is between a
prospective employee and the organization is not an easy task. It requires a
thorough investigation by both, and each must also clearly understand who
they are and what they need. Decisions about fit are too often determined
by superficial assessments that don't address the important factors that
ensure a good fit.

Selectivity applies to employees as well as employers. The Hay Group's
fifteenth annual compensation study found employees are actively seeking
organizations whose values fit with their own (M. Thompson, 2000).

Ethics, leadership, and reputation enhance recruitment (for women). A
series of interviews with 350 female executives from Canada's major cities
identified priorities in selecting an employer. Ethics of the organization
received a 9.2 rating on a scale of 10, followed by organizational leadership
(8.7), how well the organization is respected (8.6), and the extent to which
the organization offers high-quality products and services (8.6) and enables
employees to have balance between work and life (8.5). Compensation was
rated 7.8 (Marzolini, 2001).

Reputation enhances recruitment. In a study of the banking industry, the
meaning that prospective applicants associated with the organization—traits
that applicants inferred about it—accounted more for the variance in how
attractive the organization was than did job and organizational attributes
(Lievens & Highhouse, 2003).

Reputation for social responsibility enhances recruitment. For some individuals, a potential employer's commitment to social causes is an important
consideration. In 2000, 76 percent of adults surveyed indicated a company's
commitment to social causes influenced their decision about where to work
(Cone/Roper, 2001). In 2002, the number was 77 percent (Cone, 2002).[38]

The inclination to give socially desirable answers may play a part in the
strength of these responses, but even after discounting for that, the percent-
ages are still high. Therefore, organizations where commitment to social
causes is an integral part of the culture should seek out prospective employees who share social concerns.

Wholeness and Integration of Public and Private Spheres

The prospective effect on personal life is the second most important consideration when selecting a job (Galinsky, Bond, & Friedman, 1993a).

However, although most workers want work-life balance, they don't get it (Buxton, Hessler, & Schaffer, 1999). Being on one of the "100 Best Organizations to Work For" lists increases the number of applicants a company receives and improves its potential for recruiting success ("Formula for Retention," 1999).

- *U.S. workers.* In a study of working adults, 97 percent said balancing work and family was important; to 88 percent it was very or extremely important. Nearly all (95 percent) were concerned about spending more time with their immediate family; 92 percent wanted more flexibility in their work schedule to handle family needs (Heldrich Center for Workforce Development, 1999).[39]

- *Men.* In a study of two-career couples, over 50 percent of men said having a manager who is supportive of employees' work-life balance is an extremely important quality in a new employer. Two thirds of men wanted the option to customize their career paths, slow their advancement when family responsibilities are more pressing, and cut back on the fast track without harming their future chances of getting key assignments (Catalyst, 1997b).

- *Men and women.* A study of working men and women identified balancing work and family demands as the primary career concern, more than (in descending order) a competitive salary, job security, keeping skills current, and having an advanced degree or certification (OfficeTeam, 1999).[40]

- *Knowledge workers.* SAS, a software firm whose employee-friendly work environment (with sane work hours and many supports) was featured on *60 Minutes* in October 2002, had fifteen thousand job applicants in the month following the airing of the show (see Chapter 15).

- *Law school graduates.* Work-life conflict is a problem for 71 percent of male and female law school graduates with children, and for 62 percent of female law graduates and 56 percent of male law graduates without children, according to a study of fourteen hundred graduates from five top law schools (William Olsten Center for Workforce Strategies, 1999).

Current economic conditions are causing many employees to forgo attending to work-life balance issues in the short run. Nonetheless, these concerns remain a priority for employees.

- *College graduates.* The majority (57 percent) of college graduates in a 1999 survey said balancing work and personal life was their most important goal (PriceWaterhouseCoopers, 1999).[41] In 2000, 58 percent identified balance as their most important goal, and 52 percent still did so in 2001, despite the economic downturn (Shellenbarger, 2001a). They did not expect this goal to hinder their long-term career prospects.

Time and Organization of Work

Many employees are attracted to organizations where they can control when and where they work and have a manageable workload.

Flexible scheduling enhances recruitment. Flexible scheduling is the third most effective method of attracting workers—after paying above the market and offering training and development opportunities (Watson Wyatt, 1999a).

- *General population and remote work.* In a study of teleworkers, 53 percent said the ability to work from home was critical in considering a new job (Pratt, 1999).[42]

- *Technology workers.* In a survey, 55 percent of IT staff and 44 percent of managers said flexibility is important in a job, second only to job challenge (Koprowski, 2000).[43] Flexible practices have long been a staple of the high-tech industry. A survey of twelve high-tech companies (3Com, Adaptec, Adobe, Apple, Bay Networks, Dell Computer, Hewlett-Packard, IBM, Microsoft, Octel, Oracle, Tandem Computer) found that all offered flextime (Sweeney, 1997).

- *U.S. companies.* In a study of eight hundred U.S. organizations, 76 percent said flexible scheduling was important to recruiting; 47 percent said child care assistance was also important (William M. Mercer, 1996). A third (32 percent) of North American companies with flexible work options use them as a recruitment incentive, according to a study of executives (William Olsten Center for Workforce Strategies, 1999).[44]

The issue of overwork is also becoming increasingly important in job selection. The number of employees wanting to work fewer hours increased from 47 percent in 1992 to 64 percent in 1997, according to the National Study of the Changing Workforce (Bond et al., 1998; Dunham, 2001).

Resources and Tools—Dependent Care Benefits

Employees are attracted to supportive organizations; redesigning and updating benefits enhances the ability to attract all types of employees. As noted earlier, more research has been conducted on child care than on elder care and other family care benefits. But it is clear from the research that child care assistance enhances recruitment.

- The perceived value to employees of a work-site child care center was the equivalent of paying a higher wage across the company, to employees without children as well as to those who used the facility directly, according to a contingent valuation analysis of three manufacturing firms (Connelly, DeGraff, & Willis, 2002).[45]

- A study of thirty-nine companies with on-site or off-site child care centers found users of both 30 percent more likely to recommend their employer to other potential employees. It also found 30 percent of on-site center users and 20 percent of off-site users more likely to say the center influenced their decision to join the firm (Dawson et al., 1984).

- An on-site child care facility at Neuville Industries helped recruit employees in a particularly tight labor market. With local unemployment at 1.5 percent, 95 percent of new recruits surveyed in a study said they applied because of the facility (Burud et al., 1984).

- In a post-hiring survey, 27 percent of new job applicants at Union Bank reported that the on-site child care center was an important factor in their decision to apply at the bank. Of these, 61 percent did not yet have children (Ransom et al., 1989).

Retaining Employees

Retaining the right employees reduces costs, increases productivity, and is the single most important factor in keeping customers loyal, according to loyalty experts. Longer-tenured employees know the organization's products and services better than newcomers, and they know how to get things done in the organization. They also know the customers—what they want and need, and how they prefer to be handled—so they can serve customers more efficiently (at a lower cost), with fewer mistakes and less wasted effort. They are better judges of which new customers and which new employees are a good match for the organization; in addition, they tend to believe in the company and so they generate more and better employee and customer referrals (Reichheld, 1996).

While not all turnover is bad, there is no way to guarantee that the workers who leave are the ones the organization can afford to lose: the most marketable employees have the most alternatives. It is important, especially in down economies, to fully maximize an organization's resources—leveraging every element to ensure that talent remains within the organization and fully engaged (Kaye & Jordan-Evans, 2002). This is one of management's biggest challenges; Walker Information's 1999 and 2001 employee forecast surveys say only about 24 percent of employees are truly loyal (want to stay), while two thirds plan to stay for the next two years because they feel trapped—making them unlikely to go the extra mile (Drizin, 2001). Retaining loyal, engaged, and productive employees requires talent management; involving employees in decisions about how, when, and where their work gets done; and ensuring employees have the right tools and resources to be effective on the job. It should come as no surprise that adaptive practices encouraging retention also increase employee commitment.

Understanding Retention

A consistent pattern in the studies on retention over the past fifteen years shows retention is primarily a result of employees' job satisfaction and the support they receive in the workplace.

- *Job satisfaction, being cared about, and having the appropriate tools lead to retention.* A meta-analysis of fifteen studies, ranging across many industries, found employees least likely to leave had overall job satisfaction, someone—a supervisor or co-worker—who cared about them as a person, and the right materials and tools to do the job correctly (Buckingham & Coffman, 1999a).[46]
- *Support and job quality lead to job satisfaction and retention.* A national study of conditions that increase commitment, performance, and retention found that the following factors explained variations in retention (Bond et al., 1998).
  - Workplace support (flexibility, culture, respect, and so on) explained 10 percent of the variability in retention.
  - Job quality (autonomy, meaningfulness of work, opportunities for advancement) explained 16 percent.
  - Job demands (hours worked, nights away from home, job pressures) explained 2 percent.
  - Earnings and access to benefits (assuming wages are competitive and employees are treated fairly) explained only 4 percent.
- *Job content, career growth, relationships, and fair pay enhance retention.* Exciting work and challenge are the top drivers of retention,

cited by 52.9 percent of respondents in November 2000, when unemployment was 4 percent, and by 49.7 percent in January 2002, when unemployment was 5.7 percent. The other most frequently mentioned retention drivers are career growth, learning and development, working with great people and having good relationships on the job, and fair pay. These factors vary in importance depending on age, gender, industry, and job function. Having exciting work and challenges became more important after age thirty, and having meaningful work and making a difference steadily increased after age forty, illustrating the importance of understanding employees' changing needs (Kaye & Jordan-Evans, 2002).[47]

Adaptive Cultures and Practices and Retention

The research indicates that adaptive cultures and adaptive practices have a strong effect on employee satisfaction, which in turn affects employee retention. The evidence about the effect of each of these practices—those regarding cultures, talent management, the organization of work, resources and tools—is discussed below.

Adaptive Cultures Increase Retention

Culture affects how well managers and employees accept adaptive practices directed at retention. Examples of retention effects of cultures with adaptive values follow.

- *Wholeness.* At Deloitte & Touche the organizational culture and leadership of senior executives played a critical role in the success of efforts to reduce turnover, particularly of women. The firm's leaders established a high-level, visible effort to create a culture that was congruent with adaptive principles and practices. The firm was able to significantly reduce the turnover gap between men and women and reduce overall turnover for both men and women (Deloitte & Touche, personal communication with Kate Davey, 2000).

- *Flexibility and respect.* American Management Systems had a turnover rate of 16.5 percent in 1996, according to a study of company executives, compared to 25–30 percent for the high-tech industry, due primarily to a company culture that stressed flexibility and respect for employees' personal lives (Shellenbarger, 1997).

- *Aligned interests.* According to a report, Cargil is one of the hundred companies identified as best-practice (high-value) financial workplaces that "strike a balance between meeting employees' personal and professional goals and fulfilling the finance mission." Cargil has 90 percent retention among salaried finance personnel (Harris & Nyberg, 2001).

- *Flexibility.* A study of employed women before and after childbirth found those in highly accommodating workplaces were more satisfied with their jobs (73 percent versus 41 percent), worked longer into their pregnancy (98 percent versus 84 percent), and were more likely to return to the same workplace after the birth (78 percent versus 52 percent) than women working in unaccommodating workplaces (Bond, 1992).[48]

- *Empowering leadership.* Federal Express's ability to maintain a turnover rate of 3 percent is attributed to its chairman's focus on workers ("Our People, Our Assets," 1999), as is low turnover at Rosenbluth Travel. Support from supervisors and co-workers plays an instrumental part in reducing turnover of workers taking maternity leave, according to a study of pregnant women in the Midwest (Glass & Riley, 1998).[49]

- *Trust.* A study of professionals found a trusting relationship with a manager to be a key factor affecting the decision to remain. Managers who respect and trust employees' competency and pay attention to their aspirations, quality of work life, and sense of career advancement increase retention (Farren, 1999).[50]

- *Challenging work.* More than a fifth (22 percent) of women who left a job to create entrepreneurial businesses did so because of being unchallenged. When a study asked what they would do differently than the company they left, 58 percent said they would respect employees and 11 percent said they would have a more inclusive management style (Catalyst, 1998).

Talent Management Practices Affect Retention

Adaptive practices such as selective recruiting, pay for performance, and career development practices enhance the retention of key employees.

- *Pay and communication improve retention.* An analysis of employee turnover at Ryder found that HR practices such as competitive pay, performance-based compensation, communication, and advancement opportunity increased employee satisfaction, which in turn reduced turnover. Furthermore, low turnover is significantly correlated with lower workers' compensation claims, higher return on controllable assets, and higher net profit before taxes (Ulrich, Halbrook, Meder, Stuchlik, & Thorpe, 1991).[51]

- *Training and development can increase retention.* There is conflicting evidence about whether employee training and development aids retention. The human capital studies of Watson Wyatt find some support for concern that investments in training will result in employees' leaving to enrich some other organization. Training was linked to a lower shareholder value—companies providing training were worth 5.6 percent less in shareholder value—possibly because companies often fail to provide career development congruent with the training, so employees have little opportunity to deploy new skills unless they leave the company. Providing the right training at the right time and circumstances does increase retention—the shareholder value effect decreases to 3.4 percent for companies providing training during economic downturns. And companies cannot ignore training: in the Strategic Rewards 2001 survey, top-performing employees cite development opportunities as one of the most important factors in accepting a job (Pfau & Kay, 2002).

- *Specific experiences.* The following reports illustrate the impact on retention. Wegman's Grocery chain offered a six- to nine-month training program to twenty full-time employees and attributes the group's low turnover rate of 9 percent, compared to an industry average of 16.7 percent, to this program (Levering & Moskowitz, 2000). Similarly, First Data maintains a 90 percent retention rate as a result of workplace development based on an annual talent audit to identify and track the strengths of employees (Harris & Nyberg, 2001). Marriott provides training (job and life skills, work habits) to welfare recipients, guaranteeing a job to those who complete the training. After one year, 70 percent of graduates from the program were still with Marriott, compared to 45 percent of welfare recipients who did not participate in the training and 50 percent of other new hires. To Marriott, employee stability translates to a higher quality of service for guests (Kanter, 1999). At Chick-Fil-A, turnover rates among store managers are one tenth the industry average. Managers are carefully selected, paid 50 percent more than competitors' managers, given a share in profits, and not rotated among stores so employee and customer relationships are maintained. Employee turnover is lower than at other chains—120 percent compared to 200–300 percent per year, because of the managers hired and their vested interest in keeping employees for the long term (Reichheld, 1996).

Time Practices Affect Retention

Customized work schedules and career paths, reasonable workload, time off, and minimal use of time as a metric for gauging performance are all important retention strategies. By considering the effects of overwork on human assets, allowing employees to control their work schedules, and recognizing time as a shared resource, they communicate and reinforce the values of respect, trust, and aligned interests. Studies have considered the effect of time-related practices on retention of employees at different levels.

- *Financial service workers.* USAA, a diversified financial services company in San Antonio, found their turnover rate decreased by half—from 30 percent to 15 percent—within the first year of instituting a compressed workweek; the rate fell to 6–7 percent thereafter (J. S. Arthur, 1998). Through part-time positions and job sharing, Cigna retained five hundred managers and professionals (1.25 percent of its total workforce of forty thousand employees) who, according to an internal analysis, would have left the company without these practices (Wilburn, 1998).

- *Men and women.* A study of three thousand employees at Hoechst Celanese revealed 60 percent of employees regarded the ability to balance work and personal life as being of great importance in their decision to stay. Those aware of the work-family programs were 39 percent more likely to stay. Flexible hours were rated the most valuable factor (Minnesota Center for Corporate Responsibility, 1997).

- *Manufacturing workers.* Guardian Industries was able to reduce turnover at its eight-hundred-employee automotive-glass plant by 50 percent after implementation of fixed, twelve-hour day and night shifts at worker suggestion (Shellenbarger, 1997). Flexible work practices at Corning, including increased part-time work and job-sharing options, reduced employee turnover by 50 percent, according to an internal analysis, cutting attrition costs by $2 million annually (Miller, 1998).

- *Midlevel and senior women.* In a longitudinal study of managerial-level women, 81 percent said they would have left their employer or stayed only a short time without some form of flexible work arrangements, including part-time work. Many changed specific arrangements over time, but all credited the availability of part-time work schedules with their ability to remain. More than half earned promotions while working part-time (Catalyst, 2000a).[52]

- *Managers and professionals.* In a study by the Massachusetts Bar Association, 90 percent of lawyers working reduced hours reported their firm's willingness to permit the arrangement affected their decision to stay (Catalyst, 2000b). In a two-year study of part-time work arrangements of managers and professionals at two corporations and two professional service firms, 98 percent of part-time professionals agreed that flexible work schedules increase retention (Catalyst, 1997a).

- *Workload and culture enhance manager retention.* A Marriott program to increase manager retention by supporting work-life balance found that productivity, customer service, and financial performance stayed the same or improved, while managers experienced less job stress and burnout. Managers worked five fewer hours a week and cut time spent on low-value work in half because the program changed the culture, emphasizing tasks accomplished over hours worked and making it comfortable for managers to leave earlier. The number of managers who felt their jobs were so demanding they couldn't adequately take care of personal and family responsibilities decreased by half, from 77 percent to 36 percent. The number who felt the emphasis was on hours worked and not on work accomplished dropped from 43 percent to 15 percent (Munck, 2001).[53]

- *Work hours influence the advancement and retention of women and men.* A study reports that commitment to personal responsibilities was a significant barrier to women's advancement in the legal profession, particularly in environments that stress number of hours worked and continuous time in the job. Three fourths (75 percent) of women in law firms, and more than half (58 percent) of men, cite commitment to family and personal life as a barrier to women's advancement; 69 percent of women at law firms (and 65 percent of women in-house counsels) cite controlling work hours as a priority for managing work-life conflict, followed by telecommuting (55 percent; 71 percent for in-house counsel women). Only 9 percent of women in corporate legal departments and 22 percent of women in law firms believe they can use flexible work arrangements without affecting their advancement (Catalyst, 2000b).[54]

Organization-of-Work Practices Affect Retention

Adaptive practices related to flexible arrangements have a strong positive effect on retention.

- *Large firms.* In a study of Amway, Bristol-Myers Squibb, Honeywell, Kraft Foods, Lucent Technologies, and Motorola, 76 percent of managers and 80 percent of employees indicated that telecommuting and flexible work schedules improved retention (Pruchno et al., 2000).[55]

- *Top performers.* In a survey of five hundred employees designated as top performers by their organizations, 42 percent said "not enough flexibility to handle personal responsibilities" was significant in their decision to resign. Interestingly, only half as many of their employers recognized flexibility as key to their decision. Other mismatches of perceptions: 69 percent of top-performing employees said job redesign was an effective recruitment and retention tool while only 18 percent of their employers agreed; 56 percent of top performers said flexible work schedules were an effective recruitment and retention tool while only 29 percent of their employers agreed (Watson Wyatt, 1999a).

- *Women.* A survey reports that women who work for companies with flexible work options are not only more satisfied with their jobs (73 percent versus 41 percent), they are also more likely to stay (72 percent versus 58 percent; Artemis Management Consultants, 2001).[56]

- *Knowledge workers.* At Ernst & Young, internal surveys report that 80 percent of client-serving women and 55 percent of client-serving men in the assurance and advisory business considered life balance issues very important to their decision to remain with the firm. E&Y created an Office of Retention that altered the work environment; 65 percent of people profiled in the flexible work arrangements database had considered leaving the firm before the firm offered flexible work arrangements. E&Y estimates that the efforts aided employee retention, which ultimately saved $14–17 million (Casner-Lotto, 2000).

- *Service workers.* Employees in a twenty-five-person loan underwriting unit at Fleet Financial Group redesigned their work in a pilot project intended to accommodate both work and personal responsibilities. Quarterly turnover rate dropped to 4.5 percent for the pilot group versus 6.9 percent for others, and productivity was not adversely affected. The unit, though small, contributes a net profit of $21 million after taxes per month. The average percentage of time doing real underwriting (the important work of the group) rose to 60 percent from 52 percent after ninety days of the pilot, managerial goals for turnaround time were maintained, and the unit met its goals in loan size and dollars. At a second site, a parallel experiment with flextime and telecommuting found average quarterly turnover was 3.9 percent for the reporting group versus 6.6 percent for the rest of the unit (Rayman, 1997; Casner-Lotto, 2000; Bailyn & Rayman, 1998).

Updated Benefits Affect Retention

Having the right materials and tools to do the job correctly (Buckingham & Coffman, 1999b) and access to the right benefits (Bond et al., 1998) are important elements of adaptive practices that are often overlooked. According to 78 percent of benefits professionals, benefits are offered to improve retention. Therefore, it is essential to provide benefits that employees require now (MetLife, 2001). An internal study at Chubb Insurance found 60 percent of employees were in dual-career families; 50 percent had child care or elder care responsibilities and another 20 percent anticipated having them within three years. One third of employees who left the company did so in order to improve their balance of work and personal responsibilities—costing the company an estimated $3 million in 1992 and 1993 combined (Graham, 1996). The president and CEO of Scitor credits that organization's approach to employees, rooted in "fairness and understanding the human heart"— which includes strong compensation, stock incentives, longer than average vacation time, family leave policies, work flexibility, child care benefits, and training—with helping maintain turnover at 2.1 percent over a five-year period (Meade, 1993).

The inability to arrange care for family has become a chief source of turnover. Since nearly half (45 percent) of employed people have children and all adults in the household are employed, it is not surprising that child care assistance reduces turnover of both men and women (Economic Policy Institute, 2002). Parental leave policies, especially when paid, reduce the amount of nonparental child care required and are a powerful retention tool. Child care costs directly affect the rate at which women leave the workforce and the rate at which they enter, according to a meta-analysis of multiple studies (Vandell & Wolfe, 2000).[57]

- *Unpaid parental leave enhances retention.* A study at Aetna Casualty and Life found that extending unpaid parental leave up to six months cut the rate of resignations of new mothers by 50 percent (A. Johnson, 1995).

- *Parental leave enhances retention and cuts costs.* In a pre-FMLA study, 94 percent of women in a high-technology company who took parental leave returned (Staines & Galinsky, 1992).[58] The cost of parental leave was found to be 32 percent of annual pay, on average (39 percent for management and 28 percent for nonmanagement), compared to the cost of an employee's leaving, which is 150 percent of an exempt employee's pay and 75 percent of an hourly employee's pay, on average (Marra & Lindner, 1992; Phillips, 1990).

- *Paid leave enhances retention of new mothers.* When new mothers had paid family leave instead of unpaid leave, their retention increased an estimated 11.5 percent (from 80.2 percent for those with an unpaid leave to 91.7 percent with paid leave), according to an analysis of Bureau of Labor Statistics data (Dube & Kaplan, 2002).

- *Child care subsidy enhances retention.* Bank of America cut turnover by 52 percent among employees in customer service centers, call centers, and branches—those in direct contact with customers—by giving a child care subsidy of $152 per week to employees earning below $30,000 per year. In 1998, 12 percent of the bank's employees (with nearly nineteen thousand children) used the benefit (personal communication, W. Moonie at Bank of America, 2000).

- *Work-site child care enhances retention.* Union Bank experienced 2.2 percent turnover among employees using its low-cost, high-quality, on-site child care center, compared to 9.5 percent among other parents and 18 percent at the bank overall (Ransom et al., 1989). In a study of five hundred employees using seventeen different work-site child care centers, 19 percent (26 percent of managers) had chosen not to pursue or had turned down other positions because of the child care benefit. For 93 percent of parents, work-site child care was an important factor when considering a job change (Ransom et al., 1989; Simmons Graduate School of Management, 1997).

- *Child care benefits enhance retention.* A study of companies' wide-ranging child care benefits (referrals and child care facilities—on- or off-site) found that, for 94 percent of the companies, turnover rates for users of child care benefits were lower than for all other employees. In 53 percent of the companies, users of child care benefits had no turnover (Dawson et al., 1984).[59]

- *On-site child care enhances retention among manufacturing workers.* Neuville Industries, the sock-finishing firm (see the "Productivity" section), had no turnover among employees using its on-site child care in its early years; turnover eventually rose to 5 percent. Overall company turnover ranged from 5 percent to 8 percent, significantly less than the industry average of 50–100 percent. As previously noted, the company credited its company-wide low turnover to the child care center, salaries 15 percent above market, and a work environment friendly to families (Burud et al., 1984).

- *On-site child care enhances retention and performance among knowledge and service workers.* In an internal analysis, one third of employees using a New York bank's low-cost, high-quality, on-site child care center declined other outside job opportunities specifically because of the center. Among employees at other sites who could not use the center, one in three had considered quitting, were distracted at work, or had turned down extra work because of child care problems; one in four were unable to participate in professional development, felt less committed to the job, or had trouble with attendance; and one in seven reported difficulty meeting performance expectations because of child care difficulties (Burud, 2000).

Hospitals rely on child care for retention. Hospitals have a long history of using child care benefits to retain specialized workers in short supply and demonstrate the power of these practices for retaining and attracting highly skilled workers with work and personal responsibilities. Research in this area may be transferable to other knowledge or service professions with tight labor markets, tough job demands, and limited rewards. Health care requires highly skilled professionals, but working conditions are less than idyllic (rotating shifts and evening, night, and weekend work), and pay is not commensurate with responsibility. A predominantly female profession with chronic labor shortages, nursing was the first to experiment with providing child care services for large numbers of employees. In 1982, 152 hospitals had on-site child care centers—three times the number in all other industries combined (Burud et al., 1984). Over the next decade, the number of such on-site centers rose to more than nine hundred, which speaks to their recruitment and retention capacity.* Child care services resolve a major barrier to working—trouble finding or paying for child care—and they communicate respect, often in short supply. Several studies illustrate how child care enhances retention of hospital workers.

- At a western teaching hospital 58 percent of employees using its on-site child care center reported they would have left the hospital if the center had not been available. Thirty-one percent of employees with children in the center worked in hard-to-recruit positions (RNs, technologists, and computer professionals). The turnover rate among employees using the center was 0 in 1999 compared to 28 percent hospital-wide. Turnover savings were estimated to exceed $970,000 each year among center participants alone (Burud & Associates, 2000).

---

* The quality of the centers and their cost to employees significantly affects the operators' power to recruit and retain workers, with better-quality and lower-cost facilities having significantly greater effect. As hospitals began to reduce their financial support to child care programs, and the programs then raised fees and cut services, they began to shrink in attractiveness and in their capacity to retain employees.

- A ten-year internal evaluation at St. Luke Rush Presbyterian Hospital in Chicago found that 85 percent of employees using the child care facility remained employed at the hospital at least as long as they had a child enrolled at the center. With a child enrolled for five years, and often followed by a sibling, employees were then past their first five years of employment, after which turnover drops. The tenure of these employees was quite long.

- Virginia Mason Hospital in Seattle has consistently had 10 percent turnover among employees who use the twenty-year-old on-site child care facility, compared with 18 percent hospital-wide and 24 percent in the health care industry.

It is common among businesses with on-site child care facilities (when they are high-quality, affordable, and sized to accommodate the majority of employees who need such care) to have a lower average turnover rate throughout the organization. There seems to be a cumulative effect—due to an employee-friendly management approach or because employees are retained through early years of employment when turnover is higher.

In Conclusion

The substantial body of research on the effects of adaptive practices and cultures on human capital performance reveals a broad range of effects on employees that occur in most every type of employment situation. Research suggests overwhelmingly positive effects on business objectives that are pivotal to success: employee creativity, commitment, productivity, health, recruitment, and retention.

When viewed as a whole, the research raises two questions. First, can these same business objectives be achieved across a range of employees *without* the adaptive practices? The research suggests not. Second, since much of the research measures effects separately (on retention, for example), what is the combined effect when adaptive practices are implemented systemically? Does one plus one equal two? Or is there an accruing effect— does it equal three or four? Because organizations are still in the working stages of adding adaptive practices and changing their cultures deeply, the full power to achieve results has yet to be measured, although the stories of SAS and First Tennessee National (FTN) in Chapters 15 and 16 may give some indication of the systemic effect on business results. From an organizational perspective, these particular employee outcomes are critical because they affect customers and overall organizational performance. In Chapter 11 we review the research studying the effects of adaptive practices and cultures on customer results.

11

CUSTOMER RESULTS

The employee is the face of the organization to its customers: the salesperson, the customer service representative, the travel agent, the engineering and design consultant, the shipping clerk, the flight attendant, the law associate. No matter what the business, customers experience the organization through the people they meet. This chapter is about these dynamics and their effects on customers.

Much is already known about the influence of employees on customers' experience of service. Employee loyalty drives customer loyalty and thus profitability—a process described by two models: the *service-profit chain* (Heskett, Sasser, & Schlesinger, 1997) and *loyalty-based management* (Reichheld, 1996). Both show how customer experiences and purchasing decisions are the result of service created by employees. Satisfied, long-term employees know individual customers better—what they need and want— and they also know the company's products or services, processes, tools and resources, and how to get things done. These employees are motivated to deliver excellent service. When also given the power to make decisions, they simply deliver better service.

According to the service-profit chain, satisfied and empowered employees are also less expensive, generating savings that can be passed on to customers, who are then more satisfied, more loyal, and more likely to bring in new customers, causing the company's revenues and profits to grow (Heskett et al., 1997). According to loyalty-based management, longer-term customers cost less to serve and so are more profitable over time. Longer-term employees are more efficient and themselves bring in more good customers and new employees who fit well. The organization can invest these savings in product enhancements or lower prices, further improving its market position and profitability (Reichheld, 1996).

Both models apply to *service industries*—communications, transportation, financial services, utilities, and health care. They also apply to other businesses that have service activities, including the management of inventory, information, projects, and people; product design, service, and repair; product engineering; accounting; R&D; marketing; and distribution. So they apply to most every business.

EMPLOYEE–CUSTOMER SERVICE CONNECTION

USAA, a San Antonio–based insurance and investment management firm, is an example of the service-profit chain and loyalty-based management. The company has a customer retention rate of 99 percent and an employee retention rate of 95 percent as a result of having made the connection between employees and customer service (Reichheld, 1996). Its motto is *"The mission and corporate culture of this company are, in one word, service."* USAA executes this mission by

- Investing heavily in technology to enrich jobs and make customer service easier for employees
- Training and educating employees so they are able to make decisions
- Designing jobs so employees can get close to customers and make decisions (Teal, 1991)
- Providing employment and compensation policies that encourage employees to stay (Reichheld, 1996)

In this chapter we present the evidence demonstrating the financial boost customer retention can provide, the relationship between customer loyalty and profits, how employee satisfaction affects customer results, and the effects of adaptive practices on employee and customer satisfaction.

Customer Retention

The financial impact of customer retention is easy to underestimate. Longer-term customers tend to be more efficient to serve and more profitable over time, thus increasing profitability exponentially.

- *Customer retention enhances profits and growth.* According to research conducted by Frederick Reichheld (1996) across a range of industries, increasing the rate at which customers are retained by 5 percentage points (from 70 percent to 75 percent, for example) creates an increase of 35–95 percent in the lifetime profits generated by a typical customer, depending on the industry. (The increase for an advertising agency was 95 percent, software 35 percent, auto service 81 percent, branch bank deposits 85 percent, industrial distribution 45 percent.) Retention also promotes growth. According to Reichheld's research, all other things being equal, an organization that retains 5 percent more customers each year will double in size in fourteen years; without the increase it would stay the same size. An increase of 10 percent retention accelerates the doubling to seven years.

- *Customer retention enhances shareholder value.* First Tennessee National has focused on customer retention as a strategy for increasing financial performance. The bank's customer retention in consumer and business markets was 95 percent beginning in 1995 and grew to 97 percent in 1998, 9 percent above the banking industry average. The return to shareholders during the same period was 35.8 percent—49.1 percent above the return of other S&P 400 mid-cap banks and nearly double S&P 400 mid-cap companies' return of 18.8 percent from January 1, 1994, through December 31, 1998 (see Chapter 16).

Customer Satisfaction and Loyalty

Customers themselves are under increased pressure to perform. In many industries, customers have more options—globalization and e-commerce have expanded existing markets and opened new ones, but they also have created more competitors. As a result, customers' expectations of suppliers—for speed, value, and service—also continue to rise. Customers are gaining control in many industries, dictating requirements to suppliers who once could deliver value according to their definitions (Seybold, Marshak, & Lewis, 2001).

Customer loyalty is the direct result of the customer experience, as demonstrated by two decades of research across industries by TARP, an organization that studies customer satisfaction. When customers experience problems, their loyalty (their intention to repurchase) is reduced by 15–30 percentage points, regardless of how satisfied they are with the solution. Surprisingly, 50 percent of consumers and 25 percent of business customers who have problems never complain to anyone at the company (J. Goodman, O'Brien, & Segal, 2000). Although 96 percent of customers with a small ticket problem do not complain to the manufacturer, 20–50 percent complain to someone in the distribution channel. Complaints make their way through the formal service system 10–60 percent of the time (J. Goodman et al., 2000), and only 1–5 percent of customers take their complaint any further (J. Goodman, 1999). When they have a bad experience, though, customers tell twice as many people about it as when they have a good experience.

Customers are substantially affected by how their complaints are handled. If a problem is resolved so smoothly that the customer goes from being "dissatisfied" to "completely satisfied," loyalty increases by 50 percentage points (J. Goodman et al., 2000). A study for the White House Office of Consumer Affairs found that 54–70 percent of customers who complain about a problem will do business again with that company if their complaint is resolved—and 95 percent will do so if the complaint is resolved quickly (Albrecht & Zemke, 1985).

Employees are obviously critical to the service process: they affect whether a problem happens in the first place, how well the customer is listened to, and how effectively the complaint is handled. Many organizations unknowingly jeopardize relationships with customers—reducing customer loyalty by not recognizing the role stable and satisfied employees play—while at the same time working hard to create loyalty. Rotating employees so customers are always dealing with someone new commonly damages customer retention (Fournier, Dobscha, & Mick, 1998).

Although customer satisfaction drives loyalty and hence profits, merely satisfying customers does not necessarily make them loyal or profitable. Understanding what creates customer satisfaction is important if organizations are to generate and sustain it (Coyles & Gokey, 2002). Studies conducted on customer satisfaction and profitability show that the satisfaction-loyalty-profitability relationship is based on three factors.

1. *Level of satisfaction.* Only totally or completely satisfied customers are loyal (Jones & Sasser, 1995).

   - Xerox found *totally satisfied* customers were six times more likely than satisfied customers to repurchase over an eighteen-month period.

   - Opinion Research Corporation found *completely satisfied* customers were 42 percent more likely than satisfied customers to be loyal.

2. *Profitability of the customer.* "Simply put, not all loyal customers are profitable, and not all profitable customers are loyal" (Reinartz & Kumar, 2002). Segmenting customers by their profitability enables an organization to differentiate its level of service by needs and estimates of return. Having the "right customers," as Reichheld (1996) says, is as important as having the "right employees."

   - *Customer loyalty alone does not always create profitability.* Customers who are loyal in both attitude and behavior (are satisfied with and so recommend the company and buy regularly from it) tend to be more profitable than those loyal in behavior (buying) only. At a grocery retailer, customers who are loyal in both attitude and behavior generated 120 percent more profit than customers who are loyal in activity alone (made regular purchases for two years or more). For a company that provided corporate services, customers loyal in behavior and attitude generated 50 percent more profit, due to their word-of-mouth marketing (Reinartz & Kumar, 2002).

3. *The delivery of superior value.* Customers must actually receive superior value. The Internet enables customers to make comparisons among consumer goods and many durable goods at the click of a mouse. Consequently, the personal touch that only humans can deliver often determines customers' perceptions of superior value.

Employees are the key to all three elements of the satisfaction-loyalty-profitability relationship. They are key to creating highly satisfied customers, because they understand how a company's offerings fit particular customers' needs, know how to customize the service to suit them, and then know whether they are satisfied (Zeithaml, Rust, & Lemon, 2001). Employees hold the relationship with customers, so they are key to creating the attitudinal loyalty in customers that increases profitability and to evaluating future purchasing potential of customers that determines how much to invest in them (Reinartz & Kumar, 2002). They are key to delivering superior value because they are the medium through which information about customers is gathered, service is delivered, and feedback is generated, and they are the only conduit through which nimble responses can occur.

Where Customer and Employee Satisfaction Connect

Employees are the point of contact with customers, delivering the service or product and observing customer reactions. They own the customer relationship—for better or worse. Employees' experiences with their own company are often communicated to customers and affect the customers' experience, as anyone who has flown during a time of contention between flight attendants and their airline can well attest. Employee satisfaction affects performance on the job. It affects whether employees believe in the company and what it does, whether they can sell (deliver) the company's products or services with genuine enthusiasm, whether they trust the company will deliver on promises—to them and customers. Given the smaller and smaller margins upon which customer satisfaction turns, these differences can make an enormous change in customer impression.

- *Employee satisfaction and responsibility enhance customer perceptions of quality.* A multinational computer corporation was the site of a yearlong study of the connection between employee and customer perceptions. The investigation found that when employees were given more responsibility and felt more satisfied in their jobs, the customers they served were more satisfied with the service. A pay-for-performance reward system had the strongest effect on employee attitudes (Tornow & Wiley, 1991).[1]

Employees' satisfaction with their employer and job also affects their decision to stay. Employees who leave take with them their knowledge of and relationship with the customers; their customers have to form new relationships with the new person. This loss of relationship capital often frustrates customers, reducing their satisfaction with the company, affecting their willingness to do business with the company and to recommend it to others. The breakdown in satisfaction and loyalty is particularly acute in the service industries, and it reduces profitability.

- At Taco Bell, the stores with the lowest employee turnover rates had 55 percent higher profits and twice the sales of the stores with the highest employee turnover rates (Heskett et al., 1997).

Some organizations have quantified the precise effect of changes in employee satisfaction on customer activity and firm profits.

- *Employee satisfaction enhances customer satisfaction, which enhances firm performance.* A now-famous study of customer service at Sears illustrates the link between employee satisfaction and customer satisfaction and how it affects performance. Sears's quantitative path from employee satisfaction to customer satisfaction to profits shows that increasing employee satisfaction by 5 points improves customer satisfaction by 1.3 points, and yields a growth in revenues of .5 percent. Two dimensions of employee satisfaction had the most effect on employee loyalty and behavior: attitude toward the job and attitude toward the company (Rucci, Kirn, & Quinn, 1998). Also, stores with high customer service scores had employee turnover rates of 54 percent; stores with low customer satisfaction scores had employee turnover rates averaging 83 percent and a much higher use of temporary workers (Ulrich et al., 1991).[2]

- *Employee satisfaction enhances customer relationships, which enhances firm performance.* In a study of how employee satisfaction affects customer and firm performance, a 1-point increase in employee satisfaction raised the score on quality and customer relationships by .4. This difference was a 10–15 percent improvement over the average score and raised the financial performance of the marketing communications firms studied by 42 percent. Employee (as well as manager) satisfaction was affected by high standards, coaching, empowerment, fair compensation, long-term orientation and commitment, enthusiasm, and respect (Maister, 2001).[3]

- *Work environment enhances customer satisfaction.* To test whether employees' work environment affects customer satisfaction and firm profitability, a study evaluated companies on *Working Mother*'s "100 Best Companies for Working Mothers" list using their standing on the American Customer Satisfaction Index, a national quarterly survey of consumer satisfaction with products and services in the United States. Companies on the *Working Mother* list had 1-point to 7-point higher customer satisfaction ratings than other companies (Simon, 2002).[4]

- *Work environment enhances service excellence.* A study of 134 bank branches found a significant link between working conditions and service excellence, as defined by customers. Branches paying close attention to customer needs and expectations were also most likely to implement human resource policies and practices that remove obstacles to work, ensure supervisor feedback and information sharing, and provide the appropriate quality of internal service to support customer service delivery (Schneider, White, & Paul, 1998).[5]

Customers want to deal with people who understand them. Interviews with a leader of a large accounting firm illustrate how this works. Jon Madonna, of KPMG Peat Marwick LLP, said,

> *Our clients want women on their teams. We learned this the hard way a number of years ago. Our all-male client service team met with its client's leaders, including the chairman of the client company. The meeting did not go well. In fact, the next day, the chairman called me to discuss the composition of our client service team. The problem wasn't whether our team could do the job but, rather, their perception that we didn't know who their ultimate customers were—almost all women.* (Hooks, 1996, p. 51)

Adaptive Organizations and Employee Satisfaction

Since employee satisfaction affects customer performance, it is important to understand what employee satisfaction is—what contributes to it and what compromises it. Employee satisfaction is not to be confused with employee happiness, an emotional state that employers feel ill-equipped to influence. The term *employee satisfaction* as used here is not about emotional states but about a match of expectations and reality and about employees' level of engagement in their work.

Employee satisfaction is affected by a variety of factors, including many of the adaptive practices and cultures we've described. According to research, being treated with respect and recognized as whole people, working in an egalitarian environment of trust and shared responsibility, having the power to organize their own work—all values of adaptive cultures—have a profound effect on employees' ability to derive satisfaction from their work and their work experience.

Adaptive Cultures and Practices Enhance Satisfaction

Time—Customized Work Schedules

Flexible work schedules give employees a greater sense of control and latitude in managing their personal as well as work responsibilities.

- *Flexibility enhances employee loyalty.* In a study of thirty-three hundred American workers, flexible time practices enhanced employee loyalty. Employees were also more loyal when supervisors were supportive and tolerant when family responsibilities interfered with work (Roehling, Roehling, & Moen, 2001).[6]

- *Flexibility enhances employee motivation and loyalty.* A study of individuals hired into flexible work arrangements over a two-year period found a positive effect on their motivation and loyalty. All the managers in the study said employees on flex schedules were at least as motivated, loyal, professional, productive (56 percent said they were more productive), reliable, focused, and able to meet deadlines as before, if not more so. Among the employees, 87 percent said that they were just as motivated or more motivated in their flexible jobs as they were in their traditional-schedule jobs, 84 percent said that they were as loyal or more loyal, and 90 percent said they were just as results-oriented, or more so (Flexible Resources, 1999).[7]

Organization of Work—Elastic and Rewarding Job Content and Design

People are more engaged when work is challenging, when it fits their skills and stretches them. Decades of research into the state that has come to be called *flow*, led by psychologist Mihaly Csikszentmihalyi (1990), has determined that under certain conditions people feel totally involved, "lost in a seemingly effortless performance . . . 100% alive, lose track of time" and of themselves. "Intense flow . . . happens surprisingly often at work—as long as the job provides clear goals, immediate feedback, and a level of challenges matching our skills. When these conditions are present, we have a chance to experience work as 'good'—that is, as something that allows the full expression of what is best in us, something we experience as rewarding and enjoyable" (Gardner, Csikszentmihalyi, & Damon, 2001, p. 5).

- *Meaningfulness of work affects employees' level of engagement.* A series of interviews and observations at an architect firm and a summer camp—quite different work environments—found the same factors affect employee engagement. Employees were more engaged when their work was challenging, varied, creative, clearly delineated, and somewhat autonomous; when their roles carried status; when they had rewarding interactions with co-workers; when they felt it was safe to be themselves; and when they had the physical, emotional, and psychological resources to engage in their work role (Kahn, 1990).

Organization of Work—Flexible Arrangements

The ability to exercise control over their work schedules raises employees' level of satisfaction.

- Chase Manhattan Bank branch employees who had flexible work arrangements (telecommuting and flexible schedules) rated their satisfaction with the company at 73 percent, compared to 58 percent for those who wanted such arrangements and didn't have them. Among employees who did not want flexible work arrangements, 76 percent were satisfied (Chase Manhattan, 1999).

- *Control over work enhances satisfaction.* A Harris Poll of working adults found only 46 percent say they have much control over their work. Of these, 60 percent are very satisfied with their jobs—compared to 25 percent of those who feel they do not have much control. Of the 51 percent who use their talents and skills a lot, 62 percent are very satisfied with their jobs, compared to 14 percent of those who use their skills less or not at all (Taylor, 2000).[8]

Adaptive Cultures

Adaptive cultures have consistently been shown to enhance employee satisfaction, which is one of the main drivers of customer results. The process works through the whole range of adaptive practices. For example:

- *Workplace support, fair advancement, and respect enhance employee satisfaction and loyalty.* A national study of employed U.S. adults found that cultures that provided workplace support (flexibility, supervisor support, supportive workplace culture, positive co-worker relations, equal opportunities for advancement, lack of discrimination, and respect) accounted for 37 percent of the variability in employees' job satisfaction and 24 percent of the variability in loyalty to employers (Bond et al., 1998).[9]

The following sections describe various findings regarding adaptive organizations and customer results.

Adaptive Organizations and Customer Results

Studies show that adaptive cultures and practices support employees' ability to service customers effectively.

Adaptive Cultures and Practices Enhance Customer Results

Contribution-Based Performance Criteria

Customer results are enhanced through appropriate resource practices.

- *Employee perceptions of management effectiveness are related to customer satisfaction.* A study of an insurance company's fifty thousand customers found customer satisfaction was higher when employees saw management as effective. Employees saw management as effective when they received annual performance appraisals, their performance was measured against goals, and they had opportunities to pursue job and career interests; when leaders frequently asked about customer quality, satisfaction, retention, and profitability; when feedback was gathered on customer satisfaction; and when the company responded to dissatisfied customers (Schneider, Ashworth, Higgs, & Carr, 1996).[10]

Selective Recruitment

Studies show that having the right employees interfacing with customers increases customer retention.

- *Selective recruiting practices reduce customer defect rates.* Selective recruiting practices at Ritz-Carlton hotels helped reduce the customer defect rate of 27 percent in 1992 to 1 percent in 2000. Changes in interviewing and hiring practices enabled the company to identify applicants with the most potential to create customer satisfaction and helped cut employee turnover from 75 percent to 25 percent (Kiger, 2002).

- *Selective recruiting enhances customer retention.* Selective recruiting (an element of Saturn from the beginning) was also a factor in Saturn's initial success, along with extensive employee training on the product, customer service, teamwork, and factory relations. Five years after it began production, Saturn was second in auto retail sales in America, had the highest customer retention rate in the auto industry, and had the highest sales per retailer of any automobile manufacturer (Burson-Marsteller Public Relations/Public Affairs,

2000). In addition, a study of employees and customers in twenty-eight bank branches found customers' overall experience of service quality improved with human resource management practices — how work is organized, amount of supervisor feedback, reward systems, career opportunities, and new employee orientation (Schneider & Bowen, 1992).

Human Capital–Oriented Professional Development

Developing employees' skills improves customer retention.

- *Aligning rewards and professional development enhances customer retention.* The Beck Group attributes the fact that more than 80 percent of customers are repeat business to satisfied employees whose bonuses are tied to customer satisfaction and who receive on average sixty-six hours of training per year (Levering & Moskowitz, 2000).[11]

- *Employee rewards, professional development, and efforts to measure customer service enhance customer satisfaction.* A study of more than five hundred employees and almost eight thousand customers at fifty-seven bank branches found customer satisfaction connected to three areas: when the branch gathered information on ways to improve customer service and trained employees and rewarded them for delivering good customer service, customers were more satisfied (J. W. Johnson, 1996).[12]

Work Redesign and Employee Involvement

Too often employees and customers are considered stakeholders with different agendas who require trade-offs at one another's expense. In reality, their needs converge more than they diverge; successful organizations manage them as interrelated.

- *Employee control over work enhances customer service.* To deliver quicker turnaround in the on-site customer support unit, HP needed to increase the number of service hours provided, often after hours. After experiencing an increase in turnover and overtime, employees devised individualized schedules among the team that allowed them all to meet their personal needs. As a result, overtime was reduced 36 percent while customer service hours were expanded (Verespej, 2000).

- *Work redesign improves customer service ratings.* A redesign of work among twelve hundred customer service representatives at Bank of America resulted in a 4.2 percent improvement in customer service ratings within one year and a 2 percent improvement in the percentage of problems resolved with one call. Employees were involved in the redesign, which eliminated unnecessary work and increased their decision-making authority. Within a year, employee turnover also dropped from 45 percent to 31 percent at one pilot site and from 32 percent to 30 percent at the other (Casner-Lotto, 2000).

- *Work redesign increases customer satisfaction and sales.* The American Express Establishment Services unit dramatically improved customer relations, achieved the highest satisfaction ratings in its industry, and acquired more than 350,000 new customers from a work redesign effort. The unit reorganized to eliminate inefficiencies and enable employees to focus on satisfying customers. Employee training and quality programs encouraged employee participation and reward programs reinforced participation (Burson-Marsteller Public Relations/Public Affairs, 2000).

- *Physical work environment, resources, and co-worker relations enhance customer satisfaction.* A study of almost 5,000 employees and 160,000 customers in two hundred retail store branches found customer satisfaction increased when employees were satisfied with their physical working conditions and when obstacles to doing their work were reduced. Relationships among employees and a customer orientation were also positively related to customer satisfaction (Wiley & Gantz-Wiley Research Consulting Group, 1991).[13]

In Conclusion

Stable customers generate increased earnings and growth. Customer loyalty is built with the attention of employees who served them well and delivered superior value. So, the question becomes, Under what conditions do employees serve customers best? The research shows employees satisfy customers more when they themselves are in an adaptive work environment—when they have a challenging job and responsibility; when their work allows them to draw meaning from it; when they are respected and supported and have flexibility; when they have control over their time, job, and schedule; when they can make their job more efficient; when they are fairly compensated in line with their performance; when they see their management as effective; when the employer is selective about people it hires and then invests in developing them; and when they have the resources conducive to high performance. Research shows these conditions create highly satisfied employees, who in turn produce highly satisfied and loyal customers and generate superior financial performance.

In Chapter 12 we review the effects of adaptive cultures and practices on organizational performance.

12

ORGANIZATIONAL PERFORMANCE RESULTS

It may seem obvious that adaptive human capital management practices would yield positive results on the employee side—that recognizing and valuing employees as individuals, responding to their needs, and empowering them would increase their motivation, commitment, and even performance. It may also be evident that stable employees who feel respected and valued and have the resources they require to be fully present on the job will treat customers better, and that customers will in turn be more satisfied and come back for more. What is less obvious is whether these practices, which require management to shift gears (sometimes dramatically) and invest resources, would necessarily improve overall financial performance. Doesn't their cost jeopardize profits? Don't they threaten the source of value creation at an organizational level—by loosening the tight reins, reducing the emphasis on control and the ability of supervisors to see people working—that presumably ensured high performance before? Is there a net gain or a net loss? In short, is it worth it from an organizational perspective—considering the time, attention, and dollars required—to adopt these strategies?

A number of research studies have considered the effects of adaptive strategies on an organization's profitability, ability to grow, and market value. Taken together, the evidence is overwhelmingly positive—and very powerful (see Figure 5). Organizations that value and invest in human capital in these ways grow profits and revenues more impressively, sustain that growth over longer periods, and generate substantially more value to shareholders. Adaptive strategies that enable companies to use the talents of a diverse workforce contribute to that growth and market value. They must be accompanied by an effective vision and well-executed business strategy, as well as by the right customer/market strategies, financial strategies, business process strategies, and organizational learning strategies (Kaplan & Norton, 1996).

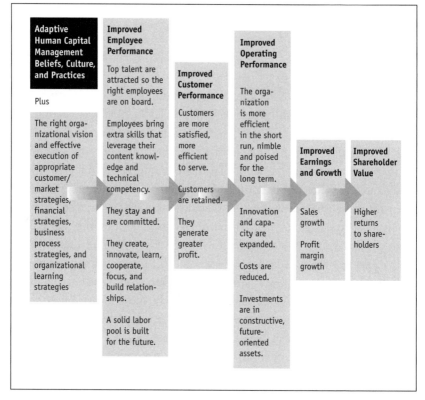

Figure 5 How Adaptive Beliefs, Culture, and Practices Build Results

Beyond this basic finding, a few clear themes emerge.

- *Context matters.* Human capital management practices that are consistent with organizational policies and business strategies produce better results than do those that are not, although positive results also occur from human capital practices alone.
- *Consistency matters.* Practices that have internal fit, that support other human capital management practices, produce much higher results than practices implemented in isolation or without regard to how well they fit with other human capital practices.
- *Culture matters.* Assumptions, beliefs, and values underlie management practices and can unfortunately undermine them as well. Failure to attend to the fit between practices and culture will reduce the positive effects of adaptive human capital management practices.

In this chapter we review this evidence. Before we present the research on overall effects on organizations, we consider whether adaptive human capital practices reduce costs.

Reducing Costs

One of the ways adaptive practices contribute to earnings and profitability (or to good financial performance for nonprofit organizations) is by reducing or eliminating certain expenditures. Adaptive human capital practices eliminate or reduce costs associated with absenteeism, turnover, stress-related illness, burnout, health, facilities, labor, and investments to attract new customers and retain old ones, as well as recruiting costs such as stock options, employment advertising, salary differentials, and hiring bonuses.

This section highlights some of the areas of direct savings to organizations resulting from human capital management practices. The studies described here are only a sample of the wealth of data that has been collected on these savings. They are intended not to be exhaustive but rather to give a sense of where cost savings occur.

Absenteeism

The cost of preventable absenteeism is high. A 1996 study conducted by the Merrill-Palmer Institute found that the annual cost of absenteeism due to child care problems among the companies it surveyed ranged from $66,000 to $3.5 million (U.S. Department of the Treasury, 1998).

- *Cost of child care–related absenteeism—$1.5 million/year.* A study of Chase Manhattan Bank's child care facility illustrates how much absenteeism happens when child care arrangements break down. The facility, which provides only short-term care for employees' children whose regular child care has fallen through (not when children are ill), was used for 6,900 employee days in the year studied. Virtually all (98 percent) of employees would have been absent otherwise, at a cost to the bank of $1,523,175 in a single year. The facility, which takes children from eight weeks to twelve years old, is subsidized by the bank at $720,000 per year. It netted a savings after expenses of $803,175 in one year (D. Friedman, 1998). Only employees who live or work within driving distance of the center use it, so these figures show only part of the bank's child care–related absenteeism.[1]

- *Cost of life challenge issues—$6 million.* According to Marriott International, a service to help employees find resources for pressing personal needs prevented a loss of $6 million by cutting absenteeism and retaining six hundred employees. Marriott's hourly workers (many are recent immigrants) face serious personal issues—domestic abuse, lawsuits, even homelessness—that reduced work time and threatened customer service. The problems took up to 50 percent of managers' time, as they were acting as makeshift social workers (Bollier, Pochop, & Meyer, 1997). Two thirds of the employees who used the service found it reduced time away from work; most found it improved productivity on the job and 64 percent were more inclined to stay because of help in resolving issues that would otherwise have caused them to leave (personal communication, K. Austin at Marriott International, 2000).[2]

Turnover Costs

Turnover can reduce earnings and stock prices, particularly in certain industries. In four high-turnover industries—call center services, high-tech, specialty retail, and fast food—earnings and stock price are reduced by an average of 38 percent because of turnover, according to a study by Princeton, New Jersey, consultants Sibson & Co. (Klaff, 2001).

- *Who leaves and why.* Employees experiencing conflict between their work and family responsibilities are three times as likely to consider quitting their jobs as those who are not (43 percent compared to 14 percent in one survey; A. Johnson, 1995).

- *The full cost.* The real cost of turnover amounts to 50–75 percent of a departing hourly employee's annual pay, and 150 percent of a salaried worker's pay. This figure includes the direct cost of finding, hiring, and training new workers and the indirect costs resulting from lost productivity and inefficiencies, which are 80–85 percent of the total cost (Phillips, 1990).* When someone leaves, productivity for everyone around—the departing employee, the replacement, and the people who work with or supervise the employee—is affected from the time the worker decides to leave until the replacement is fully up to speed. Thus, a company that loses five exempts and five hourly people (paid $60,000 and $25,000, respectively) annually is losing over $500,000 each year.

Even these figures may understate the real cost. First, they assume the replacement person is at 100 percent efficiency after 13.5 months. The more intense the knowledge or skill of the job, the longer it takes. New attorneys' billing rates and legal skills only equal their salaries, benefits, and allocated overhead after three to four years of employment; a law firm begins earning a return on a law associate between five and ten years of employment (Boston Bar Association, 1999). The turnover-cost formula also does not consider lost relational capital (the relationships held by the employee within and outside the organization) or the cost of errors, internal inefficiencies, lost ground in customer satisfaction, and lack of progress on continuous improvements while a new person is learning the ropes. It equates the economic contribution of an employee with compensation, ignoring the additional contribution the person makes to earnings.** For key employees (the ones who keep an important customer satisfied enough to stay or who generate substantial sales), this difference could be significant.

---

* Other researchers estimate it can range from as low as 50 percent of the salary of a low-cost employee to more than 200 percent of the annual salary of a high-level or difficult-to-find employee (Kepner-Tregoe, 1999).

** The cost of inefficiency is calculated by multiplying hours spent times compensation paid—to the employee, supervisors, and other affected workers.

- *The total impact.* The following firms' turnover experiences occurred after they adopted adaptive cultures and practices. (Formulas used to calculate savings were not provided by the firms.)

  - *Professionals.* Ernst & Young estimates saving $17 million in turnover-related costs during 1997 and 1998 with flexible work arrangements and a culture that made simultaneous work and personal success possible. It improved retention of employees, particularly women (65 percent of those who used flexible work arrangements had earlier considered leaving), and improved client satisfaction (Casner-Lotto, 2000).

  - *Manufacturing and technology workers.* Corning's internal analysis estimates that the company avoided a $2 million loss in turnover-related costs when employee turnover was cut in half. Corning had adopted family-friendly policies with increased part-time work and job-sharing opportunities (Miller, 1998).

  - *Service workers.* Aetna Life and Casualty's internal analysis estimates that the company saved $1 million a year by allowing part-time return after family leave. Attrition was cut by more than 50 percent over five years (A. Johnson, 1995).

  - *New mothers.* Fifty percent of women were leaving Kodak following their maternity leave—a statistic that Kodak reduced to 10 percent by modifying its maternity leave policy ("CIGNA designs flexible work plan . . . ," 1991).

Health Care Costs

Health insurance is the largest and fastest-growing element of labor costs, rising 10 percent in 2002 and expected to increase at double-digit rates through the foreseeable future (Cooper & Madigan, 2003). Health care costs are reduced by adaptive strategies, that is, when employees have sufficient resources to meet the demands they face and when they have a sense of control.

- *Depression and stress increase health care costs; adaptive cultures reduce stress.* A survey and analysis reveal that depressed employees' health care bills are 70 percent higher than those of other employees. Employees reporting high stress have 46 percent higher health care costs. Combined psychosocial problems—stress *and* depression—led to costs nearly 2.5 times those of workers who didn't report these problems (Goetzel et al., 1998). Organizations pay an additional 5–15 percent in wage costs for the lost productivity from stress and other suboptimal psychosocial work conditions. An estimated 16 percent of health care costs are preventable by reconstructing these aspects of jobs (Karasek & Theorell, 1990).[3]

- *Maternity-related medical costs.* The trend toward having children later in life is creating more complex medical issues and greater risks. Employer-provided prenatal programs that inform employees about risk factors and educate them about risk-reducing behaviors offset some of the higher costs, and a number of internal analysis projects illustrate the benefits. Maternity-related medical costs were $300 higher per birth at Haggar Clothing Company prior to an enhanced prenatal education program offered by the company. The company recovered $500,000 in 1992 (Cameron, 1993) and $200,000 in 1993 (Jacobson, Kolarek, & Newton, 1996), primarily from increasing employee participation in prenatal education, according to a company-prepared evaluation. E. A. Miller, a ConAgra beef packing plant, reduced maternity benefits from 30 percent to 10 percent of benefit costs through prenatal education and counseling programs. First Chicago NBD found costs of an average birth 31.5 percent higher among employees who did not participate in its prenatal education program — $9,986 for nonpartic-ipants and $7,593 per participant during the period 1989 through 1991. Participants had a lower frequency of cesarean-section births; C-section rates were 28 percent for nonparticipants in the program compared to 19 percent for participants. Champion International reduced the costs per maternity case of vaginal deliveries by 8.6 per-cent (and C-section deliveries by 4 percent), and reduced hospital-ization for both by 16.7 days from 1992 through 1994. C-sections dropped from 28.8 percent to 6 percent of births in two years as a result of increasing incentives to employees to participate in prena-tal education (Jacobson et al., 1996).

- *Health insurance claims and sick time.* The Los Angeles Department of Water and Power reduced health claims among new mothers by 35 percent and sick days taken to care for ill babies by 27 percent with a program that enabled mothers to continue nursing after they returned to work and provided equipment, space, and counseling on breastfeeding. An analysis found that the breastfed babies had signif-icantly fewer and less severe illnesses and their mothers were absent less than mothers of formula-fed babies (R. Cohen, Mrtek, & Mrtek, 1995).

- *Prescriptions.* CIGNA's program for breastfeeding mothers saved the company $240,000 annually in health care expenses, including what an internal analysis estimates as 62 percent fewer prescriptions (CIGNA Corporation, 2000).

Overhead

Enabling employees to telecommute or work remotely can reduce real estate–related facilities costs, according to the following evaluations.

- Ernst & Young used a policy of *encouraging* virtual work (work at home and elsewhere)—not simply *allowing* it—to eliminate one million of the seven million square feet it rents nationwide—offering employees a desk only if they were in the office more than half a day. By increasing the employee-to-desk ratio to five to one, E&Y expected to avoid $40 million in real estate costs (Pacelle, 1993).

- AT&T avoided $10 million in office space costs over five years (Minnesota Center for Corporate Responsibility, 1997), or $3,000 per teleworker, through telecommuting (Gemignani, 2000). The company also saved an estimated $80 million in 1994 by closing offices. Telecommuting employees and their managers also discovered that rather than having more distractions at home, they encountered more distractions that impeded productivity at the workplace—meetings, colleagues, and frequent interruptions, especially by telephone (Noble, 1995).

Labor Costs

Both research evidence and economic theory suggest that total labor costs required to achieve the same earnings result can be reduced in organizations that employ adaptive human capital strategies. This reduction occurs even though (in fact because) labor *rates*—salary, benefits, bonuses, and other employee costs—may be higher.

Economic theory—*efficiency wage theory*—suggests that paying above-market compensation can increase profits by attracting and keeping better workers and by motivating them to expend more effort on behalf of the employer. The theory holds that these workers are highly motivated because it would be hard to find similar opportunity and reward elsewhere.

The classic example is Henry Ford, who in 1913 doubled workers' pay from the going rate of $2.50 a day to $5 a day. His motivation was partly to counter extreme worker dissatisfaction (when he introduced scientific management and assembly-line production processes), but he also wanted to stem the 370 percent annual turnover rates among his primarily foreign-born, unskilled workforce and to increase profits. Ford, like many employers today, had no trouble attracting workers, but keeping them motivated and productive was another matter. With increased pay, turnover was reduced. The quit rate fell by 87 percent in a year; the discharge rate fell 90 percent, and absenteeism fell by 75 percent. Profits did in fact increase, although some analysts suggest they would have grown more if the wage increase had been a little less grand (Ehrenberg & Smith, 1994).

Studies of more current examples find a similar result.

- A study of auto workers found that when higher wages were paid to workers, disciplinary dismissal rates were lower (Cappelli & Chauvin, 1991).

- A study of the fast-food industry found that wages above the market rate had to be used in fast-food stores where other incentives were weak. A company paid wages 9 percent above locally owned stores to achieve the same level of performance (Ehrenberg & Smith, 1994).

Research evidence suggests that adaptive strategies can reduce labor costs *for the same output*, increasing profitability by boosting output per employee, as well as efficiency among groups and across the organization; by reducing waste (lost work time, poor concentration, mistakes, turnover, and so on); and by acting as powerful motivators for performance (see Chapters 10 and 11 for a description of how this happens). Some examples follow.

- Neuville Industries was able to run its production plant with fewer employees because productivity was higher among its workers, who were highly motivated to keep their jobs at this unusual company that offered on-site child care, higher wages, and a family atmosphere. Though the company spent more on employees, the employees produced more (Burud et al., 1984).

- First Tennessee National Corporation raised its ratio of employees to managers, reducing overhead costs by shifting greater responsibility and rewards to employees (see Chapter 16).

- Merck reduced overtime in the payroll division by 50 percent by expanding use of flexible work arrangements (Casner-Lotto, 2000).

- Bell Atlantic Corporation avoided a portion of disability leave expenses by permitting employees who would otherwise be on disability to telecommute (*Measuring Results*, 1992).

- A CPA firm that provided on-site child care during tax season increased the number of staff available and income generated (A. Johnson, 1995).[4]

Costs resulting from work slowdowns, strikes, and theft may also be reduced in organizations employing adaptive values and practices, since these problems happen more often when employees do not feel that they are respected or that their interests are aligned with those of the organization.

Stanford professor Jeffrey Pfeffer (1998a) advises organizations to distinguish carefully between labor costs and labor rates. He suggests the best yardstick is not what you are paying but what you are getting—What is the investment in labor generating for the firm? Cutting labor rates (or other investments in labor), he says, is one of the least effective ways of increasing profitability. It is the contribution to earnings and not the direct cost of labor that matters (see Chapter 15 for a description of how SAS has used this principle).

Taking a broader view, when dependent care benefits enable children to be in educational instead of custodial child care, it creates a longer-term effect on labor costs. In learning-oriented child care, these workers of the future develop higher IQs, better language and communication skills, and more sophisticated mental processing aptitudes, as well as traits like initiative, persistence, and responsibility. These skills and traits will continue with them for life and enhance their ability to be effective workers (Kotulak, 1996).

Additionally, child care benefits can reduce other social expenditures. The costs to society, which filter down to business through various assessments, are reduced when children have a better early childhood education.

- A quality preschool education brings greater success in school; increased earnings, employability, and home ownership; and lower remedial education and crime-related expenditures, at an ROI of $7.16 per dollar invested, according to a twenty-seven-year longitudinal study of three- and four-year-olds (Schweinhart, 2003).

- High-quality preschool beginning shortly after birth increased children's IQ levels and their math and reading achievement and doubled the likelihood they would attend college (Hawley & Gunner, 2000).

The savings associated with a better-educated future labor force can be enormous, considering that in 1995, 43 percent of businesses provided remedial education to workers—a dramatic increase from 11 percent in 1984 that will continue to climb (Committee for Economic Development, 1998). The trend, if unchecked, will also affect our ability to compete globally. U.S. firms now spend their training dollars on basic proficiency skills— literacy and numeracy (numerical skills)—rather than higher-level training as organizations in other developed countries do (Baker, 1999).

Quality

Many costs are associated with poor quality, including dissatisfied customers and injuries to reputation. Some costs are related directly to the issues that adaptive strategies address, as the following suggest.

- *Mistakes.* A 1992 study conducted by the St. Paul Companies found that staff who believed work was causing problems in their personal lives were much more likely (30 percent compared to 19 percent) to make mistakes than those who had few job-related personal problems (A. Johnson, 1995). Mistakes can be costly, as focus group data from a California utility demonstrate. An IT computer technician received a call at work, informing her that her mother had fallen in the nursing home where she was living. Company policy permitted two hours to be taken off during the day, but that was not enough time for the technician to reach her mother and return to work. That afternoon, distracted by worry, she accidentally erased a computer tape that was later needed for a court case. The company spent more than $2 million to reconstruct it (Burud & Associates, 1989).

- *Quality is related to employee attitude.* In a survey, NCR found the highest-quality plants had the highest employee ratings of job security, management, company performance, cooperation, goals and objectives, and other measures of employee attitude (Ulrich et al., 1991).[5]

Legal Costs

Organizations that practice adaptive strategies (not just have them on paper) can reduce their exposure to gender-discrimination claims. When applied as a whole, the strategies enable employees who are caregivers to advance and be compensated at the same levels as others. Certain strategies are key, particularly legitimizing part-time work, time-off during a career cycle, and flexible work schedules. Since most caregivers are female, the absence of strategies that make their success at work possible can constitute gender discrimination, even when suits are filed on behalf of male caregivers (see Williams, 2000). In this emerging area of litigation, a series of cases suggests the size of potential awards and settlements.

- *Award of $3 million in one case; more than $625,000 in another.* In a Title VII disparate treatment case that went to a jury in 1999, a female civil engineer who was passed over for promotions after the birth of her son was awarded $3 million. The president of the company had asked her, "Do you want to have babies or do you want a career here?" (Williams & Segal, 2003, p. 130.) Another plaintiff was granted more than $625,000 in damages and attorney fees when, after returning from maternity leave, she experienced "increased work, greater scrutiny of work, loss of schedule flexibility granted to others in her department, and demeaning comments regarding potential future pregnancies and her young child." One company has been sued three times by three different mothers.[6]

Marketing and Reputation

When it maintains customer stability, a company can avoid or reduce the cost of acquiring new customers, including staff time, advertising, and other direct costs. The increased visibility and the positive effect on reputation from recognition as a great place to work, for example, are free and can reduce investments in advertising. Public relations professionals estimate that the value of positive publicity, such as in feature articles, is two to three times that of purchased advertising in the same medium: companies featured because of their innovative management practices in articles in *Fast Company* or *Fortune* find more value from that than from equivalent advertising.

Effects on Organizational Performance

The rest of this chapter describes research on the comprehensive effects adaptive human capital strategies have on organizations—the best test of their worth from an organizational perspective.

Organizational performance is affected by cumulative dynamics of human capital and customer performance (see Chapters 10 and 11) and the cost savings described thus far. They must be accompanied by the right business strategy, executed well, and effective work processes and systems (see Figure 5). The adaptive strategies (when adopted as a whole in a congruent cultural context) contribute to a workforce that is more skilled, stable, and enthusiastic, as well as freer of distractions. These talented and focused employees are more likely to be committed to the organization's goals and deliver superior value to customers, who in turn are more inclined to be satisfied and loyal, generating strong sales. The organization is more efficient in the short run, and more profitable. It is better poised for long-term success, able to innovate, continually improve processes, and minimize overhead. Its investments are in constructive, future-oriented assets—human capital, innovation, and customer relationships—all leading indicators that stock analysts use to evaluate stock price.

Effects on Profitability, Output, and Growth

Practices that recognize both the value and the needs of human capital enable companies to grow in terms of profits and revenues, and to sustain that growth over longer periods, because they provide that critical fundamental element—getting the right people on the bus and in the right seats (Collins, 2001). The research that follows has often been conducted on clusters of adaptive human capital strategies, so we present these clusters as they most often appear in the research.

Organization of Work

Numerous studies find employee involvement is connected to rewarding, flexible, streamlined work.

- *Employee involvement enhances ROS, ROA, ROI, and ROE.* A study of Fortune 1000 companies found those with high use of employee involvement (EI) programs—high-performance knowledge development, information sharing, organization- and team-level pay for performance, and empowerment practices—performed significantly better than companies with low EI. High-EI-use companies had a 25 percent higher ROS, a 34 percent higher ROA, a 26 percent higher ROI, and a 40 percent higher ROE in 1996. In 1999, ROS was 66 percent higher, ROA was 20 percent higher, ROI was 20 percent higher, and ROE was 14 percent higher. The market-to-book ratio in 1999 for high-EI-use companies was 1.8, compared to .7 for low-performing companies (Lawler et al., 2001).[7]

- *Telecommuting enhances profitability.* An economic analysis found that when the number of employees working from home increases by 1 percentage point, the firm's profit rate increases by 0.6 percent. For the average firm in the sample, profits rose $84 million as a result. The researchers' explanation is the efficiency wage theory discussed earlier—the idea that above-market compensation (here including the opportunity to work at home) reduces turnover, absenteeism, and tardiness and increases productivity, thus increasing profitability (Meyer, Mukerjee, & Sestero, 2001).

Talent Management

Selective recruiting, investing in talent, equitable contribution-based rewards, and advancement all boost results.

- *Being a great place to work leads to higher revenue growth, higher job growth, and higher net income per employee.* Companies rated as the best places to work outgrew in revenue a matched set of comparison companies by a margin of four to one, an analysis reveals. Their net income rose 202 percent compared to 139 percent for other companies over a ten-year period. They generated seventy-nine thousand new jobs per company; the other companies lost sixty-one thousand on average. The ten-year net income per employee was $551,965 for the "contented cow companies" compared to $167,018 for the others (Catlette & Hadden, 1998). These companies—HP, FedEx, GE, Southwest Airlines, Wal-Mart, 3M—had products that were highly desired by their target markets, strong delivery mechanisms, good leadership, and competitive prices; but they also had an important element in common: the ability to generate competitive advantage from their people. Selective recruiting, fair compensation, clear direction and purpose, autonomy, accountability and responsibility, and family-responsive practices were all present. In the period since the analysis, the companies remain, despite changing competitive dynamics and industry conditions, consistent high-performers.[8]

- *Equitable rewards enhance shareholder return.* A study of the fifteen hundred largest corporations found those that awarded the biggest share of stock options to their top five executives had the lowest returns for shareholders. Companies where the top five executives received more than 40.8 percent of all options granted had total shareholder return (TSR) in 1992 through 2001 of 22.5 percent.

TSR improved significantly when stock options were shared with more people throughout the organization. Companies where the top five executives received 29–40.8 percent of all options granted had TSR of 23.1 percent; where the top five executives received 19–29 percent of all options granted, TSR was 27.7 percent; and where the top five received less than 19 percent of all options granted, TSR was 31.3 percent (Morgenson, 2002).

- *Equitable rewards enhance revenue growth.* W. L. Gore & Associates, where after a year of service all employees become stockholders, has grown in revenues at the rate of 26 percent per year over the past twenty years. Informal structures, self-defined career paths, open communication; principles of fairness, freedom, commitment; and shared responsibility have helped the company achieve this growth (Ehin, 2000).

- *Selective recruiting enhances profit and growth.* A study of recruiting practices and organizational performance found that organizations that used at least five selective recruiting practices (evaluating the effectiveness of recruiting sources, using validated tests and predictors, using structured or standard interviews, using intelligence tests, and using biographical information blanks) had significantly higher annual profit and profit growth than those that used fewer such practices (Terpstra & Rozell, 1993).[9]

Time and Resources and Tools

Two studies considered the profitability of organizations in the context of adaptive practices, one concentrating on family leave and the other on placement on various "best places to work" lists. The organizations typically provide adaptive practices regarding time and resources and tools, although which practices are offered varies from firm to firm.

- *Paid family leave enhances profitability.* An economic analysis of firms offering various adaptive practices found firms that offered paid family leave had 2.5 percent higher profits (defined as operating income as a fraction of sales) than firms that did not (Meyer et al., 2001).

- *The best places to work have higher earnings.* In a study of companies on *Fortune's* "100 Best Places to Work in America" list for the preceding five years, 73 percent had annual returns on investment higher than the average on the Russell 3000 index. The companies rated by *Fortune* as best places to work had returns of 27.5 percent, while Russell 3000 stocks had average annual returns of 17.3 percent. For the preceding ten years, the Russell 3000 averaged annual returns of 14.8 percent compared to 23.4 percent for the publicly traded "100 Best Places to Work" (Grant, 1998).

Culture

Respect, shared responsibility, trust, aligned interests, and integrity all build the bottom line. Two companies' stories (see Chapters 15 and 16) demonstrate the effect of adaptive cultures on financial performance.

- First Tennessee National Corporation has had an intensely employee-centered culture for a decade. In 2001 it was the most profitable banking company in the United States for the fourth consecutive year, according to *Forbes*, with an 18 percent five-year-average return on capital. FTN ranked fourth among the top fifty bank holding companies, with an annual revenue-per-share growth rate of 12.5 percent over the past seven years.

- SAS, a private software firm whose work environment epitomizes adaptive values and culture, had double-digit growth for the first twenty-six years of its history, until 2002. In 2002, during the economic downturn in which other software companies stagnated, SAS still had a 4.4 percent increase in revenue.

The following also illustrate the effects of adaptive cultures on financial performance.

- *Empowering leadership and alignment of interests yields higher ROI (earnings) and ROS.* A study of the effects of culture on financial performance found better performance—higher ROI and ROS—in organizations that align employee and organizational goals. Also, organizations that encourage employee participation in decisions outperformed others over time in ROI and ROS. Performance difference grew over time, with organizations having ROI and ROS similar to companies with lower scores in the beginning of the analysis, but those with more employee involvement in decision making significantly outperforming others two to five years later. The study analyzed the performance of thirty-four companies in manufacturing and services industries (Denison, 1990).[10]

- *Empowering leadership and aligned interests increase productivity and growth.* A small manufacturer of TV equipment grew more than 35 percent from quarter to quarter—in an industry that averaged 12 percent growth—by implementing a "self-organizing, shared access" environment with shared values, mission, and vision. It provided extensive training and team development (to maintain social capital) and gave employees the information—orders, bookings, revenues, margins, expenses, and profitability—they needed to gauge performance and effectiveness. The company generated $30 million in revenue the first year these changes were in place through improved productivity and growth, while reducing the workforce from 150 to 100 people through attrition (Ehin, 2000).

- *Empowering leadership and shared responsibility increase profits.* In the first seventeen years of its existence Whole Foods, the natural and organic foods retailer, grew into a publicly traded company with forty-three stores in ten states, annual revenue of $500 million, and net profits double the industry average. Its culture mandated employee empowerment, autonomy, and teamwork (Burson-Marsteller Public Relations/Public Affairs, 2000).

Following are research findings about companies that hold the value of, and maintain practices that reflect, integrity.

- *Ethics.* Companies that emphasized ethics were twice as likely to be among the top hundred financial performers, according to an analysis of 1997 S&P 500 companies ranked by *BusinessWeek* as well as the five hundred largest U.S. public corporations (Verschoor, 1998).

- *Corporate social responsibility.* In 1997, a study of the relationship between corporate social and financial performance (ROE, ROA, ROS) in 469 companies from different industries found that companies with high ROA had high levels of social performance, as did those with high ROS (both statistically significant findings). Although not significant statistically, those with high ROE also had high levels of social performance. Better-than-average social performance was a good predictor of better financial performance in the next year, and the reverse held true as well (Waddock & Graves, 1997; Weiser & Zadek, 2000).

Effects on Reputation

Adaptive strategies have a combined effect on reputation, discussed here in relationship to profitability. The absence of such strategies, cultural elements, and practices also affects an organization's reputation.

Reputation is more than an organization's identity (its products, experience, approach, customers, suppliers, investors). Reputation is the *affective* (emotional) reaction evoked by the organization's name. Good reputations create wealth, says Charles Fombrun (1996). This reputational capital makes it easier to sell products, entice investors, attract employees, and negotiate with suppliers. Enormous resources are invested in developing reputation, and rightly so.

Reputation is of particular concern to knowledge-based and service organizations, which sell intangibles—what economists call *credence goods*—goods bought on faith (Fombrun, 1996, p. 7). Faith in an organization is affected by its reputation in relation to people, including its own.

- *Reputation enhances ROE.* A study of *Fortune*'s rankings of "America's Most Admired Corporations" found two things that predicted why some companies were better regarded than others: the company's *economic* record, which must be both positive and stable, and the company's *institutional* record—its commitment to projecting an attractive image to employees and the local community. The return on equity for the ten most highly regarded companies in early 1993 averaged 25 percent in the prior year. That return held over the long term; better-rated companies had higher ten-year returns than lesser-rated companies (Fombrun, 1996).

Some companies have gained reputations for having distinct cultures and use their cultures to create and enhance their brand. Being sensitive to employees' families enhances the reputation of Johnson & Johnson and similar family-oriented-product companies. Allstate's reputation as caring, Baxter Healthcare's reputation as a company with integrity, and Patagonia's (an outdoor equipment manufacturer) commitment to the importance of play and the environment in people's lives all contribute to the organizations' brands. Each of these highly adaptive, human capital–oriented organizations has a reputation based on organizational culture and employee practices that uniquely contribute to its brand.

Effects on Shareholder Value

Shareholder value is affected by the performance of the firm as well as external forces in the marketplace. The following research suggests how the adaptive strategies can affect shareholder value.

High-Performance Work Practices

Selective recruiting, investing in talent, and contribution-based rewards and advancement contribute to organizations' performance. The studies described here measured the effects of high-performance work practices on organizational performance. "High-performance work practices" refers to a cluster of adaptive human capital management practices that include talent management (selective recruiting, contribution-based performance and advancement criteria, equitable distribution of work and rewards, human capital–oriented professional development) and the organization of work (employee involvement in work design). Three groups have conducted most of this research: Huselid and Becker; Watson Wyatt; and others.

Huselid and Becker Research. In the following section we examine the research of Mark Huselid of Rutgers University and Brian Becker of the State University of New York at Buffalo, who with colleagues have studied the relationship between high-performance work practices and firm performance extensively and rigorously (Becker & Huselid, 1998). They assert that developing high-performance work systems is not a short-term effort. They write, "Firms cannot make a one standard deviation change in their HR management system in six months and expect to see changes in market value of the magnitude described here. However, firms that take the longer perspective can develop an HR management system that strategically positions them to support their underlying core competencies and create sustained competitive advantage" (Huselid & Becker, 1995, p. 14).[11]

In short, Huselid and Becker's research has shown that investments in human capital practices affect market performance in the range of $15,000 to $73,000 per employee. Companies that invest in these practices and ensure the organization is aligned in support of them realize even stronger effects — 17 percent higher performance than those that don't do both.

The main studies summarized here are significant because the authors were able to replicate their results using different samples and different time periods, and also to isolate other factors that might affect the outcomes.

- *Selective recruiting, training, and performance-based compensation are associated with strong organizational performance.* An analysis of 590 firms found organizational performance higher in firms with progressive human resources management practices, such as selective recruiting, training, and performance-based compensation (Delaney & Huselid, 1996).[12]

- *High-performance work practices increase productivity and reduce turnover, leading to increased market value and profits.* A study of nearly a thousand companies across industries and of various sizes found a one standard deviation increase in high-performance work practices associated with a 7.05 percent decrease in employee turnover. On a per-employee basis, this change translates into an increase of $27,044 in sales, $18,641 in market value, and $3,814 in profits. In this study, high-performance work practices were defined as personnel selection including intensity of recruiting efforts (percentage of applicants hired), performance appraisals, incentive compensation, job design, grievance procedures, information sharing, attitude assessment, labor-management participation, average number of hours of training per employee per year, and promotion criteria (seniority versus merit; Huselid, 1995).[13]

- *Customizing HR practices to meet the specific needs of the organization increases market value.* Two sets of HR practices were compared. Having the first set—best practices in HR (see Huselid, 1995)— raised a firm's market value by 7–9 percent on average. The second set of HR practices was broader, including employee motivation (merit promotions and performance-based pay), the organization's HR strategy (mission, alignment with business strategy), and workforce selection and development. The use of any combination of these practices at higher than average rates raised a firm's market value by 9–13 percent on average. This translates into a per-employee increase of $38,000–$73,000 on firm market value, based on average employment at different levels of firm market performance (Huselid & Becker, 1995).[14]

- *High-performance work practices enhance market value.* To check the validity of their earlier research, Huselid and Becker evaluated changes over time across individual companies included in two studies. They isolated factors likely to distort the effects of HR practices on firm performance, such as management capabilities, marketing, or manufacturing strategies, and corrected for measurement error in data gathering. Their revised estimate revealed that a one standard deviation increase in a measure of high-performance work practices is associated with a $15,000–$17,000 increase in market value per employee (Huselid & Becker, 1996).[15]

- *More intense high-performance work practices, coupled with organizational alignment with high-performance principles, enhances market value.* Huselid and Becker subsequently studied how firm financial performance was affected by the intensity of adoption of high-performance work practices as a system, and the degree of organizational alignment with the principles of a high-performance work organization. Their study of 548 publicly held firms found—after grouping the results by clusters based on the strength of the HR system, degree of organizational alignment around the practices, and effectiveness of the HR function—that companies in the top cluster (those with strong HR systems, good alignment, and effective HR functions) are estimated to have a 32 percent higher market value than companies that are weak in all three areas. In general, the results indicate a one standard deviation increase in HR strength had an effect of 21 percent on shareholder value and an increase in market value of $42,000 per employee (Huselid & Becker, 1997).[16]

- *High-performance work systems, integrated HR systems, and organizational logic that views people as assets enhance firm performance.* Becker and Huselid (1998) also investigated how much complementary elements of organizational policies affected high-performance work practices. They specifically considered alignment of HRM (human resource management) strategies and the firm's strategies, the effectiveness with which the high-performance work systems were implemented, and whether senior management recognized the value of human capital—and the resulting effect on firm performance.

The analysis confirmed their earlier studies and found that a one standard deviation change in HR practices was associated with a 23.3 percent change in shareholder value, or $51,000 per employee. This greater impact may result from using a more comprehensive measure that included more HR practices. The fit of HRM practices within the broader system had a significant effect on firm performance, accounting for two thirds of the gain in performance. Firms that had integrated both elements into their HRM strategy—strong HR systems that build on workforce skills and motivation as a source of competitive advantage and strong organizational alignment around high-performance work practices—had clearly superior performance, both economically and statistically, compared to companies that were weak in both elements or strong in one but not the other. Strong HR systems and organizational alignment complement each other, so that firms taking advantage of both experience a 17 percent greater effect on performance (Becker & Huselid, 1998).[17]

The work of Huselid and Becker provides clear evidence that adaptive strategies for talent management affect a firm's market value in the long term. It also shows that adaptive practices are more effective and have a greater effect on results when they are supported by organizational elements (such as leadership support and alignment with overall strategy) and are part of a cohesive HR system. It is even more important that HR practices support the specific objectives of the organization—that firms use specific HR practices aligned with their business objectives. The results do not clearly show, however, whether firms adopt the practices because they operate in profitable industries and can afford to do so, or they adopt them and are profitable as a result (Huselid & Rau, 1996).

High-performance work practices and organizational elements that create the strongest improvement in market performance come from an organizational logic that regards the labor force as a strategic asset rather than a cost to be minimized (Becker & Huselid, 1998).

Watson Wyatt Studies. Watson Wyatt has also investigated the relationship between HR practices and organizational performance. Its findings corroborate those of Huselid and Becker. Its people used measures of financial performance similar to those Huselid and Becker chose, but selected larger organizations—having revenues of at least $100 million annually, compared to Huselid and Becker's at least $5 million limit. Both research groups sent questionnaires to HR executives regarding HR practices, although Watson Wyatt used different (but essentially similar) databases—Hunt-Scanlon and Standard and Poor's Compustat—to obtain financial information. One important difference is that Watson Wyatt's data are more recent. Huselid and Becker's questionnaires were sent out in 1992, 1994, and 1996, while Watson Wyatt's data for the Human Capital Index Study were obtained in 1999 and 2001. Watson Wyatt looked at three- and five-year shareholder returns, finding correlations between responses in 1999 and shareholder returns in 1997, 1998, 1999, and 2000, while Huselid and Becker looked at returns one year subsequent to each year of survey responses. Underlying both sets of research is the reasonable assumption that organizations have not just started implementing these practices; responses to survey questions reflect well-established practices.

The HR practices in the Watson Wyatt studies are broader than those used by Huselid and Becker and address the financial effects of some specific adaptive practices. (Watson Wyatt uses the term *human capital practices*, defined as recruiting excellence, clear rewards and accountability, a collegial and flexible workplace, communications integrity, and prudent use of resources.) The main difference between the two sets of studies is that Huselid and Becker evaluate effects of systems of work practices, while

Watson Wyatt looks at the effects of individual work practices. Taken as a whole, the two sets of data reinforce each other and provide compelling evidence of the importance of adaptive practices to shareholder value. The Watson Wyatt studies used surveys and analysis of financial performance. The following studies apply to all types of workers.

- *Human capital practices are associated with increased shareholder value.* A 1999 survey of four hundred North American publicly held companies indicated companies with a high Human Capital Index (HCI) had 103 percent total return to shareholders (for the period 1994–1999) compared to 53 percent for companies with low HCI. Six months after the initial analysis, high-HCI companies returned 28 percent to shareholders whereas shareholders lost 6 percent by investing in low-HCI companies. A significant improvement in thirty key HR practices (raising the result 1 point on a 5-point scale) was associated with a 30 percent increase in market value. Recruiting excellence was associated with a 10.1 percent increase in shareholder value; clear rewards and accountability was associated with a 9.2 percent increase (Watson Wyatt, 2000a). Although Huselid and Becker did not test their results to this level, the overall direction of the findings is consistent. A collegial, flexible workplace and communications integrity were not specifically addressed in the HR practices of Huselid and Becker's studies; for the HCI, they are respectively associated with a 7.8 percent and 4 percent increase in shareholder value. Most interesting when comparing the findings of the two groups of studies are those things labeled "prudent use of resources" by Watson Wyatt, which are associated with negative shareholder value creation of 10 percent. The study lists employee participation in profit sharing tied to business unit performance, employee input into peer and manager evaluations, and training programs (for advancement and when such programs are maintained during unfavorable economic conditions) as practices that should be used prudently (Watson Wyatt, 2000a). Employee participation in profit sharing and training for professional development are included in high-performance work practices in Huselid and Becker's work, although they were not tested individually. These results suggest organizations need to be careful about using these particular practices and monitor the effects of their use closely.

  - The 7.8 percent increase in shareholder value associated with a flexible, collegial workplace includes the following important practices (Watson Wyatt, 2000a): Flexible work arrangements were linked to a 1.7 percent increase in market value. A culture that encourages teamwork and cooperation was linked to a 1.5 percent gain. Offering equal perquisites regardless of position and high employee satisfaction were both linked to a 1.4 percent gain. Together, these factors represent a corporate culture and management style in which employees feel engaged and committed.

- *Human capital practices enhance shareholder value.* The 2001 survey of five hundred North American companies was merged with 250 responses from the European survey; the following results reflect both. The 2001 Human Capital Index (HCI) demonstrated that companies with high HCI scores had 64 percent total returns to shareholders (1996–2001) compared to 39 percent of companies with medium scores and 21 percent of companies with low scores. Again, recruiting excellence was important; along with retention excellence it accounted for a 7.9 percent increase in market value. Total rewards and accountability increased their effects over the prior year—representing 16.5 percent of market value. A collegial, flexible workplace increased in importance, with a 9 percent effect on market value. Communications integrity also became more important—having a 7.1 percent effect on market value. A new category, focused HR service technologies, had a 6.5 percent association with market value. The practices with potential negative effects were also stronger in these studies, accounting for a negative 33.9 percent in market value (Watson Wyatt Worldwide, 2001). Although the merged 2001 HCI results are predominately weighted with North American companies, the decision to merge the two 2001 surveys does distort the comparability of the results. Unfortunately, 2001 North America–only data were not available.

Looking at these results in more detail, it is possible to see which specific recruiting and retention practices affect market value (Pfau & Kay, 2002). Low voluntary turnover among managers and professionals was associated with a 1.7 percent increase in market value. Low voluntary turnover among employees in general was associated with a 1.5 percent increase in market value. And an emphasis within the company on job security was associated with a 1.4 percent increase in market value.

One important aspect of the research examined which came first: financial performance or human capital strategies. Approximately fifty companies participated in both the 1999 and 2001 surveys, enabling researchers to evaluate whether strong HR practices lead to strong financial performance or strong financial performance provides companies with an opportunity to improve their HR practices. By comparing the 1999 HCI score with 2001 financial performance and 1999 financial performance with 2001 HCI scores for these companies, the researchers found a much higher correlation between the 1999 HCI score and 2001 financial performance: .41 compared to .19 for 2001 HCI score and 1999 financial performance. These findings indicate that human capital practices drive financial performance rather than the reverse (Watson Wyatt Worldwide, 2001).

The link between human capital management practices and firm performance is further corroborated by evidence obtained in two other research efforts by Watson Wyatt: the Strategic Rewards and WorkUSA surveys.

- *Retention enhances shareholder value.* The 2000 Strategic Rewards survey obtained responses from three million full- and part-time employees of 410 U.S. and Canadian companies representing all major industries. Comparing responses with firm performance revealed that firms with successful retention strategies, and lower turnover as a result, had average five-year shareholder returns of 26 percent compared to 9 percent returns for companies with unchanged turnover and 7 percent returns for those with increasing turnover (Watson Wyatt, 2000b).

- *Human capital practices enhance employee commitment, which enhances shareholder value.* The WorkUSA 2000 survey, conducted in 1999, surveyed seventy-five hundred workers regarding their attitudes about the workplace and their employers. Employee commitment (Pfau & Kay, 2002) depended on

  - Leadership effectiveness and supervision
  - Work environment
  - Adequacy of technology and resources
  - Compensation and benefits
  - Teamwork and work process effectiveness
  - Communications and decision making
  - Job content and satisfaction
  - Work-life balance and flexibility
  - Diversity
  - Performance management

The study found that engaged and committed employees perform at higher levels. There was quite a payoff: companies with high employee commitment returned 112 percent to shareholders over three years compared to 90 percent for average commitment and 76 percent for low-commitment companies (Watson Wyatt, 1999b).

Other Studies. Several other studies are important to note.

- *High-performance work practices enhance productivity and financial performance.* This analysis of fifteen studies (Denison, 1990; Ichniowski, Shaw, & Prennushi, 1995) concluded that organizations with high-performance work practices have greater productivity and long-term financial performance. Companies with more innovative human resource practices (specifically training, compensation linked to firm or worker performance, and employee involvement in decision making) have higher annual shareholder returns and higher gross return on capital. The top 25 percent, those using the largest number of best practices, had an 11 percent return on capital, more than twice that of the others (U.S. Department of Labor, 1993).

- *High-performance work practices lead to higher valuations.* A study for CalPERS found companies with high-performance work practices had a higher ratio of stock price to book value than their industry peers. Companies with substandard reputation for workplace practices had lower valuations than those with high reputations. Many of the companies with the worst reputations for workplace practices either were acquired or went bankrupt (Gordon, Porter, & Pound, 1994).

- *Retention enhances shareholder value.* McKinsey's research on talent management provides clear evidence of economic benefits of retaining key employees: 88 percent of HR executives in top 20 percent companies, in terms of shareholder value, say they rarely lose employees to their competitors compared to 73 percent of middle 20 percent companies (Chambers, Foulon, Handfield-Jones, Hankin, & Michaels, 1998).

- *Talent practices related to leaders enhance shareholder return.* The same McKinsey research studied corporate officers and executives and found companies that excel at motivating and developing leaders are in the top 20 percent of shareholder value. The specific practices they excel at involve creating a great company (values, culture, good management), great jobs (autonomy, challenge, and growth), and great compensation and lifestyle packages (Chambers et al., 1998). Companies in the top 20 percent of talent-management practices outperformed their industry's mean return to shareholders by 22 percent (Axelrod, Handfield-Jones, & Welsh, 2001).[18]

- *The potential to manage talent—and improve performance further—has not been fully realized.* In 1997 only 3 percent of executives felt their companies develop people effectively and move low-performers out quickly; only 7 percent believed they hold managers accountable for the quality of their people (Chambers et al., 1998). In 2001 only 14 percent felt their companies attract highly talented people (Axelrod et al., 2001).

Time, Organization of Work, and Resources and Tools

The remaining studies in this section look at combinations of adaptive practices—those that relate to time, organization of work, or resources and tools (updated benefits in particular) and their effects on organizational performance. These practices are often referred to as *work-life programs* or *work-family benefits*, because they were originally created in response to the particular challenges of dual-focus employees (those with competing work and home responsibilities). However, most of the practices are also highly valued by employees in general. Flexible work schedules and the ability to telecommute, for example, while highly valued by workers in dual-income families with children or dependent elders, are also sought after by employees who want to avoid long commutes, go to school, or increase their discretionary time.

The work-life measures referred to in this research may include *programs* (such as alternate or flexible work arrangements), *policies* (allowing paid sick leave to be used to care for family members), *services* (referral or counseling services on dependent care), and *benefits* (parental leave, adoption assistance, child and elder care assistance). Sometimes, but less often, the research includes *cultural* elements—a climate that works for new ideal workers, for example—as reflected in advancement criteria.

- *Work-family support enhances shareholder return.* An analysis of Fortune 500 firms found decisions to provide work-family support increased shareholder returns. The study found shareholder returns increased .36 percent on the day such a decision was announced and .39 percent over the three days after the announcement (M. Arthur, 2003).[19]

- *Providing more work-family benefits enhances organizational and market performance and profit-sales growth.* A series of interviews with U.S. personnel directors found that firms with more work-family benefits had statistically significant higher organizational and market performance (as reported by the firms) and higher profit-sales growth (Perry-Smith & Blum, 2000). Work-family benefits included child and elder care, paid or unpaid parental leave, and flexible scheduling.[20]

A number of studies have investigated the shareholder performance of companies included on various best-places-to-work lists—including those prepared by *BusinessWeek, Fortune,* and *Working Mother.* These companies typically employ a combination of adaptive strategies. The studies do not isolate the effects of individual practices; instead, they measure their collective influence. The advantage of research across companies is that patterns become clear. Since the practices have the greatest effects when they are embedded within a culture and are integrated with other adaptive practices, it is perhaps more instructive to consider them collectively.

With some caveats, the results are consistent.* Companies recognized as the "best places to work" have better financial results.

- *Great places to work outperform the S&P 100 in sales and asset growth.* In this analysis, companies with better quality of life for employees had higher sales and asset growth over a five-year period than the S&P 100 companies and higher return on assets (ROA), although they did not have better return on equity (ROE). These companies were judged by their pay and benefits (good pay, unusual benefits, sensitivity to employees' family needs), opportunities for employees (training, advancement, diversity), job security, employee pride in work and company, openness and fairness (in leadership, communication, and evaluation), and camaraderie and friendliness (team environment, enjoyable workplace; Lau & May, 1998).[21]

- *Fortune's 100 Best Companies to Work For have higher share value than the S&P 500.* Shares of companies on *Fortune's* list rose 37 per-

---

* These lists do not include all best-practice companies because firms generally must apply to be on them. Also, inclusion criteria emphasize measurable practices and therefore cultural values are less often considered. Still, the applications and procedures used to evaluate many of these companies are extensive. Some collect usage data to confirm that employees are actually able to use the published practices; some (not all) gather data directly from employees. Nonetheless, the results may be distorted to the extent that practices may be concentrated in divisions or departments that are not significant contributors to total firm results. Results also may be somewhat distorted because the companies they are compared to, such as the S&P 100, may include companies that use the same practices but have not applied to be included on the list. Inclusion on the early lists (1984–1993) was based primarily on reputation; the criteria became more extensive for later lists.

cent in value compared to a rise of 25 percent for the S&P 500 for the same three-year period ending in 1999. For the five-year period ending in 1999, the average annualized stock market return for "100 Best" companies was 34 percent compared to 25 percent for the S&P 500. The average annualized stock market return for "100 Best" companies was 21 percent for the ten-year period compared with 17 percent for the S&P 500. Many of these companies were actively trying to help employees balance their work and personal lives: 89 percent offered compressed workweeks, 87 percent allowed some workers to telecommute, 71 percent offered job sharing, 70 percent had flexible schedules, and 45 percent had reduced summer hours (Levering & Moskowitz, 2000).

- *"Best Company to Work For" status enhances ROA and yields higher annual returns.* Hewitt Associates and Vanderbilt University researchers studied the operating performance and stock returns of "100 Best" companies over a period of six years, in an analysis that gave time for effects to appear. Lists for 1993 and 1998 were analyzed. Companies on both lists had higher return on average assets for most years studied than a set of companies matched by industry, size, and performance in the beginning of year 1. Cumulative annual shareholder returns for both lists of "100 Best" companies were greater than the market index for 1990–1996 and higher than the returns generated by the matched sets of companies (Fulmer, Gerhart, & Scott, 2000).

- *HR reputation signals create short-term jump in share price.* A study looked at how inclusion on "Best Companies" lists affected shareholder returns and found a 5 percent jump in share price among companies on *Working Mother's* list immediately following the award announcement. The increase was unrelated to normal market fluctuations. The temporary bump was not sustained, but it is indicative of how investors use HR signals as leading indicators of performance—an organization's ability to recruit and retain the best employees, who would presumably be more productive (Hannon & Milkovich, 1996).

- *Work environment enhances customer satisfaction, which enhances market value.* Companies on *Working Mother's* "100 Best Companies for Working Mothers" list were evaluated in regard to employee satisfaction, customer satisfaction, and firm profitability. Companies considered best for working mothers, those that advance women and have work environments that support working mothers (child care benefits, flexible scheduling, telecommuting) had customer satisfaction ratings 1–7 points higher than others, which translated into a 3–11 percent increase in market value, or $22,000 per employee (Simon, 2002). The study also found that when unemployment rates increased, market value also rose. (A 1 percentage point increase in unemployment rate results in a 1.2–2.1 percent increase in market value, or $2,400–$4,200 per employee.) This research allows comparison of whether fear or support has a stronger effect on performance; it turns out that support is three to nine times as powerful. When employees are more concerned about their ability to get another job easily (in times of higher unemployment), they are motivated to produce. When their employer respects them as whole people, removes barriers, and provides support (work-life practices), they are motivated and produce exponentially more.

In Conclusion

Adaptive human capital management cultures and practices help organizations excel in part because they reduce other expenses—real estate, legal, health care, labor, and lost productivity costs—and enable resources to be invested productively in ways that create value, solidify relational capital, and align the interests of stakeholders. They facilitate the management of people as assets and whole people. Though practices often require a substantial investment of time and financial resources, they translate to stronger financial results, generating significantly greater performance from employees and therefore for customers. In every type of organization studied, this edge has created substantial improvement in earnings and shareholder value.

While the specific effects of adaptive human capital management cultures and practices vary with each situation, the research strongly suggests a positive net result. Every organization, no matter what its size or mission, must continue to improve in any way it can to simply survive and, certainly, to thrive. Adaptive human capital management practices give organizations the potential to outdistance even other leading companies because they leverage a unique source of competitive advantage: human capital.

Certainly the adaptive strategies we've discussed are not a cure-all. Organizations must execute the basics well. Whether they are operating a steel mill, a pharmaceutical company, or a restaurant chain, corporate leaders must understand their customers, target the right market with the right products and services for those customers, execute appropriate strategies to attract them, price and promote products appropriately, and produce products efficiently. They must have access to financial capital and attend to risk management, changing regulations, and technological innovations.

Still, the research is unequivocal; adaptive cultures and practices make a significant and measurable difference in organizational performance. In Part 4 we take this evidence to the next level with stories of companies that have integrated adaptive human capital management practices and cultures within their organizations.

FOUR STORIES
OF BECOMING
ADAPTIVE

In this part of the book we relate the experiences of four very different organizations: DuPont, Baxter International, SAS, and First Tennessee National Corporation (FTN). These companies have a wide range of style, age, size, and vision. Their stories offer a window into what can happen in an organization (of whatever stripe) when it decides to adapt in a comprehensive way: how it goes about such a change and the effects the change has on business objectives and outcomes. Their stories show how adaptive principles and practices come together across an organization and advance its ability to achieve.

Each of the companies took a different route—DuPont used research, Baxter approached its transformation through values, SAS focused on work environment from its inception, and FTN used culture change. Each one also measures the outcomes of the change using a different yardstick. FTN, for example, uses multifaceted measures to assess effects on profitability and productivity, while SAS uses customer and employee retention as leading indicators to gauge results.

The stories illustrate the common threads of effective adaptation and also the variety of ways organizations can use adaptive principles to fit their specific circumstances. A research and manufacturing firm, a global health care products company, a software firm, and a regional bank—each with a different challenge and way of doing business—used their idiosyncratic expression of the adaptive strategies in this book to reach their business goals.

Rosabeth Moss Kanter describes the essential qualities that must define leaders in the new business environment. These are the qualities found, in different forms, in the leaders of these four organizations.

THE NEW LEADERSHIP
by Rosabeth Moss Kanter

Change is a condition of existence. It has been for decades. But the pace, depth, and scope of change, and how many people must get involved in coping with it, are different today. The pace and complexity of today's economy require leaders who are especially adept at leaping over barriers and converting resistance to commitment. These new leaders must be masters of change.

Change is emotionally hard. We might have to live with change, but that doesn't mean we have to love it—and we usually don't. People often resist change for reasons that make good sense to them. Resistance to change is possible even under benign circumstances. When the environment is turbulent and the impact of change revolutionary, leaders must be even more skillful at handling the human side of change.

Leaders today have to be willing to shake up assumptions about existing routines. They must wake people out of inertia. They must get people excited about something they've never seen before, something that does not yet exist. Personal passion helps a changemaster do whatever it takes to get started, to demonstrate the value of a vision, even when others cannot yet see it.

Changemasters must sell their ideas widely, attract the right backers and supporters, and entice investors and defenders. They must get buy-in from stakeholders who are in positions to help or harm the venture. In essence, changemasters build coalitions.

Coalition building begins with the minimum number of individuals necessary to launch a new vision and champion it when help is needed. A coalition needs the support of power holders early in the process. Power holders possess the resources including people, technology and funds, as well as the information and credibility that can get a new idea moving. Powerful, well-connected sponsors make ideas credible, open doors, speak on behalf of the changemaster, and quell opposition. Early coalition members help sell others; each successive round of buy-in brings more people and groups on board.

Effective coalition building proceeds through three kinds of actions. First is preselling. The changemaster speaks to many people to gather intelligence and plant seeds, leaving behind a germ of an idea that can blossom and gradually become familiar. Smart leaders pave the way for a good reception to a new idea by one-on-one preparation before convening people, and they avoid initiating discussions or holding meetings where people hear something they are not prepared for.

A second action is making deals. Having identified those likely to provide strategic support, leaders get them to chip in. Investing builds the commitment of people helping them. It lets other people in on the action, even if what they invest is minor—a little time, a little data, a staff member to serve as liaison. Investment is a good preemptive move.

A third piece of coalition building is getting a sanity check—confirming or adjusting the idea in light of reactions from backers and potential backers. Changemasters want to secure the blessings of those with experience, but they also need their wisdom to ensure they are "not out of . . . [their] minds." A coalition is generally a loose network with people chipping in various things at various levels of commitment.

Once a coalition of backers is in place, changemasters enlist others in turning the dream into reality. Leaders become producers/directors. They bring in improvisational actors who take on the task of translating an idea into implementation, a promise into a prototype. There are two parts of this job: team building and team nurturing. Team building consists of encouraging everyone to feel like a team, with ownership of goals and a team identity that motivates performance. A working team feels deep commitment and responsibility for delivering on deadlines and performance. Team building begins with allowing a set of people to embrace the goals rather than being told what to do by their manager. Team nurturing involves caring and feeding of the team as it does its work—supporting the team, providing coaching and resources, and patrolling the boundaries within which the team can freely operate. A team has a common identity, strong respect for each other as individuals, and a desire to do whatever it takes to support each other in succeeding.

Changemasters persist and persevere, staying the course through initial hurdles and midcourse corrections. They have plans, but are prepared to accept serious departures from plans and understand innovation doesn't always follow a predetermined script. Changemasters accept unanticipated consequences and prepare their teams to respond, troubleshoot, make adjustments, and make the case. They ensure there is sufficient flexibility to redirect around obstacles or to mount a second project to deal with the new challenge. When momentum slows, as it often does, changemasters revisit the team's mission, recognize what's been accomplished and what remains, and remember the differences in outlook, background, and perspective that may divide the group can ultimately provide solutions. The changemaster fights for additional resources, removes obstacles, boosts team morale, and deals with critics.

Remembering to recognize, reward, and celebrate accomplishments is the final critical leadership skill. Recognition is important not only for its motivational pat on the back but also for its publicity value; the whole organization and maybe the whole world knows what is possible, who has done it and what talents reside in the community gene pool. Recognition brings the change cycle to its logical conclusion, but it also motivates people to attempt change again. So many people get involved in and contribute to changing the way an organization does things that it's important to share the credit.

The most important personal traits a leader can bring to any kind of change effort are imagination, conviction, passion, and confidence in others. Leaders are characterized by seven qualities of mind, drawing on both analytic and emotional abilities:

- They display curiosity and imagination that allow them to envision and grasp new possibilities.
- They are adept at communication with others, near and far.
- They are cosmopolitans who are not confined to a single world view but are able to understand and create bridges of thought.
- They can grasp complexity.
- They are sensitive to the range of human needs as well as to the messages conveyed by actions that create organizational cultures.
- They work with other people as resources rather than as subordinates, respecting what others bring to the table and listening to their ideas.
- They lead through the power of their ideas and the strength of their voices more than through the authority of formal positions.

More people at more levels in more organizations must learn to master change and lead it. More of us must play leadership roles, whether we are invited to the task or appoint ourselves.

13

THE DUPONT STORY

Since 1802, DuPont has depended on a well-trained and stable workforce to invent and manufacture superior products. The company's relationship with its employees has always been one of shared interests and reciprocal obligations, but the increasing diversity of the workforce, the family responsibilities of both men and women employees, and the company's need for employees to perform at higher levels than ever before has made alignment of interests more difficult. Using research data about its employees, DuPont is undergoing a transformation, creating a work environment that leverages all the enormous talent of its very diverse workforce.

A History of Shared Responsibility and Mutual Interests

When Éleuthère Irénée (E. I.) du Pont* and his family left Paris in 1800, they left the turbulence and danger surrounding the French Revolution,

---

* While du Pont was and is the family's surname, the company officially changed the spelling of its name in the vernacular to "DuPont" in 1993. The company's full legal name still pays homage to its founder: "E. I. du Pont de Nemours and Company, Inc."

This case was cowritten with Sandra Cunningham, Ph.D.

settled on the banks of the Brandywine River in Wilmington, Delaware, and started a gunpowder manufacturing company. The gunpowder business was successful—DuPont eventually supplied 40 percent of the black powder that was used to open the American frontier and fight its wars. President Thomas Jefferson himself encouraged E. I. du Pont in his innovations aimed at developing a higher-quality, more consistent, domestic powder.

Introducing black powder was by its nature a dangerous enterprise, and explosions were common in its production. E. I. tried hard to minimize them (separating the stages of production so a blast wouldn't ignite other parts of the process and attending to every detail—down to banning metal on workers' shoes to reduce the chance of sparks). Still, explosions occurred, and they could be deadly.

Minimizing danger while providing a superior product required a stable and well-trained workforce. Safety rules and extensive training of inexperienced workers helped to minimize the risks of injury and death but were not sufficient to retain skilled and semiskilled employees. To address retention, E. I. over time developed a system of reciprocal obligations and shared interests that became the core of his relationship with his employees, offering benefits that most other companies wouldn't adopt until the early twentieth century. DuPont provided night and overtime pay, work for family members, a savings plan, and a pension plan for workers' widows and orphans. To retain skilled workers during the Depression, DuPont maintained regular rates paid to hourly employees but reduced working hours of wage earners, cutting their salaries 10 percent and instituting a five-day workweek. DuPont would later be one of the first companies in the world to institute an employee medical program, among the first to treat alcoholism as a disease, and the first to establish an employee assistance program.

E. I.'s sense of responsibility for his workers was such that he chose to build his family home five hundred yards behind the powder mill buildings so he would never lose the sense of immediate danger that workers were in—as he described it, never isolate management from the realities that employees faced. The home in which he, his wife, and seven children lived was racked by explosions multiple times and its walls regularly needed replastering.

Never isolate management from the realities that employees face.

From Skilled Labor to Human Capital

Although it has always relied on the skills of employees, in the past century DuPont has become a human capital–intensive company. In fact, DuPont—the oldest continuously operating industrial company among the Fortune 500—is in some ways a living mural of the evolution from skilled labor to knowledge work in America. Certainly the CEO's job has become more complex than it was when E. I. ran the business from a desk in his two-room office, connected to the outside world only by telegraph. But the technical sophistication of the job of the average DuPont employee has changed even more. Until World War I, the majority of DuPont employees developed, tested, and manufactured various types of blasting powder and gunpowder. Today, 37 percent of employees are professionals in engineering, research science, business administration, and information technology—creating the new products, processes, and strategies that will drive future growth.

The transformation of DuPont from an explosives company relying on skilled employees to a diversified science and technology company highly dependent on sophisticated human capital began early in the twentieth century. The company had grown significantly during World War I, increasing revenues from $35 million in 1912 to $328 million in 1918. Human assets had increased significantly as well—the number of trained executives nearly tripled (from 94 to 259) while engineering staff grew from 800 to 4,500. Peacetime provided a new challenge—how to leverage existing assets, both physical and personnel, into new products and new applications.

The success of the company's diversification efforts was due to extensive investment in research and development, acquisitions and divestitures, and the spirit, talent, and capabilities of the people who worked there. The human element was key to the company's success: a synthesis of world-class scientists and engineers conducting research while executives and managers exerted pressure for commercialization of research projects, and marketing and sales people found new markets and applications. The company hired the best scientists in the country. It also monitored research work being done in the academic world and tapped into it through consulting relationships. It encouraged scientists to explore knowledge for knowledge's sake. It formed relationships with companies in other industries, beginning with the auto industry, which enabled it to focus research efforts on products with immediate commercial application. Although the company was willing to consider the long-term potential of research, it experimented with every conceivable application for its products. It hired interior decorators, home economists, and other domestic advisers to promote new applications for its inventions. DuPont took risks—on people, on products, on research—that were considered long shots but often paid off in big ways.

The people of DuPont use their minds, determination and knowledge to take dramatic leaps forward. By unlocking the secrets of nature, they help make a better, healthier and safer world for everyone. These are The miracles of science™.

—DuPont, *Into Our Third Century*

Human capital continues to be the cornerstone of the company's growth strategy. Nowhere is the creative yet prudent management of human capital more evident than in its use of *Knowledge Intensity*. Knowledge Intensity is a favorite DuPont term meaning "getting paid for what the company knows rather than simply for what it makes. Knowledge Intensity is the opposite of capital intensity. It's creating value from two centuries of experience, know-how and brand equity." The DuPont Safety and Protection business leverages two hundred years of experience working with dangerous products and substances—a clear example of the commercialization of knowledge.

Senior Vice President for DuPont Global Human Resources Dennis Zeleny observes that a company that has constantly transformed itself for more than two hundred years could not have remained competitive if its focus was on product transformation alone. Rather, the method of supporting current employees—and attracting and retaining new ones—had to evolve, as well. "This company's focus has always been on business growth powered by the knowledge of our outstanding workforce," Zeleny says. "What our work-life initiatives have done is anticipate the changing demographics of the U.S. workforce, and the changing responsibilities of our employees. Not only are there more women in the workforce, but men are taking greater responsibility for work-life issues, and more families are caring for both children and their aging parents. It was imperative that we create initiatives to help our employees address these issues."

The Process of Discovery Through Research

In the early 1980s, DuPont found itself in a more turbulent operating environment—faced with economic recession, the loss of important markets to competitors, and a possible takeover. The company was challenged to improve productivity while continuing to develop new products and new applications. Employees—their knowledge and expertise, imagination and commitment—were critical to the success of these two objectives. "We have great technology packages, but if the people left, they'd be meaningless," stated Chip Schussler, HR manager, DuPont Central Research and Development.

DuPont senior leadership has always regarded employees as a major company stakeholder on par with shareholders, customers, and the communities in which it operates. In the early 1990s, the company had identified three significant changes in its labor force. First, diversity and leadership were coming to the forefront as interrelated issues that required attention if the company was to access all of its talent. Second, the role of women in the company was changing: women were filling more professional and managerial jobs. Third, more employees came from dual-income families, and their competing responsibilities came to the attention of management as a workforce issue.

In keeping with its scientific tradition and emphasis on discovery, DuPont undertook a series of research studies over two decades to analyze the meaning of these changes in its workforce. It was essential that DuPont manage and preserve its greatest asset—the innovation and expertise of its people.

What DuPont Learned

DuPont discovered that its approach to managing people, although effective for decades, had become less than a perfect fit and in some ways was impeding the performance that DuPont needed to achieve its goals. At various points in its history, the company had changed management practices upon realizing they no longer suited the current circumstances. It was time to do it again.

The willingness to undertake profound change to remake the company is in the "DNA" of DuPont. Our predecessors never shrank from it.

—Chad Holliday, chairman and CEO

In 1985 the first in a series of studies conducted for DuPont by Work/Family Directions (WFD) identified the nature of workforce trends, particularly the growing number of employees across the company with primary responsibility for children and older family members. This trend suggested that employees would need resources that DuPont employees had not typically needed before, such as child care and elder care services, which were not then readily available. As a result, the company instituted a number of initiatives to meet the needs of employees and emphasized their importance in conferences and manager training.

In 1995 DuPont commissioned a follow-up study, also by WFD, to consider the progress it had made in ten years. The intent was to honestly assess the value of the initiatives it had adopted. If they were not working, DuPont was prepared to do away with them. The 1995 study also measured the relationship between employees' dual responsibilities and organizational commitment. It made three significant discoveries that reinforced the direction DuPont had been taking.*

- *Workforce composition.* By 1995 most of the company's workforce had both home and work responsibilities; 60 percent of employees were in dual-earner families—a startling finding. A third had primary caregiving responsibility either for an older relative or for children under thirteen. The average DuPonter worked forty-seven hours per week; managers worked fifty-five hours per week. Many employees worked what amounted to a second shift at home. When home and work responsibilities were combined, employees with children and no elder care responsibilities worked ninety-one hours per week; those with no young children and no elder care responsibilities worked seventy-six hours. Only 34 percent of exempt men and even fewer exempt women (5 percent) were married to a nonemployed spouse who handled the home front. Clearly the old assumptions that employees could be singularly focused on work no longer applied.

---

* The study also found that employees with dual responsibilities who did not feel supported by the organization experienced higher levels of stress and burnout and were less able to pursue advancement opportunities.

- *Employee commitment.* Employees who had used the initiatives felt more supported in the workplace in their dual roles as employees and family members, were more committed to the company, were more satisfied with their work, and were less likely to feel overwhelmed or burned out. Employee commitment was revealed in discretionary effort, a willingness to recommend the company to others, and a sense of alignment with corporate goals.

- *Leadership.* Considerable evidence indicated that managers were unaware of the significant challenges faced by employees with dual responsibilities. For example, exempt men (presumably many of them managers) were *more* likely to have a spouse at home than was true ten years earlier. If DuPont wished to have leaders who understood its labor force and wanted to continue its founder's intention *never to isolate management from the realities that employees faced,* it would need to influence how leaders thought about these issues.

Clearly, the various programs DuPont offered had made a difference in the lives of employees. What was not clear, however, was whether managers (many of whom might not be using the programs) were aware of the powerful business case for integrating employee support into the culture. While the initiatives were the building blocks of the new corporate culture, management had yet to become the cement.

Current CFO Gary Pfeiffer remembers how the research data triggered what senior management calls a BFO—"a blinding flash of the obvious." The research's key finding was that employees who were aware of or used the initiatives were among the most productive in the company.

> *We had a BFO—"a blinding flash of the obvious."*
>
> —Gary Pfeiffer, senior vice president and CFO

Pfeiffer and then-senior vice president Joe Glass took the findings to the office of the chief executive. The issue was adopted as a strategic necessity for DuPont. Senior leadership recognized that the company must, as always, use all of the talent of its diverse workforce if it was to achieve its objectives. What had initially been seen (after the 1985 studies) as a social responsibility and ethic of valuing people also became a *business imperative*: Supporting employees in meeting their dual responsibilities was not just "the right thing to do" but also "the right business thing to do."

The DuPont Response

DuPont has undertaken a series of responses over two decades, which have evolved as the company has learned more about the workforce and become more convinced that the new approach is essential to the business. Initial pilot projects designed to provide some of the most obvious resources needed by those with dual responsibilities, like child care, developed into a continuum of resources for employees to choose from as their situations change.* They have become, as Elena Bingham, the manager of College Relations and Recruiting in DuPont Human Resources, put it, "bricks" that have built a culture and eventually morphed from "initiatives" to become embedded in the company. DuPont institutionalized the change efforts by making them a departmental function within DuPont HR, eventually aligning them with the diversity function. It also undertook a company-wide training program of managers to communicate the strategic importance and encourage use of the initiatives.

Changing the Culture

DuPont has made a major cultural change by recognizing employees' sometimes competing priorities and supporting them concretely. Managers are encouraged to manage employees more flexibly; some senior leaders build training about the use of these new management tools into critical operating tasks upon which their direct reports are judged.

> Employee access to the [initiatives such as flexible work arrangements] is critical to our success; it has to be integral to our business plan, and it's within the accountability of our leadership.
> —Hemispheres, May 1996, p. 33

The founder's core values in managing human capital have been recalibrated into a respectful environment where people share common values, bring diverse backgrounds, work as team members, function in more ambiguous conditions, and have opportunities to grow on the job.

---

* DuPont continues its research to keep a finger on the evolving needs of the labor force. In 2000 the aging of the stable workforce meant that employees' family responsibilities were shifting from caring for young children to caring for elderly relatives.

A TIMELINE OF WORK-LIFE
PROGRAMS AND INITIATIVES

1985

- Creation of the Work Force Partnering Division within DuPont Human Resources
- Expansion of family leave including paternity, adoption, and serious illness of a family member, and adoption of flexible spending accounts for dependent care
- Grants to establish community-based family care referral services
- Increased investments to expand and improve the quality of local child care resources in communities where DuPont employees live and work
- Creation of a near-site child care facility

1985–1990

- Formation of the Flex Team to develop flexible work practice principles and guidelines; flexible work arrangements available included reduced-hour jobs, job sharing, flextime, telecommuting, compressed workweeks, and sabbaticals
- Expansion of family leave to six months and to include a gradual return-to-work option
- Expansion of grants to improve child care where DuPont employees live and provision of a national dependent care referral network
- A conference with delegates from more than fifty DuPont sites.
- A pilot "Just in Time Care" program—a subsidized emergency backup system for elder care and child care at corporate headquarters

A TIMELINE OF WORK-LIFE PROGRAMS AND INITIATIVES (CONT'D)

After 1990

- A U.S. company-wide conference on work and family–related issues with thirty-five site committees represented
- A national child care and elder care resource and referral service to provide information on family care and school to all U.S.-based employees
- Training for managers on flexibility practices
- Expanded child care benefits

After 1995

- Emphasis on communicating to managers the business value of the initiatives to encourage greater usage; increased communication to employees also on the initiatives
- "Managing Smart" through WFD, a training program for managers as problem solvers in partnership with employees on work and personal life integration
- Site fund to assist DuPont office and plant sites with regional work-life balance
- Payment of work-related travel dependent care expenses; on-site child care facility near DuPont headquarters; lactation program to assist nursing mothers
- Expansion of convenience services (banking on site, dry cleaners, sundry stores)

As DuPont made changes over time, it became clear by the range of circumstances that arose—spouses being relocated, school assessments, and health matters, as well as family issues—that one size did not fit all.

"We began to understand clearly that everybody needs special treatment sometime," says Rosemary Truitt, global HR director—Crop Protection. Instead of a set menu of responses, she continues, "It is always about the conversation, the relationship and understanding people's needs—that people recognize that they have choices and that someone is willing to work with them about it. And we know that if people aren't fully present, it doesn't matter, anyway. After we changed [to this new way of managing], we got twice the performance, because they became fully engaged."

"We have come to understand that our workforce is diverse not only with respect to such aspects as culture, ethnicity, gender, age, and sexual orientation, but also diverse in terms of family situations," says Sandra M. Bowe, director of Global Diversity and WorkLife. "We now understand that this change requires creative responses from management to help our employees successfully address their needs."

The following real-life examples illustrate how the changes have been realized.

Ellen Kullman, Senior Vice President, DuPont Safety & Protection

Having proven her ability to manage a critical business unit and deliver results when she was solely career-focused, Ellen was promoted to manage the global business team, where she managed 8,600 people. When she and her husband Michael, who works for DuPont in Corporate Marketing, began to have children—first a daughter and then twin boys, both DuPont and she wanted to find a way for her to continue to manage the group. As her children (now twelve and eight) have grown, Ellen has maintained a flexible work schedule, which often finds her home for dinner with the children; some mornings she drops them at school. She and the CEO, to whom she reports, typically do meetings by phone at 9 P.M., which works for both, given equally full schedules.

Ellen emphasizes that she has not replaced one set schedule for another—she is not home every night for dinner. What distinguishes the new culture is a different approach—meeting schedules and communication revolve around both work needs and personal needs, with recognition that both are legitimate and important. But it is always about getting the business goals accomplished. Ellen finds she has developed more effective leadership skills since living life as a parent: "You clearly develop patience and become a more holistic leader, because you understand better how people live. Being a DuPonter, which we say is a '24/7' job, is very much like being a parent, which is also '24/7.'" Ellen is an example of the new generation of proven leaders who didn't understand why it couldn't be done another way.

She says, "We used to rate people on activity ('Can I see you here working hard?'). Now we rate people on results."

Gary Pfeiffer, Senior Vice President and CFO

"Twenty years ago I would not have been considered 'serious' if I left a meeting for a family responsibility. Earlier in my career, I remember vividly my boss checking to be sure I was back at my desk the day after my daughter was born, despite my wife's difficult delivery. A few years ago, when my oldest son graduated from high school, I realized I had blinked and missed it. I said to myself that was not going to happen with my second son. I am proud to say that I have not missed a single school conference, performance, or soccer game—I coach his soccer team. I recall being in the middle of a senior leadership meeting and the CEO—realizing it was three o'clock and my day to coach the team—asked me, "Gary, don't you have to leave?" I offered to stay. He said, "No, you go, that's important.""

How Things Change

The flexibility of the DuPont work environment today is a far cry from that remembered by a twenty-five-year veteran when he first began work in the Finance group. On the glass door entry to the department, just under the department name, was painted the religiously observed lunch hour—12:20 to 1:20 P.M. The DuPont of today seeks to offer greater balance for its employees and to shift the point of decision making from company to employee.

"There is a difference between fair and respectful work practices and paternalism," says Elena Bingham. "One empowers and enables employees to make their own choice. Paternalism seeks to foster dependence. Today employees are more apt to question and want to manage their own lives. Still, it isn't about integrating work and personal life so they become as one. One's personal life should stay that way—separate from work, but one should not overwhelm the other."

Chad Holliday put it this way, as he pondered what it means to adapt this large, diverse business to the reality that the average worker cannot always be singularly focused on work. For him it is not a question of whether DuPont should change but how.

The challenge for an organization our size is to figure out how you get back to where you would go naturally—to treat people right—which would be obvious if you were a small enterprise. We need to figure out a way to get beyond the rules that have been created over time to help us manage an organization this size. We must remember that it is more than a set of programs, but instead an atmosphere. . . . It is certainly not about excusing poor performance. And it is not a one-time event either, but an evolutionary process that takes time. In fact, our next wave issue on this subject—that I personally worry about—is how to deal with the stress of the 24/7 lives we all lead.

The Results

"It is about creating a work environment where each person is valued and respected in the work they do. When people feel that all of who they are is valued, they produce more," says Willie C. Martin, vice president of Diversity and WorkLife and president of the North American Region.

Gary Pfeiffer, in considering the value to DuPont of its changes, says that it makes *the* difference in company performance.

It's not enough for DuPont to have smart people; we only hire smart people. Talent isn't enough; it's our starting point. To succeed, we need smart people who are highly motivated to do their job well. We must have that extra edge—it is what makes the difference. Our research showed when employees used the new initiatives we created for their competing work and personal responsibilities, they felt more supported by the company, were willing to work longer hours, were more loyal to the company, and were willing to do whatever it took. When we first saw these findings, our initial reaction was one of skepticism, but we scrubbed the data and ultimately were convinced. There was absolutely a direct relationship. We have also built up an enormous bank of goodwill.

Asked how a company as large and complex as DuPont would know if these changes in how it manages human capital are worth the investment, CEO Chad Holliday responded, "The value is so obvious that I have a hard time describing it."

In 2000, a new round of workforce research evaluated the improvements that the company's fifteen-year change effort had brought. This study added new measures of the connection between burnout, commitment, and employees' sense of being supported by the company and its managers in their personal responsibilities.

Employee Commitment, Burnout, and Support

Employees surveyed in 2000 who felt supported in both their work and personal responsibilities were more committed at work. Similarly, employees who felt supported reported less burnout. The average support score—the number of employees who felt supported—had risen by 18 percent since 1995. Employees who felt supported were less likely to turn down projects that involved increased pressure or non-daytime work, turn down promotions, or refuse overtime. The average number of employees reporting stress and burnout from managing their work and personal responsibilities had dropped by 8 percent since 1995, and employees reported high individual effort and a willingness to go the extra mile.

Ellen R. Doran, senior specialist, Central Research and Development, describes her reaction in these terms.

> I've taken advantage of parental leave, flexible work hours, and telecommuting for twelve years and it has made a big difference in my personal life and in my personal productivity. I'm a senior scientist and I hope a valued employee, but don't know if I would have remained with DuPont had I not had this flexibility. When I adopted my third child in 1990 I was very close to leaving and becoming a stay-at-home mom, but because I was able to work half time I stayed with the company. When my youngest child started school I went back full time, but worked a flexible schedule. I work from home when I need space to concentrate on something (for example, writing programs, trying experiments—with computers, not lab work—or just figuring something out). I also work from home when I have a sick child, or there is a snow day. I'm a very creative person, but I need mental and intellectual space in order to do my best work and I believe this type of arrangement and flexibility gives me that space. I've figured out new and different approaches to problems dur-

ing "work at home" days that I don't know I would have thought of at work. Having this type of support for my home life means as much, or more, to me than my paycheck and my benefits. Because of it, I can continue to work at a very intense scientific level, yet I don't struggle with feeling like I am shortchanging my children.

A Stable Workforce

Almost three fourths of DuPont employees under forty predicted in the 2000 survey they would stay for fifteen years or more, which is especially impressive in a booming economy that offers many enticing opportunities to those with scientific training. Its culture and work-life policies have clearly helped DuPont retain talented employees.

Jane Swinehart, a senior consultant in the Personnel Relations Section of DuPont Human Resources, sums it up this way.

In July of 1989 I had been with DuPont ten years when my husband and I adopted our daughter, Cate. . . . I did not know whether I would continue to work or resign. Under the company's Family Leave initiative . . . I took off five months without pay and worked one month at part-time. Then I went back to work on Flex hours that allowed us to minimize the time our daughter was at the babysitter's. I was the first person in an Exempt position at that particular site to both take an LOA and come back to work on Flex hours. . . . If I had to return to work [when she was six weeks old] I would have resigned. Even at five months it was a difficult choice for me. I went back to work with the attitude that I would try balancing working and raising a child for three months. If it wasn't working out I would resign at that time. Thirteen years later I'm still happily employed.

Enhanced Reputation

The changes the company has implemented have enhanced its reputation as a good place to work, particularly for employees with significant family responsibilities—important in its ability to attract the best talent. It is consistently recognized among the top U.S. companies for its people practices, including being among *Fortune*'s "America's Most Admired Companies," *BusinessWeek*'s "Top Ten Family-Friendly Companies," *Child*'s "30 Great Companies for Working Dads," *Working Mother*'s "100 Best Companies for Working Mothers" (fourteen out of seventeen years possible), and the *Wall Street Journal*'s "Best Employers for Women and Parents."

A New Employee Contract

DuPont has found that human capital practices, especially those that recognize employees' personal as well as work responsibilities, make the difference in attracting and retaining talent. Says Dennis Zeleny,

> *Companies cannot make the same promises of twenty years ago, so employees are in a world of uncertainty. The old deal was if you got a good education, kept your nose clean, and hooked up with a good company, you were set. Not so any more. The current research on why people come and why they stay often misses what motivates most people to stay for the longer term. Our company's new practices, which recognize that people have personal responsibilities that they bring to work, are more systemic and are a powerful tool for getting and keeping the right talent.*

DuPont Corporate Vision: Work and Life

DuPont established a corporate vision for work and life.

> *DuPont believes it will be beneficial to the company, the communities in which it operates, and future generations if the company's increasingly diverse workforce is enabled to lead full and productive lives, both at work and at home.*

> *The company is committed to making changes in the workplace and fostering changes in the community that are sensitive to the changing family unit and the increasingly diverse workforce.*

> *DuPont believes this will result in healthier and more productive employees, better able to drive the company to compete more effectively in the global marketplace.*

Current Challenges

DuPont continues to face challenges—from global competition, rising raw materials costs, worldwide economic conditions, and price pressures. Productivity is more important than ever—productivity in manufacturing, research, marketing, and operations—leveraging every dollar spent to produce more value than the competition. The company is aggressively pursuing a three-pronged growth strategy that is dependent, more than ever before, on the capabilities and commitment of every member of the team:

- Integrated science that provides the innovation and technological edge to grow its businesses

- Knowledge Intensity that creates new business models that capture a larger share of downstream value from the company's innovation, brands, and know-how

- Productivity that drives excellence in sales and operations

Recognizing this, the company has made people a high priority. "In the last five years DuPont has undertaken a workforce renewal effort—which will continue into the foreseeable future—focusing on hiring at the recent college graduate level," says Dennis Zeleny. "People want to come here because they know they will be able to make contributions that are relevant to business, and they know that they will be recognized and valued for the unique individuals they are."

Tough times are nothing new. This two-hundred-year-old company has faced them before and triumphed—always as a result of its employees. The difference today is that triumph can no longer be based solely on the efforts of the company's leaders and its brilliant scientists; it must come from leveraging all the talent of all its people and leveraging that talent in new ways. A diverse workforce is critical to meeting the challenge.

14

THE BAXTER
INTERNATIONAL STORY

The core values of respect, responsiveness, and results have become the driving force behind the transformation of Baxter International—a transformation that has improved talent management and increased returns to shareholders.

The Catalyst for Change

Baxter International produces blood-related and drug delivery products—critical for people with life-threatening conditions like hemophilia, immune deficiencies, kidney disease, and cancer. The stakes are high, and confidence in the integrity of the company among its customers—hospitals, doctors, and patients—is about as essential as it gets.

In 1993 Baxter got a loud wake-up call alerting it to the need for change. A key customer wrote to Chairman and CEO Vernon Loucks about a discrepancy between Baxter's rhetoric, how Baxter said it operated, and its action, the customer's actual experience. At the same time, the U.S.

This case was cowritten with Sandra Cunningham, Ph.D.

Department of Veterans Affairs accused Baxter of overselling products and eventually banned Baxter products from its hospitals. Baxter had a stated policy of just-in-time ordering and delivery of products that reduced overstocking and understocking, minimized costs of storing unused items, and eliminated periodic large expenditures that caused spikes in cash outlay. Baxter adhered to the policy most of the year, but, when the end of the year rolled around and Baxter needed to boost the bottom line as it prepared to release earnings numbers, it encouraged customers to stock up on its products.

This circumstance could have been dismissed as an isolated problem, but Baxter chose to use the episode as an opportunity to take an honest look at itself: at what it was and what it wanted to be. Vernon Loucks was just planning the leadership succession for his departure, so it was an opportune time. The incident raised questions of whether other discrepancies existed between rhetoric and action throughout the organization. What did the company believe in? What were its values? What would it need to be to enter the twenty-first century? What kind of leadership would be required?

Discovering a New Identity

Baxter embarked on a serious exploratory effort to discover the answers to these questions. It launched a multifaceted examination, internally and externally. It held company-wide focus groups, interviewed managers, surveyed employees, and benchmarked admired companies. The strategic effort, which reported directly to the president's office, eventually spanned eight years.

The exploratory process identified a faster pace of change, the importance of new knowledge and creativity to fuel innovation, the need to fit Baxter's offerings to customer needs, and globalization as key elements of Baxter's future growth. Baxter determined that if it were to thrive in the context of such challenges, it must first have a strong rudder—a set of core values that would keep the company on course. Because the discrepancy found in 1993 had been one of conflicting values or lack of clarity about them, any solution would need to be about values as well. Baxter needed to be both unambiguous about its values and transparent in its execution of them, so that its integrity was never in question.

With a clear set of values, the right thing to do in any situation would be obvious. What the company expected of business units and employees would be unequivocal. Customers, the public, everyone could count on it—*integrity*.

Integrity has come to suggest a moral standard, but the root of the word means "of one piece"—complete, all parts fitting together. It was also this kind of integrity that Baxter needed.

Baxter identified a fundamental value that would be essential to its efforts—*respect*. Respect would be the value that defined the company. It applied to all stakeholders—customers, shareholders, employees, suppliers, and the communities in which Baxter operated. Respect would push decision making closer to the customers, improve understanding of their issues, and position the company publicly in a more favorable light. From this value all else, including business performance, would flow.

Respect was the key to operating with integrity—to instilling confidence that Baxter could be counted on to deliver what it promised. Without respect it would be impossible to get empowered employees, teamwork, innovation (employees bringing their best ideas), or the quality it would take to meet the needs of customers. With respect, individuals and teams would accept responsibility for their actions, honesty would be at the forefront of decision making, and people would be treated with dignity and be encouraged to challenge assumptions and provide valuable feedback.

With respect as its first core value, Baxter developed a set of Shared Values that included *responsiveness* and *results*. These three values became behavioral guidelines for everyone in the organization to use in their actions with one another, customers, and shareholders.

A Newly Defined Workforce

Recognizing that company practices are carried out by people, and that its people would be the ones living the values, Baxter was determined to ensure it was not making assumptions about its employees any more than it made assumptions about the consistency of its practices. It undertook an equally thorough analysis to understand what a value system rooted in respect would mean for employees.

Working with an outside consulting firm (MK Consulting), the company spent eighteen months studying employees and managers; randomly selected employees participated in 125 focus groups, a hundred managers were interviewed (more than half of all officers), and employees were surveyed (Koblenz, 2000). The depth of the analysis alone was a reflection of how determined Baxter was to genuinely understand the dynamics of its people.

Having originally conceived of respect for employees as listening to them, communicating with them, and attending to their professional development, Baxter discovered a new dimension.

When employees and managers were asked what they needed from Baxter to be the best team members they could be, the answer was surprising. Employees said it was essential that they be regarded as whole people, not just employees. They said they couldn't give their best at work if their whole lives weren't supported in the workplace. Managers and nonmanagers alike needed the authority and flexibility to manage both work and personal obligations so they could be more successful at both. The ability to do that was the cornerstone upon which the value of respect rested for most employees.

Upon closer examination, the reason became clear, as the study revealed how dramatically different the current workforce was: a full two thirds (66 percent) of employees in the focus groups either were part of a dual-income couple or were single parents with significant family responsibilities.

Not About Employee Programs

Another eye-opener was that people still had problems of seismic proportions being both excellent employees and responsible family members, even though Baxter already had an array of programs for dual-focus employees. In fact, Baxter was considered a leader in work-life balance programs. Existing programs included family leave, informational programs to help employees find child care and elder care, and allowing employees to use sick days to care for family members.

Even with these services in place, employees had conflicts, which could have had a dramatic effect on the company. Employees found it so hard to balance competing work and personal responsibilities that 41 percent were looking for a new job. More men than women had been exploring other job opportunities—49 percent of men compared to 39 percent of women.

Subtle issues were causing problems for employees, such as the amount of time they were required to work. Managers were incorrectly assuming that money (overtime pay or salary increases) compensated for the control over their time that employees needed. In the study, one fourth of employees said they were willing to slow their career and salary advancement to achieve maneuverability to balance work with other responsibilities.

The resulting effect on the company was troublesome. Employees who felt their managers were unsupportive of their personal obligations said they invested less discretionary effort. They cited examples: exerting minimum effort on a task and then passing it on incomplete to someone else, not sharing suggestions about how to improve processes, and bad-mouthing the company to customers.

Baxter and MK Consultants developed a conceptual framework to demonstrate how the issues fit together and how to deal with them. It became a seminal work that other companies would find enlightening as well.

Dubbed the "Work and Life Pyramid of Needs," it was modeled on Abraham Maslow's hierarchy of needs and summarizes sources of conflict and resolution in ascending order (see Figure 6).

The pyramid has four levels. At the base is "Respect," defined as whether employees are treated with dignity at work and whether the whole person, including responsibilities and interests outside work, is recognized and validated. Respect is necessary for all employees but poses the biggest problem for hourly employees, who typically have the least control over their work and schedules (Koblenz, 2000).

Figure 6 Work and Life Pyramid of Needs

The next level is "Balance," whether time devoted to work in relation to other activities is at a comfortable ratio for employees. Balance, by this definition, is affected most by workload. Exempt employees tend to struggle most with this since they can work long hours, and often do.

The next level is "Flexibility," which considers whether the parameters of when and how work is accomplished are flexible and can accommodate a variety of personal needs. The top level is "Programs"—what Koblenz (2000) defines as "programmatic support for employees' needs in specific areas, including financial, health, family, convenience assistance, and time off."

Respect and balance are considered entitlements by employees, and there is more risk to employers for not providing them than reward for providing them (see Figure 7). Employees perceive these top two levels—flexibility and programs—as benefits rather than entitlements. The return to the company in employee appreciation is potentially greater for flexibility and programs than for balance and respect, which employees see as a given.

These four levels operate in order of pain felt by the employee, with the bottom—respect, then balance—causing the greatest pain when they are absent. Employees experiencing pain at the levels of respect and balance do not express need for flexibility or programs. In fact, without the essential levels satisfied—for example, without a context of basic respect—the top levels are apt to be considered lip service and backfire on the employer.

This framework helped Baxter understand why the conflicts employees were facing could not be resolved by employee programs alone. Baxter rebuilt its approach to employees around respect: trusting, empowering, and encouraging employees to manage and balance both their personal and work lives responsibly.

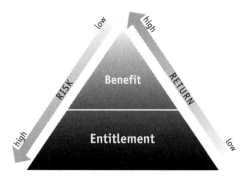

Figure 7 Risk and Return

BAXTER'S GUIDEBOOK FOR
MANAGERS AND EMPLOYEES

Baxter's leadership is built on several core strengths: technological expertise, manufacturing and quality excellence, and global presence. Baxter needs to be quick, flexible, and constantly available in order to maintain its market position and grow. And Baxter needs to do this with a workforce that is dramatically different from the one that took us through the Industrial Age. At a time when the need for employee focus and dedication couldn't be greater, employees have more distractions and competing priorities than ever before. It used to be in most families there was a person to take care of "work" and another to take care of "life." Now more people work, but life hasn't stopped. Therefore, we need a new model for working. A model that recognizes two diverse sets of needs, the company's needs and the employee's needs, and enables us to successfully fulfill our responsibilities in both realms. (Baxter Healthcare, 2000)

Making the Values Real . . . Leadership

The values clarification process resulted in the selection of Harry Jansen Kraemer as the new CEO. Kraemer, Baxter's then-CFO, exemplified the challenges of the workforce he was to lead and Baxter's new values. He also reflected its new demographics. A forty-something father of five children, with a banker wife who was employed until the birth of their fifth child, he had always been actively involved with the children. First as CFO and later as CEO, he left the office by 6 P.M. to eat dinner with his children, play a little baseball, or help with homework, finishing his own work between 10 P.M. and 1 A.M. after the kids were in bed. He routinely left executive committee meetings to pick up a sick child from school, laughing at the prospect of considering anything else when the school called. He worked with his daughter's softball team and taught Sunday school at his church, believing that investing in your community is important, no matter how busy you are. He deliberately made these actions visible, writing news about family exploits on the company home page, to establish that respect for everyone's balanced life is real at Baxter, not just talk.

The sports news in the Kraemer household was baseball. I was the co-manager of Suzie's 4th grade softball team. The games had some humorous moments, particularly early in the season when we struggled to get everybody to be focused and disciplined about the rules (sound familiar?). The classic situation was when we had the bases loaded with no outs and the next batter hit a slow roller to third. For reasons that are difficult to explain, the runner on third base started running back to second base! . . .

I took two vacation days last week to help prepare the children for school. I had a great time walking everybody to school and meeting the teachers. (Casner-Lotto, 2000, p. 97)

In talking about how he manages his complex life, Kraemer says, "It is all about how to prioritize, where to allocate resources—particularly time." It is the same skill required to run the company effectively. On his conference table sits a sign, "I can handle any crisis—I have kids."

Kraemer also exemplifies Baxter's clarity of focus on values. His mantra is "Do the right thing." For Kraemer, a respectful organization exhibits at least four essential elements of a respect-based, values-driven, culture.

- Everyone's talent is a corporate asset.
- Good ideas are more important than being right.
- Employees bring their whole selves to work.
- The way you get results is as important as the results you get.

Even though Kraemer means this last point emphatically—in fact it is the corporate anthem—there is no question in his mind that better results come from Baxter's values-driven way of operating.

When you have shared values, you have a company of people who want to do the right thing, not prove that they are right. People check their egos at the door and it optimizes ideas.

—*Harry J. Kraemer Jr.*

Integrating Values Throughout the Organization

How does an organization as large and complex as Baxter instill values evenly?

"The question is, How in a large organization do you create a culture, a process, a discipline, and a communication system?" observed Harry Kraemer when discussing the dissemination of the Shared Values—respect, responsiveness, results—to forty-two thousand Baxter employees. "The first thing you do is to create shared values and then demonstrate that you really mean it. The only thing worse than not having a great set of values is saying you do and not acting on them."

Baxter communicated and methodically integrated the newly adopted Shared Values throughout the organization as the backbone of expected behavior with employees, customers, and shareholders. The values are integrated into the metrics that measure success for all employees, business units, and leaders. They are put in practice through Baxter's Key Goals of *Best Team, Best Partner, Best Investment,* and *Best Citizen.* In turn, these goals are the core for the corporation's annual business objectives developed by each team within the organization. Their annual "Balanced Scorecard" states the objectives used to measure the performance of teams and team leaders.

The Shared Value of respecting employees as whole people with lives and responsibilities outside work is an important part of the package. Alice Campbell directs the strategic initiative that enables employees to give quality time to both family and career. She serves on the Baxter Shared Values Committee Working Team so she can oversee the integration of the employee values into Baxter's systems. New systems ensure that employees can adjust their own schedules, telecommute, and be active in the design of their jobs. It has changed a once one-way employee-employer relationship to a two-way street; as one employee put it, "If you only care about me because you want to get the work done, then you don't really care about me."

A new standard for attracting and retaining employees was designed and implemented in 1997 by Baxter's Operating Management Team. This new mandate reads as follows.

We are committed to the provision of ongoing development and feedback and the creation of a workplace that supports employees in achieving their maximum potential. Managers and employees will share responsibility in achieving a healthy balance between work and personal life.

The decision to share responsibility came out of a 1996 survey that identified employees' ability to manage work and personal life simultaneously as one of eight critical drivers of overall performance. Managers' success in sharing responsibility is measured in a 360-degree performance evaluation system.

To Alice Campbell, the most important change has been creating an environment of trust where conflicting needs and responsibilities can be discussed openly. The following box describes the new atmosphere in which employees' and Baxter's needs are negotiated.

Baxter is clear to employees about their responsibility in the equation. Employees are responsible for communicating their personal situations and seeking out the assistance they need. They must communicate openly, exhibit personal accountability, find their own solutions first, be realistic and flexible, use available resources, and constantly reevaluate and change.

For Harry Kraemer, the employee aspect of living Baxter's values is both doable and critical to the company. He says,

If you want values, and you want values to be more than words, and you seriously want to be respectful with employees, then you must create an environment to optimize people's lives. There are two great lies about doing that. First, that it's really complicated. I don't think so. It's only complicated if the company has to come up with the answer. I don't even know what the problem is. The second great lie is that people will take advantage. You either believe people are basically good or not; it's a basic trust issue. In my experience, people who work flexibly are more productive; they will be retained longer and we don't have to replace that expertise. It simply doesn't make any sense not to manage this way, when we are economically better off.

The Essence of Baxter

The systemic nature of the change at Baxter can be lost when discussions of Baxter focus on Harry Kraemer. Harry Kraemer's place at the helm is as much a reflection of the change at Baxter as the change at Baxter is of his place at the helm. There is integrity—a wholeness—to what Baxter is about that has equipped everyone to know how to do the right thing. It is clear that managers can trust employees and Kraemer can trust company-defining moments to others.

BAXTER'S GUIDEBOOK FOR MANAGERS AND EMPLOYEES WORK/LIFE IN THE WORKPLACE
A Framework for Understanding and Taking Action

Two Sets of Needs

In every workplace there are two sets of needs: the needs of the business and the personal needs of the employee. There are choices about how to respond to these two sets of needs.

Two Approaches . . . Competitive vs. Collaborative

The company and the employee can each take a "my needs first" approach that will no doubt lead to increased work/life conflict, or they can take an "our needs" approach that seeks collaborative solutions.

Solutions . . . The BEST TEAM Approach

Management, employees, and the infrastructure of the company all have a role to play in order to create and foster an environment at work that can produce win-win solutions for the employee and for Baxter.

Impact of Conflicts

At times, the two sets of needs may seem to be competing. How the company and employee respond when their needs conflict will ultimately determine whether they create 1) a mutually supportive environment that respects the goals of the other, or 2) a competitive environment that requires one side to lose in order for the other to win.

Baxter now uses a Collaborative Approach to addressing the convergence of employee and company needs. It is "one where each party holds the perspective that the other's needs must be incorporated into the solutions in order for 'me' to be successful."

Collaborative Company Perspective

When an employee's personal needs interfere with the company's needs to get the job done, the personal needs must be considered or the employee may not be able to perform the job.

Collaborative Personal Perspective

When work interferes with an individual's ability to take care of personal needs, the employee needs to search for solutions that meet business as well as personal needs or else s/he is not fulfilling his/her obligations to either.

Source: Baxter Healthcare, 2000

The newly defined Baxter has had several moments of truth. One such moment began in August 2001 in Madrid when a series of patients died after dialysis. It was not clear whether the cause was connected to products made by Baxter's newly acquired renal division, Althin. It could simply have been that the patients were old and medically fragile, which many dialysis patients are. It could also have been a problem with the solution, a 3M product, that was used to test the Althin-made dialysis filters (Hammonds, 2002).

In the midst of the crisis, the Spanish government blamed Baxter's product, even though Baxter's own internal analysis indicated no evidence of a malfunction. Before it was clear where the fault lay, Baxter made a $10 million decision to recall all Althin filters. Alan Heller, president of Althin, simply felt there was too much commonality among the deaths, which would rise to fifty-three and include some in Croatia and the Spanish city of Valencia, to be a coincidence.

After intense exploratory research and testing by toxicologists and physicians at Althin and Baxter, the source of the problem was found—bubbles that indicated trace amounts of liquid: a solution made by 3M that was used in testing the filters was found to have not been totally evaporated. The liquid was not toxic, but when heated to body temperature in the bloodstream it apparently could become gaseous and cause a fatal pulmonary embolism. Research and test results confirmed that the solution was indeed the source of the problem. The next day, Alan Heller called Harry Kraemer at home to tell him the test results. Kraemer was packing the car for a camping trip with his daughter. They talked through the strategy and then, K. H. Hammonds (2002) reports, "Kraemer told Heller, 'Let's make sure we do the right thing.' Then he went camping. . . . 'If I didn't think Al would do the right thing on this one, I had a much bigger issue.'"

Even though an outside company's products (3M) were involved, Baxter didn't point fingers, wait to pull the filters from the market, or pull them quietly. It could have groused about the lack of foreign government cooperation that slowed Baxter's ability to pinpoint the problem. Instead, Harry Kraemer did several highly unusual things and he did them right away and unequivocally. "He told the truth. He took responsibility when it would have been easy not to" (Hammonds, 2002). And he apologized.

Baxter and its executives were willing to make sacrifices to do the right thing. The first product recall cost $10 million. Refreshingly, that cost was seen in the context of potential cost to patients. Baxter eventually took a $156 million after-tax loss to close factories that produced the filters and pay legal settlements (Hammonds, 2002). Kraemer recommended that his board cut his performance bonus by 40 percent and those of other senior executives by 20 percent.

The decisions were costly, but they were clear, because what Baxter was about was clear. Values drove the decision; it was simply a matter, as Harry Kraemer would say, of "doing the right thing." The end goal that Baxter had been working toward for almost ten years—creating a rudder that would guide the company without question and make its integrity unequivocal— had indisputably been accomplished.

Baxter's handling of this very visible crisis left a "lasting imprint on the company's relationships with patients and doctors, with employees, and of course, with investors. . . . 'In the short run, our results are probably worse for the way we handle things. But in the long run, they'll be better,' Alan Heller said" (Hammonds, 2002).

Kraemer has noticed that how when he visits customers, about a third of the time they mention having read about Baxter's values. Does this recognition give Baxter an advantage? "I think so," he says with assurance.

When Kraemer was asked in 2002, "Which is it for you; is this first the *right* way to run a business and it turns out to also be the *smart* way, or vice versa?" he responded,

I don't know many CEOs who are more bottom-line oriented than I am. In 1993 the market capitalization of Baxter was $4–5 billion. Nine years later [after the reorientation around Shared Values] it is $34 billion. How did the value increase eightfold in nine years? Yes, we had some spin-offs, but if I could name one variable, it is the Shared Values. How? People are more engaged. It is okay to argue and disagree here. That drives a significant improvement in talent management. In my mind, it is those more qualitative variables that drive the financial variables. I always wanted to run a business this way, but it had to be done at a net zero economic impact. (It couldn't create a loss.) The homerun is that it is the right thing to do—socially and spiritually; the special bonus is that it is the right economic thing. (Hammonds, 2002)

The Right Economic Thing

Baxter's financials tell the rest of the story. In 2002, when the median growth in revenues among the Fortune 500 was 1.2 percent and aggregate revenues sank by 6 percent, Baxter had revenue growth of 10 percent; Baxter's five-year revenue growth from 1998 to 2003 was 69 percent. In 2002 Baxter had earnings of 15 percent, compared to a median among the Fortune 500 of 14.2 percent and aggregate earnings that plunged by 66 percent (Harrington, 2003).

Even with a drop in stock value that occurred in 2003, Baxter's five-year average shareholder return was 4 percent from 1998 through the first quarter of 2003, compared with −7.1 percent for the S&P 500 and 2.7 percent for the S&P Healthcare Composite. This performance clearly reflects Baxter's reorientation around Shared Values and Harry Kraemer's leadership, which began in 1998. By comparison, for the ten-year (1993–2003) averages that include the period before Baxter implemented these changes, Baxter's shareholder return at 11 percent was better than the S&P 500's return of 8.6 percent, but lagged the S&P Healthcare Composite's return of 18.1 percent.

Two employee stories illustrate some of what has contributed to Baxter's economic success and growth.

- Steve Meyer is the treasurer; his department manages Baxter's assets. He makes sure his team knows he will help find creative solutions when their lives change. When an employee who was familiar with Baxter's tax and accounting systems and skilled at handling investments told Steve that she was pregnant with a third child and would have to quit, Steve suggested a creative alternative. He asked her to take responsibility for a second-tier project that could not be assigned to anyone else — at her own pace, from home. The rest of the team members' plates were already full; otherwise the project would have to be postponed to the following year. This story illustrates his approach to conserving the worth of a knowledge worker; without this arrangement her underlying knowledge — her technical knowledge and contextual knowledge of Baxter — would have been lost. Whatever she could accomplish on the project would be "gravy." They agreed she would work on it at whatever level she could and come into the office only on occasion. The flexibility she had and the company's willingness to work around her needs created a dynamic that Baxter sees playing out all over the company. As a result of this arrangement, according to Steve, her work realized "tens of millions of dollars" in revenue to Baxter because the assets were handled a year sooner. Steve says, "Because I can manage people this way, I get access to the best people."

- In 2001 Sue Halliday, vice president of the internal accounting and accounts payable department, formed a set of employee teams to re-examine work processes. Even as VP, Sue works a 75 percent schedule, and 90 percent of her 115 team members use some form of alternative work arrangements, working a wide variety of schedules. One of the team goals was to reduce workload. Workload had arisen in the research as an issue compromising employees' ability to have balance. The teams reorganized the work, implemented new technology, and redesigned the performance review system. In an eight-month period, they decreased workload, reduced headcount by 7 percent, increased the volume of work processed by nearly 40 percent, and saved a total of 450 workdays. "You create a culture of people who are held accountable for getting results rather than just being there. The three R's [the Shared Values of respect, responsiveness, and results] force managers to manage people in a more balanced way—to get results without dead bodies in the corner," she adds.

There is no question about where Baxter stands. It has, in the process of reorienting itself around its Shared Values and making sure they are real, found a way to stay poised for change, to innovate through highly engaged people, and stay true and whole at the same time. It has shown the world that it sticks by its values no matter what. After all, principles matter most—when they're not convenient to follow; it's when they're inconvenient that they really mean something. In a time when "the business section reads like the police blotter" (Hammonds, 2002), that's called integrity.

15

THE SAS STORY

SAS founders operate by a simple philosophy—create the same work environment for every employee that they would want for themselves. They believe that by hiring the right people—people who enjoy the work itself—and making SAS a place where employees want to be, employees will stay. They find that stable employees serve customers best and that loyal customers are the source of their company's success.

A Marathon Runner, Not a Sprinter

SAS Institute, a privately held North Carolina statistical software company, is known for coloring outside the lines on its human resource practices, and for its iconoclastic co-founder and CEO. The truth is that Jim Goodnight is much more concerned about substance than flash.

When GQ asked to schedule a photo shoot of Goodnight in front of his car (part of a series of such CEO photos), he was stumped. Why would they want a picture of him in front of his Ford station wagon? When someone explained to the then-sixty-fourth richest man in the world that the other

CEOs had fancy cars, Jim Goodnight wondered aloud how they would haul their junk to the dump (Bankert, Lee, & Lange, 2000).

The work atmosphere at SAS—like Goodnight's personality—is the subject of much publicity that implies the work environment is built on flash. It is not. SAS does not want to be known as a great place to work in order to attract good employees; it actually wants to be a great place to work.

SAS has two reasons for this desire. First, that's how Jim Goodnight wants to work himself, and he thinks he's no different from—and no better than—anyone else. Second, it builds incredibly loyal employees, who in turn create the incredibly loyal customers who are the source of SAS's success.

Clearly, this business model—stable, happy employees lead to stable, happy customers—has worked. SAS had 3–4 percent turnover rate among employees throughout the dot-com craze when many in the high-tech industry had 20 percent, and it resubscribes an astonishing 98 percent of its customers annually. Founded in 1976, SAS has never had a down year; in fact SAS had twenty-seven straight years of growth and profitability.*

Who Is SAS?

SAS produces innovative and customized software to help clients manage information strategically. It is the largest privately held software company in the world, with $1.18 billion in sales in 2002. SAS has nine thousand employees worldwide—five thousand in the United States, with thirty-eight hundred at a single campus in Cary, North Carolina.

SAS writes software that converts data into information, what SAS calls "business intelligence and analytics." Initially a tool for statisticians, SAS now has 90 percent of the Fortune 500 as clients. "Marriott uses it to manage a frequent-visitor program, Merck & Co. and Pfizer Inc. use it to develop new drugs, and the U.S. government uses SAS to calculate the Consumer Price Index" (Fishman, 1999, p. 87). According to SAS (2002), the U.S. Marines used it to save $89 million between 2000 and 2002 by pinpointing the true cost of services. SAS has more than 8,000 customers, 40,000 different customer sites in 118 countries, and 3.5 million users.

---

* SAS had twenty-five straight years of double-digit growth; in its twenty-sixth year revenues grew by 4.4 percent.

SAS has deliberately chosen a business model that forces it to stay tuned to customers. It resubscribes customers every year, so every year customers have a chance to walk. SAS generates 80 percent of its revenue by renewing contracts, so it must know how the software is working and how the customer feels about it long before the year ends. Jim Goodnight's philosophy is simple: "Listen to the customers. Give them the software they want" (Bankert et al., 2000).

About 20 percent of the software that SAS delivers to a customer (particularly with solutions implementation software) is customized to that client. SAS makes improvements based on the customer's experience—a highly individualized process. So having the developer who initially wrote the code available as the improvements are made creates an enormous advantage in efficiency and results and makes retaining employees a factor in SAS's customer-driven success.

SAS is an ecosystem—a highly interdependent enterprise. The developers rely on the marketing people to interpret what's happening in the marketplace, and they both rely on technical communicators who write the manuals to make the technology understandable. Interdependency is one reason that most everyone who works in connection with SAS is an SAS employee, whether the job is tending the gardens, printing the brochures, teaching swimming, or developing software. It gives SAS control over the quality of every aspect of the business.

The other reason for creating that atmosphere for *everyone* is that it's the kind of place Goodnight wanted to work and the only kind of place he'd want to lead. The spirit at SAS is genuinely egalitarian, which is what makes the printer who prints the software materials and the visual artists and video creators who create the technological wizardry for marketing events as committed to the company's success as the software developers.

What's Behind the SAS Culture?

A set of beliefs underlies the SAS culture and work environment.

- *Reciprocity.* "If you take care of people, they will take care of the company" (Jim Goodnight, quoted in Pfeffer, 1998b, p. 5).

- *Egalitarianism.* Employees are no different from the people who run the place, and the people who run the place are no better than employees.

- *Health and balance.* Well-rounded, healthy, rested people are better employees.

- *Invest!* SAS invests in R&D, employee well-being, and customer relationships because it expects to have the same employees and customers for a long time.

- *Hire hard, manage easy.* Once past the rigorous selection process, employees have much room to be creative and innovative in their work.

- *Accountability.* "SAS expects the best. I knew before I came to SAS that you couldn't come to SAS and play around," says Nicole Jones, software tester. Every SAS product manual lists the names of the developers and testers who created or upgraded the software (Fishman, 1999, p. 94).

SAS Is a (Really) Great Place to Work

No question—the SAS work environment is unusual, so unusual that *60 Minutes* thought it worth airtime—twice (Safer, 2003). Employees have an on-site medical facility with doctors and nurses employed by SAS, a pianist to serenade them at lunch (where a quarter of the staff can be seen eating with family members visiting the office), a 77,000-square-foot complex of recreation and fitness facilities, two artists in residence, beautiful light-filled offices, four excellent child care facilities for which parents pay a nominal fee, ubiquitous employee break rooms with an endless supply of free snacks, and on and on and on.

SAS consistently ranks as one of the best places to work in America by almost any criteria. *Fortune* ranked SAS number nineteen in its 2003 list of the "100 Best Companies to Work For in America." In 2001 *Computerworld* ranked SAS among the "100 Best Places to Work in IT," for diversity, training, career development, benefits, hot projects, and retention (SAS, 2002). It was in the top ten of *BusinessWeek's* "1997 Best Companies" for enabling employees to balance work and family (Cohen & Prusak, 2002) and has been in the "100 Best Companies" listed by *Working Mother* thirteen times. SAS is named in two books, *Companies That Care* and *100 Best Companies to Work For in America.* It was featured on *Oprah's* "Best Place to Work" show.

The SAS Work Environment

The SAS work environment is different from almost every other company's, even best practice companies. But the real difference is not quantitative, but qualitative; it doesn't just have *more* (although it does), it has a different goal behind what it does. SAS's intent is to create a place that is good for employees in all of who they are, in and out of work.

Executives in other companies have a typical reaction to what SAS does—first envy, then dismissal as not replicable. We have included SAS as a demonstration of what's possible and because it has a number of takeaways relevant to all companies.

- SAS has been successful because of its work environment, not in spite of it.

- Managing people as assets is qualitatively different from managing them as expenses, both in approach—SAS's health care services versus traditional health benefits—and results.

- The payoff from investing in human assets can be extensive, depending on the level of investment, the innovativeness of approach, and the attention paid to the effort.

- Practices reinforce values and vice versa. What happens when you hire the right employees and give them an inch (or more)? They don't take a mile; they go a mile—and more.

Nonphysical Aspects of the Work Environment

The most important aspects of the SAS environment—to employees and in terms of creating loyalty and high performance—are the least observable aspects, and they have been present since the beginning. From its founding, SAS has not wanted employees to live only for work; SAS had a standard thirty-five-hour workweek, and employees had control over their work schedules. Employees shared in SAS's financial results through profit sharing. It also had an atmosphere of trust.

Atmosphere of Trust

SAS management doesn't spend much time looking over employees' shoulders. People manage themselves, which works because they are hired carefully and are in jobs they enjoy. The CEO spends time programming. When told most other CEOs wouldn't do the same, he said, "I don't know what they do all day; probably poking their nose where it doesn't belong" (Fishman, 1999). SAS's emphasis is on "intrinsic motivation and trusting people to do a good job . . . on coaching and mentoring rather than monitoring and controlling. On trust and respect" (Pfeffer, 1998b, p. 6).

The sense of trust includes a sense of job security. SAS has never had layoffs. Some employees have quit, like the woman who was surprised to learn that no one was going to tell her what to do. SAS employees say as long as you do your job well and keep learning, there will be a place for you at SAS.

Time

SAS still encourages people to get their work done in thirty-five hours, although salaried employees may need to work longer to complete their work. For example, while it is rare that SAS is behind its internally set schedule for a product release, sometimes when release dates approach employees may work longer hours.* Still, the "high norm"—the most hours typically worked, even for exempts, is about forty-five hours per week, a far cry from the standard weeks at most other high-tech firms.

The gates of the SAS campus close at 6 P.M., and most employees leave by 5 P.M. Goodnight believes that rested people do better work: "I've seen some of the code that people produce after these long nights and it's garbage. You throw it away the next day and start over. . . . You have got to be alert and sharp to be a good programmer. . . . I'd rather have sharp focused people that write good code that doesn't need as much testing. I recently came back from a Microsoft conference and they said that now Microsoft has three testers for every programmer." SAS Institute "has substantially fewer testers" (Pfeffer, 1998b, p. 9).

SAS employees take a lunch hour. At the Cary campus they eat and relax in one of several cafés, where their spouse or their children, picked up from the on-site child care center, often join them. Some employees use their lunch hour to take an on-campus class offered by SAS, like belly dancing, or to work out in the fitness complex.

---

* SAS does not publicly announce product release dates to avoid external pressure to release a product before it has met an SAS-set standard of quality.

The pace is efficient but not frenetic. SAS was dubbed "Sanity, Inc." by Charles Fishman (1999), who called it perhaps "the world's sanest company" for its relaxed mood, stable workforce, and the balanced lives that its employees live. Fishman said that, while SAS might meet the definition of a "fast company" in terms of its growth, it has gotten there without the withering pace that characterizes other such companies.

The seven-hour workday was originally adopted so that employees' families could eat dinner together (Fishman, 1999). Other practices also give employees family time. Some employees arrange their day to meet a schoolchild's bus in the afternoon. Since 1989, employees have received an extra week off between Christmas and New Year's, in addition to their normal three to four weeks of vacation time. There is no limit on the number of sick days employees can take, and they can stay home to care for family members.

Although employees can flex their work schedules, most SAS employees at the Cary campus work full-time. Few SAS employees work reduced work hours or telecommute. The abundance of campus-based family care and other life support services, the relatively easy commute most employees have, the reasonable work hours, and the relatively low-stress environment—along with the premium value people at SAS place on personal interaction—may explain why there has been little call for part-time work or telecommuting. Perhaps, as the founders intended, SAS is such an enjoyable place that people simply want to be there.

Physical Environment

A lot of attention at SAS is paid to the physical environment. "I believe a person's surroundings have a lot to do with how a person feels. We try to have nice surroundings here," said Jim Goodnight in classic understatement (Fishman, 1999, p. 89). The bucolic 250-acre campus has twenty-one buildings, a lake, lush rolling hills, and grounds dotted with sculptures.*

- *Artwork.* The artwork is part of a deliberate intent to inspire creativity company-wide; three thousand works of art grace the various buildings,

---

* Other SAS work sites also pay attention to aesthetics—a chateau outside Paris, a large manor house on the Thames River in England, and chateaux in Sydney and Belgium house SAS employees (Pfeffer, 1998b).

not just the executive suite. SAS has the second-largest fine art collection in the state—art glass sits on the tables and original art hangs on the walls of each building.

- *Ergonomics.* A staffed Ergonomics Department helps employees ensure that their work space is ergonomically sound and that they are physically comfortable and safe (in concert with safety staff), which earns SAS lower insurance rates.

- *Architectural design.* Buildings are designed for aesthetics as well as efficiency, such as maximizing natural light to employees, whose offices in new buildings line exterior walls. This design creates what might be considered an inner core of wasted space; in the R&D building, it is a beautiful atrium. Every employee at SAS has always had a private office, with the exception of one group that recently chose to experiment with a different office layout. Building plans are designed to foster a sense of group belonging (Pfeffer, 1998b).

- *Break rooms.* Every floor on every building has a break room fully stocked with free juice, soft drinks, coffee, and snacks. Three days a week a special snack is delivered, for example, fruit on Mondays and M&Ms on Wednesdays—22.5 tons of them each year. The idea is that if employees are hungry, there should be something for them to eat.

Employee Services

SAS is best known for its tangible services, which fall into three groups: health, recreation and fitness, and work-life balance. Altogether, well over a hundred services are provided, and new programs are added regularly even in an economic downturn.[*] Potential offerings are evaluated by whether they fit with the SAS culture, would serve a significant number of employees— they don't have to serve a majority—and whether the perceived value would be at least as high as the cost (Fishman, 1999). We will not attempt to describe them all, but have selected some that demonstrate the breadth, depth, and spirit of the SAS approach. Most examples are from the main campus, but employees at other sites also enjoy substantial services.[**]

---

[*] These services are coordinated through a joint wellness committee and exist in addition to traditional benefits and leave policies, which fall within the Human Resource function.

[**] As an example, employees at the German site have all of their public transportation costs paid by SAS.

Health Center

SAS operates a 7,500-square-foot on-site medical facility with a fifty-five-member staff to provide twenty-four-hour coverage to employees. The staff includes eleven family nurse practitioners, three family practice physicians, two nutritionists, ten nurses, a nurse psychotherapist, and two physical therapists. All services are covered under the company's health plan: they are free to employees and have been so since they were first created in 1983.

The company is self-insured, not to minimize costs but as part of its long-term approach to employment. SAS believes that healthier people are more productive and will ultimately be less costly to the company. Appointments are managed with a five-minute average wait time, which, combined with saved travel from being on-site, recovers thousands of hours annually.

About 90 percent of Cary-based employees used the health center in 2002, which handled 36,000 family visits during the year, about 120 per day. (SAS had just expanded the facility by 50 percent to meet increased demand.) Half of employees use it as their primary source of health care. Family members use it as well, including the children in the SAS child care facilities.

Recreation and Fitness Center

The SAS Recreation and Fitness Center (RFC) is a 77,000-square-foot complex with indoor and outdoor fitness, wellness, and recreation facilities. Indoors are two basketball courts, three racquetball courts, a 19,000-square-foot ten-lane swimming pool, volleyball and wallyball courts, aerobic exercise rooms, strength-training equipment, cardiovascular equipment, Ping-Pong tables, locker rooms, meeting space, and a café that serves healthy food throughout the day. Outdoors are soccer, softball, and Frisbee fields; miles of walking, jogging, and biking trails; tennis courts; an oval track; horseshoe pits; a putting green; and a 3,000-square-foot picnic shelter.

The RFC, which is free and available to all SAS employees and their families, dependents, and significant others, is staffed by seventeen highly trained fitness personnel. It holds organized events and team activities (leagues, tournaments, and clinics) in every conceivable sport. There are sports lessons, personal trainers, a nutritionist, fitness counseling, and competitive sports. There are wellness seminars, fitness testing, and extramural sports leagues and lessons. Reward systems encourage participation; 90

percent of SAS employees in Cary use the programs or facilities each year, and 70 percent use them regularly. The RFC's performance goal is that "employees are happier when they leave than when they arrived."

Nonathletic recreational activities, such as group travel and organized events, are also part of the RFC, as are services designed to save employees time—a hair salon, massage therapy, dry cleaning pickup and delivery, book and outdoor clothing sales, and car service and detailing. These services guarantee that appointments will be on time; the goal is to save employees two hours each week. The saved hours are the employee's; participants are not expected to use the extra time at work.

In 2001, 120,000 visits were logged by SAS employees, children over the age of eighteen, spouses, and domestic partners.* SAS has won the North Carolina Governor's Award for Fitness and Health in Business five years running.

Work-Life Balance

SAS has a five-person department whose goal is to create a work environment that fosters and encourages the integration of the company's business objectives with employees' personal needs (SAS, 2002). One of those needs is family. "Families are a big part of our lives and with them come responsibilities," says Diane Fuqua, who manages the group. The department has services for any shape or form of family responsibility or personal interest. There are seminars, counselors, a lending library, and film, book, and discussion groups on all sorts of topics—raising teens, college counseling, retirement, living single. The staff organizes learning programs and resource fairs, and facilitates mentoring. Employee interest groups have facilitators to help form networks of support, for example, in dealing with divorce or parenting teens. In 2001, seventeen hundred SAS employees attended a work-life balance seminar on campus. Most of the services, such as the geriatric counselor, are free, but small fees are charged for some classes.

The SAS approach to child care illustrates its unique approach. SAS provides on-site child care, and has since 1980, but that's where the similarity with other firms ends. First, SAS continually attempts to provide child

---

* Children in the SAS child care centers and the adolescents and teens who are in the SAS summer and vacation camps can also schedule time to use the facilities. SAS pays the tab for SAS employees who don't work at the Cary site to join a local fitness center.

care for all employees who need it. It has aggressively expanded its child care services and now has four centers at the Cary campus alone. Altogether they serve more than six hundred children—three times the national norm in terms of capacity relative to the size of the workforce. There are summer and vacation programs and activities for adolescents and teens, a population rarely addressed by employers.

Second, SAS has kept the quality of the child care high even though high-quality care is expensive to produce; high quality is rhetoric that is commonly espoused but rarely lived over time. The first SAS centers were learning-oriented Montessori schools; they are still going strong and have an educational consultant, art teacher, and speech therapist in addition to teaching staff. None of the SAS child care centers are daycare centers as the term is commonly used. They are learning centers with teaching staff trained in child development and early childhood education.

Third, SAS pays most of the cost itself. Child care at SAS was free to employees until a few years ago. Today, employees pay $300 per month for children from six weeks through kindergarten, less than a third the real cost.* Further, children are considered an integral part of the SAS community—the café has booster seats and highchairs to encourage parents to eat with children. Older children in the summer programs swim in the pool and use the picnic facility.

The quality of the learning environment is so good in the SAS child care facilities that Jim Goodnight's son attended one. A favorite story—part of SAS folklore—is that one morning, the center director called Goodnight and asked him to accompany his son to the center. When they arrived, the director explained that Goodnight's son had colored on the bathroom walls the day before and that his father had been invited to be there when he cleaned up the walls—standard operating procedure for parents of children in the center. Goodnight did that happily and then went on to the rest of his day running the company—another example of the egalitarian principle at SAS in action.

These examples illustrate SAS's intent, which is to do whatever it takes, in fact to do everything it can, to give employees what they need. That is what makes SAS so rare.

---

* Although other SAS locations do not have a high enough employee concentration to allow the same services as the Cary campus, SAS often provides a similar benefit. For example, it provides an equivalent child care subsidy for employees at other U.S. sites; SAS pays all but $300 of employees' child care expenses at a licensed facility.

The Results

SAS has not felt the need to measure all the effects of its employee practices, because it already knows the approach is working: 98 percent of its customers resubscribe; employee turnover is consistently about 4 percent; it has an endless pool of great talent from which to draw; and it has had twenty-seven consecutive years of revenue growth and profitability.

Employee Stability and Quality of Talent

The value of the SAS approach shows most clearly in the longevity and quality of the company's workforce. The company has a lock on both retention and recruitment.

Retention

Company-wide, SAS turnover was 3–4 percent each year throughout the 1990s; it has never risen above 5 percent. At the Cary campus it was 2.3 percent in 1999 (Pfeffer, 2000). In an industry with an average turnover rate between 15 and 20 percent in normal economic times, SAS's stability is extraordinary, particularly with 150 other technology firms five miles away in Research Triangle Park. Turnover is low even among the SAS sales force, most of whom are in regional offices, not in Cary; in 2002 it was 8 percent in North America, compared to 20 percent industry-wide.

The difference between a 4 percent and a 20 percent turnover rate company-wide is worth $67.5 million a year, assuming an average employee salary of $50,000 per year (a conservative estimate—SAS does not release actual figures; Fishman, 1999). The total is based on a formula that calculates the full cost of turnover to replace an exempt employee at 150 percent of annual salary or 75 percent for an hourly employee. (Other analysts put the cost as high as 250 percent—see Fitz-enz, 2000). This figure recognizes that 85 percent of replacement cost is nonproductive time spent by the employee who is departing, the incoming employee, and the colleagues and supervisors affected by the transition. The balance (15 percent) are direct costs such as recruiters' salaries and advertising fees. The 75/150 percent formula assumes that the learning curve time for an employee to become fully up to speed is 13.5 months (Phillips, 1990), which may be a gross underestimation for knowledge workers like those at SAS. The $67.5

million savings does not include the additional value an employee adds in efficiency, institutional memory, or relational capital after being on the job more than a year. And since the average salary of many other software firms is well above $50,000 per year, savings would also be higher by whatever proportion average exempt salaries were above $50,000.

It's a simple economic trade-off to SAS. "We can spend money on employees or we can spend it on headhunters," says Jim Goodnight.

Some organizations may consider such employee stability a disadvantage that can create stagnation. But SAS encourages internal employee movement; people at SAS change careers three to four times. They move from sales to development, from one project to another, to different facilities, and from individual contributor to manager and back, with no reduction in pay (Pfeffer, 1998b). They even move from being child care teachers to working in line functions. People keep growing, which is what makes the longevity work—and the relationship capital grow.

Recruitment

SAS pretty much has its pick of talent, with little direct recruiting expense. In the month following the second *60 Minutes* show featuring SAS, which aired in October 2002, SAS received fifteen thousand job applications, roughly three times the number of jobs at SAS (not openings, *jobs*) in the United States (Safer, 2003). In a more typical period, SAS had 45,432 applicants. Since it had at the time 4,638 U.S. positions through 2001 and had filled 920 positions that year, it had just under ten applicants for every position (or forty-nine for each opening). This proportion of applicants to positions is nearly the same as at Microsoft (10.32 applicants per position), although that company enjoys substantially more visibility than SAS (Levering & Moskowitz, 2003). Direct recruiting costs are reduced because of unsolicited applications. In the first quarter of 2003, SAS got only .5 percent of its new hires from search firms to whom it paid fees, down from 12 percent in 2001 and 5 percent in 2002.

Besides the sheer size of the applicant pool, SAS managers report that they see many applicants who require little training, such as senior programmers. These people are attracted by the autonomy SAS offers, which they cannot get elsewhere. The level of their expertise results in a short learning curve.

Employee longevity translates into an experienced workforce. The average tenure of an SAS employee is twelve years (Safer, 2003), but at a 4 percent turnover rate each year, an employee could be expected to stay at SAS for twenty-five years.

SAS has a higher proportion of female employees than most other software firms—about half its employees (49 percent) and half its managers are female, which means it is more effectively tapping this half of the labor pool. Stanford Business School professor Jeffrey Pfeffer considers this an unrecognized advantage for SAS. Although there are no data to prove it, it is reasonable to assume that the company's work environment is at least part of the reason. Even compared to other software firms rated among the best places to work, SAS excels in its family-related benefits and in its employment of women.

Managers at SAS note that women with families often bring skills they have developed in their private lives to work, making them highly effective. They exhibit a heightened ability to listen and interpret nonverbal signals, to compromise, to negotiate, and to nurture others, along with emotional skills such as patience that help them adapt to change and deal with emotional situations that come into the workplace.

Relationship Capital Leads to Efficiency and Nimbleness

SAS is a premier example of how relationship capital works—the value that is created by human networks. As economist Robert Reich describes, in a business where value-added comes from knowledge-generating relationships with co-workers and customers, an environment where people know each other well and trust each other enables the work to be done better.

At SAS people know each other well. They come into contact with people throughout the company. They have often played on a volleyball team together, had children in child care together, taken a jewelry-making class or been in an elder care support group together. They have relaxed time and space to bond on many levels—over lunch and in break rooms, or on trips to the theater or a ballgame. The stability of the workforce and the policy of moving people around the company have further expanded working relationships over the years and eventually formed highly durable networks (Prusak & Cohen, 2001).

This knowledge of one another—true at all levels—is what enables work to be done better and more efficiently and the quality of collaboration to be more consistent over time. People know who to call—who does what, who knows what, and who knows whom.

SAS enjoys—and profits from—a spirit of cooperation, which employees report is partly the result of the peace of mind that the total SAS work environment produces. That spirit, the relational capital at SAS, and the fact that people are not burned out all seem to increase efficiency and enable SAS to go to market quickly. It also allows SAS to be constantly poised to react to change.

The sense of mutuality—interest in the good of the whole—has become embedded in SAS's processes. For example, everyone affiliated with a given work effort comes together as a group, instead of parceling out the work into steps and reviews. The mail room participates in the design of marketing materials, for example, advising that by changing the size or shape of a brochure, the company can take advantage of cheaper bulk rate printing or postage. The health center works closely with the fitness facility staff and the ergonomics staff to coordinate health and safety processes. The maintenance staff makes suggestions to the architectural design staff that improve the building design and reduce maintenance costs. As a result, turnaround time to open a new building is rapid and smooth, from the market search through build-out to signage.

As SAS has grown, this continual fostering of relationships has become even more critical to its smooth running. Often when firms become larger their size creates disconnection and bureaucracy; processes to capture institutional knowledge can become entrenched. SAS's age has instead become an asset; it can leverage its institutional memory in a fluid way.

Overhead Costs

The investment in people and the relationship capital result in cost savings.

Labor Costs

As Jeffrey Pfeffer notes, it's important to distinguish between labor rates and labor costs (1998a). A company can cut labor *rates* and cause labor *costs* to rise if lower productivity results. The reverse is also true: SAS's higher benefit investments may actually yield lower labor costs overall if higher performance is achieved. The full cost of labor should be weighed when considering various labor practices.

SAS may invest less in salaries overall than comparable firms; it certainly invests substantially more in benefits. But how the performance achieved compares to the total investment is what's important.

Salaries at SAS are not disclosed externally or internally, but the company tracks market data closely to keep salaries "competitive." One thing for sure, at many other firms salaries are augmented by signing bonuses and stock options (perhaps less so in the economic downturn); at SAS they are not (Levering & Moskowitz, 2003).* Even with annual bonuses and an SAS-funded retirement plan, overall direct compensation at SAS may be lower than at other software firms. For employees, this difference is obviously more than offset by the wealth of benefits and the work environment. One software engineer said, "I just can't imagine leaving SAS and I have felt that way for a very long time. If somebody offered to double my salary, I wouldn't even think about it" (Safer, 2003). That makes a big difference to SAS. All the elements combine to create a lower marginal cost of labor, even without the estimated $67.5 million in turnover-related savings that SAS achieves every year because of its workforce stability.

Medical Costs

The full-service on-site medical services cost SAS half what it would otherwise pay for medical insurance, which amounts to $500,000 saved each year. Additional savings result from short wait times and the on-site location, eliminating lost work time. Figured at 1.5 hours saved per visit, that time is worth an additional $500,000 per year in productive time, according to

---

* There are no stock options. The company typically contributes the maximum allowed by the IRS into employees' profit sharing retirement plans (15 percent) and no employee contributions are required. (The only exceptions occurred in 2001 when SAS contributed 10 percent and in 2002 when it contributed 5 percent, when profits were lower.) Salaries are competitive, and annual bonuses typically range from 5.5 percent to 8 percent. Financial incentives are deemphasized at SAS as a source of motivation, but they are also structured to support the goal of being customer-focused. Sales employees, for example, are not paid on the basis of sales commissions (nor are individual sales results highlighted), because commissions do not encourage long-term relationships and a customer orientation. This compensation approach has caused employees to migrate to SAS to get away from other high-tech sales environments where high pressure discourages customer-focused behavior (Pfeffer, 1998b).

SAS's calculations.* As SAS plans for retiree health benefits, the fact that employees have been healthier over time will mean substantial additional savings to SAS.

Workers' Compensation Insurance Costs

SAS has a low claims history, presumably because of its ergonomics and safety activities and its employee-friendly culture, which enables SAS to qualify for lower workers' compensation insurance rates. SAS has an experience modification that each year ranges 20–40 percent below the industry norm calculated by the National Council on Compensation Insurance. That results in a 20–40 percent credit on workers' compensation insurance rates. Risk Manager Mari-Jo Hill also notes, "We don't have people staying out of work just to collect workers' comp benefits; they would rather be here at work."

Customer Performance

SAS retained 98 percent of its customers in 2002, and two thirds of them expanded their "share of wallet" spent at SAS. In other words, they not only came back, they bought more SAS products—purchasing more of the vertical products that accompany the basic offering.

SAS credits at least three things with influencing customer retention. SAS has an *accurate read of customers*. The company's annual subscription model forces SAS relationship managers to stay in touch with customers and know truthfully how satisfied they are. SAS knows which things are working and which are not. Its employee longevity provides for *continuity of relationships* that enable individual customers to stay connected to the software developers who prepared their initial purchases. The stability of SAS's employee population means that updating the code is done more quickly with fewer bugs than it would be if a person unfamiliar with the original code attempted the job. Continuity brings *accountability* into play. When software designers develop original code, they know they will be around to help modify it in the future; they will have to deal then with any problems they ignore during development.

---

* An SAS visit takes thirty minutes on average (including travel time), compared to a community average of two hours.

SAS signed on thirteen hundred new customers in 2001 and eleven hundred new customers in 2002.

Growth

As noted, SAS has had a twenty-seven-year unbroken track record of revenue growth and profitability. Its revenue nearly doubled in seven years—from $562 million in 1996 to $1.34 billion in 2003.

SAS's ability to innovate in response to changes in the marketplace and to mine existing customer relationships to develop specific customer solutions has enabled the company to continue to grow despite a difficult technology market and increased competition (Whiting, 2003). At a time when some software firms lost revenue and others relied on services to drive growth, SAS's software license revenue grew by 4 percent, making SAS the fifth-largest independent software company worldwide by software license revenue. Growth followed SAS's focus on specific industries, with the most significant growth in financial services and banking at 25 percent and in insurance at 7 percent (SAS Institute, 2003).

The SAS workforce tripled in size from three thousand to nine thousand employees between 1994 and 2003. In 2002, a year when other technology firms were cutting back, SAS had job growth of 9 percent. By comparison Microsoft had 4 percent job growth; Adobe lost 1 percent, Xilinx lost 5 percent, Cisco lost 7 percent, and Agilent lost 20 percent ("100 Best Companies to Work For," 2003). SAS deliberately expanded sales staff by 5 percent during the downturn to poise itself for when the market picked up. It has also invested heavily in R&D. In 2002, SAS increased R&D staff by 6 percent and invested a higher percentage in research and development than any other large software company—25 percent, twice the industry average. SAS has invested 25–30 percent in R&D each year it has been in business.

Profitability

SAS is a privately held company and thus does not publish earnings statements. Financial data about SAS are closely held. It may be tempting to conclude that being privately held is what makes SAS so different from publicly held companies (subject to short-term pressures for profitability and growth), that the lessons of SAS don't apply. In reality, managers in publicly held companies have greater control over the decision to focus on short-term results and stock appreciation than they think. Some companies, realizing the dangers of ignoring long-term effects of management decisions in favor of short-term hits, have already decided to eliminate monthly earnings releases.

Perhaps the best indication of SAS profitability is the fact that despite the lavish provisions the company makes (Goodnight might say because of them), Goodnight, who owns two thirds of the company, has a net worth of $4.8 billion and by 2002 had become the fifty-third richest person in the United States (having moved up several places since the GQ shoot mentioned earlier in the chapter). Co-founder John Sall, who owns the other third, has a net worth of $1.5 billion and is 131st on the U.S. wealth list. Both were described as "self-made men," whose wealth was created by SAS (Kroll & Goldman, 2002).

Well-Being in Action: The Story of Bernard

SAS has always seen itself as a marathon runner rather than a sprinter—in for the long haul, focused and disciplined. Bernard's story offers a prime illustration of how the SAS work environment helps accomplish its aim. The story also answers the question, What happens when an organization is structured around a principle of caring about employees—all of who they are—not just so they will do work better, but because it is actively interested in the well-being of people who work there?

Bernard Penney is a small, energetic man, popping out of his chair with eagerness to tell his story. To look at him, it is unimaginable that for most of his adulthood he had chronic debilitating asthma and in fact found it difficult to walk up steps. His doctor had told him that exercise would help, but he had never been able to make it a reality. He worked long hours as a software product developer at IBM for nearly twenty years, then at an Internet start-up that went bankrupt after two years. In 1999 he came to SAS.

A Turnaround

According to Bernard, "It's one thing for a company to have a gym, another to give you the time to use it." In his experience, gym staff are usually there just to check badges; at SAS they get involved, very involved. First the SAS

Health Center's on-staff nutritionist advised Bernard that he should change his diet from the strict vegetarian regime he had been following to a higher-calorie Mediterranean diet. He also began to participate in athletic activities at the SAS Recreation and Fitness Center—running and swimming—and began to meet people outside his work group.

The RFC staff got him involved in more programs and stayed with him. "I stunk, but they kept encouraging me," he says. He joined the master swimming group, where he was trained in how to swim, the master running group, where he was trained in how to run, and the master biking group, where he was trained in how to bike. He began regular swimming, running, and biking, and later added weight training. In 2002, this man—who two and a half years before had had trouble walking up steps—reported, "Two weeks ago I completed my own triathlon. They talked me into a half Iron Man this summer. See if I can make it."

His overall health has done a 180. "Before I was at SAS I was lethargic and totally addicted to asthma drugs; these are steroids, narcotics. I have more energy than I have had in my entire life. I work eight hours a day. I get up at 5 A.M. and run, bike, or swim before I come to work."

When Bernard works out, he is with other SAS employees, including John Sall, the chief administrative officer (CAO). Sall, one of the founder-owners, is a sixty-year-old who in 2001 completed the Iron Man Triathlon. Three SAS employees participate on the national biathlon team, competing at world champion levels, which requires a heavy investment of time. When the CAO is in the pool too, working out or swimming in the SAS Olympics, employees believe the time investment is genuinely acceptable. The incredible facilities and staff also send that message, but if the senior leaders did not use them, they would communicate a different standard for employees than for leaders. At SAS there is no such difference. "These guys have real jobs here, and they compete with professionals. It's a very healthy organization; you don't feel like it's a bad use of your time; you're encouraged to do it," explains Bernard.

That's half of Bernard's story.

Something New

Eighteen months ago Bernard came up with an idea. SAS's business has up to this point been entirely in complex, expensive software run on mainframes of large organizations—Fortune 100 companies—and universities. Bernard's idea was to produce a small, affordable "Learning Edition" of SAS software geared toward students that would simultaneously appeal to their desire to acquire SAS skills and prime the market they would later work in. He proposed to develop this software, which would be an entrée for SAS into an entirely new market.

His entrepreneurial efforts were rewarded, which is typical of SAS. His proposal was approved after the usual close review and contributions of ideas by SAS leadership. It would be the first product of its kind for SAS.

He was given charge over the product from start to finish: it was his baby. Once the proposal was approved, he and the SAS team generated the final product from development through production (developing the software, the training manual, and the tutorial, and producing the CD and the packaging) in an amazing seven months. Bernard compares the lean process at SAS with inordinately more process-bound cultures he had worked in before. SAS Learning Edition 1.0 hit the market in June 2002, timed perfectly for the school purchasing cycle. This is nimbleness.

The cycle time was possible because of the efficiency and relationship capital that accrues at SAS—the result of experience together across the SAS campus, including in the pool. "Things are faster and more fun here."

"SAS has changed my life" is a phrase Bernard repeats often.

The Marathon Continues

Bernard's experience is a reminder that SAS itself is a marathon runner, not a sprinter. It is going for endurance, willing to endure the pain of constant investment and to exercise the discipline of a long-term orientation. Marathon runners make a series of decisions that cumulatively build their strength over time, which is precisely why they last. When the day of the race arrives, the marathon runner can outdistance even a more powerful competitor who trained for the short sprint.

SAS did not undergo a transformation to create its extraordinary work environment. In that, it is different from the other businesses we describe. It has been on the same path, following the same philosophy, since it began. It also has not had the constraints of a public company. CEO Goodnight says that keeping it privately held means he does not have the pressure of making decisions based on what any one year's business results are. He believes that pressure—to prime business results for the specificity that the stock market demands—does not always lead to good business decisions.

SAS has deliberately chosen to stay private in order to maintain the freedom to think and act for the long term—to invest heavily in employees and in the development of new ideas. SAS is, therefore, an example of what happens if you follow the approach of creating a work environment that is truly good in all ways for employees in all that they are and what that practice in turn means to the ability to develop and market new ideas.

The results have been unequivocally positive. As quintessentially plain-spoken Jim Goodnight says, "It has worked for us" (Safer, 2003).

It's simple.

If employees are happy, they make the customers happy. If the customers are happy, they make me happy.

—Jim Goodnight (quoted in Safer, 2003)

16

THE FTN STORY

To remain independent, First Tennessee National Corporation (FTN) transformed itself, creating an employee-centered culture. In a rare instance where strategy was driven by measurable human capital and customer results, the bank retained an astonishing 95–96 percent of customers and has been the most profitable banking company in the United States for the past four years.

Employee-Focused Culture Change

The story of FTN is the story of a bank that undertook a complete transformation of its culture over a ten-year period and tenaciously measured the results. It credits the success during this time—when total assets grew from $8.9 billion to $24.8 billion—to employees' ability to work together as owners, which was the objective of the cultural transformation.

Today, FTN has more than eleven thousand employees in almost six hundred locations in more than forty states. It is a diversified financial

This case was cowritten with Sandra Cunningham, Ph.D.

services company with $24.8 billion in assets and $5 billion in market capitalization as of March 31, 2003. The holding company, First Tennessee National Corporation, has four primary lines of business:

- *First Horizon:* Home loans and short-term financing products
- *FTN Banking Group:* General financial services
- *FTN Financial:* Financial services for the institutional investment community
- *Transaction processing:* Credit card merchant processing (First Horizon Merchant Services), nationwide bill payment processing and check clearing operations (First Express Remittance Processing), and other products and services

What Prompted FTN's Culture Change

The early 1990s were extraordinary times in the financial services industry. Mergers and acquisitions ruled the day, with independent banks like FTN becoming prey to the voracious appetites of a few financial mega-organizations. Neither Ralph Horn—then CEO—nor the company's shareholders wanted to give up the company's independent status. Despite strong commitment from senior leaders, the company had little chance to remain independent without demonstrating strong financial returns to shareholders. Pat Brown, senior vice president for workforce optimization, summarized the challenges facing FTN at the time. In 1992 "the bank was looking at a $5 million to $6 million gap in earnings—a five to six percentage point gap—between how quickly the retail commercial bank could grow its business and what the high performers in the industry could continue to achieve. Although adding other business lines, such as mortgage banking and transaction processing, would be helpful in closing the gap, it could not erase it" (Casner-Lotto, 2000, p. 130).

Customer Retention: The Key to Profitability

During the latter part of the 1980s the company had been systematically collecting data on its customers. The effort was triggered in part by the conviction that reliable data about customer satisfaction and loyalty could help drive long-term strategies. The research reinforced the effect of customer loyalty on profitability. While most organizations believe in the relationship between customer behavior and profits, few actually collect data to enable them to act with confidence.

The customer research findings were the first critical step in the evolution of FTN's culture. Once FTN had the data to reinforce the effect of customer retention on profitability, it began to focus attention on measuring drivers of customer satisfaction and loyalty. An early study revealed that retail banking branches with the highest customer retention also had the highest employee retention.

What Created Loyal Customers

Customers consistently reported that what they wanted most was to see a familiar face when they did business at the bank. They wanted "relationships with the people who handled their money" (Flynn, 1997). Instead, because of employee turnover, they often saw a new face—and often that of a trainee. Customers said "they wanted to be seen as individuals rather than as part of a group, to be treated with flexibility, and certainly, to have their banking problems solved in a friendly, caring fashion" (Casner-Lotto, 2000).

The Employee–Customer–Profit Connection

FTN's internal research was discovering the same causal relationship that management authors were writing about. This notion—dubbed the "service-profit chain"—said that employee commitment and retention affected customer service, satisfaction, and retention, and that in turn increased profitability, and *you could measure by how much.* "We knew that customer retention drove profitability and that customer satisfaction strengthened it if we kept employees longer," says Sarah Meyerrose, executive vice president of corporate and employee services.

Internal research revealed that FTN branches with an average employee tenure of two years had a customer retention rate of 83 percent. When employee tenure increased to four years, the customer retention rate increased to 92 percent (Flynn, 1997).

FTN was able to explain 34 percent of the variance associated with customer loyalty by citing employee factors. The remainder came from product, convenience, image, and pricing factors. Improvements through process automation, opening new markets, and adding other business lines had already been put in place. The employee side seemed to offer the greatest opportunity for gain.

Increasing employee retention also offered a substantial cost-saving opportunity. The company estimated that it could save $75,000–$100,000 by retaining a commercial loan officer and $5,000 in direct costs by retaining a teller. With opportunities to reduce turnover, the company could create cost savings that would have a significant effect on earnings.

Reordering Priorities

It was at this point that Ralph Horn had an "aha! moment." It happened in 1992, in a strategy meeting with senior leaders to consider how FTN could outsmart the forces that were pushing against them. As the leaders surveyed the list of four key stakeholders commonly recognized as important—customers, shareholders, employees, and the communities in which they operated—Ralph recognized what the bank needed. He rearranged the order of the groups FTN served, listing employees first among the company's constituencies—employees, customers, shareholders, and communities—and announced that from that day forward, "Employees come first." The rest flowed from there. Employees focus on creating value for customers; loyal customers lead to profitability; profitability benefits shareholders and allows the company to invest in the community.

The pivotal decision represented a radical shift for this 139-year-old financial institution—motivated by a belief that the company's survival depended on making a substantial change in the way it had been operating. FTN put all its financial eggs in this strategy basket and undertook the change not in a piecemeal way, but full throttle. It makes FTN's experience a good one for others to study, but it includes an essential lesson that could easily be missed. The phenomenal business results that occurred thereafter would probably not have been achieved if FTN had taken an incremental approach to its cultural transformation.

Discovering Employee Success Factors

Once the link between employees and customer retention and profitability was clear, the question for senior leaders became, What will make employees more committed and engaged? FTN surveyed 150 senior leaders, talked with 200 employees in focus groups, and conducted a demographic and barrier survey of 3,500 employees.

Employees were asked how they fared in the current environment.

Interviewers found [employees] loyal to customers as well as to the company. Employees wanted to serve customers well, but often felt that managers were getting in their way because they were treating them in the old autocratic style of management, "as though employees were fourth graders." In essence, employees were saying, "When you don't respect me, when you don't treat me like an adult, you take away my incentive to help make this a better company." "That was really our key learning point," Brown recalls. (Casner-Lotto, 2000, p. 130)

Employees said what they needed most was empowerment.

* *Empowerment on the job.* Employees wanted to make decisions about how to better serve their customers. This meant employees needed to be able to make decisions with minimum involvement from managers.
* *Empowerment to manage their responsibilities outside work.* Employees wanted flexibility. Having no say in their work schedules frustrated them and thwarted the continuous improvement programs.

As an example, a decades-old policy required vacations to be taken in two-week blocks (Flynn, 1997). Some employees with school-age children preferred to take vacation time in days, so they could stay home when the child's school was closed or schedule a doctor's appointment while still giving their manager advance notice. When they cannot take single or half vacation days, employees have to claim that they are ill to avoid being censured, and take an unscheduled absence, which is more difficult to manage.

A substantial number of employees had significant personal and family responsibilities. Ninety percent of employees' spouses were employed in 1997; half of the employees had dependent children, and 75 percent of the latter group were women (Flynn, 1997).

How FTN Reinvented Its Culture

The goal was to create an *employee-centered* culture. Since this dramatic and important change would affect FTN's financial future, senior leaders knew the whole organization needed to believe in it. FTN's new culture was to be built on putting employees first. This culture—called *Firstpower*—would become the cornerstone for how the company does business.

In the early 1990s, Firstpower was defined with three key elements: empowerment, continuous improvement, and Family Matters. Today, a company document states,

> *Firstpower is the attitude of ownership and teamwork that each employee brings to the job every day. As owners, we:*
>
> - *Recognize that a job well done is the first order of business*
> - *Are empowered to take care of our customers, internal and external*
> - *Create a flexible work environment so we can embrace both our personal lives and responsibilities at work*
> - *Know that what we create at work is a reflection of ourselves and as such, only the absolute best is good enough*

The first key step in the change process was to make sure everyone knew that this effort was not a cosmetic restatement of values or a flavor-of-the-month HR initiative—it was a real, long-term change in how each individual in the organization must operate. Every leader attended a meeting with Ralph Horn about the new strategy; Horn explained what it was and why it was the key to the company's future. Leaders in particular had to embrace it, understanding that it was critical to achieving FTN's financial goals for shareholders and therefore to its ability to remain independent. The introduction of the employee-focused culture had to accomplish two major goals: to prepare leaders to manage according to the new culture—in a Firstpower way; and to enable employees to be successful at work *and* in life.

Firstpower was accompanied by the development of a new skill set for managers, who were now held responsible for retention and recruitment of quality employees, finding out what employees value and developing a sense of accomplishment among employees, recognizing and rewarding employees and providing opportunities for employee development and advancement, and creating a team environment (Casner-Lotto, 2000).

Retooling managers was considered more important than adopting any new program or benefit. FTN already had a team environment in place, but this effort took it a step further. Managers had to be reeducated to focus on employee outputs, such as performance, rather than inputs such as attendance.

If you are going to take away the rule book, you have to have decision-making, problem-solving, process-type skills. (Casner-Lotto, 2000)

In 1993 more than a thousand managers at FTN attended three-day training sessions in which they learned how to lead in ways that recognized employees for their contributions and built an empowered team. The off-site training sessions centered around open communication and personal stories that caused leaders to realize that they shared the same personal and family dilemmas that their team members had and that the new approach would also improve their own quality of life.

FTN began its multiyear culture change by emphasizing to employees that they were important as individuals and that their personal needs counted. In the early and mid-1990s FTN focused on communicating and demonstrating this message to employees. It was also essential that employees understood their role in the company's ability to remain independent. It included communicating the importance of ownership and teamwork company-wide. It required two initiatives.

- *Retraining employees.* Employees had to see that their ideas and actions were valued by the organization and to learn to make decisions on their own. It required training employees to think like owners. As Pat Brown put it, "Treat your piece of the business as if you own the company, and if you do that, then we trust that you are going to be making the right decisions for yourself, for your co-workers, and for the company and your customers" (Casner-Lotto, 2000, p. 132).

- *Providing resources to assist with personal issues.* "Family Matters" was the term used in the early stages of the Firstpower culture change to define FTN's commitment to putting employees first. Under the Family Matters umbrella, FTN provided employees with resources to support their lives at work and at home. By 1998 FTN provided a dependent care reimbursement, family leave, a dependent scholarship program, family care informational services, an Employee Assistance Program (EAP), and sick child care resources. In addition, the company invested more than a million dollars to strengthen parental involvement with the schools. The definition of *family* has always been highly individual; family responsibilities range from child care to helping friends or relatives in need. Later, FTN evolved from using that term to speaking of "personal lives" in recognition of the breadth of important issues.

It was not until a few years later, when the commitment to employees was clear, concrete, and embedded in FTN's Firstpower culture, that the leaders began to put more focus on what the company needed back from employees—high performance.

The small firm size and cohesive leadership team that had enabled leaders in 1992 to consider the total cost of turnover in its decision to invest in employees also allowed the focus to remain consistent and coordinated over time. Former CEO Ralph Horn and the current CEO, Ken Glass, created a council of senior executives to meet regularly to discuss issues related to employee value and loyalty and ways to advance the Firstpower culture. The leadership team was able to consider how other strategic decisions would effect the Firstpower culture. The team applied systems thinking— looking at the big picture and how decisions in one area of the business affected other areas, including the culture and employee performance. In other organizations, senior management may be more removed from what is happening with employees, and the interrelationship of various management decisions less readily apparent.

Key Elements of the Firstpower Culture

The Firstpower culture creates an environment of ownership and teamwork where employees can make decisions to respond to customer needs, take more control of their personal and work lives to maximize their performance, count on leaders for support, and contribute to the company's financial success. Several characteristics distinguish it.

Empowered Employees

Empowered employees are the competitive differentiator. FTN knows that products, services, and technology are easily replicated by competitors; employees and their skills and attitudes are not. Empowered employees at FTN are well-trained decision makers who take responsibility for their actions with the ongoing support of their leaders. Leaders believe they must also continually create value and build loyalty with employees one opportunity at a time.

Emphasis on employee development. Because ongoing training and professional growth opportunities are vital for empowered employees, FTN is committed to employee development. Employees have an average of forty hours annually devoted to personal development (70 percent in on-the-job training, 20 percent classroom, and 10 percent self-study, which includes career-mapping workshops). Career and professional development are emphasized.

Open communication throughout the organization. Because the culture centers on employees' acting like owners, information is critical. Employees not only understand their own work and unit, they are also encouraged to understand the work and products across the company.

A monthly Strategic Orientation program for leaders and high-performing employees throughout the company enables them to hear presentations and have small-group discussions with senior executives about FTN's business strategies and their focus on employees. They have an informal question-and-answer session over lunch with CEO Ken Glass.

A dedicated financial center, Employees First Financial Services, gives discounts and extended hours exclusively to FTN employees. When employees use it they understand the company's products and can more effectively recognize and act on cross-selling opportunities.

Employees are on a first-name basis with the executive team, and the executives are highly visible. They make a point of finding out how things are going for employees. Doors are always open. New employees are encouraged to get to know members of the leadership team and share honest feedback in interactions with them. The goal is to use every means to continue to improve the organization whose best interests they all share.

There is an effort to use branding language to reinforce consistent messages throughout FTN. Firstpower, the name for the culture, is an example.

Atmosphere of Trust

Early in the evolution of Firstpower, the CEO orchestrated a ceremony in which he literally burned the attendance policy. The event has become a cultural artifact that is often repeated to reinforce Firstpower. Attendance is important, but the other practices have enabled (and required) it to be deemphasized in favor of motivating employees to contribute their best.

With the removal of a restrictive, one-size-fits-all policy, departments create their own attendance guidelines, beginning first with customer needs and business requirements, then considering individual employee needs and coverage plans. As a result, work teams have ownership of their attendance guidelines and are accountable to one another for coverage. With the recognition that high-performing employees have family responsibilities that result in legitimate absences, attendance guidelines are flexible. The emphasis instead is on performance and teamwork.

> *It's just letting go and trusting people. That's what really happened here.* (Casner-Lotto, 2000)

People have a strong sense of "we-ness"—a team orientation. "We just figure it out." "We cover for each other." These are phrases used by line employees to describe how the culture actually works. At an operations center, where multiple daily deadlines must be met, employees volunteer to fill in for each other when a personal need arises, knowing that one day they will need somebody to fill in for them. The team, not the leader, typically rearranges the coverage, and members cross-train so the coverage works. Even though they acknowledge that a few people will abuse such a system, teams have a strong collective sense that it all evens out.

The role of a team leader has changed dramatically; it is to get employees what they need, rather than to set and implement rules. Leaders set goals and hold employees accountable for achieving them. From the team leader's perspective, "It's about building teams you can trust."

Two-Way Matching

With each hire, the goal is to match the job to the employee and the employee to the culture. FTN no longer searches exclusively for employees who fit the company's job descriptions. Rather, staffing specialists consider applicants for qualities such as their sense of ownership and responsibility, and new leaders are selected based on their fit in FTN's Firstpower environment.

Engaged Employees

Employees take tremendous pride in their personal and team accomplishments because they own both the process and the results. Teams in this energized organization set high standards and strive to deliver beyond company and customer expectations. In 1997, 90 percent of employees said with the new culture they were more productive and better able to serve customers; 88 percent said their commitment to staying with FTN had risen; 90 percent felt management had a sincere interest in them (Casner-Lotto, 2000).

Ongoing Assessment

FTN monitors what it calls "employee value" continually through employee surveys, which it considers a critical organizational metric. The score is considered a more informative measure for leaders than "revenue per employee," because as a leading indicator it permits midcourse corrections. The score measures employee perceptions of their leaders' effectiveness and their overall experience of working at FTN. In 2001, the Employee Value Survey, which had remained flat for the five years prior, showed a 12 percent rise in employee value scores—to 74 percent. (There was an additional 3 percentage point rise in 2002 scores.) The bank attributed the increase primarily to employees' having a better understanding of Firstpower and how it improves their day-to-day jobs. The score is the percentage who give positive ratings on such items as

- Employees' sense of accomplishment
- Employees' sense of responsibility
- Employees' perception of flexibility in completing job duties and tasks
- Employees' sense that their individual opinions count
- Employees' sense of pride in being part of FTN
- Employees' view of the company as a place to work in comparison with others in the area
- Employees' overall work experience

Employer and Employee Interests Are Aligned

FTN encourages employees' whole life success. Based on 2002 employee surveys at FTN, 94 percent of employees report they have flexibility in completing their job duties; nearly half report working some form of flexible arrangement on a regular basis—an astounding fact, given the nature of the business—from financial centers to operations facilities.

Flexibility

Flexibility is one of FTN's most important strategies; it enables employees to embrace their responsibilities both at work and in their personal lives. The "flexibility principle" first identifies business needs and then identifies the flexible work options that are possible given those business needs. Employees at FTN know the ultimate goal is to achieve the organizational objectives and that there are times when work tasks come first and other times when personal responsibilities come first.

New employees are told, "Flexibility is the 'foundation of our culture.' We encourage you to talk with your leader about ways to flex your schedule when personal conflicts arise that require you to be away from work. This way you don't have to use sick or vacation days for routine family needs like late babysitters or doctor's appointments. Then you can rest on your vacation!" (This statement comes from "Newcomer Celebration," the new hire orientation brochure.)

Employees know they can use flexible work arrangements without it counting against them. Team members and managers evaluate work by performance, not when or where the work is performed. Results count—meeting deadlines matters, but employees have wide-open flexibility about how work is scheduled and organized to achieve those results. Reduced work schedules and flexible options are available on a variety of shifts and across nearly all positions. Departments don't necessarily use all possible flexible work arrangements, but most have found a way to implement some form of flexible work.

At an FTN operations center, for example, employees work one of three different schedules within a certain shift and if they need to adjust on a given day, they make up the lost time by working longer another day.

In a department that reconciles accounts, the beginning of each month is intensely busy. The department employees restructured the regular work schedule so that they work twelve-hour days at the beginning of each month and take time off at the end of the month. Afterward, the accounts were reconciled in half the time—four days instead of the eight it had taken before (Flynn, 1997)—and customer satisfaction improved, without additional cost (Martinez, 1997). Management set the guidelines for what had to be accomplished and employees devised the system. Absenteeism has been minimal since the changeover, as employees schedule personal business such as dental appointments on their days off.

Employees choose from a variety of shifts plus a "prime-time" option—twenty to thirty-two hours per week—without the stigma or reduced benefits and advancement potential often associated with part-time work. Prime-time scheduling can be on a temporary basis (after childbirth or surgery) or a long-term arrangement.

The company maintains enough relief staff—financial centers have floating tellers, for example—to provide coverage to meet customer needs and support employee flexibility. Employees' stress and well-being are monitored. Midlevel managers are encouraged by senior leaders to use the flexible options and lead by example.

Employees know it is about meeting the work goals. It is a challenge to meet the tight deadlines—as many as twelve a day in an operations department where FedEx shipment deadlines are essential to making one-day deposits. Everyone is clear that the culture has to work within the framework of delivering results, but, given that, almost anything is possible. Speed, accuracy, and availability of funds are required, and the department is successful at achieving all three. FTN does not seek to resolve employees' work and personal issues for them, but rather to create an environment where teams and individuals can fulfill their needs and be successful at work and in their personal lives.

Ownership Outlook

Employees act like the owners they are. The power that employees at all levels have to make decisions means that continuous improvement is often led by employees. Members of an operations group, for example, took it upon themselves to dissect the tasks for hand-processing a commercial multiple-entry statement. Collectively empowered to take on the whole problem, not just a piece of it, they turned a fourteen-hour process into one that now requires six hours.

Employees don't just act like owners, they *are* owners. Through stock options to all employees and a system of rewards to and investments in employees, employees in fact became owners. Stock options grants (subject to approval by the board of directors) are typically granted to *all* full-time, prime-time, and part-time employees each year (currently fifty shares per year that vest in three years). An active employee who worked at FTN when the shares were first granted in 1995 would have a take-home profit of at least $16,000 before tax as of the first quarter of 2003.

Our employees own this company, and that ownership feeling has got to come through in this whole effort because we've got to have everybody in this company every day thinking about, "This is my com-pany. This is my job. What can I do today to help us be the best we can be and to figure out how to do things more efficiently." The purpose [of the stock options] is to give our employees an ability to benefit personally and financially from the company doing well, to make people feel like they are owners, which they are . . . so that the decisions that they make every day will be in alignment with our overall goals.

—*Roundtable with Ralph Horn, November 29, 2001*

There is a palpable sense that when an employee has an idea, it is heard, taken seriously, and often implemented. For example, a financial center manager developed a special reward for tellers who spot bad checks—a card worth time off. Since any bad check can mean a substantial loss, the savings generated were worth hundreds of thousands of dollars and the idea spread to other financial centers.

Shared responsibility and pride in results is what enables the company to manage lean.

The elements of the Firstpower culture—the principles, language, leadership and employee training, rewards, models of behavior—are highly aligned and aggressively nurtured. FTN seems to be a well-tuned machine, with an enormously energized, motivated, and proud group of employees across all levels. Its rhetoric and action match, and all levels share a rare sense of egalitarianism. The relational distance between the senior leaders and line employees is not great; the comfort level between them is rarely seen in an organization of any size. The sense of empowerment and commitment the ordinary employee (who is not so ordinary) has is remarkable.

The Business Results

The business results are described here in chronological stages. We start with the initial stage, then describe an intervening financial storm, and then present the results of recent years.

The First Six Years

By the end of 1998, six years after its introduction, the work to remold the culture was clearly paying off. FTN continued to meet its goal of remaining independent.

During this period, FTN was also able to execute a number of important business strategies, including the national expansion of its mortgage banking and transaction processing businesses and increasing the breadth of product offerings of FTN Financial. This growth would not have been possible without the performance improvements that resulted from the FTN culture. The five essential results from this first phase were

- Increased customer satisfaction
- Extraordinary customer loyalty and retention
- Increased productivity
- Stronger recruitment and retention and employee satisfaction
- Excellent profitability and shareholder returns

Increased Customer Satisfaction

Introduction of the Firstpower culture contributed to greater employee and customer satisfaction and retention.

By 1998, 98 percent of customers of the Loan Operations Division had rated it "good" compared to only 38 percent "good" ratings in 1992. This division was considered a microcosm of the overall company culture (Casner-Lotto, 2000). Customer satisfaction was directly connected to employees' sense that their leader was supportive of their ability to embrace both work and personal responsibilities: leaders rated as less supportive in these areas had a 61 percent lower rating on customer service than more supportive leaders.

Extraordinary Customer Loyalty and Retention

Customer retention increased in both the consumer and business markets to 95 percent beginning in 1995 and continued to grow to a record 97 percent in 1998, 9 percent above the banking industry average.

Customer retention was influenced by leaders' supportiveness of employees' dual responsibilities (at work and home). When employees rated their managers as more supportive it made a 7 percent difference in customer retention.

FTN developed a model for identifying the most important factors of customer loyalty. As noted earlier, the company was able to explain about one third of customer loyalty with employee factors, with the remaining two thirds related to "other factors" of product, convenience, image, and pricing.

To understand what *specific* employee factors created customer loyalty, FTN analyzed the data further. It discovered that three things made the difference in customer loyalty: how employees rated managers *(leadership)*, the length of tenure of the team *(experience)*, and the strength of employees' job satisfaction *(job value)*. Leaders received high scores on the employee survey when they empowered employees, supported their personal responsibilities, were good role models of the Firstpower culture, set direction, and worked toward continuous improvement. Employee job value scores were high when employees reported they gained a sense of responsibility and accomplishment from their jobs, felt their ideas counted, had flexibility about how to do the work, and felt a sense of pride in FTN.

Understanding these dynamics enabled FTN to predict the financial effect of changes in these scores. According to internal company research from the late 1990s, when the employee rating of leaders increased by 0.50, it led to a 2.08 percent increase in customer loyalty, which would result in an increase of $16.3 million over five years. Similar results would result if employee scores for experience and job value increased by 0.50, resulting in a five-year revenue increase of $10.3 million and $21.7 million, respectively.

Increased Productivity

Productivity increased across the organization. Reducing the amount of time required to fill positions, a result of FTN's reputation for being an outstanding place to work, yielded a gain of fifteen thousand workdays of productivity—a $1.5 million gain in productivity per year.

The Loan Operations Division more than doubled its volume of business from 1992 to 1998. Although original projections indicated an additional 122 FTE (full-time equivalent employees) would be required to accomplish the additional work, the department processed the increased volume without any increases in staff. The performance boost came because the stable workforce understood the process and was more engaged and efficient than newcomers would have been, and the learning curve time associated with turnover was avoided.

Stronger Recruitment and Retention and Employee Satisfaction

National recognition for organizational success, workplace excellence, and being one of the best companies to work for, coupled with an excellent local reputation for its people practices, reinforced FTN's ability to attract and retain top talent. FTN has been recognized regularly by *BusinessWeek*, *Fortune*, and *Working Mother* as a great place to work since 1995. In 1996 *BusinessWeek* named FTN the number one family-friendly company in America.

Despite a highly competitive job market, FTN filled open positions in a fraction of the time other banks required. In 1990, FTN exceeded all other banking organizations, taking about twenty days to fill an open position. By 1997, while FTN retained the twenty-day fill rate, others were taking nearly twice as long, and the difference was attributed to FTN's reputation as a good place to work (Casner-Lotto, 2000). Supportive leaders (those rated by employees as supportive of the ability to embrace both work and personal responsibilities) had tripled the employee value scores and retained employees at twice the rate of less supportive managers.

Among a high-risk group of employees, 85 percent were retained specifically by prime-time, which allows a shorter workweek while retaining full-time benefits and the same advancement potential as full-time employees (Flynn, 1997).

Excellent Profitability and Shareholder Returns

In January 1999, FTN topped the *Forbes* Platinum List of profitability at 19 percent for its five-year average return on capital—the result of increased employee performance and retention, increased customer retention, and reduced costs. Return on assets in the 1992–1997 period increased to 2.07 percent from 1.49 percent; return on equity increased from 15.4 percent to 22.5 percent.

The return to shareholders soared to 35.8 percent for the five-year average, which was 49.1 percent above the return of other S&P 400 mid-cap banks and nearly double S&P 400 mid-cap companies' return of 18.8 percent for the period January 1, 1994, through December 31, 1998.

Weathering the Financial Storm of 2000

FTN had documented the effects of its culture change between 1992 and 1998 and was convinced that it had found the solution to remaining financially independent. A year later, however, fourth-quarter earnings unexpectedly pointed to signs of upcoming turbulence that dampened the 1999 financial performance. No one, including FTN, could foresee the financial toll that 2000 would take on the nation's financial institutions. Critics watched closely to see if FTN's culture would work in these tough financial times. Even though the tumult knocked FTN out of the highest-performer group, which had a 12–15 percent annual earnings per share growth rate, and disrupted a decade-long growth trend, executives never questioned the commitment to employee-centered practices, now deeply embedded in the FTN culture. In fact, FTN leaders were relying on its employees and its business strategy to climb back into the high-performer group.

Chairman Horn summarized what happened in 2000.

Last year a set of conditions involving pricing pressures, rising interest rates, and inverted yield curve combined to strangle earnings in our mortgage operation and our capital markets business. In the mortgage company, refinancing dried up as interest rates rose; at the same time, our reliance on wholesale mortgage originations left us with excess capacity in our back office and a need to create volume in a price-sensitive market. As a result, the profitability in our mortgage company was hit hard. In Capital Markets, an active first quarter quickly became only a pleasant memory as an inverted yield curve took the energy out of customer demands for many of our more historically successful products. The net effect of this "storm" was a year of diminished earnings and only a modest increase in our stock price. . . .

Last year did nothing to quell my optimism. I believe our strategy is better than ever. I know our people are the best and our culture allows them to develop relationships with our customers, providing them with All Things Financial.

—Chairman's message, 2001 First Quarter Report, April 17, 2001

Results of Recent Years

FTN emerged from financially troubled 2000 with its Firstpower culture firmly in place. The culture was credited with helping FTN rebound to its previous status in the industry even more quickly than analysts expected.

Customer Loyalty and Retention

Customer retention in 2002 was 95.3 percent for the consumer target market, which FTN now uses as *the* measure of customer satisfaction.

Productivity and Growth

From 1990 through 2000, FTN produced one of the best average annual growth rates in the industry—17 percent. Even with the financial storm of 2000, the earnings per share average growth rate of 14 percent over two years put FTN among the ten fastest-growing bank holding companies, its 2001 First Quarter Report points out. Other indicators include the following.

- One third of the $350 million in fee income produced by FTN Financial was generated by new products and services not offered before midyear 2000 (2001 First Quarter Report). (FTN Financial includes Capital Markets, Equity Research, Investment Banking, Strategic Alliances, and Correspondent Services.)

- Bloomberg ranked FTN Financial among the top ten in total underwriting volume in U.S. agency bonds for 2001.

- The *span of control*—the ratio of employees to managers—increased in many areas as a result of the Firstpower culture. As employees are empowered to make decisions about their work, leaders are able to focus on value-generating activities.

Recruitment, Retention, and Employee Satisfaction

Continued exposure as a great place to work attracts great employees to FTN; being a great place to work keeps them.

Business Ethics recognized FTN as one of the "100 Best Corporate Citizens" in 2003. FTN is one of only twenty-six companies included on *Fortune*'s list of the "100 Best Companies to Work For in America" for the six consecutive years since the list was created. *Working Mother* listed FTN among the "100 Best Companies for Working Mothers" from 1994 to 2002.

The Employee Value Score, which measures employee perceptions of their experience of working at FTN, continues to increase. In 2002, the overall score was 77 percent; other results include the following.

- Ninety-two percent of employees consider their overall compensation to be of greater value because of the family-friendly benefit programs and resources.

- Ninety-four percent of employees have flexibility in completing their job duties and tasks.

- Ninety-four percent of employees report that someone at work cares about them as a person.

- Ninety-three percent of employees are likely to recommend FTN as a great place to work.

- Eighty-nine percent of employees report that their leader is supportive of their ability to embrace both work and personal responsibilities.

- The voluntary turnover rate was 12 percent in 2002. Since FTN salaries are at the market level, its turnover rate is particularly instructive. Job applicants often come to FTN because of its reputation and media exposure as a company that respects people and as a great place to work.

- A new phenomenon is noted by recruiters—a boomerang effect, a larger than usual number of employees coming back to FTN after employment elsewhere.

Profitability and Shareholder Returns

In 2001 FTN was rated the most profitable banking company in the United States for the fourth consecutive year, according to *Forbes* (Forbes Web site, 2001). The company has made the *Forbes* list of the "400 Best Big Companies" from 2000 to 2003, with an 18 percent five-year average return on capital.

In 2002, FTN ranked third among the top fifty bank holding companies, with an annual revenue per share growth rate of 15.3 percent over the past five years. Total return to shareholders for FTN was 24.03 percent, compared to the Top 50 at 18.64 percent and the S&P 500 at –2.84 percent. Dividends increased annually from 1998.

FTN outperformed market expectations each quarter in 2001 and 2002, and the first quarter of 2003. Earnings of $376.5 million in 2002 represent an 18 percent growth from 2001 earnings of $318.2 million. Return on average shareholder's equity was 24 percent for 2002 compared to 22.7 percent in 2001, as reported in the 2003 annual report. Five-year annual growth rate of earnings per share is 14 percent and continues to be 11 percent for dividends.

By the end of 2002, FTN had total shareholder returns slightly higher than its peer group of The American Banker Top 50 and significantly higher than the S&P 500, according to the 2003 FTN Proxy Report.

"Firstpower is what makes all our strategies succeed," says Sarah Meyerrose. "It's the way we approach our work every day with an attitude of ownership and teamwork. FTN is a company focused on people. Employee value is a business imperative and a strategic advantage for us."

President and CEO Ken Glass and Chairman of the Board Ralph Horn sum up the company's success in a company report (2003).

The real key to our ability to produce exceptional growth (an average annual earnings per share growth rate of 17 percent since 1990) is our culture and the careful attention given to our four constituent groups: employees, customers, communities, and shareholders. For the sixth consecutive year Fortune magazine selected First Tennessee as one of "100 Best Companies to Work For," and Working Mother magazine picked us for their list of "100 Best Companies for Working Mothers" for the eighth straight year. That's a testimony to our unique culture that allows our employees to develop and enhance relationships with their customers without sacrificing their personal lives. Every year we survey all employees on a variety of subjects related to their satisfaction with their jobs and the leadership provided to them. The results guide us in improving our culture, allowing us to retain and motivate those high-performing employees who give us our competitive edge. There is no question that there is a substantial bottom-line payoff for engaged, motivated employees.

AFTERWORD

People live and work differently today than they did in the past. They invest more of themselves in their work because their work requires it. They seek more satisfaction from their work and want more say over it. They have 24/7 work lives that overlap with 24/7 personal lives.

These people—the new human capital—expect more, require more, and offer more. Powerful, capable, and torn in two directions, they hold the reins to organizational performance because their creativity, knowledge, and relationships determine whether or not an organization flourishes. Understanding what makes them tick—what they need, what they care about, and how they think—is essential to organizational survival. Managing in line with this knowledge is the organization's lifeline.

Organizational systems that have promoted and rewarded those with a singular focus on work must now shift, acknowledging that this focus is simply not possible for most people. Managers must promote leaders who are able to manage a workforce of multidimensional, complex human capital. They must reward results instead of time invested and recognize that employees' time is no longer an unlimited resource at their disposal. They must support career patterns that enable people to move in and out of organizations and even interrupt work altogether. They must facilitate rather than dictate, because in this environment dictating just doesn't work.

Leaders and managers must pay attention to their people in all their complexity. They must recognize and foster a new set of skills that were invisible before, including self-awareness, relational skills, and an orientation toward others. They must encourage the individuality of the people who work for them, because individuality is the source of personalized service, innovation, fully engaged employees, and happy customers. They must abandon one-size-fits-all policies and instead embrace individualized policies that value diversity. They must rethink their benefits philosophy, redefine equity, and realize that this new human capital requires new tools to be fully present at work, that is, services to replace what the stay-at-home partner once did. Leaders must be willing to look deeply into their organizational psyche, be honest about what they believe about people and how a business should run, and have the courage to abandon what has worked in the past because it's not going to work anymore. They must be willing to invest in a long-term change effort that makes explicit values and beliefs that have been unspoken.

Leaders will ask, Why do we need to do this? The answer is that their organizations will not be able to compete otherwise. The ground has shifted; it is not something they can control. The threads of the change in the society and the marketplace have come together to weave an entirely new environment. To get the best talent and to free their people to produce all that they can, organizations must reinvent themselves.

To those who would ask, What is the return on investment? we say that, without question, it is sizable—as evidenced by the enormous body of research reported in this book. But we would add that we believe this question is the wrong question; it understates the value and oversimplifies the basis for such a significant decision. The right question is, What is it worth? What is it potentially worth to the organization

- To expand the range of ideas and problem solvers?

- To create new knowledge in an atmosphere of mutuality (where employees openly share knowledge with colleagues and managers, contributing their best ideas to further the interests of the organization rather than their self-interest, knowing they will be treated fairly)?

- To increase the sense of loyalty and affiliation across the organization?

- To attract and keep a higher level of knowledge capital and increase the workforce's ability to focus, attend to priorities, build relationship capital, and exercise creativity?

- To achieve cohesion and alignment of purpose and culture across the organization—within and among managers, between managers and employees, and across business units?

- To increase the proportion of employees who are fully engaged in the work of the organization—who have a sense of ownership and sense the organization holds values they share?

- To increase the proportion of talent who are motivated by the substance of their work and require minimal oversight by management, who understand how they contribute to organizational results, who agree with and feel ownership of organizational goals and strategy, who can be trusted to organize their own work for highest maximum yield, and who have a sense of pride in their work and employer?

- To replace the sense of a "transactional relationship" (I will get mine) between managers and employees with a sense of mutual commitment to common goals?

- To reduce waste, errors, and mis-hires, counteract employee burnout, excessive absenteeism, and turnover?

- To maximize the satisfaction and retention of customers?

- To increase the breadth and depth of relationships with partners, sub-contractors, vendors, and the community?

This book is not about a new management technique, a new tool or initiative to get more out of people. It asks leaders and managers to summon the personal and organizational courage to examine what they believe and how they operate, and to change from the inside out. It offers in return the opportunity to leverage this new human capital for all it's worth. For those who do, the dividends can be enormous.

NOTES

Chapter Three

1. Women were not typically prepared for or employed in occupations with the same earning potential as men. When they were employed, it was in female-dominated professions like teaching, clerical work, and retail sales, in which pay was substantially lower.

2. One in six married-couple families had a sole breadwinning father. Among married couples with children there were nearly three times as many where both Ozzie *and* Harriet were employed as ones in which just Ozzie was—that is, 53 percent had both employed fathers and mothers and 19 percent had only the father employed (in 2000). The remainder of married couples with children had only the mother employed (5.4 percent), no one employed (16 percent), or other employment combinations (6.2 percent; Bureau of Labor Statistics, 2001a).

3. The U.S. Census Bureau reports that median household income in 2000 was $41,994, even considering that most of these households had more than one earner. In 1999, more than a fourth (29 percent) of families had incomes below $25,000 per year (2002a). About 6 percent of earners hold down more than one job—6.6 percent of women who are widowed, divorced, separated, or single and 5.8 percent of married men with a spouse present (2002c, Table 586). Increases in family income are the result of more hours worked and more earners in the family (Mishel, Bernstein, & Schmitt, 2000). The difference in wages from the top rung to the bottom has grown, so the bottom 10 percent of earners earned less in real terms in 2000 than they did in 1973 (91 percent of what they had earned three

decades before). Those in the eighth 10 percent earned 107 percent more than they had in 1973 (Ehrenreich, 2001).

4. Between 1979 and 1995 alone, wages for the median male worker fell 15 percent (Mishel, Bernstein, & Boushey, 2002, p. 125; see also Ellwood et al., 2000). The amount men could expect their earnings to rise over their lifetime also dropped dramatically. The real earnings of men born between 1926 and 1935 had jumped 61 percent by the time they reached midcareer in the 1960s; those born in the next age group, who reached midcareer in the mid-1970s, had an earnings increase of only 24 percent (Spain & Bianchi, 1996).

5. The median family income in 2001 for a couple with both spouses employed was $70,834, compared to $40,792 for a married couple with a nonemployed wife, and $25,745 for a single female head of household (U.S. Census Bureau, 2001).

6. Today the total opportunity cost in forgone earnings for a college-educated stay-at-home mother is an estimated $1 million (Crittenden, 2001). A separate analysis put the opportunity cost at half a million dollars for a woman earning $23,600 who reduced her work hours while raising children but continued working (*U.S. News & World Report*, March 30, 1998, cited in Business Women's Network, 2002).

7. In 1910, 23 percent of all women (55 percent of black women) worked for wages (Levine & Dworkin, 1983).

8. In 1942, 87 percent of American school districts forbade hiring married women; 70 percent fired single women who married (Dubeck & Borman, 1996).

9. With greater life spans both women's and men's earning years lengthen, which makes the economic trade-off of women's investment in employability greater. In the early 1960s, the average age of the U.S. worker was thirty; by 2005, the average age will be forty-one (Keilly, 2002). In 1999, one in four families had a single mother as head of household (Acs & Nelson, 2001); and almost half (46 percent) of single-mother families with children under six fell below the poverty line, compared to 9 percent of families in general (U.S. Census Bureau, 2002a). Women are better educated, which potentially gives them access to a wider range of jobs. In 1950, 5 percent of American mothers with children under twelve had completed four years of college; by 1990, more than 18 percent had (Sandberg & Hofferth, 2001).

10. By 1998, wives' hours in the paid workforce had grown by 42 percent on average since 1979. Middle-income wives with children added 479 hours over this nineteen-year period, close to three months of full-time work (Mishel et al., 2000). In a similar development, 43 percent of women worked year-round in 1970, while in 1990 57 percent did. The number of full-time year-round employed mothers rose from 14 percent in 1970 among those born between 1925 and 1936 to 42 percent in 1990 among those born between 1956 and 1965. Meanwhile, although it is often presumed that most men work full time year-round it is not entirely true. Only 66 percent of men born between 1956 and 1965 worked full time year-round in 1990 (Spain & Bianchi, 1996).

11. The majority of children under six (58.6 percent in 2000) have all parents in the household employed (U.S. Census Bureau, 2002a).

12. In a study of dual-career couples conducted for Catalyst by Yankelovich Partners, 55 percent said "more freedom in career choices" was a plus factor in the two-

career marriage. Two thirds (67 percent) said that as a result of having a wage-earning spouse, they are more likely to leave their company if they aren't satisfied—an increase from 20 percent in 1981 (Catalyst, 2000a).

13. Married couples work thirty-six hundred hours combined per year on average, which is nearly full time—there are two thousand working hours in a year (Mishel et al., 2000).

14. This number is made up of the 45 percent of employed people with children who have all adults in the household working (Economic Policy Institute, 2002) and the 21 percent of employees who provide care for an elderly or disabled adult (Fredriksen-Goldsen & Scharlach, 2001) minus some overlap because some families care for both adults and children at the same time.

15. Those who cannot afford to contract out child care sometimes work tandem shifts; 35 percent of married couples with children under five work nontraditional shifts—undergoing stress indicated by their divorce rate, which is three to six times that of other couples with children of similar age (Presser, 2003). In other cases young children and other family members are left in "self-care" or in the care of siblings, because the alternative is for the family to go without necessary income.

16. More than half of the employees who care for adult family members lose time from work because of these duties; they work two to four fewer hours per week and between one and three fewer weeks per year. A third must change their work schedules. Metropolitan Life Insurance Company estimates these work disruptions affect 25 percent of full-time employees and cost $1,142 per year per employee in lost productivity (Fredriksen-Goldsen & Scharlach, 2001).

17. In 2000, persons reaching age sixty-five had an average life expectancy of eighteen more years than those who reached that age in 1950 (Bureau of Labor Statistics, 2003).

18. A 2002–2003 study of ten California companies by Arizona-based Summa Associates found that 51 percent of employees—male and female—would choose to reduce their pay in order to work fewer hours if they had the opportunity. Among men who responded to the question, 41 percent said they would choose to reduce their pay in order to work fewer hours (Summa Associates, 2003). A Work in America Institute survey of unionized employees found that almost one quarter (23 percent) would prefer to work incrementally less than their current full-time schedule, for example, 10–20 percent less, even if it meant reducing their pay and benefits proportionately. A third (34 percent) of the unionized employees would strongly consider part-time positions if they had good pay, benefits, and job security (W. Friedman & Casner-Lotto, 2003).

Chapter Eight

1. In a national study of child care centers, care for the very youngest—when their brains were most affected by their environment—was the worst; 40 percent of the care was rated "poor," which meant, for example, that caregivers did not interact with the children; children wandered aimlessly; they were rarely held, talked to or played with, or encouraged to sit up or speak. These "poor" centers also had bad general health practices; for example, caregivers did not wash their hands between

changing a series of children's diapers and preparing food for them (Helburn & Bergmann, 2002). There were few toys or materials to engage children's curiosity and problem-solving skills. Children's natural drives to be active, curious, exhibit initiative, and become self-motivated were stifled. The experiences most critical to the development of children's critical thinking, creativity, and active imagination were absent. Children were not learning how to learn (Cost, Quality, and Child Outcomes Study Team, 1995).

Chapter Ten

1. A combination of interviews and questionnaires of research managers, scientists, program officers, research officers, managers and support staff was used.

2. Participants were members of twenty-two project teams from seven U.S. companies in three industries (chemical, high-tech, and consumer products) who completed daily questionnaires about the day's work, the environment, and their level of creativity during the entire project.

3. Researchers evaluated creativity levels prior to the announcement of a downsizing initiative, during the downsizing period, and after the restructuring was complete using surveys and interviews with more than 750 employees.

4. Surveys were completed by 584 employees of the consumer products company, mostly machinists, line operators, tool and die makers, and technicians, and by 158 high-tech employees including program managers, accountants, buyers, and business analysts.

5. This study of 265 employees, 97 percent of whom were women, took place in three knitwear companies in Bulgaria. The results may differ from a similar study if done in U.S. firms.

6. Data were obtained during face-to-face interviews with 745 respondents to the 1991 General Social Survey conducted by the National Opinion Research Center.

7. Alumni of graduate business programs at two Northeastern U.S. universities were surveyed.

8. The two-year study used focus group discussions, in-person and telephone interviews, and surveys of colleagues, supervisors, senior management, human resources, systems people, alumni, recruits, clients, and other employees as well as the participants.

9. The small sample size (188 employees from five insurance companies), single industry, and homogeneity of worker type limit the extent to which this study pertains to other situations.

10. Individual companies have conducted studies of the effects of flexible work arrangements on organizational commitment. These case studies do not employ the statistical sampling that many other studies do, but they reflect concrete experiences.

11. The study selected women executives at random from a list provided by the American List Council and matched them with a male peer. No significant differences were found between respondent and nonrespondent type. Although the final sample size was small, the procedures to obtain the sample ensure it is representative of the entire population of women executives.

12. Researchers asked 367 individuals, who were employees of various types of organizations, about their perceptions of how supportive their organizations and supervisors were as well as their degree of affective commitment (emotional attachment) to their organizations.

13. Nine months after the survey (July 1983), employment records were examined to determine which of the 445 employees surveyed had actually left the organization and for what reasons.

14. Surveys were completed by 130 members of the Medical Library Association.

15. The panel, surveyed in 1995, is made up of individuals from the United States, Canada, Europe, and Australia who have experience with implementing work-life programs.

16. Both groups were absent the same average number of days in 1986, the year before the center opened.

17. This study randomly assigned employees to control groups and used data from company attendance and employment records as well as questionnaires.

18. Flexible arrangements included consistent flexible schedules that did not vary from day to day, schedules that could be flexed daily, and telecommuting.

19. The employee-driven changes resulted in a reduction in overtime hours from 7 percent of hours to 2.7 percent. Employees working the compressed schedule completed sixty-three transactions per day, while those working the normal 8-to-5 schedule averaged thirty-seven per day. This evidence was gathered from a pilot study of thirty-eight out of sixty financial center employees in Colorado Springs.

20. Catalyst conducted a two-year study of managers and professionals working part-time at two corporations and two professional services firms using discussions, interviews, and surveys of supervisors, co-workers, and participants.

21. In a two-year study of 1,300 employees and 150 managers at Amway Corporation, Bristol-Myers Squibb Company, Honeywell, Kraft Foods, Lucent Technologies, and Motorola, job satisfaction scores were 29.5 for daily flex users (out of a possible 40), 29.4 for flex users whose schedule did not change daily, 28 for telecommuters, and 27.8 for employees not using flexible work practices. Controlling for demographic differences, employees using the flexible arrangements were more attached to the company.

22. These researchers surveyed managers of more than two hundred women working flexible jobs in marketing, finance, human resources, sales, and other professions in the Boston, New York, and Los Angeles metropolitan regions..

23. This one-year pilot study at Fleet Financial Group was one of the most extensive studies of the impact of work redesign on employee productivity. It used surveys, interviews, and analysis of company records to explore workplace innovations that would help employees better integrate work, family, and community aspects of their lives. At the Framingham location, cost pressures had led to the relocation of operations and increased commute times, an emphasis on quantity of loans processed rather than quality, cuts in administrative staff that required underwriters to perform clerical tasks, and a reorganization that split the sales and underwriting functions into two separate groups. These changes were made based on underlying assumptions that workers were easily replaced, economies of scale existed,

administrative responsibilities were not important, and functional goals were more important than business goals. It became evident that these assumptions were actually very costly. A work redesign effort that enabled both the underwriters and administrative staff to concentrate on tasks best suited for their skills resulted in increased productivity for both groups.

24. The survey did not ask participants to identify productivity enhancements achieved.

25. Telephone survey of 247 teleworkers. This same study quantified the effects of this increase in productivity as a net gain of $685 per worker, including the 10 percent who found their productivity dropped when telecommuting

26. The data were gathered from the 276 women managers and their co-workers in interviews between October 1995 and October 1996. The second phase with the same women continued until November 1999 and included a 360-degree survey. Two-thirds were upper-middle managers or executives; most were midcareer and highly paid.

27. The National Sleep Foundation surveyed a thousand employed U.S. adults in 1997.

28. The benefits included a full-service summer camp for employees' school-age children and on-site child care and other services for employees' families, along with more traditional benefits. Worker appreciation of the benefits offered was enhanced by supportive relationships with supervisors and co-workers. The study examined organizational records to measure employee behavior.

29. Based on surveys of four thousand employees at forty manufacturing plants during 1995–1998.

30. The data were gathered in telephone interviews of twenty-eight hundred wage and salaried workers selected randomly from the general population as part of the 1997 National Study of the Changing Workforce conducted by Louis Harris and Associates. *Job quality* was defined as autonomy, learning opportunities, meaningfulness of work, opportunities for advancement, and job security. *Workplace support* was defined as supervisor support, supportive workplace culture, positive co-worker relations, absence of discrimination, respect in the workplace, equal opportunity, and flexibility in work arrangements.

31. Observation and interviews were used to obtain data about female engineers in a high-tech company.

32. According to Donald Kruse, who has analyzed thirty-one studies on employee stock ownership plans, employee satisfaction, and firm performance, "A number of studies have attempted to control for self-selection bias resulting from the types of companies that adopt employee ownership plans, but these corrections have made little substantive difference in the results" (Kruse, 2002, p. 72).

33. The study included surveys of 105 publicly held companies regarding the extent of stock options granted and the dates such plans were implemented plus analysis of these companies' financial performance as well as the performance of 395 companies that had announced the adoption of broad-based stock option plans. Performance levels were analyzed during three time periods: 1985–1987 (before the companies had adopted their plans), 1995–1997 (when the plans were

adopted), and during 1997. Broad-based plans for this study are defined as those granting at least 20 percent of options to employees; in fact, surveyed participants in this study averaged slightly higher participation rates—45 percent of employees were granted stock options.

34. Surveys of job characteristics and health status of 21,300 U.S. nurses from 1992 through 1996.

35. A survey of twelve hundred employees selected at random from private sector U.S. companies in 1992 and six hundred workers in 1991 found that allowing flexible scheduling of work hours reduced those reporting burnout by eleven percentage points, from 39 percent on average across companies to 28 percent.

36. The National Study of the Changing Workforce, a study of the general population of employed people conducted by Louis Harris and Associates.

37. This survey of forty-six thousand employees at six major U.S. companies tracked medical bills over a three-year period.

38. According to telephone interviews of two thousand adults in 2000 and one thousand adults in 2002.

39. Per a February 1999 telephone survey of one thousand adults in the U.S. workforce.

40. The survey addressed 687 working men and women, 26 percent of whom identified balancing work and family demands as their primary career concern, followed by 23 percent who cited earning a competitive salary, job security (17 percent), keeping skills current (16 percent), and having an advanced degree or certification (9 percent).

41. The 1999 survey included twenty-five hundred graduating students from thirty-six universities on five continents.

42. Telephone surveys of approximately 250 teleworkers, identified through random-digit calling of thirty thousand households in 1999, revealed how important it is for those who work remotely to continue to do so.

43. Survey of 11,700 information technology staff and 10,700 managers, conducted in 2000.

44. A survey of 160 executives from a variety of North American companies found those with more than 10,000 employees offered flexible work options.

45. This contingent valuation analysis was performed on three small Southeastern manufacturing firms, two with on-site child care centers and one without. It found that the perceived value of the benefits to employees (both employees with and without children) was the equivalent of paying a higher wage across the firm. The benefit was valued monetarily by employees with children and, surprisingly, also by those without children. The center created a recruitment value in attracting new employees that was worth one and one third to two times the cost of the service, before the effects of the centers on attendance or retention or other effects were considered.

46. This analysis was conducted as proprietary research for various organizations in an effort to uncover the variables most often associated with turnover. The studies represented a large number of employees, numerous business units, and a variety of industries.

47. According to a survey of 6,255 individuals.

48. The study interviewed twenty-six hundred prenatal women and nineteen hundred of them postnatally, and looked at the factors determining when women stop working, how they perform on the job, how long they stay on leave, and whether they return after childbirth.

49. In this study, 324 women were interviewed in 1991 and 1992; they were patients of four hospitals in one Indiana county.

50. According to a survey of five hundred professionals by Mastery Works Inc.

51. The Ryder analysis used 1988 employee attitude surveys, actual turnover, and 1988–1989 financial performance for twelve districts (covering 983 employees) to determine how HR practices affected employee satisfaction and turnover. The results indicate HR practices such as competitive pay, performance-based compensation, communication, and advancement opportunity had a positive impact on employee satisfaction, and that satisfaction affected turnover.

52. Catalyst has studied the effects of reduced work hours and flexible work arrangements on both employers and employees, particularly on managerial-level women, for more than a decade. This longitudinal study tracked twenty-four of the women and two of the men who had been part of the 1989 and 1993 studies. Many participants moved from full-time work to job-sharing, to part-time work, and back to full-time work—and sometimes back to part-time again over the period studied. Thirteen of the twenty-four earned promotions while working part-time.

53. Marriott initiated this pilot flexibility program in 2000 at three hotels.

54. A study of graduates of five law schools examined why women, who have made up at least 40 percent of law students since 1985, are only 15.6 percent of law firm partners and 13.7 percent of general counsels in Fortune 500 companies.

55. A two-year study of 1,300 employees and 150 managers.

56. This was based on a study by the National Council of Jewish Women.

57. Child care costs also influence the type of child care used; more stable forms of child care are used by higher-income families. Lower-income families use unregulated, informal care that breaks down more often, resulting in absenteeism that can lead to disciplinary action and ultimately to termination.

58. Data were obtained from a 1991 survey of 331 managers who had supervised a leave by subordinates.

59. Data from thirty-nine companies were used in 1982–83 to study the effects of different types of employer-provided child care benefits (referrals and child care facilities—on or off the work site) on employee retention and morale.

Chapter Eleven

1. The study covered a division that provides payroll, tax, accounting, and HR services. Opinion surveys were obtained from 667 employees and 633 customers in thirty districts over a twelve-month period. A strong positive relationship was found between customers' perception of the service climate and employees' overall satisfaction with the company and their level of responsibility, and also between customers' satisfaction and employee opinions about management practices, culture

for success, work group climate, job satisfaction, personal responsibility (commitment to organizational success, personal development, and safeguarding organizational assets), reward for performance, and overall satisfaction with the company.

2. Sears used surveys, interviews, and focus groups to develop a quantitative model of the linkage between employee satisfaction, customer satisfaction, and profits. By analyzing employee turnover, workforce composition, and customer satisfaction scores of 771 out of 800 stores, the researchers found that those stores with high customer service scores had employee turnover rates of 54 percent and a higher percentage of employees working a forty-hour week or a regular twenty-hour part-time week.

3. The researchers studied 139 offices from twenty-nine marketing communications firms.

4. Companies make the *Working Mother* 100 Best list by instituting policies helpful to women with children: they advance women and provide child care benefits, flexible work schedules, telecommuting, and other adaptive practices.

5. Based on surveys of two thousand employees and thirty-one hundred customers in 1990 and twenty-five hundred employees and twenty-three hundred customers in 1992.

6. Telephone surveys of a representative sample of American workers between the ages of eighteen and sixty-four from the 1992 National Study of the Changing Workforce.

7. A 1999 survey of two hundred individuals hired into flexible work arrangements with various companies during the prior two years, and of the managers who employed them.

8. A nationwide telephone survey of 695 working adults conducted between November 13 and 18, 2000.

9. Telephone interviews with 3,551 employed adults in the United States conducted by Louis Harris and Associates as part of the 1997 National Study of the Changing Workforce. Results were compared with a similar survey conducted in 1992 and the 1977 Quality of Employment Survey conducted by the U.S. Department of Labor.

10. Quarterly surveys of seven thousand employees and fifty thousand customers of an insurance company, selected at random, assessed the progress of a quality initiative addressing customer satisfaction and retention, customer-focused quality, profitability, sustainability, and employee growth and development. In every quarter, customer satisfaction and employees' perceptions about management effectiveness showed a significant correlation.

11. The Beck Group mandates a minimum of forty hours of training a year—employees actually average more than 50 percent above that figure.

12. Surveys from 538 employees and 7,944 customers at fifty-seven branches of a retail and commercial bank were received during the third quarter of 1993.

13. A survey of 4,854 employees in two hundred retail store branches in 1988, a survey of 158,878 customers of those retail branches in a similar time period, and an analysis of retail sales and net income of fifty-six of the two hundred stores was undertaken in order to identify the aspects of the work environment that are most conducive to high levels of customer service. All stores had been in operation for at least eighteen months; employee turnover was high—around 50 percent.

Chapter Twelve

1. Internal case study of usage of Chase Manhattan Bank's emergency child care in 1996. The loss figure of $1,523,175 included employee salary costs for days missed only; it did not include the extra costs of absenteeism—time spent by supervisors, lost efficiency, and the like.

2. Internal evaluation of Marriott International's Associate Resource Line, established to help employees find resources for other pressing personal needs.

3. This analysis was based on a synthesis of health research including an analysis of occupational and health data coupled with random surveys of employed men that controlled for other risk factors.

4. A thirty-eight-person CPA firm in Kern County, California, found that the absence of child care services that fit long tax season hours limited the firm's ability to conduct its full capacity of business.

5. In 1988 NCR compared employee opinions from surveys of twelve plants with performance and quality ratings of each plant.

6. At district court level, in *Walsh v. National Computer Systems, Inc.*, plaintiff charged Title VII claim under disparate treatment, hostile work environment, constructive discharge, and retaliation theory.

7. The Center for Effective Organizations at USC has been studying how Fortune 1000 companies implement and use different organizational effectiveness programs including reengineering, total quality management, and employee involvement since 1987. Results given here refer to surveys of the Fortune 1000 companies conducted in 1996 and 1999.

8. An analysis of financial results and published research on twelve companies compared companies rated as the best places to work on a variety of indices with similar companies matched by industry type.

9. This survey of 201 U.S. companies with more than two hundred employees was drawn from the 1989 *Dun's Business Rankings* and investigated staffing practices and organizational performance from 1986 through 1990.

10. These findings are from one of the first studies to examine how employees affect organizational performance; it used longitudinal data over a fifteen-year period. The data were obtained from the Survey of Organizations and the Organization Survey Profile (collected from 1966 through 1981) and compared with performance data obtained from Compustat for the five-year period after data were collected for the surveys (Denison, 1990). Approximately thirty-four companies are included in the final analysis (having both survey and Compustat data), representing diverse industries from aircraft parts to telephone communication equipment and including services such as transportation, banking, and investments.

11. Much of this research has been published in peer-reviewed journals. The researchers use surveys and analysis; results apply to all workers.

12. This study addressed both for-profit and nonprofit firms from the National Organizations Survey.

13. Senior HR executives representing 968 companies selected from the Compact Disclosure database completed questionnaires in 1992 about their HR practices in

effect during 1991. Questions involved practices considered to be associated with high performance. Across a diverse range of industries and company sizes, the results consistently demonstrated that companies could make investments in employees that increased their productivity and reduced their tendency to leave, and, as a result, reap significant financial returns from that investment.

14. The analysis was made by reexamining the data obtained during the 1992 study of 968 companies and by sampling an additional 740 companies from the Compact Disclosure database in 1994 regarding HR practices in effect during 1993. Both the 1992 and 1994 analysis found a significant positive effect on firm performance from the use of HR best practices as well as above-average use of a combination of HR practices.

15. To do a validity check on the 1992 and 1994 studies and test their measurement approach, Huselid and Becker analyzed the companies that had participated in both the 1992 and 1994 studies in a different way. They adjusted for bias created by looking at changes in the same firm over time (using longitudinal data) as opposed to comparing results across different firms that used different practices (using cross-sectional data). The study had complete data for both years on 218 firms. The authors believe the two effects—measurement errors and possible bias—have been corrected in this study.

16. In 1996, using methods similar to those from previous studies, the authors collected data from 548 publicly held firms with more than a hundred employees and $5 million in sales regarding their HR practices in 1995 and obtained financial performance information from the Compact Disclosure database. These results are similar to earlier studies but measure the effects of a more comprehensive HR system.

17. Data were collected in 1996 and reflected HR practices used by approximately five hundred firms in 1995. The publicly held firms were again selected from a commercial database of firms with more than a hundred employees and $5 million in sales. An index composed of mean scores from each element of a high-performance system was created, so an organization could not receive a high score for doing an especially good job with recruiting, for example, while using a low-performance compensation system (Becker & Huselid, 1998).

18. McKinsey surveyed 350 corporate officers and 5,500 executives from 77 companies in 1997. They found companies in the top quintile (20 percent) of shareholder value outperform those in the middle quintile in thirteen of nineteen practices related to motivating and developing leaders.

19. Announcements of decisions to provide work-family support were culled from the *Wall Street Journal* for the period 1971 to 1996. Firms in the high-tech industry had greater increases in shareholder returns than firms in other industries. Work-family initiatives included dependent care, flexible work arrangements, and family stress and general work-family supports.

20. Telephone interviews with personnel directors at 527 U.S. firms, based on data obtained from the National Organizations Survey, investigated whether organizations providing a greater range of work-family benefits had better organizational performance.

21. A study compared sales and asset growth, return on assets (ROA), and return on equity (ROE) data from January 1990 to December 1994 for fifty-eight companies identified in the 1994 edition of Levering and Moskowitz's book, *The 100 Best Companies to Work For in America* (Levering & Moskowitz, 2000), with eighty-eight companies from the S&P top 100 companies (those recognized as leaders in growth and profitability). The researchers concluded that a company can afford to satisfy employees, enjoy exceptional growth, and be profitable (Lau & May, 1998). In our view, using the S&P 100 as an index is particularly instructive about the nature of the competitive edge these practices can give.

REFERENCES

Ackerman, T. (2002, Saturday, June 8). Study indicates low-control job can increase risk of dying early. *Houston Chronicle*, p. 28A.

Acs, G., & Nelson, S. (2001). "Honey, I'm home": Changes in living arrangements in the late 1990s. Washington, DC: Urban Institute.

Albrecht, K., & Zemke, R. (1985). *Service America!: Doing business in the new economy*. Homewood, IL: Dow Jones-Irwin.

Allen, N. J., & Meyer, J. P. (1990). The measurement and antecedents of affective, continuance, and normative commitment to the organization. *Journal of Occupational Psychology, 63*(1), 1–18.

Amabile, T. M. (1997, Fall). Motivating creativity in organizations: On doing what you love and loving what you do. *California Management Review, 40*(1), 39–58.

Amabile, T. M., & Conti, R. (1999). Changes in the work environment for creativity during downsizing. *Academy of Management Journal, 42*(6), 630–640.

Amabile, T. M., Hadley, C. N., & Kramer, S. J. (2002). Creativity under the gun. *Harvard Business Review, 80*(8), 52–61.

Amar, A. D. (2002). *Managing knowledge workers: Unleashing innovation and productivity*. Westport, CT: Quorum Books.

American Association of University Professors. (2002). Statement of principles on family responsibilities and academic work. Retrieved May 7, 2002, from http://www.aaup.org/statements/re01fam.htm.

Amick, B. C., & Mustard, C. (2003, June). *Labor markets and health: A social epidemiological perspective.* Paper presented at the Workplace/Workforce Mismatch: 1, Work, Family, Health, and Well-Being conference, Washington, DC.

Anderson, D., Binder, M., & Krause, K. (2003, January). The motherhood wage penalty revisited: Experience, heterogeneity, work effort, and work-schedule flexibility. *Industrial and Labor Relations Review, 56*(2), 273.

Ansberry, C. (2001a, June 4). Odd numbers: States discover it is hard work to figure their jobless rate—Ohio shows how problems in data, analysis skew key economic indicator—no bad times for calendars. *Wall Street Journal*, p. A1.

Ansberry, C. (2001b, July 6). Private resources: By resisting layoffs, small manufacturers help protect economy—many opt not to sacrifice hefty investments they made to find workers—Extrude Hone's new process. *Wall Street Journal*, p. A1.

Aon Consulting. (2000). US @ work. Workforce Commitment Report, 2000.

Appelbaum, E., Bailey, T., Berg, P., & Kalleberg, A. L. (2000). *Manufacturing advantage: Why high-performance work systems pay off.* Washington, DC: Economic Policy Institute.

Appelbaum, E., Bailey, T., Berg, P., & Kalleberg, A. L. (2002). *Shared work valued care.* Washington, DC: Economic Policy Institute.

Appelbaum, E., & Berg, P. (1997). *Balancing work and family: Evidence from a survey of manufacturing workers.* Washington, DC: Economic Policy Institute.

Artemis Management Consultants. (2001). Facts about work/life issues. Retrieved May 10, 2001, from http://www.artemismanagement.com/Pages/WorkLifeSub/ Facts.html.

Arthur, J. B. (1994). Effects of human resource systems on manufacturing performance and turnover. *Academy of Management Journal, 37*(3), 670.

Arthur, J. S. (1998). Flexible balance. *Human Resource Executive*, 71–72.

Arthur, M. M. (2003). Share price reactions to work-family initiatives: An institutional perspective. *Academy of Management Journal, 46*(4), 497.

Atkinson, R. D., Court, R. H., & Ward, J. M. (1999). *The state new economy index.* Washington, DC: Progressive Policy Institute.

Axelrod, E. L., Handfield-Jones, H., & Welsh, T. A. (2001). War for talent—part 2, *McKinsey Quarterly, 2*, 9–11.

Bailyn, L. (1993). *Breaking the mold.* New York: Free Press.

Bailyn, L., Drago, R., & Kochan, T. (2001). *Integrating work and family life: A holistic approach.* Boston: Alfred P. Sloan Foundation Work-Family Policy Network.

Bailyn, L., & Rayman, P. (1998). *Creating work and life integration solutions.* Cambridge, MA: Radcliffe Public Policy Institute and Fleet Financial Group.

Baker, T. (1999). *Doing well by doing good: The bottom line of workplace practices.* Washington, DC: Economic Policy Institute.

Bank of America. (2002). Values. Retrieved June 23, 2002, from http://www. bankofamerica.com/careers/index.cfm?template=car_life_values.cfm.

Bankert, E., Lee, M. D.,& Lange, C. (2000). *SAS Institute: A case on the role of senior business leaders in driving work/life cultural change.* Philadelphia: The Wharton Work/Life Integration Project, The Wharton Work/Life Roundtable.

Barkema, H. G., Baum, J. A. C., & Mannix, E. A. (2002). Management challenges in a new time. *Academy of Management Journal, 45*(5), 916–930.

Bashaw, R. E., & Grant, E. S. (1994). Exploring the distinctive nature of work commitments: Their relationships with personal characteristics, job performance, and propensity to leave. *Journal of Personal Selling and Sales Management, 14*(2), 41–56.

Baxter Healthcare. (2000). *Work/life in the workplace: A guidebook for managers and employees.* Retrieved November 8, 2001, from http://www.baxter.com/job_seekers/worklife/index.html.

Becker, B. E., & Huselid, M. A. (1998). *Human resources strategies, complementaries, and firm performance.* Retrieved January 15, 2002, from http://www.mgt.buffalo.edu/departments/ohr/becker/negotiation/#Selected Papers.

Bennis, W. G., & Thomas, R. J. (2002). *Geeks and geezers: How era, values and defining moments shape leaders.* Boston: Harvard Business School Press.

Blasi, J., Douglas, K., Sesil, J., Kroumova, M., & Carberry, E. (2000). *Stock options, corporate performance, and organizational change.* Oakland, CA: National Center for Employee Ownership (NCEO).

Bollier, D., Pochop, L., & Meyer, K. A. (1997). *Donna Klein and Marriott International (A)* (Vol. 9–996–057). Palo Alto, CA: Business Enterprise Trust.

Bond, J. (1992). The impact of childbearing on employment. In D. Friedman, E. Galinsky, & V. Plowden (Eds.), *Parental leave and productivity: Current research* (pp. 1–16). New York: Families and Work Institute.

Bond, J., Galinsky, E., & Swanberg, J. E. (1998). *The 1997 national study of the changing workforce.* New York: Families and Work Institute.

Boston Bar Association. (1999). *Facing the grail.* Boston: Author.

Boston College Center for Work & Family. (2002). *The standards of excellence in work/life integration.* Unpublished manuscript, Boston.

Brandenburger, A. M., & Nalebuff, B. J. (1996). *Co-opetition: 1. A revolutionary mindset that combines competition and cooperation; 2. The game theory strategy that's changing the game of business.* New York: Currency/Doubleday.

Brannick, J. (2001). Seven strategies for retaining top talent. *Journal of Business Strategy, 22*(4), 28–31.

Bravo, E. (2003, February 27). *Women and the work/life agenda.* Paper presented at the Designing the Future conference, Orlando, FL.

Britt, T. W. (2003). Black Hawk Down at work. *Harvard Business Review, 81*(1), 16–17.

Buckingham, M., & Clifton, D. O. (2001). *Now, discover your strengths.* New York: Free Press.

Buckingham, M., & Coffman, C. (1999a). Appendix E: The meta-analysis. In *First, break all the rules: What the world's greatest managers do differently* (pp. 255–267). New York: Simon & Schuster.

Buckingham, M., & Coffman, C. (1999b). *First, break all the rules: What the world's greatest managers do differently.* New York: Simon & Schuster.

Budig, M. J., & England, P. (2001). The wage penalty for motherhood. *American Sociological Review, 66*(2), 204–225.

Bureau of Labor Statistics, U.S. Department of Labor. (2000). Employee benefits in private industry, 2000. Retrieved April 30, 2003, from http://www.bls.gov/news.release/ebs2.nr0.htm.

Bureau of Labor Statistics, U.S. Department of Labor. (2001a, April 19). Employment characteristics of families in 2000. Retrieved September 19, 2001, from ftp://146.142.4.23/pub/news.release/History/famee.04192001.news.

Bureau of Labor Statistics, U.S. Department of Labor. (2001b). Working in the 21st century. Retrieved April 30, 2003, from http://www.bls.gov/opub/working/home.htm.

Bureau of Labor Statistics, U.S. Department of Labor. (2001c). Statistical tables: Employment and the labor force. Washington, DC. Retrieved May 18, 2002, from http://www.bls.gov/opub/rtaw/pdf/table06.pdf.

Bureau of Labor Statistics, U.S. Department of Labor. (2002). Labor force statistics from the current population survey. Retrieved February 5, 2003, from ftp://ftp.bls.gov/pub/special.requests/lf/aat10.txt.

Bureau of Labor Statistics, U.S. Department of Labor. (2002–3a). Table 4. Families with own children: Employment status of parents by age of youngest child and family type. Retrieved July 5, 2004, from http://www.bls.gov/news.release/famee.t04.htm.

Bureau of Labor Statistics, U.S. Department of Labor. (2002–3b). Table 6. Employment status of mothers with own children under 3 years old by single year of age of youngest child, and marital status. Retrieved July 5, 2004, from http://www.bls.gov/news.release/famee.t06.htm.

Bureau of Labor Statistics, U.S. Department of Labor. (2003). A profile of older Americans: 2002—the older population. Retrieved July 5, 2004, from http://www.bls.gov/news.release/famee.t06.htm.

Burggraf, S. P. (1999). *The feminine economy and economic man: Reviving the role of family in the post-industrial age.* Reading, MA: Perseus Books.

Burson-Marsteller Public Relations/Public Affairs. (2000). *Customer service leadership.* New York: Burson-Marsteller Knowledge Development Division.

Burton, T. M., & Silverman, R. E. (2001, March 30). Lots of empty spaces in Cerner parking lot get CEO riled up: E-mail scolding of employees gets posted on a Web site; stock price takes beating. *Wall Street Journal,* p. B3.

Burud & Associates. (1989). *Study of child care for a Los Angeles utility.* Unpublished paper.

Burud & Associates. (2000). *Hospital child development center: Return on investment analysis.* Unpublished paper.

Burud, S. (1984). *Productivity impact study of the Kathy Kredel Nursery School.* Unpublished paper.

Burud, S. (2000). *Child care analysis for bank: Executive summary and key findings.* Unpublished paper.

Burud, S., Aschbacher, P. R., & McCroskey, J. (1984). *Employer-supported child care: Investing in human resources.* Dover, MA: Auburn House.

Business Women's Network. (2002). Working mothers and worklife. Retrieved October 29, 2002, from http://www.ewowfacts.com/wowfacts/pdfs/women/2workingmothers&worklife.pdf.

Business: The ultimate resource. (2002). Cambridge, MA: Perseus Publishing.

Buxton, J., Hessler, P., & Schaffer, C. (1999). *Capitalising on the international workplace revolution.* London: Gemini Consulting.

Cairncross, F. (2002). The company of the future: How the communications revolution is changing management. *Ubiquity, 3*(1). Retrieved February 19, 2002, from http://www.acm.org/ubiquity/book/f_cairncross_1.html.

Cameron, M. (1993, May). Prenatal care: A big investment begets a big return. *Business and Health,* 50–53.

Campbell, A., & Koblenz, M. (1997). *The work and life pyramid of needs.* Deerfield, IL: Baxter Healthcare Corporation and MK Consultants.

Cannon, D. F. (1998). Better understanding the impact of work interferences on organizational commitment. *Marriage & Family Review, 28*(1/2), 153–166.

Cappelli, P. (1999). *The new deal at work: Managing the market-driven workforce.* Boston: Harvard Business School Press.

Cappelli, P., & Chauvin, K. (1991). An interplant test of the efficiency wage hypothesis. *Quarterly Journal of Economics, 106,* 769–787.

Carson, K. D., Carson, P. P., Roe, C. W., Birkenmeier, B., & Phillips, J. S. (1999). Four commitment profiles and their relationships to empowerment, service recovery, and work attitudes. *Public Personnel Management, 28*(1), 1–13.

Casner-Lotto, J. (2000). *Holding a job, having a life: Strategies for change.* Scarsdale, NY: Work in America Institute.

Catalyst. (1997a). *A new approach to flexibility: Managing the work/time equation.* New York: Author.

Catalyst. (1997b). *Two careers, one marriage: Making it work in the workplace.* New York: Author.

Catalyst. (1998). *Women entrepreneurs: Why companies lose female talent and what they can do about it.* New York: Author.

Catalyst. (2000a). *Flexible work arrangements III: A ten year retrospective of part-time arrangements for managers and professionals.* New York: Author.

Catalyst. (2000b). *Women in law: Making the case.* New York: Author.

Catlette, B., & Hadden, R. (1998). *Contented cows give better milk.* Germantown, TN: Saltillo Press.

CCH. (1998). 1998 CCH unscheduled absence survey: Employee absenteeism jumps 25 percent, hits 7-year high as work, real life collide. Retrieved June 18, 2001, from http://www.cch.com/press/news/1998/empab.htm.

CCH. (2002). 2002 CCH unscheduled absence survey. Retrieved January 6, 2003, from http://www.cch.com/absenteeism/.

Chambers, E. G., Foulon, M., Handfield-Jones, H., Hankin, S. M., & Michaels, E. G. I. (1998). The war for talent. McKinsey Quarterly 3, 44–57.

Chase Manhattan. (1999). Improving profitability through development programs and practices. In The Chase Manhattan Value Chain (p. 10). Unpublished paper.

Cheever, B. (2001). Selling Ben Cheever: Back to square one in a service economy. New York: Bloomsbury.

Cheng, Y., Kawachi, I., Coakley, E. H., Schwartz, J., & Colditz, G. (2000). Association between psychosocial work characteristics and health functioning in American women: Prospective study. National Report on Work and Family, British Medical Journal, (20), 1432–1436.

Chin, K. (1997). Moving towards a common goal. Chemical Engineering, 104(12), 133.

Chodorow, N. (1978). The reproduction of mothering: Psychoanalysis and the sociology of gender. Berkeley: University of California Press.

CIGNA Corporation. (2000, June 15). UCLA Study of CIGNA Corporation lactation program proves that helping working moms breastfeed is good business. Press release.

CIGNA designs flexible work plan to enhance recruitment, retention. (1991). National Report on Work and Family, 4(18), 1–2.

Cohen, A. (2000). The relationship between commitment forms and work outcomes: A comparison of three models. Human Relations, 53(3), 387–417.

Cohen, D., & Prusak, L. (2002). In good company: How social capital makes organizations work. Boston: Harvard Business School Press.

Cohen, P. N., & Bianchi, S. M. (1999, December). Marriage, children, and women's employment: What do we know? Monthly Labor Review, 24–30.

Cohen, R., Mrtek, M. B., & Mrtek, R. G. (1995). Comparison of maternal absenteeism and infant illness rates among breast-feeding and formula-feeding women in two corporations. American Journal of Health Promotion, 10, 148–153.

Collins, J. (2001). Good to great: Why some companies make the leap . . . and others don't. New York: HarperBusiness.

Collins, J. C., & Porras, J. I. (1994). Built to last: Successful habits of visionary companies. New York: HarperBusiness.

Committee for Economic Development. (1998). The employer's role in linking school and work. Washington, DC: Committee for Economic Development.

Cone, Inc. (2001). 2001 Cone/Roper corporate citizenship study. Boston: Author.

Cone, Inc. (2002). 2002 Cone corporate citizenship study. Boston: Author.

Connelly, R., DeGraff, D. S., & Willis, R. (2002). If you build it, they will come: Parental use of on-site child care centers. Populations Research and Policy Review, 21(3), 241–273.

Cooper, J. C., & Madigan, K. (2003). Sobering stats that evaded the radar: The employment cost index shows companies struggling to curb benefits. BusinessWeek, (3820), 25.

Cost, Quality, and Child Outcomes Study Team. (1995). *Cost, quality, and child outcomes in child care centers.* Denver: Economics Department, University of Colorado.

Coussey, M. (2000). *Getting the right work-life balance: Implementing family-friendly practices.* London: Chartered Institute of Personnel and Development.

Coyles, S., & Gokey, T. C. (2002). Customer retention is not enough. *McKinsey Quarterly, 2.*

Crittenden, A. (2001). *The price of motherhood: Why the most important job in the world is still the least valued.* New York: Henry Holt.

Csikszentmihalyi, M. (1990). *Flow.* New York: HarperCollins.

Csikszentmihalyi, M. (1993). *The evolving self.* New York: HarperCollins.

Csikszentmihalyi, M. (2003). *Good business.* New York: HarperCollins.

Cubed, M. (2002). *The national economic impacts of the child care sector.* Conyers, GA: National Child Care Association.

Davenport, T. H. (2002). The rise of the knowledge manager. *Futurist, 36*(2), 14–15.

Davenport, T. H., & Beck, J. C. (2001). *The attention economy: Understanding the new currency of business.* Boston: Harvard Business School Press.

Davenport, T. H., & Prusak, L. (1998). *Working knowledge: How organizations manage what they know.* Boston: Harvard Business School Press.

Davenport, T. O. (1999). *Human capital: What it is and why people invest it.* San Francisco: Jossey-Bass.

Dawson, A. G., Mikel, C. S., Lorenz, C. S., & King, J. (1984). *An experimental study of the effects of employer-sponsored child care services on selected employee behaviors.* Foundation for Human Service Studies and CSR.

Delaney, J. T., & Huselid, M. A. (1996). The impact of human resource management practices on perceptions of organizational performance. *Academy of Management Journal, 39,* 949–969.

Denison, D. R. (1990). *Corporate culture and organizational effectiveness.* New York: Wiley.

Dess, G. G., & Shaw, J. D. (2001). Voluntary turnover, social capital, and organizational performance. *Academy of Management Review, 26*(3), 446–456.

Dixit, A. K., & Nalebuff, B. J. (1991). *Thinking strategically: The competitive edge in business, politics, and everyday life.* New York: Norton.

Dixon, K. A., Storen, D., & Van Horn, C. E. (2002, Winter). *Standing on shaky ground: Employers sharply concerned in aftermath of recession and terror; Americans' attitudes about work, employers, and government: Work trends* (Heldrich Work Trends Survey, V. 3.4). New Brunswick, NJ: John J. Heldrich Center for Workforce Development, Rutgers University.

Drizin, M. J. (2001, November). Recruitment, retention, and loyalty. *Stakeholder Power.* Retrieved October 31, 2002, from http://www.stakeholderpower.com/story.cfm?article_id=169.

Drucker, P. F. (1993). *Post-capitalist society*. New York: HarperCollins.

Drucker, P. F. (1995). *Managing in a time of great change*. New York: Truman Talley Books/Dutton.

Drucker, P. F. (1999). *Management challenges for the 21st century*. New York: HarperBusiness.

Drucker, P. F. (2001, September 15). The next society. Graduate seminar. Claremont, CA: Claremont Graduate University.

Drucker, P. F. (2003, July 11). The organization of the future. Lecture. Claremont, CA: Claremont Graduate University.

Drucker, P. F., Dyson, E., Handy, C., Saffo, P., & Senge, P. M. (1997). Looking ahead: Implications of the present. *Harvard Business Review, 75*(5), 18.

Dube, A., & Kaplan, E. (2002). *Paid family leave in California: An analysis of costs and benefits*. Berkeley: Labor Project for Working Families.

Dubeck, P. J., & Borman, K. (1996). *Women and work: A handbook*. New York: Garland.

Dunham, K. J. (2001). Stressed out: Seeking the new, slimmed-down workday: 9 to 5—what were once considered normal hours are luxury for burnt-out employees. *Wall Street Journal*, p. B1.

Eaton, S. C. (2001). *If you can use them: Flexibility policies, organizational commitment, and perceived productivity* (Faculty Research Working Papers No. RWP01–009). Cambridge, MA: John F. Kennedy School of Government, Harvard University.

Economic Policy Institute. (2002). *Challenges facing the American workplace: The American workplace report 2002*. Washington, DC: Author.

Ehin, C. (2000). *Unleashing intellectual capital*. Boston: Butterworth-Heineman.

Ehrenberg, R. G., & Smith, R. S. (1994). *Modern labor economics* (5th ed.). New York: HarperCollins.

Ehrenreich, B. (2001). *Nickel and dimed: On (not) getting by in America*. New York: Henry Holt.

Ellsworth, R. R. (2002). *Leading with purpose*. Stanford, CA: Stanford University Press.

Ellwood, D. T., Blank, R. M., Blasi, J., Kruse, D., Niskanen, W. A., & Lynn-Dyson, K. (2000). *A working nation: Workers, work, and government in the new economy*. New York: Russell Sage Foundation.

Employment Policy Foundation. (2002). Human resources and public policy implications of the changing working household. Retrieved October 29, 2002, from http://www.workandfamily.org/research/indepth/id1.asp?page=4#7.

Farren, C. (1999). Manager's trust: A key factor in employee retention. *ACA News, 42*(10).

Finegold, D., and Mohrman, S.. (2001, January 25–30). *What do employees really want: The perception vs. the reality*. Paper presented at the World Economic Forum annual meeting. Los Angeles: Korn/Ferry International.

Fishman, C. (1999, January). Sanity Inc. *Fast Company, 21*, 84–96.

Fitz-enz, J. (2000). *The ROI of human capital.* New York, AMACOM.

Fletcher, J. (1999). *Disappearing acts: Gender, power, and relational work.* Cambridge, MA: MIT Press.

Fletcher, J. (2001). *Disappearing acts* (Paperback ed.). Cambridge, MA: First MIT Press.

Flexibility: Compelling strategies for a competitive workplace. (1991). San Francisco: New Ways to Work.

Flexible Resources. (1999). *Research on the non-traditional workplace.* New York: Author.

Flowers, V. S., & Hughes, C. L. (1973). Why employees stay. *Harvard Business Review, 51*(4), 49.

Flynn, G. (1997, March). Making a business case for balance. *Workforce,* 68–74.

Fombrun, C. J. (1996). *Reputation: Realizing value from the corporate image.* Boston: Harvard Business School Press.

Formula for retention. (1999). In *The chief executive guide: The war for talent* (pp. 21–24). New York: Chief Executive Magazine.

Fournier, S., Dobscha, S., & Mick, D. G. (1998). Preventing the premature death of relationship marketing. *Harvard Business Review, 76*(1), 43–51.

Frank, J. F. (1995, July–August). IBM mobile workforce thrives. *Total Quality Review.*

Fredericks, J. O., Hurd, R. R., & Salter, J. M., II. (2001). Connecting customer loyalty to financial results. *Marketing Management, 10*(1), 26–32.

Fredriksen-Goldsen, K. I., & Scharlach, A. E. (2001). *Families and work: New directions in the twenty-first century II.* New York: Oxford University Press.

Friedman, D. (1998). *ROI: Making the case for Chase with arithmetic.* Watertown, MA: Bright Horizons.

Friedman, L., & Friedman, D. E. (1998, September 16–18). *Overcoming resistance to flexibility: A case study of changing attitudes at Chase Manhattan.* Paper presented at the Work/Family Congress, New York.

Friedman, S. D., & Greenhaus, J. H. (2000). *Work and family—allies or enemies? What happens when business professionals confront life choices.* New York: Oxford University Press.

Friedman, W., & Casner-Lotto, J. (2003). Significant number of union workers feel the time squeeze. *Alliance for Work-Life Progress, 3*(4).

Fulmer, I. S., Gerhart, B., & Scott, K. S. (2000). *Are the 100 best better? An empirical investigation of the relationship between being a best employer and firm performance.* Lincolnshire, IL: Hewitt Associates.

Galinsky, E., Bond, J., & Friedman, D. (1993). *The changing workforce: Highlights of the national study.* New York: Families and Work Institute.

Gardner, H., Csikszentmihalyi, M., & Damon, W. (2001). *Good work: When excellence and ethics meet.* New York: Basic Books.

Gemignani, J. (2000). There's no place like home . . . for today's teleworkers. *Business and Health, 18,* 30–36.

Genasci, L. (1993). Flexible scheduling popular with some workers. *Minneapolis Star Tribune* (Metro ed., p. 01J).

Ghoshal, S., & Bartlett, C. A. (1997). *The individualized corporation.* New York: HarperBusiness.

Glass, J., & Riley, L. (1998). Family responsive policies and employee retention following childbirth. *Social Forces, 76*(4), 1401–1435.

Goetzel, R. Z., Anderson, D. R., Whitmer, R. W., Ozminkowski, R. J., Dunn, R. L., & Wasserman, J. (1998). The relationship between modifiable health risks and health care expenditures. *Journal of Occupational and Environmental Medicine, 40,* 843–854.

Goodman, E. A., Zammuto, R. F., & Gifford, B. D. (2001). The competing values framework: Understanding the impact of organizational culture on the quality of work life. *Organization Development Journal, 19*(3), 58–68.

Goodman, J. (1999, June). Basic facts on customer complaint behavior and the impact of service on the bottom line. *Competitive Advantage,* 1–5.

Goodman, J., O'Brien, P., & Segal, E. (2000). Turning CFOs into quality champions. *Quality Progress, 33*(3), 47.

Gordon, L. A., Porter, T., & Pound, J. (1994). *High-performance workplaces: Implications for investment research and active investing strategies.* Report to the California Public Employees' Retirement System. Waban, MA: Gordon Group.

Graham, B. W. (1996). The business argument for flexibility. *HR Magazine, 41*(5), 104.

Grant, L. (1998, January 12). Happy workers, high returns. *Fortune, 137*(1), 81.

Greene, K. (2001, March 29). A new push to help workers with elder care. *Wall Street Journal,* p. B1.

Greenhaus, J. H., & Beutell, N. J. (1985). Sources of conflict between work and family roles. *Academy of Management Review, 10*(1), 76.

Grisaffe, D. (2001, November). Marrying customer relationship management and loyalty measurement. *Stakeholder Power.* Retrieved October 29, 2002, from http://www.stakeholderpower.com/story.cfm?article_id=170.

Grover, S. L., & Crooker, K. J. (1995). Who appreciates family-responsive human resource policies: The impact of family-friendly policies on the organizational attachment of parents and non-parents. *Personnel Psychology, 48,* 271.

Guaspari, J. (1998, March). The next big thing. *Across the Board,* 18–25.

Hall, D. T. (2002). *Careers in and out of organizations.* Thousand Oaks, CA: Sage.

Hallowell, E. M. (2000, July 1). The human moment at work. *Harvard Business Review OnPoint Enhanced Edition.* Available from Harvard Business School Press at http://harvardbusinessonline.hbsp.harvard.edu/b01/en/common/item_detail.jhtml;jsessionid=O41VWHBT1QIXICTEQENSELQ?id=4436&_requestid=32745.

Halpern, D. (2003, June 16–18). *Psychosocial factors that link workplace/workforce mismatch and health.* Paper presented at the Workplace/Workforce Mismatch: Work, Family, Health, and Well-Being conference, Washington, DC.

Hammonds, K. H. (2002, November). Harry Kraemer's moment of truth. *Fast Company* (64), 92.

Hannon, J. M., & Milkovich, G. T. (1996). The effect of human resource reputation signals on share prices: An event study. *Human Resource Management, 35*, 405–424.

Harrington, A. (2003). The 2003 Fortune 500. Honey, I shrunk the profits: Accounting made a bad year look a whole lot worse. *Fortune.* Retrieved March 31, 2003, from http://www.fortune.com/fortune/fortune500/articles/ 0,15114,437426,00.html.

Harris, R., & Nyberg, A. (2001, September). Good work: An analysis of 100 companies identifies best practices for financial workplaces. *CFO Magazine, 8.*

Hawley, T., & Gunner, M. (2000). Starting smart: How early experiences affect brain development. Retrieved from http://www.ounceofprevention.org/downloads/publications/Starting_Smart.pdf.

Heintz, J., Folbre, N., & The Center for Popular Economics. (2000). *The ultimate field guide to the U.S. economy.* New York: New Press.

Helburn, S. W., & Bergmann, B. R. (2002). America's childcare problem: The way out (II). New York: Palgrave/St. Martin's Press.

Heldrich Center for Workforce Development (1999). *Work and family: How employers and workers can strike the balance* (Vol. 1). New Brunswick, NJ, and Storrs, CT: John J. Heldrich Center for Workforce Development, Rutgers University, and Center for Survey Research and Analysis, University of Connecticut.

Heldrich Center for Workforce Development. (2000). *Nothing but Net: American workers and the Information Economy.* New Brunswick, NJ, Storrs, CT: John J. Heldrich Center for Workforce Development, Rutgers University, and Center for Survey Research and Analysis, University of Connecticut.

Herman, R. E., Olivo, T. G., & Gioia, J. L. (2003). *Impending crises.* Winchester, VA: Oakhill Press.

Herzberg, F. (1966). *Work and the nature of man.* New York: New American Library.

Heskett, J. L., Sasser, W. E., Jr., & Schlesinger, L. A. (1997). *The service profit chain.* New York: Free Press.

Hesselbein, F., Goldsmith, M., & Beckhard, R. (1997). *The organization of the future.* San Francisco: Jossey-Bass.

Heymann, J. (2000). *The widening gap: Why America's working families are in jeopardy and what can be done about it.* New York: Basic Books.

Hitt, M. A., Bierman, L., Shimizu, K., & Kochhar, R. (2001). Direct and moderating effects of human capital on strategy and performance in professional service firms: A resource-based perspective. *Academy of Management Journal, 44*(1), 13–28.

Hochschild, A. (1983). *The managed heart: The commercialization of human feeling.* Berkeley: University of California Press.

Hochschild, A. R. (1997). *The time bind: When work becomes home and home becomes work II.* New York: Metropolitan Books.

Hock, D. (1999). *Birth of the Chaordic Age*. San Francisco: Berrett-Koehler.

Hooks, K. L. (1996). Diversity, family issues and the Big 6. *Journal of Accountancy, 182*(1), 51–56.

Huitt, W. G. (2003). Maslow's hierarchy of needs. Retrieved June 13, 2003, from http://chiron.valdosta.edu/whuitt/col/regsys/maslow.html.

Huselid, M. A. (1995). The impact of human resource management practices on turnover, productivity, and corporate financial performance. *Academy of Management Journal, 38*(3), 635–672.

Huselid, M. A., & Becker, B. E. (1995). *Strategic impact of high performance work systems*. New Brunswick, NJ: School of Management and Labor Relations, Rutgers University.

Huselid, M. A., & Becker, B. E. (1996). Methodological issues in cross-sectional and panel estimates of the human resource–firm performance link. *Industrial Relations, 35*(3), 400–422.

Huselid, M. A., & Becker, B. E. (1997). *The impact of high performance work systems, implementation effectiveness, and alignment with strategy on shareholder wealth*. New Brunswick, NJ: School of Management and Labor Relations, Rutgers University.

Huselid, M. A., & Rau, B. L. (1996). *The determinants of high performance work systems: Cross-sectional and longitudinal analyses*. New Brunswick, NJ: School of Management and Labor Relations, Rutgers University.

Ichniowski, C., Shaw, K., & Prennushi, G. (1995). *The effects of human resource management practices on productivity* (Working Paper 5333). Cambridge, MA: National Bureau of Economic Research.

Intracorp. (1997). *Intracorp work/life study: Corporate culture matters*. Philadelphia: Author.

Iverson, K., & Varian, W. T. (1998). *Plain talk: Lessons from a business maverick*. New York: Wiley.

Jackson, M. (2002). *What's happening to home: Balancing work, life, and refuge in the information age*. Notre Dame, IN: Sorin Books.

Jacobson, M., Kolarek, M. H., & Newton, B. (1996). *Business, babies, and the bottom line: Corporate innovations and best practices in maternal and child health*. Washington, DC: National Business Partnership to Improve Family Health, Washington Business Group on Health.

Johnson, A. (1995). The business case for work-family programs. *Journal of Accountancy, 180*(2), 53–59.

Johnson, J. W. (1996). Linking employee perceptions of service climate to customer satisfaction. *Personnel Psychology, 49*, 831–851.

Johnson, S. (2001). *Emergence: The connected lives of ants, brains, cities, and software*. New York: Scribner.

Jones, T. O., & Sasser, W. E., Jr. (1995). Why satisfied customers defect. *Harvard Business Review, 73*(6), 88–99.

Kahn, W. A. (1990). Psychological conditions of personal engagement and disengagement at work. *Academy of Management Journal, 33*(4), 692–724.

Kanter, R. M. (1997). Restoring people to the heart of the organization of the future. In F. Hesselbein, M. Goldsmith, & R. Beckhard (Eds.), *The organization of the future* (pp. 139–150). San Francisco: Jossey-Bass.

Kanter, R. M. (1999). From spare change to real change: The social sector as beta site for business innovation. *Harvard Business Review, 77*(3), 122–132.

Kaplan, R. S., & Norton, D. P. (1996). *The balanced scorecard: Translating strategy into action.* Boston: Harvard Business School Press.

Karasek, R., & Theorell, T. (1990). *Healthy work: Stress, productivity, and the reconstruction of working life.* New York: Basic Books.

Kaye, B., & Jordan-Evans, S. (2002). *What keeps 'em? Updated findings from on-going research into retention drivers: Statistical summaries of retention data.* Scranton, PA: Career Systems International and Jordan Evans Group.

Keilly, S. A. (2002, February 7–9). *Preparing for an aging workforce: Implications for employers.* Paper presented at the Alliance of Work/Life Professionals conference, San Francisco.

Kellogg, K. C. (2001). *Institutionalized frenzy: Daily work activities, individual work-personal life integration, and employee creative thinking time in a knowledge-based workplace.* Boston: Center for Gender in Organizations, Simmons Graduate School of Management.

Kelloway, E. K., & Gottlieb, B.H. (1998). The effect of alternative work arrangements on women's well-being: A demand-control model. *Women's Health: Research on Gender, Behavior and Policy, 4*(1), 1.

Kepner-Tregoe. (1999). *Avoiding the brain drain: What companies are doing to lock in their talent* (Research Monograph 1). Princeton, NJ: Kepner-Tregoe.

Kiger, P. (2002). Why customer satisfaction starts with HR. *Workforce, 81*(5), 26–32.

Klaff, L. G. (2001, January 28). Employers don't see hidden costs of high turnover: Soft costs eat away at a company's profits. *San Jose Mercury News,* p. 1PC.

Know your assets. (2001). *Ubiquity, 2*(24). Retrieved August 7, 2001, from http://www.acm.org/ubiquity/interviews/b_libert_1.html.

Koblenz, M. (2000). Baxter Healthcare Corporation: The evolution of a work/life strategy. In J. Casner-Lotto (Ed.), *Holding a job, having a life: Strategies for change* (p. 195). Scarsdale, NY: Work in America Institute.

Kohn, A. (1998). How incentives undermine performance. *Journal for Quality and Participation, 21*(2), 6–13.

Koprowski, G. J. (2000, October 16). Flexibility in the workplace is an increasing concern. *InformationWeek,* 212–218.

Kossek, E. E., Colquitt, J. A., & Noe, R. A. (2001). Caregiving decisions, well-being, and performance: The effects of place and provider as a function of dependent type and work-family climates. *Academy of Management Journal, 44*(1), 29–44.

Kotulak, R. (1996). *Inside the brain: Revolutionary discoveries of how the mind works.* Kansas City, MO: Andrews McMeel Publishing.

Kroll, L., & Goldman, L. (2002, February 28). The world's billionaires. *Forbes*. Retrieved July 26, 2002, from http://www.forbes.com/2002/02/28/billionaires.html.

Kruse, D. (2002, February 13). Research evidence on prevalence and effects of employee ownership. *Journal of Employee Ownership Law and Finance, 14*(4), 65–90.

Lambert, S., Hopkins, K., Easton, G., Walker, J., McWilliams, H., & Chung, M. S. (1993). *Added benefits: The link between family-responsive policies and work performance at Fel-Pro Inc.* Unpublished manuscript.

Lau, R. S. M., & May, B. E. (1998). A win-win paradigm for quality of work life and business performance. *Human Resource Development Quarterly, 9*(3), 211–226.

Lawler, E. E. I. (1999). Employee involvement makes a difference. *Journal for Quality and Participation, 22*, 18–20.

Lawler, E. E. I., Mohrman, S. A., & Benson, G. (2001). *Organizing for high performance*. San Francisco: Jossey-Bass.

Leach, D. J., Wall, T. D., & Jackson, P. R. (2003). The effect of empowerment on job knowledge: An empirical test involving operators of complex technology. *Journal of Occupational and Organizational Psychology*, (76), 1.

Ledford, G. E. J., Lawler, E. E. I., & Mohrman, S. A. (1995). Reward innovations in Fortune 1000 companies. *Compensation and Benefits Review, 27*(4), 76.

Lee, T. W., & Maurer, S. D. (1999). The effects of family structure on organizational commitment, intention to leave, and voluntary turnover. *Journal of Managerial Issues, 11*(4), 493–513.

Lee, T. W., & Mowday, R. T. (1987). Voluntarily leaving an organization: An empirical investigation. *Academy of Management Journal, 30*(4), 721–744.

Levering, R., & Moskowitz, M. (2000). The 100 best companies to work for. *Fortune, 141*, 82–110.

Levering, R., & Moskowitz, M. (2001). 100 best companies to work for: America's top employers. *Fortune, 143*(1), 148.

Levering, R., & Moskowitz, M. (2003). 100 best companies to work for. *Fortune, 147*(1), 127.

Levine, S. B., & Dworkin, S. (1983). *She's nobody's baby*. New York: Simon & Schuster.

Lewis, M. D. (2003). From master builder to servant leader: The changing role of the community college president. The Ninth Annual Sally Loyd Casanova Distinguished Alumni Lecture. Claremont, CA: Center for Educational Studies, Claremont Graduate University.

Lievens, F., & Highhouse, S. (2003). The relation of instrumental and symbolic attributes to a company's attractiveness as an employer. *Personnel Psychology, 56*(1), 76–102.

Lipman-Blumen, J. (1996). *The connective edge: Leading in an interdependent world*. San Francisco: Jossey-Bass.

Locke, E. A., & Henne, D. (1986). Work motivation theories. In C. L. Cooper & I. Robertson (Eds.), *International review of industrial and organizational psychology*. New York: Wiley.

Lombardi, J. (2003). *Time to care.* Philadelphia: Temple University Press.

Low, J. (2002). The invisible advantage: Getting a grasp on intangible assets. *Perspectives on Business Innovation* (Valuing Intangibles). Retrieved July 5, 2004 from http://www.capgemini.com/adaptive/media/invisibleadvantage.pdf.

Maciariello, J. A. (2000). *Lasting value: Lessons from a century of agility at Lincoln Electric.* New York: Wiley.

Madjar, N., Oldham, G. R., & Pratt, M. G. (2002). There's no place like home? The contributions of work and nonwork creativity support to employees' creative performance. *Academy of Management Journal, 45*(4), 757–767.

Magretta, J. (1993). Introduction: Managing in the new economy. In J. Magretta (Ed.), *Managing in the new economy* (pp. vii–x). Boston: Harvard Business School Press.

Maharaj, D. (1998, November 22). Layoffs: A company's strategy of first resort. *Los Angeles Times*, p. 1.

Maister, D. H. (2001). *Practice what you preach: What managers must do to create a high-achievement culture.* New York: Free Press.

Malone, T. W., & Laubacher, R. J. (1993). The dawn of the e-lance economy. In J. Magretta (Ed.), *Managing in the new economy* (pp. 145–157). Boston: Harvard Business School Press.

Marra, R., & Lindner, J. (1992). The true cost of parental leave: The parental leave cost model. In D. Friedman, E. Galinsky, & V. Plowden (Eds.), *Parental leave and productivity: Current research* (pp. 55–78). New York: Families and Work Institute.

Martinez, M. N. (1997). Work-life programs reap business benefits. *HR Magazine, 42*, 110–114.

Marzolini, A. (2001). *Moving forward 2001: The experiences and attitudes of executive women in Canada.* Toronto, Ontario: Pollara.

McGregor, D. (1960). *The human side of enterprise.* New York: McGraw-Hill.

Meade, R. (1993). Fueling the passion for productivity. In E. J. Miranda & B. E. Murphy (Eds.), *Work-family: Redefining the business case.* New York: Conference Board.

Measuring results: Cost-benefit analysis of work and family programs. (1992). Washington, DC: Bureau of National Affairs.

Mendels, P. (2002). How investing in dependent care pays off. *BusinessWeek Online.* Retrieved February 10, 2002, from http://www.businessweek.com/careers/ content/oct2000/ca20001.011_781.htm.

MetLife. (2001). *The MetLife study of employee benefits trends: Findings from a 2001 national survey.* New York: Author.

Metropolitan Life Insurance Company. (1997). *The MetLife study of employer costs for working caregivers.* New York MetLife.

Meyer, C. S., Mukerjee, S., & Sestero, A. (2001). Work-family benefits: Which ones maximize profits? *Journal of Managerial Issues, 13*, 28.

Miller, B. E. (1998). *Reinventing work: Innovative strategies re-linking life and livelihood to benefit business and staff.* Mill Valley, CA: Artemis Management Consultants.

Minnesota Center for Corporate Responsibility. (1997). *The bottom line value of work/life strategies.* Minneapolis: Author.

Mintzberg, H. (1993). *Structures in fives: Designing effective organizations.* Englewood Cliffs, NJ: Prentice Hall.

Mishel, L., Bernstein, J., & Boushey, H. (2002). *The state of working America 2002–03.* Ithaca, NY: Cornell University Press.

Mishel, L., Bernstein, J., & Schmitt, J. (2000). *The state of working America 2000–01.* Ithaca, NY: Cornell University Press.

Mitchell, A., Stoney, L., Dichter, H., & Ewing Marion Kaufmann Foundation. (2001). *Financing child care in the United States: An expanded catalog of current strategies.* Kansas City, MO: Ewing Marion Kaufmann Foundation.

Mom As CEO. (2003, July 15). ExchangeEveryDay (772). Retrieved July 15, 2003, from http://www.ccie.com/eed/issue.php?id=340.

Morgenson, G. (2002, November 10). When options rise to top, guess who pays. *New York Times,* 1, 10, 11.

Moskowitz, M. (2002, February 6–9). Addressing the Alliance of Work/Life Professionals conference, San Francisco, CA.

Mowday, R. T., Steers, R. M., & Porter, L. W. (1979). The measurement of organizational commitment. *Journal of Vocational Behavior, 14,* 224–247.

Munck, B. (2001). Changing a culture of face time. *Harvard Business Review, 79*(10), 125–131.

National Association of Manufacturers & Center for Workforce Success. (2001). *The skills gap 2001: Manufacturers confront persistent skills shortages in an uncertain economy.* Washington, DC: National Association of Manufacturers.

National Sleep Foundation. (2000). Omnibus sleep in America poll. Retrieved May 18, 2001, from www.sleepfoundation.org/publications/2000poll.html.

National Women's Law Center. (2001). *Women's stake in improving the availability, affordability, and quality of child care and early education.* Washington, DC: Author.

Newel, S., Robertson, M., Scarbrough, H., & Swan, J. (2002). *Managing knowledge work.* New York: Macmillan.

Nilles, J. M. (2000). *Telework in the US: Telework America survey 2000.* Silver Spring, MD: International Telework Association & Council.

Noble, B. P. (1995, July 30). Nudging workers from comfy nests—AT&T pushes for telecommuting. *New York Times,* p. 310.

Northwestern National Life Insurance Company (1991). *Employee burnout: America's newest epidemic.* Minneapolis, MN.

Northwestern National Life Insurance Company. (1992). *Employee burnout: Causes and cures.* Minneapolis, MN.

OfficeTeam. (1999, March 26). Business meeting vs. baseball practice: Survey respondents rank work-family balance as number one career concern for new millennium. Retrieved August 27, 2000, from http://www.officeteam.com/OT/ Dispatcher?file=/OT/Press032699.

Ohmae, K. (1990). *The borderless world: Power and strategy in the interlinked economy* (McKinsey & Company, Trans.). New York: HarperBusiness.

O'Reilly, B. (1994, June 13). The new deal: What companies and employees owe one another. *Fortune*, p. 50, extracted from footnote.

O'Reilly, C., & Pfeffer, J. (1995). *Southwest Airlines: Using human resources for competitive advantage* (A) (No. HR-1A). Stanford, CA: Graduate School of Business, Stanford University.

Our people, our assets. (1999). In *The chief executive guide: The war for talent* (pp. 3–6). New York: Chief Executive Magazine.

Pacelle, M. (1993). Vanishing offices: To trim their costs, some companies cut space for employees. *Wall Street Journal* (Eastern ed., p. A1.).

Parkinson, D. (1996). *Work-family roundtable: Child care services* (Vol. 5). New York: Conference Board.

Perry-Smith, J. E., & Blum, T. C. (2000). Work-family human resource bundles and perceived organizational performance. *Academy of Management Journal, 43,* 1107–1117.

Petzinger, T. (1997, January 3). Self-organization will free employees to act like bosses. *Wall Street Journal*, p. 31.

Pfau, B. N., & Kay, I. T. (2002). *The human capital edge.* New York: McGraw-Hill.

Pfeffer, J. (1994). *Competitive advantage through people.* Boston: Harvard Business School Press.

Pfeffer, J. (1998a, May–June). Six dangerous myths about pay. *Harvard Business Review, 76*(3), 109–119.

Pfeffer, J. (1998b). The SAS Institute: A different approach to incentives and people management practices in the software industry. White paper. Stanford CA: Graduate School of Business, Stanford University.

Pfeffer, J. (2000). SAS Institute: The decision to go public. Stanford CA: Graduate School of Business, Stanford University.

Phillips, D. J. (1990, December). The price tag of turnover. *Personnel Journal, 69*(12), 58.

Pierce, J. L., & Newstrom, J. W. (1983). The design of flexible work schedules and employee responses: Relationships and process. *Journal of Occupational Behavior, 4*(4), 247–262.

Pratt, J. H. (1999). *Cost/benefits of teleworking to manage work/life responsibilities.* Silver Springs, MD: International Telework Association & Council.

Presser, H. (2003, February 28). *From 9-to-5 to 24/7.* Paper presented at the Designing the Future conference, Orlando, FL.

PriceWaterhouseCoopers. (1999). *International student survey.* New York: Author.

Procter & Gamble. (2002). *Purpose, values, and principles.* Retrieved June 23, 2004, from http://www.pg.com/company/who_we_are/ppv.jhtml#values.

Pruchno, R., Litchfield, L., & Fried, M. (2000). *Measuring the impact of workplace flexibility.* Boston: Boston College Center for Work & Family.

Prusak, L., & D. J. Cohen (2001). How to invest in social capital. *Harvard Business Review, 79*(6), 86.

Quinn, J. B. (1992). *Intelligent enterprise: A knowledge and service based paradigm for industry.* New York: Free Press.

Randall, M. L., Cropanzano, R., Bormann, C. A., & Birjulin, A. (1999). Organizational politics and organizational support as predictors of work attitudes, job performance, and organizational citizenship behavior. *Journal of Organizational Behavior, 20*(2), 159–174.

Ransom, C., Aschbacher, P., & Burud, S. (1989, October). The return in the child-care investment. *Personnel Administrator,* 54–58.

Rapoport, R., & Bailyn, L. (1996). *Relinking life and work: Toward a better future.* New York: Ford Foundation.

Rapoport, R., Bailyn, L., Fletcher, J. K., & Pruitt, B. H. (2002). *Beyond work-family balance: Advancing gender equity and workplace performance.* San Francisco: Jossey-Bass.

Rayman, P. (1997). *Radcliffe-Fleet project team report.* Cambridge, MA: Radcliffe Public Policy Institute.

Rayman, P., Krane, D., & Szostak, A. (2000). *Life's work: Generational attitudes toward work and life integration.* Cambridge, MA: Radcliffe Public Policy Center.

Reich, R. (2003, February 27). *Designing the future.* Paper presented at the Designing the Future conference, Orlando, FL.

Reichheld, F. (1996). *The loyalty effect.* Boston: Harvard Business School Press.

Reinartz, W., & Kumar, V. (2002). The mismanagement of customer loyalty. *Harvard Business Review, 80*(7), 86–94.

Rhoades, L., Eisenberger, R., & Armeli, S. (2001). Affective commitment to the organization: The contribution of perceived organizational support. *Journal of Applied Psychology, 86*(5), 825–836.

Rodgers & Associates. (1995, July). *DuPont work/life study.* Unpublished paper.

Rodgers, C. S. (1998). *The drivers of employee commitment.* Boston: Work/Family Directions.

Roehling, P. V., Roehling, M. V., & Moen, P. (2001). The relationship between work-life policies and practices and employee loyalty: A life course perspective. *Journal of Family and Economic Issues, 22*(2), 141–170.

Rousseau, J.-J. (1911). *Emile* (B. Foxley, Trans.). London: Dent.

Rucci, A. J., Kirn, S. P., & Quinn, R. T. (1998). The employee-customer-profit chain at Sears. *Harvard Business Review, 76,* 82–97.

Ruderman, M. N., Ohlott, P. J., Panzer, K., & King, S. N. (2002). Benefits of multiple roles for managerial women. *Academy of Management Journal, 45*(2), 369–386.

Safer, M. (2003, April 20). The royal treatment. *60 Minutes*, CBS Television.

Sandberg, J. F., & Hofferth, S. L. (2001). *Changes in children's time with parents, W.S. 1981–1998* (PSC Research Report No. 01–475). Ann Arbor: Population Studies Center, University of Michigan.

SAS. (2002). SAS wins CRM Excellence Award for third consecutive year. Retrieved April 21, 2003, from http://www.sas.com/news/feature/23sep02/crm.html.

SAS Institute. (2003). SAS continues annual revenue growth streak: Worldwide revenue increases 4.4 percent in 2002. Retrieved May 23, 2003, from http://www.sas.com/news/preleases/031003/news1.html.

Scandura, T. A., & Lankau, M. J. (1997). Relationships of gender, family responsibility, and flexible work hours to organizational commitment and job satisfaction. *Journal of Organizational Behavior, 18*(4), 377–391.

Schein, E. (1992a). The dynamics of culture change and leadership in young organizations. Chapter 15 in *Organizational culture and leadership*. San Francisco: Jossey-Bass.

Schein, E. (1992b). Uncovering the levels of culture. Chapter 2 in *Organizational culture and leadership*. San Francisco: Jossey-Bass.

Schneider, B., & Bowen, D. E. (1992). The service organization: Human resources management is crucial. *Organizational Dynamics, 21*, 39–52.

Schneider, B., Ashworth, S. D., Higgs, C. A., & Carr, L. (1996). Design, validity, and use of strategically focused employee attitude surveys. *Personnel Psychology, 49*(3), 695.

Schneider, B., White, S. S., & Paul, M. C. (1998). Linking service climate and customer perceptions of service quality: Test of a causal model. *Journal of Applied Psychology, 83*(2), 150–163.

Schroeder, M. (2003, February 10). Job market grows a bit stronger but lacks vigor to lift economy. *Wall Street Journal*, p. A2.

Schulman, K. (2000). *The high cost of child care puts quality care out of reach for many families*. Washington, DC: Children's Defense Fund.

Schweinhart, L. J. (2003). *High-quality preschool program found to improve adult status*. Ypsilanti, MI: High/Scope Educational Research Foundation.

Senge, P. (1990). *The fifth discipline: The art and practice of the learning organization*. New York: Currency/Doubleday.

Seybold, P. B., Marshak, R. T., & Lewis, J. M. (2001). *The customer revolution: How to thrive when customers are in control*. New York: Crown Business.

Shellenbarger, S. (1997, November 19). Employers are finding it doesn't cost much to make a staff happy. *Wall Street Journal*, p. B1.

Shellenbarger, S. (2001a, November 21). Job candidates prepare to sacrifice some frills and balance—for now. *Wall Street Journal*, p. B1.

Shellenbarger, S. (2001b, September 20). Some employers begin to find what helps shiftworker families. *Wall Street Journal*, p. B1.

Shellenbarger, S. (2002, May 16). From office catnaps to lunchtime jogs: Tales of grabbing "undertime" at work. *Wall Street Journal*, p. D1.

Shore & Families and Work Institute. (1998). *Ahead of the curve: Why America's leading employers are addressing the needs of new and expectant parents.* New York: Families and Work Institute.

Simmons Graduate School of Management. (1997). *The benefits of work-site child care.* (Report). El Segundo, CA: Bright Horizons.

Simon, D. (2002). *Happy employees, happy customers: Understanding the relationship between work-life policies, labor market opportunities, and customer satisfaction.* Unpublished paper.

Sims, W., Joroff, M., & Becker, F. (1996). *Managing the reinvented workplace.* Atlanta, GA: IDRC Foundation.

Smith, L. J. (1996). Providing family benefits can boost bottom line. Best's Review: *Property/Casualty Insurance Edition, 97,* 16.

Spain, D., & Bianchi, S. M. (1996). *Balancing act: Motherhood, marriage, and employment among American women.* New York: Russell Sage Foundation.

Staines, G. L., & Galinsky, E. (1992). Parental leave and productivity: The supervisor's view. In D. Friedman, E. Galinsky, & V. Plowden (Eds.), *Parental leave and productivity: Current research* (pp. 21–32). New York: Families and Work Institute.

Stamps, D. (1997). The 10 million best companies to work for in America. *Training, 34*(12), 42–44.

Stewart, T. A. (1997). *Intellectual capital: The new wealth of organizations.* New York: Currency/Doubleday.

Stewart, T. A. (1999). *Intellectual capital.* New York: Currency/Doubleday.

Summa Associates. (2003). *Study of work/life needs in Ventura County.* Tempe, AZ: Project Work/L.I.F.E. of Ventura County—A Project of the Child Care Planning Council.

Survey: The new demographics. (2001). *Economist, 360*(8239), 5.

Survey: The new workforce. (2001). *Economist, 360*(8239), 8.

Survey: Will the corporation survive? (2001). *Economist, 360*(8239) 16.

Sweeney, K. (1997). *High-tech companies work/life survey.* Watertown, MA: Bright Horizons.

Tam, P.-W. (2003, June 5). Palm to buy Handspring as hand-helds morph into phones. *Wall Street Journal*, p. B1.

Tapscott, D. (1996). *The digital economy: Promise and peril in the age of networked intelligence.* New York: McGraw-Hill.

Taylor, H. (1998). Harris poll on child care. Retrieved January 28, 1998, from http://www.harrisindia.com/harris_poll/index.asp?PID=200.

Taylor, H. (2000). Three factors appear to have big impact on job satisfaction. Retrieved December 20, 2000, from http://www.harrisindia.com/ harris_poll/ index.asp?PID=208.

Teal, T. (1991, September–October). Service comes first: An interview with USAA's Robert F. McDermott. *Harvard Business Review*, pp. 117–127.

Terpstra, D. E., & Rozell, E. J. (1993). The relationship of staffing practices to organizational level measures of performance. *Personnel Psychology, 46*(1), 27–48.

Thomas, R. R. (1999). *Building a house for diversity.* New York: AMACOM.

Thompson, C., Beauvais, L., & Lyness, K. (1999). When work-family benefits are not enough: The influence of work-family culture on benefit utilization, organizational attachment, and work-family conflict. *Journal of Vocational Behavior, 54*(3), 392–415.

Thompson, M. (2000, January 25). *Hay report: Compensation and benefits strategies for 2000 and beyond.* Philadelphia: The Hay Group.

Tierney, P., & Farmer, S. M. (2002). Creative self-efficacy: Potential antecedents and relationship to creative performance. *Academy of Management Journal, 45*(6), 1137–1148.

Tornow, W. W., & Wiley, J. W. (1991). Service quality and management practices: A look at employee attitudes, customer satisfaction and bottom-line consequences. *Human Resource Planning, 14*(2), 105–115.

Towers Perrin. (2001). *The Towers Perrin talent report 2001: New realities in today's workforce.* Valhalla, NY: Towers Perrin.

Tulgan, B. (2000). *Managing Generation X: How to bring out the best in young talent.* New York: Norton.

Ulrich, D., Halbrook, R., Meder, D., Stuchlik, M., & Thorpe, S. (1991). Employee and customer attachment: Synergies for competitive advantage. *Human Resource Planning, 14*(2), 89–103.

U.S. Census Bureau. (2001). Historical income tables—families, table F-7. Type of family (all races) by median and mean income: 1947 to 2001. Retrieved February 17, 2003, from http://www.census.gov/hhes/income/histinc/f07.html.

U.S. Census Bureau. (2002a). DP-3 profile of selected economic characteristics: 2000. Retrieved October 26, 2002, from http://factfinder.census.gov/servlet/QTTable?ds_name=D&geo_id=D&qr_name=DEC_2000_SF3_U_DP3&_lang=en.

U.S. Census Bureau. (2002b). Civilian labor force and participation rates with projections: 1980 to 2008. Retrieved April 7, 2003, from http://www.census.gov/prod/2002pubs/01statab/labor.pdf.

U.S. Census Bureau. (2002c). Labor force participation rates by marital status, sex, and age: 1970 to 2000. Retrieved April 7, 2003, from http://www.census.gov/prod/2002pubs/01statab/labor.pdf.

U.S. Census Bureau. (2002d). Employed civilians by occupation, sex, race, and Hispanic origin: 1983 and 2000. Retrieved April 7, 2003, from http://www.census.gov/prod/2002pubs/01statab/labor.pdf.

U.S. Department of Commerce & Bureau of Economic Analysis. (2002). Gross domestic product by industry in current dollars, 1994–2001. Retrieved October 28, 2003, from http://www.bea.doc.gov/bea/dn2/gpoc.htm#1994-2001.

U.S. Department of Labor. (1993, July). *High performance work practices and firm performance.* Washington, DC: Department of Labor.

U.S. Department of Labor. (1998). *Meeting the needs of today's workforce: Child care best practices.* Washington, DC: Department of Labor.

U.S. Department of Labor. (2003). *Dictionary of occupational titles.* Washington, DC: Department of Labor, Office of Administrative Law Judges Law Library.

U.S. Department of the Treasury. (1998). Investing in child care: Challenges facing working parents and the private sector response. Retrieved March 21, 2004, from http://www.treas.gov/press/releases/docs/chdcare.pdf.

Vandell, D. L., & Wolfe, B. (2000). *Child care quality: Does it matter and does it need to be improved?* Madison, WI: Institute for Research on Poverty, University of Wisconsin.

Verespej, M. A. (2000). Flexible schedules benefit all. *Industry Week, 249,* 25.

Verschoor, C. C. (1998). A study of the link between a corporation's financial performance and its commitment to ethics. *Journal of Business Ethics, 17*(13), 1509–1516.

Vistnes, J. P. (1997). Gender differences in days lost from work due to illness. *Industrial and Labor Relations Review, 50*(2), 304–324.

Waddock, S. A., & Graves, S. B. (1997). The corporate social performance-financial performance link. *Strategic Management Journal, 18*(4), 303–319.

Waldfogel, J. (2001). Family and medical leave: Evidence from the 2000 surveys. *Monthly Labor Review, 124*(9), 17–23.

Walsh, K., Bartunek, J. M., & Lacey, C. A. (1998). A relational approach to empowerment. In C. L. Cooper & D. M. Rousseau (Eds.), *Trends in organizational behavior* (Vol. 5, pp. 103–126). New York: Wiley.

Washington State University Cooperative Extension Energy Program. (1998). Case study: Holland America Line Westours Inc. Retrieved July 26, 2002, from http://www.commuterchallenge.org/cc/csholland.html.

Watson Wyatt. (1999a). *Strategic rewards: The new employment deals.* Bethesda, MD: Author.

Watson Wyatt. (1999b). *WorkUSA 2000 study.* Bethesda, MD: Author.

Watson Wyatt. (2000a). *The human capital index: Linking human capital and shareholder value.* Bethesda, MD: Author.

Watson Wyatt. (2000b). *Playing to win: Strategic rewards in the war for talent.* Bethesda, MD: Author.

Watson Wyatt Worldwide. (2001). *Human capital index: Human capital as a lead indicator of shareholder value.* Washington, DC: Author.

Weiser, J., & Zadek, S. (2000). *Conversations with disbelievers: Persuading companies to address social challenges.* New York: Ford Foundation.

WFD Consulting. (2001, Summer). *Three things you need to know about your workforce . . . and creative ways to measure them.* Watertown, MA: Author.

Wheatley, M. (2001). Foreword. In C. Desjardins (Ed.), *The leading edge: Competencies for community college leadership in the new millennium.* Mission Viejo, CA: League for Innovation in the Community College/National Institute for Leadership Development.

Wheatley, M., & Chodron, P. (1999, November). It starts with uncertainty. *Shambala Sun, 58–62.* Retrieved March 21, 2004, from http://www.margaretwheatley.com/articles/uncertainty.html.

Whiting, R. (2003, April 28). Going above and beyond. *InformationWeek, (937)*, 49–58.

Whyte, D. (1994). *The heart aroused.* New York: Currency/Doubleday.

Whyte, D. (2001). *Crossing the unknown sea: Work as a pilgrimage of identity.* New York: Riverhead Books.

Wichert, I. C., Nolan, J. P., & Burchell, B. J. (2000). *Workers on the edge: Job insecurity, psychological well-being, and family life.* Washington, DC: Economic Policy Institute.

Wilburn, D. A. (1998, October). The 100 best companies for working mothers. *Working Mother Magazine.*

Wiley, J. W., & Gantz-Wiley Research Consulting Group. (1991). Customer satisfaction: A supportive work environment and its financial cost. *Human Resource Planning, 14*(2), 117–127.

William M. Mercer. (1996). *Mercer work/life and diversity initiatives benchmarking survey.* New York: Author.

William Olsten Center for Workforce Strategies. (1999). *Managing workplace technology.* Melville, NY: Olsten Corporation.

Williams, J. (2000). *Unbending gender.* Oxford, England: Oxford University Press.

Williams, J., & Calvert, C. T. (2001). *Balanced hours: Effective part-time policies for Washington law firms* (Final report, 2nd ed.). Washington, DC: Project for Attorney Retention, Program on Gender, Work & Family, American University, Washington College of Law.

Williams, J., & Segal, N. (2003). Beyond the maternal wall: Relief for family caregivers who are discriminated against on the job. *Harvard Women's Law Journal, 26,* 78–162.

Wright, T. A., & Cropanzano, R. (1998). Emotional exhaustion as a predictor of job performance and voluntary turnover. *Journal of Applied Psychology, 83*(3), 486–493.

Zeithaml, V. A., Rust, R. T., & Lemon, K. N. (2001). The customer pyramid: Creating and serving profitable customers. *California Management Review, 43*(4), 118–142.

Zemke, R., Raines, C., & Filipczak, B. (2000). *Generations at work: Managing the clash of Veterans, Boomers, Xers, and Nexters in your workplace.* New York: American Management Association.

INDEX

absenteeism: adaptive practices effect on, 187, 235–236; child care-related, 236; costs of, 235–236; flexible work arrangements effect on, 189; productivity effects of, 186
accountability, 116
adaptability, 61–62
adaptation levels, 73
adaptive beliefs: description of, 108; about human nature, 112–116; model of, 118–120; about nature of business, 109–112; about nature of work, 117–118
adaptive culture: description of, 108, 114, 118; employee commitment affected by, 182–183; employee satisfaction and, 228–229; management commitment to, 156; retention of employees increased by, 207–208; stress reduction in, 199
adaptive organizations: career planning in, 140; child care supported by, 145; communication in, 164–166; description of, 122; employee satisfaction and, 226; flexibility offered by, 150; managers in, 140; managers' role in, 160–161; technology for, 152
adaptive practices: absenteeism reduced by, 187, 235–236; commitment increased by,

179–181; employee commitment increased by, 179–181; employee turnover reduced by, 236–238; health care costs reduced by, 238–240; labor costs reduced by, 240–243; leadership support for, 159–160; legal costs reduced by, 243–244; marketing costs reduced by, 244; for organization of work, 131–135; overhead reduced by, 240; productivity affected by, 186–196; quality enhanced by, 243; reputation enhanced by, 244; resources and tools, 141–152; retention of employees affected by, 209–211; stress reduction using, 199; for talent management, 136–141; technology effects on, 151–152; for time, 122–131
adaptive strategies: assumptions. *See* assumptions; beliefs. *See* beliefs; characteristics of, 74–75; fit, 155–167; Huselid and Becker's research regarding, 251–254; invest in people. *See* investing in people; list of, 74; organizational culture. *See* organizational culture; profitability affected by, 234; transforming management practices, 121–153; Watson Wyatt's research regarding, 254–258
adhocracy, 26